In Search of Elegance
Towards an Architecture of Satisfaction

What is architecture? How is it made? How is it judged? These fundamental questions have intrigued architects for centuries. While the questions are philosophical, the answers have important ramifications for architectural practice. *In Search of Elegance* provides answers to these complex questions and, in so doing, develops a new theory for the practice of architecture and urban design.

Michel Lincourt calls for a dignified architecture, centred around the concept of elegance, that will provide satisfaction to both its users and the surrounding society. Elegance, defined as the symbiosis of excellence and magnificence, is the ultimate attribute of any creative endeavour and achieving it is the architect's prime motivation. Using this concept, Lincourt develops a set of archetypes for designing a more satisfactory architecture and provides an in-depth analysis of three examples of architectural elegance: the Palais-Royal and the Fondation Rothschild Worker's Residence in Paris and the Municipality of Outremont in Montreal.

In Search of Elegance defines the essential components of architecture, articulates non-self-referential design criteria based on societal values, and develops a proactive design process that incorporates the concept of archetype as a privileged means for achieving a coherent design. It will be an indispensable reference book for architects and urban planners as well as students and scholars of architecture.

MICHEL LINCOURT is professor of architecture, École Nationale Supérieure des Arts et Industries de Strasbourg, and visiting professor, Institut National de la Recherche Scientifique du Québec.

In Search of Elegance

Towards an Architecture of Satisfaction

Michel Lincourt

Illustrations by Louise Beaupré-Lincourt

Liverpool University Press

McGill-Queen's University Press
Montreal & Kingston · London · Ithaca

© McGill-Queen's University Press 1999
ISBN 0-7735-1753-7 (cloth)
ISBN 0-7735-1827-4 (paper)

Legal deposit first quarter 1999
Bibliothèque nationale du Québec

Printed in Canada on acid-free paper

Published in the European Union by
Liverpool University Press.
ISBN 0-85323-524-4 (cloth)
ISBN 0-85323-534-1 (paper)

This book has been published with the help of
a grant from the Humanities and Social Sciences
Federation of Canada, using funds provided by
the Social Sciences and Humanities Research Council
of Canada.

McGill-Queen's University Press acknowledges
the financial support of the Government of Canada
through the Book Publishing Industry Development
Program for its activities. We also acknowledge
the support of the Canada Council for the Arts
for our publishing program.

Canadian Cataloguing in Publication Data

Lincourt, Michel, 1941–
In search of elegance: towards an architecture
of satisfaction
Includes bibliographical references and index.
ISBN 0-7735-1753-7 (bound) –
ISBN 0-7735-1827-4 (pbk.)
1. Architecture – Aesthetics. 2. Palais-Royal (Paris, France).
3. Architecture – Quebec (Province) – Outremont.
4. Working class – Dwellings – France – Paris.
I. Beaupré-Lincourt, Louise. II. Title.
NA2500.L55 1998   720'.1   C98-900938-6

British Cataloguing-in-Publication Data

A British Library CIP record is available

Typeset in Times New Roman 10.5/13
by Caractéra inc., Quebec City

CONTENTS

Illustrations   vii

Acknowledgments   xi

1 Introduction: A Theory for the Practice of Architecture   3

2 A Theory Based on Phenomenology   7

3 Unveiling Architecture   45

4 Values and Design Criteria   85

5 Palais-Royal: A Perennial Elegance   123

6 Fondation Rothschild Workers' Residence: An Honest Elegance   169

7 Outremont: A Convivial Elegance   209

8 Reveiling Architecture   245

9 Archetypes of Elegance   319

10 Conclusion: Elegance for an Architecture of Satisfaction   351

Notes   359

Bibliography   381

Appendix: Sample of the questionnaire used for the survey conducted at the Fondation Rothschild Workers' Residence   399

Index   403

ILLUSTRATIONS

1 Children, Palais-Royal 2
2 Café, Palais-Royal garden 8
3 Trees, Palais-Royal garden 39
4 Street facade, Fondation Rothschild Workers' Residence 40
5 Ferme Outre-Mont 42
6 Feeding birds, Palais-Royal garden 44
7 Demonstrators in the streets of Paris 84
8 Galerie d'Orléans portico 124
9 Schematic plan, Palais-Royal 126
10 Conseil d'État, Palais-Royal 128
11 Palais-Royal entrance, galerie de Nemours 131
12 Cour d'Honneur, Palais-Royal 142
13 Palais-Royal garden 146
14 Galerie d'Orléans 147
15 Sitting in the Palais-Royal garden 153
16 Study of proportions, garden façade, Palais-Royal 156
17 Gathering places, Palais-Royal 158
18 Fountain, Palais-Royal garden 160
19 Galerie d'Orléans 164
20 Palais-Royal 167
21 Detail, Fondation Rothschild Workers' Residence 170
22 Rue de Prague façade, Fondation Rothschild Workers' Residence 172
23 Schematic of ground-floor plan 174
24 Schematic of typical floor plan 174
25 Schematic of plan and neighbourhood 178

26 Square Armand-Trousseau 179
27 Marché de Bauveau and place d'Aligre food market 181
28 Fondation Rothschild Workers' Residence 183
29 Central courtyard, Fondation Rothschild Workers' Residence 186
30 Urban-design diagram, Fondation Rothschild Workers' Residence 194
31 Schematic floor plan of typical flats, Fondation Rothschild Workers' Residence 197
32 Stone and brick façades, Fondation Rothschild Workers' Residence 200
33 Courtyards, Fondation Rothschild Workers' Residence 204
34 Janitor's lodge, Fondation Rothschild Workers' Residence 206
35 Mont-Royal, Outremont 208
36 Schematic plan, Municipality of Outremont 210
37 Twin houses, Outremont 213
38 Front porch, Outremont 215
39 Plan of Outremont, 1875 220
40 Institutional buildings, Outremont 223
41 Street archetype, Outremont 225
42 Street space, Outremont 226
43 Three-storey row houses, Outremont 231
44 Knoll, Mont-Royal 233
45 Easy access to parks, Outremont 234
46 Outremont house, 1890 238
47 Walking in Outremont 240
48 Fountain, Parc Outremont 243
49 Garden, Palais-Royal 244
50 Design strategy diagram, phase one 248
51 Design strategy diagram, phases one, two, three 251
52 Design strategy diagram, seven phases 257
53 Palais-Royal garden 272
54 Mount Royal cemetery, Outremont 279
55 Street, Outremont 287
56 Main gate, Fondation Rothschild Workers' Residence 289
57 Small house, Outremont 291
58 Conviviality, Palais-Royal 293
59 Corinthian capital, Tholos of Epidaurus 296
60 Vegetables, Chinese market 298

61 Shaker cloak   299
62 Portico, Palais-Royal   305
63 Rue de Rivoli portico, near place du Palais-Royal   311
64 Portico, school in Strasboug   315
65 Andrea Palladio's basilica, Vicenza   316
66 Wedding party, Parc Pratt   318
67 Inspiration: archetype for a residence   321
68 Residence archetype of elegance   327
69 Residence archetype of elegance   330
70 Inspiration: archetype for a community park   333
71 Park archetype of elegance   336
72 Park archetype of elegance   338
73 Inspiration: archetype for a city square   341
74 Public square archetype of elegance   345
75 Public square archetype of elegance   346
76 Design objective   352

All photos are by the author. Sketches are by Louise Beaupré-Lincourt. All other drawings were done by the author with the help of Céline Klipfel.

Figures 9, 25, 73: City of Paris Planning Department
Figures 23, 24, 30, 31, 67: Fondation Rothschild
Figures 36, 39, 70: City of Outremont Planning Department

ACKNOWLEDGMENTS

I wish to express my gratitude to the many people who helped me with this work, most notably: Jean Wineman, Robert Craig, John Peponis, Ronald Williams, David Seamon, Thomas Galloway, Akira Yamashita, Leonard Warshaw, Pierre Dansereau, Victor Goldbloom, Martine Courant-Vidal, Alain-Charles Perrot, Jean-Pierre Hervé, Marie-Jeanne Dumont, Jean-Paul Flamand, Jacques Boulet, Pierre Dupuis, Pauline Marie Rosenau, and Monique Rochon.

Also, Mary Williams edited the manuscript, Jonathan Clements helped me with the translation of some French texts, and Céline Klipfel did some of the technical drawings.

In Search of Elegance

At the Palais-Royal, children play in an architecture of respect

I

INTRODUCTION
A THEORY FOR THE PRACTICE OF ARCHITECTURE

Society considers that the architect's mission is to assume the prime design responsibility in the vast industry entrusted with making the places where people live. It follows that the architect's professional credibility rests upon the success of his mission.[1] What is required of the architect is nothing less than to perform his duties at the highest possible level of efficacy. To do so, the architect needs to be knowledgeable, sensitive, competent, and creative.

The architect's sine qua non undertaking is the architectural design practice, a multifaceted professional activity that seeks to meet people's habitation needs by supplying architectural products. Simply put, the architect exists in society for the purpose of making architecture. He is asked to design – produce, construct – buildings and other kinds of places that are not only useful and solid, but also relevant and beautiful. The effective conduct of this complex trade requires a skilful and carefully thought-out manipulation of an extremely large and diversified knowledge base. Beyond technical and managerial skills, a conceptual framework is necessary to structure the architect's study procedure, channel his creative outflow, and buttress his design judgement. In other words, the practice of architecture necessitates a theory of architecture. The formulation of such a theory is the topic of this work.

INTENTION

Based on phenomenology, the architectural and urban design theory presented in this work introduces the quest for elegance as the predominant design objective, and suggests an approach for designing a more satisfactory and respectful architecture. This theory is supported by a description of three enduring architectural artefacts: the Palais-Royal and the Fondation Rothschild Workers' Residence on rue de Prague, both in Paris, and the municipality of Outremont in Montreal.

DEFINITIONS

The preceding statement of intention requires further definition, because even the most familiar ideas are often shrouded in confusion. This work is about formulating a theory. The definition of a theory of architecture used here is inspired by Stephen Hawking's conception of scientific theory (Hawking 1988, 9).[2] I suggest that a theory of architecture is a good theory if it satisfies two requirements: it must, as accurately and comprehensively as possible, describe the designed environment in a way that contains only a few arbitrary elements; and it must propose a method of designing this environment in response to human needs.[3] Such a theory is a coherent body of ideas that has two dimensions, descriptive and prescriptive.

Architecture is the object of the theory, and refers to both process and product. As process, it is the art, science, and practice of designing and constructing buildings. As product, it is a vast assemblage of built artefacts and a synonym for the manmade or designed environment, which also includes the tamed natural environment that surrounds it. No distinction is made between a certain type of building, sometimes described as architecture, and another kind of building, sometimes considered as mere construction. By definition, the architectural product has a physical presence. It has to be constructed in order to exist. Before it is built, it is not architecture. It is a vision, perhaps, a set of drawings or models. If it is demolished, it ceases to be architecture. If ruins remain, it becomes archaeology. The architectural product is always in the present, a cultural object as opposed to a natural object, like a pen as opposed to a pebble. The difference is purpose: a cultural object – an architectural product – is always made for a purpose (Lyotard 1991, 98).

As architectural products are material entities, it is paramount that the architect master the techniques for building them. This fundamental requirement has transcended all design theories, with perhaps one recent exception: some postmodern ideologues argue for the preeminence of what students call "paper architecture" (Bayer 1992, 7). The paper architects' strange position is difficult to uphold, simply because if architecture is not built, then what *is* what is built? And how does one distinguish between paper architecture and graphic design? If one follows this logic and concludes that the image of a building is architecture, then one concludes also that the image of a dish is gastronomy, or that a ten-thousand-volt electrical diagram on a chart will blast a deadly jolt. While such a statement appears obvious, some of the discourses used in architecture schools today make it necessary to present it.

The theory is also concerned with urban design. Although it is generally recognized that urban design possesses characteristics that distinguish it from architecture proper, it could be considered as larger-scale architecture, since it deals with the public domain as a structural framework integrating private components.[4]

The proposed theory is buttressed by phenomenology. Invented by German philosopher Edmund Husserl at the beginning of the twentieth century, phenomenology is a far-reaching system of thought that advocates a return to things themselves in order to describe those things as they appear to consciousness; that is, as phenomena perceived outside any preconceived ideology. The two main methodological *démarches* of phenomenology are the "epochè" and the "constitution." The former engages in a reduction of the phenomenon under scrutiny in order to obtain an enhanced consciousness of its essence, while the latter undertakes to reconstitute the phenomenon in its full reality, in the light of the enhanced consciousness obtained through the preceding epochè. Within this theory, epochès and constitutions of the architectural phenomenon are conducted.

Values and criteria are two notions called upon to support architectural judgement. Here, value is understood as a societal principle, a beacon guiding individual and collective aspirations; criterion is defined as a standard by which a thing is assessed.

Elegance is the key concept introduced by this theory. Although elegance is undoubtedly an inborn or acquired attribute of a person, it can also be a characteristic of a constructed thing, such as a work of architecture. It incorporates features affecting the entire architectural object. It is defined as the symbiosis of excellence and magnificence, and positioned as the ultimate attribute of any design process or creative endeavour. The quest for elegance is presented as the architect's prime design motivation and the necessary condition for creating an architecture of satisfaction. Facing a problem, the architect seeks to conceive the elegant solution; that is, to solve the problem thoroughly and fully with a frugality of means, and to erect buildings and cities that will endure and be considered elegant by present and future generations.

The main practical means of applying the theory is provided by the notion of archetype. In architecture, *archetype* is understood as "first form"; it serves as a model for a design endeavour. An applied archetype is necessarily built, has a form, and is referred to as either a type or, merely, a single architectural artefact.

ATTITUDE

This work is meant to be neither a rejection of the past nor a return to it. It deals with the actual, perpetual, yet constantly changing presence of architecture, and looks towards the future while remembering the past. It accepts the contextual characteristics of architecture without negating the possibility of some universal, humanist values. It says, for instance, that not everything can be defined as structure, yet structures are to be found in phenomena. What it tries to do is detect some coherence in the chaotic, discover continuity in the disjointed, uncover creativity in the systematic, and draw simplicity out of complexity. Undoubtedly, obscurity will remain, but, as Heidegger points out, obscurity is a necessary condition of clarity (Heidegger 1957, 56).

The reader will notice that my approach in this work is inclusive. For me, the world is too complex to be perceived as a Manichean confrontation between good and evil. Ambiguities have existed since the emergence of human consciousness. Each point of view carries the germ of its contrary; each action triggers its reaction. Philosophical debates and ideological quarrels amply demonstrate that all schools of thought – humanism, positivism or existentialism, modernism or postmodernism, contextualism – contain inherent contradictions (Rosenau 1992). There is no need to demonstrate their existence, only to reconcile them. As we shall see, Descartes influenced both phenomenology and the present theory of architecture. At the beginning of his most famous text, the *Discours de la méthode*, the great French philosopher warned his readers that his goal was not to teach them the sort of method each person must follow in order to reason well, but only to show them how he has tried to conduct his own. His attitude has inspired my own.

2

A THEORY BASED ON PHENOMENOLOGY

A COMPLEX PROBLEM

In architecture, as in other problem-solving procedures, analysis always starts with observation. The architect observes the world and scrutinizes his own design activities within it. It does not take long for him to realize that the prime problem of architecture is how to fulfil a client's needs properly. Every contract he obtains, every mandate he assumes, every proposal he makes, every design he creates, is an attempt to meet one or several of such human habitation needs. As a rule, the architect strives to solve the prescribed problem to the best of his ability.

Three Classical Questions

Is he successful, however? A simple enough query, perhaps, but certainly one that itself raises three fundamental questions that begin to frame the architectural problem statement. First, what is this designed environment the architect is trying to design? Second, why should his client – indeed, society as a whole – accept the sort of design he is producing? Third, how can he design his product in such a way that the client and society in general are fully satisfied with it? An architectural theory is precisely the sort of mental construct needed to find meaningful answers to these three questions.

Admittedly, such a tripod is unabashedly classical and inspired by Aristotle. In his introduction to Aristotle's *Politics* and *Poetics*, American philosopher Horace Kallen summarized the approach of Alexander's mentor by stating that "Aristotle asked of man and the universe three major

People enjoy sitting at the terrace of a café in the serene atmosphere of the Palais-Royal garden

questions: First, What is it? This is the question, which the sciences of nature and metaphysics purport to answer. Second, What is it good for? This is the question to which the so-called 'normative' sciences, especially ethics and aesthetics – and politics as an extension of ethics – are held to provide answers. Third, How do we know? This last question sets the task for logic, epistemology and every other variety of knowledge" (Kallen 1979, xiii).

The questions raised by a contemporary architectural theory are simpler than those raised by Aristotle, and could even by understood as subsets of the Greek philosopher's existential issues. Nonetheless, although focused on a specific domain of human activity – architecture – the three interrogations are undoubtedly complex and far-reaching. Since before Aristotle's time, all architects have agonized over them, and none have ever been able to formulate a permanently satisfactory answer. Yet, over the years, numerous doctrines have been applied, and countless buildings, good and bad, erected. Architects, together with all the other participants in the construction industry, never cease to structure our designed environment. They are, however, the first to admit that their practice is based on a body of knowledge riddled with uncertainties, half-truths, partial data, and controversial assumptions. The fact that a few architects of great talent have always been able to reach beyond ambiguity and create masterpieces does not change the basic situation. Exceptional architectural works are precisely that: exceptions to the rule. The real problem is how to deal with the rule, how to harness the mainstream of architecture. When practitioners turn to theoreticians for guidance, they are often met with a display of intellectual scepticism – no doubt well founded – and a barrage of criticism – no doubt well documented – that do nothing more than shake the very foundation of their beliefs.

What, then, should be done? Architects cannot espace their destiny. Every day, a new architecture has to be designed. If architects refuse the challenge of their mission, they will be pushed aside by entrepreneurs eager to usurp their title. In fact, this eroding process has already started. The architect's permanent *crise de conscience* would not be at issue if the works of "alternate" designers were satisfactory. But such is not the case. Although one set of individuals has replaced another, severe architectural problems remains. A simple observation of the state of the designed environment around the world convinces us that, indeed, there is room for improvement. Architects, practitioners, and theoreticians alike are not responsible for all the problems of society. They are not even responsible for all the problems related to the designed environment, but they do share in this responsibility and must help to find solutions. The three questions I have posed constitute the backbone of the architectural problem.

Unavoidable Complexity

Are these questions too broad to yield meaningful answers? If, in fact, they are, then we may wind up in a quandary. What course of action should be taken if one realizes that the solution to architectural problems lies precisely in the answers to these seemingly unanswerable broad questions? One could certainly argue that these broad questions cannot be ignored, because they reflect the complex architectural reality, and because architectural design always implies a similar complex synthesis of many elements. And, if for unknown reasons one has to select more restricted questions when reflecting on architectural theory, how can one insure the relevancy of these partial questions? After all, architects do not have the leisure to study useless questions. Is there, in architectural theory, a shield against triviality?

Indubitably, architecture is a multifaceted reality. For example, the user's requirements, either for a simple villa or a large hospital, are governed by myriad, varied imperatives deeply entrenched in human values and behavioural patterns. Construction, alone, is a complicated assemblage of numerous materials and systems. Planning, designing, and erecting sections of cities or urban infrastructures requires multidisciplinary analyses that baffle the sharpest minds. Every step of the way, the architectural praxis is twisted by political and social necessities, tamed by financial and economic constraints, and coloured by cultural peculiarities. Recognition of the compounded fact that complexity is a fundamental characteristic of architectural reality and that complexity cannot be avoided if one seriously wishes to address environmental problems constitutes a vital dimension of the architectural problem.

Social Accountability

In architecture, the obligation of relevancy is paramount because the architect never designs for himself, except perhaps when he designs his own home, which is seldom, if ever. Even when he does, his work is submitted to the critical assessment of others. Whether he likes it or not, whether he negates it or not, the architect is always accountable to society, which supports his training, regulates his trade, and, in the final analysis, pays his bills.

Even though they may be issued by private clients, architectural mandates always imply a public responsibility. Design briefs are meant to respect environmental regulations. Any individual building is a part of the public townscape. Since people's habitation needs and aspirations are both personal and collective, it is up to the architect to see that the attainment of individual objectives finds its proper place in the list of common goals. This is a complex, elusive task. In any analysis of society, one cannot fail to notice that social consensus cohabits with contradiction, that emancipation is frustrated by alienation, that progress is curbed by injustice or disaster – in sum, that this immensely complex world of ours does not evolve in a straight line. Within this meander, however, one can detect certain patterns of order, which are often illustrated by the sort of enduring architectural artefacts that have reached the status of historical monument. Although many things change – as, for instance, have the perception of others and standards of comfort – other things – such as the will to survive, the need to sleep, the urge to learn, and the desire to have a home – last. Relevancy in architectural design requires proposals that try to integrate individuality within community, diversity within harmony, and innovation within continuity. Reaching the proper equilibrium between private objectives and public aims is a delicate yet indispensable undertaking that must rest on society's values. The architect must endeavour to understand these values because they may constitute the foundation of his design decisions. His social accountability is nothing more than his responsible attitude towards society's values.

Environmental Mediocrity

Clearly, today's society is not satisfied with the present condition of the design environment. Signs to this effect are numerous and voiced in many ways: United Nations reports (Sachar 1993), mayors' appeals ("Cities" 1993), the lobbying efforts of citizens' groups, the exposés of social critics, and riots in the streets. At its 1993 meeting, the United Nations Economic and Social Committee's Commission on Human Rights endorsed a report on the right to adequate housing that documented "the enormity of the global housing crisis being faced today. According to indicators compiled by the United Nations Centre for Human Settlements, over 100 million persons live in a state of absolute homelessness, while in excess of one billion persons are forced by circumstances to reside in desperately inadequate housing conditions, threatening their health, security, safety and dignity" (Sachar 1993, 2). Observers generally concur: by and large, the present designed environment is in a state of appalling mediocrity. A walk in a city anywhere in the world, and in many rural settlements, readily confirms the prevalence of this environmental desolation. The ugliness and degradation of most Eastern European suburban residential districts make them as perverse and alienating as parts of Calcutta, Cairo, Hong Kong – or even New York.

Living conditions in most North American inner-city districts are no better than those in South American *favelas*. In a 1989 issue of *Human Rights Quarterly*, social critic Scott Leckie wrote that "shelter dilemmas are not only endemic to poorer countries. In the United States, the National Coalition of the Homeless estimates that two to three million people are homeless, while in the Netherlands 1.7 million people have registered with their local governments to obtain better accommodations" (Leckie 1989). In its 1 November 1993 issue, *U.S. News and World Report* magazine claimed that American mayoral candidates are once again concentrating on the basic quality-of-life issues because the environments of their cities are deteriorating at an alarming rate. For example, "in New York, the proportion of districts with fewer than half the streets rated acceptably clean rose from 13.6% in 1989 to 25.4% in 1992" ("Cities" 1993). Dirty streets are not a trivial issue: they are a symptom of a more pervasive mediocrity.

The World Health Organization has clearly established the link between environmental health and housing conditions. In many epidemiological analyses, the demonstration was made that housing – understood in the broad context of dwellings together with their neighbourhoods and their amenities – is the environmental factor most frequently associated with disease conditions. For example, inadequate and deficient housing is invariably correlated with higher mortality and morbidity rates. A recent study on living conditions in Third World cities showed that in them hundreds of millions of people inhabit overcrowded dwellings, and have no clean water, no sewers, and no health care. There is no garbage-collection service, and drains have not been installed to prevent flooding. In many squatter communities, children are fifty times more likely to die before reaching the age of five than their counterparts in more affluent neighbourhoods.

Environmental mediocrity infiltrates all corners of the designed environment. It manifests itself in a lack of basic amenities, deficient urban services, decrepit or overstressed infrastructures, squalid and overcrowded residential quarters, crumbling public buildings, sordid schools, public places that serve no coherent purpose, dangerous barren areas, sprawl and waste of all sorts, dirt, deafening noise, pollution, and ugliness. Poor planning, deficient design, and ill-advised architectural doctrines are not the sole causes of environmental mediocrity. Other powerful factors – such as poverty, blind political ideology, racism, bureaucratic lunacy, and pure, simple ignorance – also contribute. But desolate American inner cities and sprawling suburbs, as well as the endless stretches of anonymous residential towers found in European suburbs, are direct products of the Modern Architecture doctrine, as expressed, for instance, by Le Corbusier's *Plan Voisin* and Frank Lloyd Wright's *Broadacre City* (Le Corbusier 1948; Wright 1963; Brolin 1976; Jencks 1984; Wales 1989; Frampton 1992). Wealthy downtown Houston, for instance, is nothing but a vast parking lot surrounding scattered office towers – a modern, glistening, but inhuman and dangerous environment (Kostof 1992, 287).[5]

Examples of this rampant mediocrity are far too plentiful to enumerate, and so I will relate a personal experience, if only as one telling illustration. In the fall of 1993, I was an urban design studio instructor at the Georgia Institute of Technology in Atlanta. My students were asked to study East Lake Meadows, an Afro-American residential community situated in East Atlanta, and propose means of upgrading this "campus" of 640 housing units built with federal money some thirty years earlier. Since opening, East Lake Meadows had been the perfect slum, a place of horrendous poverty made worse by horrible design. In this indistinct compound, thirty-two two-storey walk-up brick barracks were scattered across barren patches of earth amid desolate parking lots. When I saw them, both buildings and grounds had deteriorated beyond repair because there had never been any incentive to maintain a place that clearly belonged to no one. Residential units that had not been abandoned were overcrowded. To visitors, the prevailing impression was one of desperate environmental confusion. To residents, the community was a place to stay, but definitely not a satisfactory home because privacy had been negated. At East Lake Meadows, as soon as one walked out of a building – often through a door opening directly into a bedroom – one stepped into a no-man's-land where anyone felt entitled to do anything. It is not surprising that such a field of spontaneous confrontation had nurtured violence, a brutality so offensive that residents nicknamed their community "Little Vietnam." At the beginning of the exercise, the Georgia Tech authorities had declared Little Vietnam too dangerous to visit and no official site inspection was organized for the students. However, I was proud to see that they chose to ignore this directive. And we discovered a miracle: although living conditions in East Lake Meadows are an affront to human dignity, very dignified, honest, and deserving people were surviving there, crying out for a better environment. People like the East Lake Meadows residents are living in similar places all over the world, urging architects to propose better design solutions.

The perception of deserving people living in a mediocre environment is another fundamental element of the architectural problem. Of course, in the midst of this overall mediocrity, one finds high-quality pockets, flashes of genuine beauty, sometimes even places that are magnificent tributes to humanity's wisdom and creative genius.

Odd Neglect

While many architects are sensitive to the magnitude of the architectural problem, most have retreated into some sort of intellectual cocoon, oblivious to the basic purpose of their professional mission. In his inaugural address at the Harvard Graduate School of Design, Dean Peter Rowe reflected on this issue and stated that it is "abundantly clear, for example, that we do rather well at what might be termed the high end of design. The signature buildings and landscapes which grace the pages of magazines are, by most accounts, beautiful and fitting in their own ways. When it comes to the quality of endless suburban tracts, or deteriorating inner-city slums, by contrast, nothing could be further from an ideal. Professionally speaking, they have been neglected at best, or simply abandoned" (Rowe 1993, 4).

It seems that, through an odd twist of its dialectic, it is the postmodern ideology that has fuelled this neglect. The situation's irony is that postmodernism came into being as a reaction to the environmental mediocrity caused largely by the preceding Modern Architecture ideology (Jencks 1984). In the same Harvard address, Rowe affirmed that "although the relatively recent post-modern critique and the critique arising from the 'philosophy of difference' have been most constructive," he saw "a very serious danger, within the broader educational scheme of things, of design falling totally into the realm of personal visions, a fetished concern for marginality, and a kind of not particularly prepossessing art for art's sake. Unfortunately, these and other similar trends have other consequences. Among them is a perceived, if not real, loss of authority on our part as designers over the permeation of design quality in broader societal terms. In short, we can quickly become reduced to providing the 'window dressing' or a 'gloss on otherwise lacklustre terms'" (Rowe 1993, 3). The current postmodern neglect constitutes an aggravating factor of the architectural problem.

Ill-Equipped Architects

The postmodern emphasis on triviality or, in Fredric Jameson's words, on "contrived depthlessness," may be a symptom of a much more profound malaise (Jameson in Harvey 1990, 59). Perhaps it is because many architects feel inadequate that they shy away from difficult problems and are content with becoming sceptical, detached observers, often advantageously disguised as avant-garde intellectuals.

Fortunately, other architects have reacted and have proposed, once again, that the architectural profession's perennial existential problems be put at the top of the agenda. That is why, on 23 October 1993, a symposium on architectural practices was held at the Harvard Graduate School of Design. In his opening remarks, Dean Rowe explained to a group of distinguished architects[6] that one of the reasons for convening this meeting was that "there is a sense of crisis among design professions, which is centrally concerned with professional well-being, or at least with the survival of the profession as we know it" (Rowe 1993, 36). Rowe's diagnosis of crisis was a cry that has often been heard throughout the twentieth century, which indicates that the malaise is perhaps deeply rooted.[7]

The GSD symposium panellists offered a series of explanations for the current crisis and ways of curbing it. British architecture historian Andrew Saint professed his optimism about the future of architecture, but said that the architect's real challenge "is to ride and control this exciting, undisciplined, licentious, and dangerous beast, this irresponsible lust for image which pervades our culture" (Saint 1994, 39). Professor of architectural practice Carl Sapers, after describing some of the profession's prevalent difficulties, declared: "The forces of change I have described, the debasement of the profession, the influence of liability insurers, the loss of control, the growth of design/build project delivery systems, the degradation of the fiduciary relationship, and the popularisation of the team approach – all these forces are the more powerful because they push in the same direction. Without some strong countervailing force, their effect on architectural practice will, I predict, be devastating." And he added: "What are the contrary forces which might be marshalled? First, architects must move toward embracing, rather than avoiding, responsibilities" (Sapers 1994, 40–41). *Progressive Architecture* magazine executive editor Thomas Fisher criticized the architects' neglect, and said that "if this profession is to survive, it must see its primary mission as public service" (Fisher 1994, 43). Practising American architect Elizabeth Padjen commented that the current trends "tend to redefine architecture in very narrow terms. A focus on architecture as mere art will tend to marginalize the profession; a focus on architecture as mere fashion will tend to trivialize the profession; and, most dangerously, a focus on architecture as a luxury product either unavailable or unnecessary to the majority of people will ultimately destroy the profession" (Padjen 1994, 44).

The architectural profession's malaise is not limited to the United States. In Canada, a 1986 report on the profession commissioned by the federal government, *The Barnard Report*, named after its principal author, Peter Barnard, clearly identified the profession's problems: real or perceived arrogance on the part of many architects who put their own interests before those of their clients, inadequate management practices, failure to remain abreast of technological developments, and insufficient research to buttress relevant design solutions and solid construction techniques (Barnard 1986). Consequently, insisted Barnard, architects are losing credibility and business and will continue to do so if they do not mend their ways. Six years later, another Canadian study, commissioned this time by the Royal Architectural Institute of Canada, offered a very interesting comment. According to the nonarchitects who participated in various groups within the study, architects possess special skills to solve some of society's problems, but are conspicuously absent from social debate. Also in 1992, in the United Kingdom, a government initiative to deregulate the architectural profession almost succeeded. The argument of those behind it was simply this: Why should British society pay for a five-year university programme to train people who are doing nothing more than decorating building façades? Indeed, why should society maintain architecture as an exclusive liberal profession for such a superficial activity?[8]

Extending beyond corporate anxieties, this malaise uncompasses the current deficiencies displayed by architects. It is sad to say that design proficiency, which should be an architect's strong point, has become appallingly weak. The glaring design mistakes and ugliness of existing constructions, such as East Lake Meadows, are a constant reminder of these shortcomings. In his doctoral dissertation on architectural education, architect Michael Jones demonstrated that "unfortunately, examples of incompetence, negligence, design and construction errors, and fraud in the building industry are all too frequent" (Jones 1989, 346).

If architects are ill equipped to face the twenty-first century's enormous environmental challenge, it is largely because of the shortcomings of their education. Michael Jones was quoting a 1988 *Progressive Architecture* survey when he wrote in his dissertation: "Sixty-eight percent of the readership who responded to the survey (over 1,500 responses) supported the idea of a work-study program which they believe would better prepare graduates for practice than the conventional courses in a professional school" (Jones 1989, 337). Through this response, the *Progressive Architecture* readership was saying that the schools of architecture (in the United States) were not adequately training young architects. Although Jones warned that one must be careful in interpreting the survey's responses, he noted that "many architects place the blame for their dissatisfaction with their careers on their education ... even respondents who were satisfied with their own education did not think too much of architectural education in general today." He added, "this indicates that the critics are right; today's schools are not preparing their students well enough for practice ... ninety percent agreed that schools were out of touch with reality." In addition to concerns about design education and training, and the lack of focus on practice, the respondents identified other shortcomings in architectural education: lack of management and business-practice training, insufficient connection between design studio and other courses, too little emphasis on communication skills, insufficient instruction in technical matters, and too little opportunity to study other disciplines (Jones 1989, 376, 378).

In its September 1995 issue, *Progressive Architecture* published a long article arguing once more that "the rift between the architecture schools [in the United States] and practitioners has never been greater," and that the schools are "failing the profession" (Crosbie 1995). Aloof architectural education is another dimension of the architectural problem.

Fragmented Profession

Ill-trained architects are not supported by their profession, which is divided against itself. Perhaps the design profession has always been this way. Today, however, the balkanization of architecture seems to be accelerating. The design profession's disjointed disciplines are removed from the building-engineering disciplines[9]. There is a further split between the professionals and the contractors/construction workers. Practicing architects who absolutely need to bring disciplines together in order to erect a building are cut off from theoreticians, historians, and critics – precisely those people who might help them with this integration. Other disciplines important to high-quality architecture, such as psychology and behavioural science, rarely make it to construction sites or classrooms. This vast field, which could be immensely rich because of its multidimensionality is, in fact, impoverished by its divisions.

The profession's harmful fragmentation starts at the university, where disciplines are taught in separate programmes. This sets the tone for the practice's subsequent dislocation. The point could be made that the lack of pedagogical cohesion is one of the main reasons for the absence of a common professional language, which explains the practitioners' confusion and, ultimately, the designed environment's poor quality. Things done in a disjointed, haphazard way are rarely coherent and purposeful. This is another element of the problem.

Theory/Practice Schism

Now, at the close of the twentieth century, two trends seem to dominate the field of what is called architectural theory. The first is a shift from practice to academia. Prior to World War II, the profession's most influential theoreticians were practitioners; since the war, most of its prime thinkers have been university professors. The main prewar thinkers were Otto Wagner and the other Secession activists centred in Austria, Walter Gropius and the Bauhaus team in Germany, Frank Lloyd Wright in America, and Le Corbusier and his Esprit Nouveau associates in France. These giants shaped the Modern Architecture doctrine.[10] In the thirties, Nazi persecution displaced numerous European intellectuals, and American universities retrieved some of the leading architectural ideologues. For instance, Gropius was appointed director of Harvard Graduate School of Design, while Mies van der Rohe was offered a similar position at Chicago's Illinois Institute of Technology.

After World War II, the trend towards universities accelerated, and it became irresistible in the seventies. For the past twenty-five years, the most influential architectural ideas have originated in schools of architecture. Robert Venturi, Charles Jencks, Robert Graves, and Peter Eisenman, for example, disseminated their messages from university platforms: clearly, the post-modern and deconstructivist movements germinated in university seminars. While the first generation of postmodern architectural luminaries moved on to practise extensively, many of their followers were exclusively university teachers. Today, in America at least, nonpractising architects produce almost all of the writings in the area of what is called architectural theory.

The second trend proceeds from the first. Because today's architectural writers are rarely practising architects, their writings are more and more removed from practice. The breach between university-based writers and practising architects is widening at an alarming rate, fuelling suspicion between the two groups. In her presentation at the Harvard seminar mentioned earlier, Elizabeth Padjen described the practitioners' feelings in strong terms: "As architecture schools examine the culture of the profession, they should also examine their own culture of academia, to understand better the fit between the two. It is no surprise that the introduction of PhD programs is generally viewed with deep suspicion by practitioners, who fear that a new mandarin class of theoreticians is seizing control. Suspicion seems to be a two-way street; practitioners who visit schools as visiting critics, fellows, and guest jurors frequently report that the faculty are either disdainful or defensive around the outsiders" (Padjen 1994, 44).

If the mandarins' rôle is to develop an architectural theory, then one is entitled to ask if they are really doing so. Indeed, what is the objective of a theory of architecture? Most architects would answer that architectural theory is developed in order to explain the architectural artefact and aid the practice of architecture. Yet, few architectural writings today attain this goal. It is interesting to note that the most popular texts in architecture doctoral seminars, even the required readings of PhD programmes, are written by nonarchitects on subjects sometimes far removed from architecture, such as social criticism, semiology, structuralism, hermeneutics, history of art, and even literary criticism.[11]

One may certainly point out that it is within design that one finds the aim of architectural theory; hence the call for a design education leading to a practice more solidly grounded in theory. But to accomplish this, theoretical writings in architecture must be more than what they are today, more than mere speculative discourses. They must strive to fill the gap between theory and practice, and present positive contributions to a real architectural theory. There is no doubt that practising architects need theoreticians to help them articulate their design knowledge. It is, however, up to the theoreticians to speak a language that meets the practicing architects' concerns. The theory/practice schism is another element of the architectural problem.

A Theory Needed

Baffled by the immensity of the environmental problem, architects need a theory that recognizes that the present confusion within the architectural profession is, in part, responsible for the designed environment's unacceptable mediocrity. This two-tiered problem is the ultimate issue to tackle, and improving the designed environment becomes the only aim of both architectural theoreticians and practitioners. Instead of retreating into separate worlds and indulging in sterile rationalization and mutual recrimination, they should join forces to attain this overriding goal.

Within this widespread environmental mediocrity, pockets of excellence do exist. Perhaps the solution resides there. The reasons that these all-too-rare, high-quality, and very beautiful places thrive are still to be investigated. One may ask what is so special about these places that people are inspired to preserve them at any cost, to rebuild them if they are destroyed, to make homes of them, and to identify them as a cherished part of their cultural heritage. These places may be used as models for producing a more satisfactory architecture elsewhere, everywhere, so that quality and beauty become the norm rather than the exception.

The proposed theory calls for a renewed harmony between creativity and relevancy, a stronger continuum between history and actuality, and a more pertinent definition of the fundamental traits of architecture. It probes into the forgotten attribute of architecture that may encompass all others: the attribute of elegance. It argues that the search for elegance has become a necessary undertaking. The current environmental mediocrity and the architectural profession's difficulties result, in part, from the contemporary architect's ignorance of the attribute of elegance. Should he choose to reintroduce this attribute in all aspects of his work, he will be compelled to master the lost dimensions of his trade and become more efficient and relevant. In order to accept such a change in his attitude, however, he needs a strong motive and a persuasive rationale. The proposed theory seeks to provide a convincing argument to this effect, as well as a useful contribution to architectural knowledge. That is why the main theme of this work is the search for elegance as a route towards an architecture of satisfaction.

A PHENOMENOLOGICAL METHOD

Phenomenology is called upon to serve as the methodological underpinning of the theory. Increasingly frustrated by the inadequacy of both experimental science and the traditional philosophies as tools to explain the world, German philosopher and mathematician Edmund Husserl proposed a third option. He developed what he called the science of phenomena, a new system of thought devoted to the description of the essence of things as they appear to consciousness. According to American philosophers David Stewart and Algis Mickunas, phenomenology is characterized by "a return to the traditional task of philosophy, the search for a philosophy without presuppositions, the intentionality of consciousness, and the refusal of the subject-object dichotomy" (Stewart and Mickunas 1974, 5).

Remaining above ideological turmoil, phenomenology has been the most fertile basic philosophy of the twentieth century. It gave birth to some of the most influential contemporary philosophies, such as Heidegger's ontology, Sartre's existentialism, and Gadamer's hermeneutics (Dumas 1990; Trotignon 1967). It has extended philosophical enquiry into numerous segments of human knowledge or preoccupation. For example, Enzo Paci developed a phenomenology of nature. Maurice Merleau-Ponty wrote phenomenological studies of flesh, movement, and perception. His book *Phénoménologie de la perception* became a classic in phenomenological literature mainly because perception is the point of departure of all awareness, a central theme in phenomenology. Henri Duméry conceptualized a phenomenology of the religious experience, complemented by Emmanuel Lévinas's phenomenology of God. Mikel Dufrenne wrote a monumental phenomenological exploration of the aesthetic experience. Paul Ricœur, in addition to his extensive work on Husserl, developed a phenomenology of the will. Gaston Bachelard wrote phenomenological essays on fire, dreams, water, and architectural space. Anna-Thérésa Tymieniecka worked on a phenomenology of invention and creativity. Jacques Derrida did a phenomenology of language that led him to his concept of deconstruction. Jean-François Lyotard started his career with a treatise on phenomenology, published some fifteen years before the influential *La condition post-moderne: Rapport sur le savoir* (Gaston Bachelard 1949, 1964, 1973; Cumming 1991; Derrida 1967; Dufrenne 1973; Husserl 1950, 1970; Lyotard 1954, 1991; Merleau-Ponty 1945; Trotignon 1967).[12]

What explains phenomenology's fertility may be precisely what differentiates it from the other systems. Phenomenology's governing attitude is that the broadest possible definition of its own subject matter and approach should be embraced. It is an open-minded method that always begins by freeing itself from preconceived ideologies. It neither excludes nor negates anything, only temporarily suspends judgement on things. One could suggest that such a method is what is needed for a theory of architecture: a method of enquiry as extensive as architecture itself.

Facts

The phenomenological method starts with the observation of facts. Merleau-Ponty wrote that the first instruction Husserl gave to those who wanted to practice phenomenology was to return to the things themselves (Merleau-

Ponty 1945, ii). In the conclusion to the *Cartesian Meditations*,[13] Husserl insisted that the research depicted in his lectures was "nothing but the beginning of the radical elucidation of the meaning and origin of concepts such as: world, nature, space, time, being, animal, man, soul, organism, social community, culture, etc." (Husserl 1986, 132). These concepts arise from the reality they depict, that is, from facts.

In architecture, facts are singular, spatio-temporal architectural artefacts. In other words, they are bare buildings and places. Together, they constitute a physical whole called the designed environment. However, bare facts are of little interest to phenomenologists and architects; what begins to be relevant is perceived facts.

Phenomena

Enlarged by human perception, facts emerge from their so-called objective isolation and become phenomena. Lyotard explained that a phenomenon is "that which appears to consciousness, that which is given" (Lyotard 1991, 32). Phenomena are known through the senses. Since they do not exist outside human perception, they are "humanized" facts. In architecture, a phenomenon can be described as "inhabited space perceived by the people who experience it." However, an architectural phenomenon is more than "people in space": it is people energizing space, people intrinsically, organically linked to their physical environment in the most intimate fashion. Architectural phenomena form a category of phenomena. Together, they constitute the generic idea of the architectural phenomenon, which constitutes the object of this theory.

Life-World

By broadening one's comprehension of all phenomena, including the architectural phenomena, one accomplishes the symbiosis of an infinite number of phenomena and reaches the idea of the life-world. The life-world is phenomenology's all-encompassing object par excellence.

Expressing not only his own opinion but also the position of Husserl, Swiss philosopher André de Muralt insisted that "the life-world (*Lebenswelt*) [is] is pregiven to all scientific knowledge" (de Muralt 1974, 246). In this context, the designed environment is a part of the life-world's physical manifestation. The environment is pregiven to the designed environment, and design knowledge flows out of the description of the designed environment.

Subject

If phenomena are what are given, then phenomena are given to me. "I" grasp phenomena with, as Antony Flew wrote, the "scrupulous inspection of my consciousness" (Flew 1984, 19). You? You may practise phenomenology as you also grasp phenomena. As we all experience reality, we all, as humans, may also practise phenomenology. Are these disjointed practices? "Absolutely not!" the phenomenologists answer, because humans overcome their individuality as they become part of their community, part of humanity. American philosopher Mark Taylor explained that "the task of the phenomenologist is to describe all being as being-for-consciousness. Through this description, it becomes apparent that every object of experience is the product of the constituting subject. This subject is the 'transcendental ego' that projects the world of experience through its 'intentional' activity" (Taylor 1988, 19).

Transcendental has to be distinguished from transcendent. The latter refers to a relationship between humans among themselves and as a dimension of phenomena, and the former to a relationship between me as a human and the life-world. Phenomenology asserts that it is the combined effect of this double transcendence that provides universality in the consciousness of phenomena.

But who is this "I" who perceives the phenomena? To answer this question, phenomenologists have turned to René Descartes. The seventeenth century French philosopher said that the "I" is the thinking man – or, better, the doubting man. Descartes argued that the doubting process is what pushes us towards the primordial statement of the human condition, a statement so fundamental that it becomes the self-evident, indubitable foundation of all knowledge. It is the "cogito, ergo sum."[14] In architectural theory, one could suggest that the subject be a special kind of man. Not only is he thinking and doubting, but he is also creating architecture, a sine qua non condition of his existence and reality as architect. In this theory, the subject is the thinking and doubting architect.

But the thinking and doubting architect does not lose his human condition. He makes architecture for other humans like himself, and he makes it for himself, as well. As an architect, he is different from other humans because he is the one who conceives and constructs the designed environment; the others merely occupy and use it. As a human being, he joins the other members of his community because he also occupies and uses the same environment. Hence, the subject-object dichotomy is shattered, and the theory's subject joins the theory's object in a symbiotic whole.

"But what is it that I am?" asked Descartes. And he answered: "It is a thing that thinks. What is a thing that thinks? It is a thing that doubts, conceives, affirms, negates, does not want, imagines also, and feels" (Descartes 1979, 81).[15] With this one sentence, Descartes offered an admirable description of the architect's essential activities:

§ The architect doubts: He is sceptical, he questions and analyses.

§ He conceives: He conducts his principal mission, which is to design; but he also develops a theory to buttress his design endeavour.

§ He affirms: For the architect, the ability to affirm is a necessity; the act of building requires affirmations; never has he the intellectual luxury of remaining aloof in the comfortable nirvana of scepticism; his mission requires of him to descend to the level of clay and stones, mud and water, in order to construct a building with material components.

§ He negates: Of course, by affirming a particular design solution, the architect negates all others.

§ He does not want: The architect remains a free person with the opportunity to express his judgement; by saying what he does not want, he takes risks, acknowledges the fact that he makes mistakes, and claims the right to correct them.

§ He imagines also: The fact that it introduces imagination is one of the most important reasons Descartes' approach is so relevant to architecture; what Descartes is saying is that to imagine is to perform an act of cognition in the noblest sense of the word; to employ the imagination is to employ a means as legitimate as rationalization for developing knowledge; the architect's capacity to imagine defines him as architect; it cannot be ignored, and it constitutes a necessary component of the most rigorous rational discourse; architectural design requires imagination.

§ And he feels: The process of making architecture requires sensitivity, a perception of the world beyond rational explanation.

Consciousness and Intentionality

When I voluntarily observe the world in which I am intrinsically integrated, I become conscious of the world and of my lived experience as part of this world.[16] Husserl's professor, Franz Brentano, demonstrated that consciousness is always the consciousness of something else (Stewart 1974, 8), and this projection, this grasping of phenomena, this consciousness of something else is what is called "intentionality." Husserl adopted Brentano's concept and made it the principle of his method. As it is the projection of humans towards their world, intentionality forges the bond between the subject and the object in an existential symbiosis. States of consciousness are states of intentionality. Phenomenology, thus, reveals a consciousness that "bursts outward, a consciousness, in sum, which is nothing if not a relation to the world" (Lyotard 1991, 34).

I project my intentionality towards the architectural phenomenon and establish a relationship with architecture. In so doing, I proceed to seize and describe the architectural phenomenon. Phenomenology insists that the proper way of grasping phenomena is not by trying to explain it, but, rather, by describing it. It argues that the mere attempt at explaining distorts comprehension. Architecture vividly demonstrates this point, since many dimensions of the architectural phenomenon defy explanation. Being larger than explanation, description encompasses it.

Total consciousness of the pure ego within the essence of all phenomena is, of course, the ultimate destination of the phenomenological journey. But it is an elusive goal, beyond the reach of any of us.

Reflection and Logic

Intentionality is accomplished by two intellectual means that are constantly active in the phenomenological method: rational discourse and intuitive apprehension.

Rational discourse can also be called the practice of reflection. Phenomenology insists that it is not sufficient to experience phenomena through empirical perception. One must probe deeper than the common-sense perception of reality, and, by reflecting on it, grasp the meaning behind the meaning. Reflection implies meditating, asking questions, and developing answers. It is a personal quest that ensues from Descartes's approach, a filiation well recognized by phenomenologists. Husserl insisted that Descartes was his mentor, and de Muralt showed that Cartesianism buttresses every step of the phenomenological method. Descartes's method is a masterpiece of simplicity and has influenced knowledge development for more than three centuries. It was in the *Discours de la méthode* that the French philosopher outlined his logical, deductive approach, adding that he, himself, proceeded very slowly, as a man walking in the dark (Descartes 1991, 16).

Descartes's method comprises four methodological precepts. The first stipulates that arguments should be based only on demonstrably truthful statements. Obviously, one has to define what truthful is, and then identify truthful statements. The architectural theory will try to do this. The second precept states that one needs to subdivide the problem into the smallest possible parts in order to facilitate a resolution. This is now a well-understood approach: since Descartes, and probably well before him, practically all researchers and designers have adopted it. This precept will also apply to the present theory. The third precept indicates that one should proceed systematically from the simplest problem components to the most complex ones, a procedure that establishes relationships between components that may not be immediately self-evident, but will emerge from the exercise. The fourth precept stipulates that, in the course of a work, comprehensive reviews must be conducted on a regular basis in order to insure that nothing is forgotten. The architectural theory will also endeavour to follow these last two precepts.

By definition, Descartes's method is a logical discourse, and so is phenomenology. André de Muralt explained that "phenomenology, in its deepest sense, is a logic, a logic based on a criticism of science, advancing through a formal logic of being and of knowledge, and ending in a constitutive logic of being. It advances from a logical criticism to an objective-analytic philosophy, then to a subjective-synthetic philosophy. This philosophical logic – which is a science of both being and knowledge, hence a science of intentionality – is a dialectic" (de Muralt 1974, 104).

The theory of architecture formulated here is based on this logic. It is a logic of correlation, one that brings things into their mutual or reciprocal relationship. In this logic, said de Muralt, "the object (noema) must therefore always be distinguished from the consciousness of the object (noesis)" (de Muralt 1974, 287). *Noesis* is the intellectual apprehension of an object; and *noetic* means to be related to noesis. *Noema* signifies that this object has meaning. Husserl said that the fundamental aim of all consciousness is not only an experience but also an experience that has a meaning, a noematic experience. What is significant in a phenomenon is its noematic structure.

Correlation is not specific to phenomenology. It is a logic that is applied to many other human activities. This is, for example, the logic of creative endeavours in visual art, music, or poetry. By all accounts, it is a logic well adapted to architecture.

Imagination and Intuition

The second means of probing phenomena is the harnessing of imagination and the mobilization of intuition. *Imagination* is "the power of forming mental images," and *intuition* is "the immediate apprehension of truth, or supposed truth, in the absence of conscious rational process" (*Webster's* 1988). Descartes insisted that imagination and intuition are also a part of the philosophical process. Standing on Descartes's shoulders, Husserl said that imagination is phenomenology's weapon par excellence, and added that "the free images are occupying a privileged position with respect to perception; this superiority affirms itself even up to the phenomenology of perception" (Husserl 1950, 225). Gaston Berger, quoted by Ricoeur, maintained that "phenomenology is a philosophy of the creative intuition" (Ricoeur in Husserl 1950, l.c. xxx). All phenomenologists have placed imagination and intuition at the centre of their method. All have insisted that intuition and imagination are not only necessary means of probing phenomena, but also potent instruments for describing their essence.

No doubt intuition and imagination are tools as important as rational discourse for the shaping of our world. Mozart's *Magic Flute*, Shakespeare's *Hamlet*, and the Katsura Villa are convincing illustrations of this assertion. What is more important? What is more real? Is it the rational discourse leading to Newton's law of gravitation and the other principles of aerodynamics that permit aeroplanes to fly, or is it the creative imagining leading to Beethoven's Ninth Symphony that disposes people to sing the "Hymn of Joy"? Both approaches are necessary and complementary. In architecture, a method of enquiry that accepts intuition and imagination as valid instruments for describing the life-world has a certain chance of being pertinent, because architecture deals simultaneously with rational, experimental concepts similar to the law of gravitation, and with intuitive gestures such as the one that created the Ninth Symphony.

Epochè

The procedure by which "I" project my intentionality towards phenomena is called the "epochè." By adopting the phenomenological attitude, I engage in a process of systematically removing the constitutive layers of the phenomenon under scrutiny, of temporarily suspending the discarded elements, of bracketing them; I do all this in order to get behind its appearance and probe deeper and deeper into its essence; this exploring journey is called the epochè (Husserl 1950, 1986; Stewart 1974, 15–34). De Muralt explained further that the Greek word *epochè* designates the notion of "the point of view from which one withholds oneself." He added that "the epochè and the reduction must be distinguished as two moments of a single operation, and they must be regarded in an efficient ordering of antecedent [epochè] and consequent [reduction]" (de Muralt 1974, 253). However, many authors do not make this distinction, and treat *epochè* and *reduction* as synonyms.

Because of the extraordinary importance of the epochè in phenomenology and in this theory of architecture, it is necessary to present it by using Husserl's own definition, as it appears in the original French version of the *Cartesian Meditations*. He wrote that "The epochè is the putting into parentheses of the objective world, and that it does not place us in front of nothingness." However, what "becomes ours, or better, what becomes mine, the meditating subject," insisted Husserl, "is my pure life with the ensemble of my pure state of living and its intentional objects; that is, the universality of phenomena, phenomena understood in the special and enlarged way of phenomenology." He added that:

the epochè is the radical and universal method through which I grasp myself as pure ego, with the life of pure consciousness, which belongs to me, a life in which, and through which, the objective world exists for me. All that is world, all that is spatial and temporal – and exists for me precisely because I experience it, perceive it, remember it, think about it, in one or another way – an this carries existential or value judgements, desire, and so on. We know that Descartes designates all this by the term "cogito." In truth, the world is not for me anything other than what exists and has value for my consciousness in a similar "cogito". (Husserl 1986, 17)[17]

Merleau-Ponty asserted that "the true meaning of the famous phenomenological reduction [the epochè] is like a return to a transcendental consciousness before which the world unfolds in absolute transparency." He also stated that the best formulation to describe the epochè was given by Husserl's assistant, Eugen Fink, when he talked about an amazement at the world. As related by Merleau-Ponty, Fink said that the "reflection does not retire from the world toward the unity of consciousness as the foundation of the world; rather, it steps back in order to see the bursting of transcendences, it loosens up the intentional threads which tie us with the world in order to bring them to light, it alone is the consciousness of the world because it reveals it as strange and paradoxical" (Merleau-Ponty 1945, ix).[18] This is exactly what this theory proposes to accomplish regarding the architectural phenomenon.

It is at this point that one may join François Lyotard in asking: "What is the result of this reductive operation?" Lyotard's answer was, "insofar as the concrete ego is interwoven with the natural world, it is clear that it is itself reduced; in other words, I must abstain from all theses concerning the self as existing. But it is no less clear that there is an 'I' who properly abstains, and who is the 'I' even of the reduction. This 'I' is called the pure ego, and the epochè is the universal method by which I grasp myself as pure ego" (Lyotard 1991, 47). Merleau-Ponty, however, reminded us that "the greatest lesson of the reduction is the fact that a complete reduction is impossible" (Merleau-Ponty 1945, viii).

Eidetic Concepts

When I project myself towards a phenomenon that I perceive and that has become a part of my lived experience, when I probe this experience, when I put in motion towards it the full force of my imagination and my reflection, and when I systematically peel off the phenomenon's successive constitutive layers, then I generate in my mind images of this experience. By unfolding the description of the phenomenon, I formulate an imagery that increases my consciousness of the life-world.

These creations of the mind are called "eidetic concepts." They form an imaginary representation that seeks to describe the essence of the phenomenon under scrutiny. Such ideas are the formulation of an increasing consciousness of the world. Two notions emerge here: voluntary formulation of eidetic concepts, and increasing consciousness. When combined, they constitute the inherent, necessary motivating factor of the epochè.

Constitution

Discussing the concept of the phenomenological constitution, American philosopher Marvin Farber wrote that "after the reduction, which defines the domain of philosophical inquiry, the aim of phenomenology becomes the 'constitution' of meanings and structures" (Farber 1967, 3). Czech philosopher Jan Patocka echoed Farber when he indicated that the epochè was only one half of the phenomenological method, and that the other half was the reversed epochè, or the constitution. Patocka argued that the epochè is useless without the subsequent constitution. Furthermore, he said that in Husserl's mind, the epochè and the constitution make a systematic whole, resting on a single foundation. He continued, explaining that "these two fundamental ideas find themselves in some sort of antagonistic linkage, one deconstructing, the other constructing, one serving to uncover, the other trying to set foot in the newly uncovered land, in order to conduct its exhaustive exploration" (Patocka 1988, 249–61).[19]

The constitution is the "re-making" of the phenomenon's composition in light of the enhanced awareness generated by the preceding epochè.

Applied to architecture, the phenomenological constitution's final destination is the reconstituted built artefact, the only exhaustive architectural reality that can ultimately be perceived and described. With the epochè, one uncovers the essence of the architectural phenomenon; with the constitution, one reconstructs the phenomenon in a radical way. In this sense, in architecture, the ultimate constitution implies both design and construction.

Universals

During the first phases of the epochè, the phenomenon is described mainly through its contextual characteristics. However, as one penetrates deeper, one uncovers its universal attributes. Without negating or rejecting contextualism, phenomenology accepts the idea of universals, and offers arguments to support the double claim that universals do exist and can be described.

The word *universal* is normally used as an adjective that denotes what "is general, for everything or everyone" (*Webster's* 1988). In a philosophical context, it is also employed as a noun that has the same basic meaning: a general proposition that deals with everything that exists. Universals are opposed to singulars: "A universal: humanity is the genus, while the individual man like Socrates is the singular reality" (*Hachette* 1990).[20] In logic, a universal is an attribute that belongs to every member of a class. The mere fact that logic involves the concept of convention is the main evidence that universals exist: the idea of convention is the universal attribute of human discourse. And rules of logic are described in any treatise on logic.

In architecture, the existence of universals may be grounded in the observation of human beings because they are at the same time the origin and destination of all architectural works. The purpose of architecture is found in people. Before people become involved in social struggles, adopt a particular lifestyle, and decide to settle in a certain location – in sum, before they are influenced by local and temporal constraints – they are what they are: living, sensitive, and intelligent creatures. By this I mean that each possesses the same basic physical and psychological characteristics. Like medicine, architecture caters to these fundamental human traits. At all times, everywhere, architecture has offered the same universal response to the same basic human needs: it has provided the protective shelter humans need to survive and prosper. Moreover, people have used universal notions ever since they first learned to express simple ideas, perhaps because simplicity itself is a universal concept. The world would be chaotic without people's ability to conceive all-encompassing categories and structure their knowledge and activities accordingly.

The acceptance of the concept of the universal is fundamental in phenomenology because it opens the door to the larger concept of essence.

Essence

The operational objective of phenomenology is to grasp the essence of phenomena through the conduct of epochès. The essence is the soul of the phenomenon. It defines the phenomenon's reality and assembles the attributes without which the phenomenon would cease to be what it is. Lyotard suggested that "the essence, or eidos of the object, is constituted by the invariant that remains identical throughout the variations" (Lyotard 1991, 39). But Lyotard's definition is partial: eidos is only the first of the two dimensions of essence. The other is telos, the phenomenon's apodictic destiny. Eidos is the essence of what a phenomenon is; telos is the essence of what it wishes to be. In architecture, the eidos of the architectural phenomenon is acquired by a method of enquiry; the telos by design.

Phenomenology and Architecture

As one canvasses the literature of architectural theory and phenomenology, one is able to identify few, yet significant, essays that establish not so much a formal link between the two disciplines as a new awareness of certain dimensions of the architectural reality.

In his *Phénoménologie de la perception*, published in 1945, Maurice Merleau-Ponty studied the phenomenological perception of space. Exploring the human experience of space, he showed that space is "not the milieu in which one places things, but rather the means by which the positioning of the things becomes possible." When he said that he was transferring his focus from "spatialized" space to "spatializing" space – "de l'espace spatialisé à l'espace spatialisant" – he was indicating that he was exploring "the original experience of space, underneath the distinction of form and content." He argued that existence is "spatial," and that "the experience of perceiving this spatial existence leads to the primordial meeting with the being, and that being is being in space." For him, "experiencing the structure [of a space or an object] is not receiving it in a passive way; it is rather 'living' it, recapturing it, assimilating it, and finding its immanent meaning" (Merleau-Ponty 1945, 281–397).

Exploring the immanent meaning of the phenomenon of dwelling is what Gaston Bachelard did in his *La poétique de l'espace*. Adopting a phenomenological approach, Bachelard studied "the house as an instrument for analysing the human soul" (Bachelard 1964, 19). He did not look at the house itself, but rather at the way poets describe it. Penetrating the world of the poetic imagination, he developed a series of themes related to the notion of dwelling: the sense of the hut; the house as a microcosm of the universe; the meaning of the drawers, coffers, and cupboards; the nest and the shell; the corners; the miniatures; the complementary ideas of intimacy and immensity; the indoor-outdoor dialectic; and the phenomenon of the round. To best illustrate the spirit of Bachelard's insightful essay, it may be necessary to quote a few passages:

an empty drawer cannot be imagined, it can only be thought ... only one who has learned to nestle can inhabit with intensity ... any truly inhabited space carries the essence of the notion of the house ... in its thousand cavities, space contains compressed time ... no true intimacy repels ... the native house is an inhabited house ... the vaulted ceiling is the great principle of the dream of intimacy: endlessly, it reflect intimacy toward its centre ... a lamp in the window the eye of the house ... inhabited space transcends geometric space ... through the poet's window, the house engages an exchange of immensities ... there are always more things in a closed coffer than in an open one: checking kills images ... the nest is [a] bouquet of leaves that sings ... never, in imagination, are entering and exiting symmetrical images ... life is the cause of forms, and form is the habitation of life ... space is nowhere: space is in one like honey in the hive.

As related by Christian Norberg-Schulz, Martin Heidegger published an essay called *Building Dwelling Thinking* in 1951 that explored in a phenomenological way "the basic existential structures of the functions of building and dwelling" (Heidegger 1971; Norberg-Schulz 1980, 6). This essay influenced not only Norberg-Schulz, but also other writers who were exploring the meaning of architecture and the environment – writers such as Edward Relph and David Seamon.

Admittedly inspired by Heidegger, Norberg-Schulz, in his 1980 book *Genius Loci: Toward a Phenomenology of Architecture*, rejected the scientific method for exploring architecture and embarked on the development of "a phenomenology of architecture, or the conquest of [its] existential dimension." He began by defining the phenomenon of place in terms of its character, its structure, and its spirit. Like Bachelard, he said that "to dwell in a house ... means to inhabit the world" (Norberg-Schulz 1980, 5, 9). Then

Norberg-Schulz applied this definition to the two basic sorts of place: the natural and the man-made. This gave him a foundation to conduct a phenomenological description of three cities: Prague, Khartoum, and Rome. He concluded his essay with a series of comments on the notion of place, which he applied to both traditional and contemporary places. For example, he argued that one's understanding of the spirit of a place, its "genius loci," is based on what that place gathers. He wrote, "a thing is a thing by virtue of its gathering. Structure, instead, denotes the formal properties of a system of relationships. Structure and meaning are hence aspects of the same totality" (Norberg-Schulz 1980, 166). He insisted that man is an essential component of the spirit of a place; in fact, it is man who gives the place its identity.

The first part of his conclusion was a severe criticism of the sort of place created by Modern architects. It showed that, since World War II, "the qualities which traditionally distinguish human settlements have been corrupted or have got irreparably lost ... spatially, the new settlements do not anymore possess enclosure and density ... the character of present day environment is usually distinguished by monotony ... in general, [these] symptoms indicate a loss of place ... indeed we may talk about an environmental crisis." The conclusion's second part, however, was optimistic. In it, Norberg-Schulz expressed the opinion that it was possible to recover a sense of place, and the new generation of Modern architects – Louis Kahn, Alvar Aalto, and Robert Venturi – could be the one to introduce a more meaningful architecture. The last sentence of his book was this: "Today man is mainly educated in pseudo-analytic thinking, and his knowledge consists of so-called 'facts.' His life, however, is becoming ever more meaningless, and ever more he understands that his 'merits do not count if he is not able to dwell poetically' ... only when understanding our place, may we be able to participate creatively and contribute to its history" (Norberg-Schulz 1980, 189–95, 201).

Norberg-Schulz's subsequent book, *The Concept of Dwelling: On the Way to Figurative Architecture*, was a continuation of his phenomenological exploration of architecture, and, notably, the notion of dwelling. Here, he put forward a definition of dwelling: "The word dwelling means more than having a roof over our head ... it means ... to meet others for an exchange of products, ideas and feelings, that is to experience life as a multitude of possibilities ... to come to an agreement with others, that is to accept a set of common values" (Norberg-Schulz 1985, 7). As we shall see, the idea of shared values plays an important role in this theory.

In his interesting essay *Place and Placelessness*, geographer Edward Relph used phenomenology to explore the meaning of place. As he explained in the preface, the essay comprises four sections. First, Relph discussed the relationship between space and place in order to demonstrate the range of place experience and concepts. Second, he explored the different components and intensities of place experience, arguing that there are profound psychological links between people and place. Third, he analysed the identity of places, and the identification of people with places. And fourth, he looked at the ways in which sense of place and attachment to place are manifest in the making of places. Relph then concluded that "the essence of the argument relating these themes is that distinctive and diverse places are manifestations of a deeply felt involvement with those places by the people who live in them, and that, for many, such a profound attachment to place is as necessary and significant as a close relationship with other people" (Relph 1976, i).

This description of the concept of place lead Relph to define the essence of place according to a set of attributes:

a place is a centre of action and intention; it is a focus where we experience the meaningful events of our existences ... places are thus incorporated into the intentional structures of all human consciousness and experience ... places are the contexts or backgrounds for intentionally defined objects or groups of objects or events, or they can be objects of intention in their own right ... places are basic elements in the ordering of our experiences of the world ... the essence of place lies in the largely unselfconscious intentionality that defines places as profound centres of human existence ... [quoting French philosopher Gabriel Marcel] an individual is not distinct from his place; he is that place.

Relph ended his essay with these words: "But one thing at least is clear – whether the world we live in has a placeless geography or a geography of significant places, the responsibility for it is ours alone" (Relph 1976, 42, 147).

Between 1983 and 1993, a series of twenty-nine essays on the environment were written by American writers who, collectively, could be characterized by the loose denomination of "existential phenomenologist." These essays were grouped into two books: the first was edited by professor of architecture David Seamon and environmentalist Robert Mugerauer and appeared in 1989 under the title *Dwelling, Place and Environment*; the second, edited by Seamon, was published in 1993 under the title *Dwelling, Seeing, and Designing*. The authors of these essays worked in diverse disciplines. Seamon, Mugerauer, Botond Bognar, Kimberly Dovey, David Saile, Francis Violich, Gary Coates, Randolph Hester, Catherine Howett,

Clare Cooper Marcus, Mark Riegner, Murray Silverstein, and Ronald Walkey were in architecture, landscape architecture, or environmental science. Anne Buttimer, Miriam Helen Hill, Edward Relph, and Joan Nogué i Font were geographers. Henri Bortoft, Walter Brenneman, Joseph Grange, Michael Zimmerman, and Karsten Harries were in philosophy. Bernd Jager and Richard Lang were psychologists, and Murray Schafer was a musician.

Three themes linked these essays: they all discussed the ideas of place and dwelling, they all used phenomenology as the philosophical underpinning of their argument, and they all made references to Heidegger more than to any other leading phenomenologist. In different ways, they supplied answers to the following questions (as presented on the back cover of the second book): What is a sense of place? How can architecture, policy, and education support it? Why are places important to people? Can designers create better places; that is, places that are beautiful, alive, and humane?

In his historical essay, *Architecture and the Crisis of Modern Science*, Alberto Pérez-Gómez argued that "modern architecture and the crisis it faces, has its roots in a historical process touched off by the Galilean revolution, a process whose development is marked by two great transformations ... in the first transformation [at the end of the seventeenth century], the assumption, which had been inherited from medieval and Renaissance cosmology, that number and geometry were a *scientia universalis*, the link between the human and the divine, was finally brought into question by philosophy and science ... [and] around 1800, a second great transformation took place ... faith and reason were truly divorced." It follows, wrote Pérez-Gómez, that "once it adopted the ideals of a positivistic science, architecture was forced to reject its traditional rôle as one of the fine arts ... deprived of a legitimate poetic content, architecture was reduced to either a prosaic technological process or mere decoration" (Pérez-Gómez 1983, 10, 11).

After presenting the evolution of the ideas of number, proportion, and geometry in architecture, from Claude Perrault to J. N. L. Durand, Pérez-Gómez stated:

only contemporary phenomenology, with its rediscovery of the primacy of perception, where structure or *mathesis* is given and yet embodied in the mutable and specific, has been capable of overcoming the fundamental dilemma that modern philosophy inherited from Descartes. By revealing the limitations of mathematical reason, phenomenology has indicated that technological theory alone cannot come to terms with the fundamental problems of architecture. Contemporary architecture, disillusioned with rational utopias, now strives to go beyond positivistic prejudices to find a new metaphysical justification in the human world; its point of departure is once again the sphere of perception, the ultimate origin of existential meaning. (Pérez-Gómez 1983, 324, 325).

The present theory strives to accomplish precisely what Pérez-Gómez advocates.

Methodological Underpinning

Many justifications exist for the adoption of phenomenology as the methodological underpinning of the theory. Like architecture, phenomenology is all-embracing. The ultimate object of phenomenology is the entire lifeworld that, like a set of Russian dolls, comprises the ecological world that, in turn, encompasses the designed environment. In this sense, any architectural artefact is viewed as a life-world subset, not as an isolated icon. Central to the phenomenological method is the indissoluble link between the subject and the object, a feature that resolves the object/subject dilemma. The so-called Cartesian duality, which, according to architecture historians Joseph Rykwert and Pérez-Gómez, is at the root of the present difficulties of architecture, is reassembled into one phenomenological paradigm (Rykwert 1980; Pérez-Gómez 1983). Phenomenology requires an attitude that embraces the reality of architecture as a human phenomenon that transcends time: architecture is always made by people for people. By integrating the intentionality of both the architect and the artefact's user, phenomenology tells us that consciousness is a flux of lived experiences that, as Gaston Bachelard said, range from intimacy to immensity (Bachelard 1964, 168–90).

In both its descriptive epochès and prescriptive constitutions, phenomenology associates rational reflection with intuition and imagination, complementary approaches that also constantly cohabit in the perception and design of architecture. Like architecture, phenomenology constructs. Its deconstructivist epochès are carried out for the sole purpose of providing a solid foundation for developing, afterwards, a more enlightened consciousness of things through the constructivist constitution. Because it is engaged in a constant search for the essence of phenomena, phenomenology is a system of thought that is conducive to a value-oriented description of architecture. It is therefore a comprehensive approach that is not self-referential, and it opens the door to a larger societal, cultural, and humanist relevancy. By the very nature of its approach, it is a method that frees itself from existing viewpoints, thus permitting the broadest vision of architecture possible.

Three Fundamental Tasks

As stated earlier, three basic questions await an answer. The first is: What is the design environment? Or, if one recalls Vitruvius's pointed question – "Ex quibus rebus architectura constet?" –[21] and takes a broader perspective, one launches an investigation into the architectural phenomenon's inherent components (Vitruvius 1965, 24). A thorough understanding of the artefact within the architectural phenomenon is indispensable for the architect, because an inaccurately described object cannot be successfully designed. Both common sense and the most sophisticated strategy proclaim that knowledge of what to do precedes attempts to do it. And knowledge is obtained through a detailed description of the artefact, either at the scale of a single building or at the scale of an assemblage of buildings. Developing a means of describing the architectural artefact as accurately as possible becomes the first task of the theory.

The second question may take many forms: Why is a proposed scheme better than another? (And this immediately raises the problem of defining what "better" signifies.) Or, why do we say that a particular place is better than another? Or, why do people wish to live in certain places and reject others? Another way of presenting the same question is this: When the architect tries to obtain design mandates from a client, he argues that the client's investment will serve to improve things, that the place will be better after than before. But how can the architect demonstrate this claim? How can the architect, the client, indeed society as a whole, decide whether or not the architect's proposed scheme is actually enhancing the existing designed environment? A fifth way of posing the same question is this: On what foundation can the architect ground his design decisions? The rationale behind this multidimensional question is that all design endeavours require a complex sequence of decisions bolstered by the sort of value judgement that distinguishes between success and failure, between quality and mediocrity, between relevancy and frivolity, and between beauty and ugliness. The second task of the theory is to identify and validate architectural assessment criteria.

The third question is this: How can one design a successful environment; that is, an environment that meets users' and society's needs? An approach is required that restructures design knowledge into a practical activity. It is only on this condition that the theory becomes useful. The third task of the theory is to develop an action-oriented design strategy; it is a task that amounts to a quest for an operational principle of a satisfactory architecture. And this principle, I hope to show, comprises the ideas of elegance and archetype. Elegance is defined as the symbiosis of excellence and magnificence and the ultimate attribute of architecture, and archetype as an exemplary model for design; these concepts are paired in order to generate an operational means for making an architecture of satisfaction.

The first of these three tasks responds to the theory's descriptive side; the other two are related to its prescriptive dimension.

Procedure

Here, I suggest a procedure for properly answering the three questions that are raised by the theory. It is a procedure that calls for the conduct of successive epochès and constitutions.

a. To answer the first question, which concerns the definition of architecture, two successive epochès are conducted: the epochè of architectural theories; and the epochè of the architectural phenomenon.
Both these epochès deal exclusively with the architectural reality, irrespective of any value judgement. The first one is a general epochè of architectural theories, as architects presently understand them. Its purpose is to clear the deck and get to the architectural phenomenon as it presents itself in its existential bareness. The second epochè penetrates the architectural phenomenon in order to uncover its apodictic components – apodictic in the sense that they are the necessary ingredients for an eventual design. It seeks to uncover the architectural phenomenon's essence in terms of its eidos, and by so doing develop a knowledge framework for design.

b. To produce meaningful answers to the second question, which concerns the assessment of architecture, one epochè and one constitution are conducted: the epochè of values; and the constitution of design criteria.
This epochè undertakes the reduction of society's values through their most universal statements, the charters of rights, in order to uncover the telos of the architectural phenomenon. Based on this, a constitution of value-grounded design criteria is conducted, and design criteria are suggested.

c. To evaluate critically the procedure's validity with respect to the first two questions, three additional epochès are conducted: the epochè of the Palais-Royal, in Paris; the epochè of the Fondation Rothschild Workers' Residence, also in Paris; and the epochè of Outremont, in Montreal.
These epochès are based on the preceding theoretical epochès and the first constitution, which have provided the necessary instruments for a

In the Palais-Royal garden, lines of chestnut trees create multiple enclosures and promenade areas

The street façade of the fondation Rothschild Workers' Residence blends into the townscape of Paris

meaningful phenomenological – factual and judgmental – description of existing architectural artefacts. It is necessary to conduct these epochès of existing artefacts because architecture is not an exclusively abstract construct, and consciousness of it cannot remain at the level of theoretical discourse and still be proclaimed useful. To achieve their purposefully, those who are investigating the architectural phenomenon need to wrestle with reality. That is why the exercise leading up to a more insightful cognition of architecture is applied to existing artefacts: the Palais-Royal, the Fondation Rothschild Workers' Residence, and Outremont. These artefacts have been chosen because they are urban complexes that have endured, retaining over the years their original intentions and principal functions. All three places are a part of their respective cultural heritages. To a certain extent, they are complementary. Built mainly during the seventeenth, eighteenth, and nineteenth centuries, the Palais-Royal is a multiuse urban complex. It represents urbanity, historicity, and European culture at the high end of the socioeconomic scale. The Fondation Rothschild Workers' Residence is a subsidized housing project built in 1909 by a private philanthropic foundation. Located in Paris's faubourg Saint-Antoine, it caters to the proletariat, which inhabits the low end of the economic scale. The residence represents social awareness and cultural relevancy. Outremont is a predominantly residential neighbourhood of Montreal, built almost entirely during the first half of the twentieth century. It serves a middle-class Canadian population. The municipality represents domesticity, modernity, and a mixture of North American and European cultures. All three artefacts were designed by more than one architect – architects who were, in their time, considered competent but certainly never revered by their respective peers. Through the phenomenological description of these artefacts, I hope to reveal the reasons for their lasting success. In other words, by probing the Palais-Royal, the Fondation Rothschild Workers' Residence, and Outremont in the light of the design criteria formulated here, I will not only test the method of the factual epochè, but will also conduct a judgmental epochè.

d. To answer the third fundamental question regarding the making of architecture, three constitutions are conducted: the constitution of a design strategy; the constitution of the concepts of elegance and archetype; and the constitution of architectural archetypes.
If, as Heidegger said, a method implies a journey towards a more meaningful knowledge, the design strategy can be associated with the road, the concept of elegance with an arrow sign pointing in the desired direction,

The Ferme Outre-Mont is one of the rare nineteenth-century farmhouses in existence today; it gave its name to the Municipality of Outremont

and the concept of archetype with the vehicle that brings us to our destination. The road is constructed by a coherent sequence of practice assignments or necessary tasks for designing and implementing an architectural project. The sense of direction is given by the artefact's attributes. The vehicles are manufactured by redefining the methodological necessity, in architecture, of handling simultaneously the qualitative and quantitative dimensions of its reality.

After this book is closed, the ultimate journey starts. That journey is the actual design endeavour. It is undertaken by purposefully reassembling the architectural phenomenon's constitutive elements that were reduced and temporarily suspended in the course of the preceding epochs. Through these prescriptive assignments, a transformed paradigm of the architectural reality is reconstituted at the service of architects for the benefit of users. By becoming operational, the theory becomes useful.

A fine ecological gesture: children feed birds in the Palais-Royal garden

3

UNVEILING ARCHITECTURE

The journey towards an enlarged awareness of the architectural phenomenon necessitates the conducting of two successive epochès. The first suspends all existing theoretical knowledge in order to uncover the architectural phenomenon as it presents itself to our consciousness. The second probes the architectural phenomenon through the removal of the successive veils that drape its factual reality, uncovering its eidos.

EPOCHÈ OF ARCHITECTURAL THEORIES

By "architectural theories," I mean the successive attempts at explaining the architectural phenomenon. Even though theories of architecture are as old as architecture itself, few writings produced before the Renaissance have survived, at least in the Occident. Some speculations by Ancient Greek philosophers, Vitruvius's treatise, and a few texts by medieval mastermasons, are among the exceptions. From the fifteenth century on, however, countless texts were published. Today, this body of opinion and precept takes the form of interpretations of history; doctrines, many of which were fuelled by political or philosophical movements; and a rather pervasive collection of idées reçues, expressed mainly in critical essays and manifestos.[22] While these theories and attitudes have framed our ability to construct bigger buildings and larger cities, they have not insured a continuous increase in their quality, beauty, or social relevancy.

Such difficulties are not restricted to architecture. Husserl made the point that science in general, indeed the entire realm of human knowledge, is facing a similar crisis of confidence. That is why he proposed an upward paradigm shift, a move from what he called the natural, prephilosophical attitude up to the philosophical or phenomenological attitude. Only this change of attitude made through the conduct of epochès, argued Husserl, will provide us with a more truthful awareness of the life-world. Such a paradigm shift, however, requires the temporary suspension of all knowledge models that lie between the natural attitude and the phenomenological one. Husserl showed that these structured explanations, because of their limited methodologies and circumscribed scope, have introduced distorted views of the life-world. Their bracketing has therefore become necessary. In *Crisis*, Husserl wrote:

clearly required before everything else is the epochè in respect to all objective sciences. This means not merely an abstraction from them, such as an imaginary transformation, in thought, of present human existence, such that no science appeared in the picture. What is meant is rather an epochè of all participation in the cognition of the objective sciences, an epochè of any critical position-taking which is interested in their truth or falsity, even any position on their guiding idea of an objective knowledge of the world. In short, we carry out an epochè in regard to all objective theoretical interests, all aims and activities belonging to us as objective scientists or even simply as [ordinary] people desirous of [this kind] of knowledge. (Husserl 1970, 135)

I propose to carry this general statement to architecture.

Bracketing of Historical Interpretations

Historical interpretations of architecture are inherent components of architectural knowledge. Historians may perhaps disagree, but it seems that it was in France in the middle of the seventeenth century that intellectuals began to search for guiding principles in architecture. The famous quarrel between the Ancients and the Moderns clearly demonstrated that different visions of architecture were not only possible, but also in opposition to one another (Charles Perrault in Fichet 1979, 183–203; Rykwert 1980, 23–52). About one century and many points of view later, Marc-Antoine Laugier (1713–69) expressed the opinion that the origin of art was in the imitation of nature,[23] and that the primitive hut was architecture's primal principle (Laugier in Fichet 1979, 367–86). Anthony Vidler explained that "for Laugier, the hut as origin assumed a paradigmatic status for all architecture … the vertical branches gave the idea of columns; the horizontal members inspired the invention of entablatures; the inclined roof beams formed the first pediments" (Vidler 1987, 19). Later still, contemporary historians offered different interpretations of the evolution of architecture. For example, Christian Norberg-Schulz suggested that "architecture ought to be understood in terms of meaningful (symbolic) forms. As such it is part of the history of existential meanings" (Norberg-Schulz 1980, 5).

Another pervasive historical interpretation of architecture is the idea of style. It seems extremely difficult nowadays to discuss the history of architecture without resorting to the notion of style, which appears to be one of the few means of depicting the design of a particular period, or in a particular geographic area.[24] While perhaps fifteen different styles were sufficient to cover three thousand years of architectural evolution, that is, up until the end of the nineteenth century – an average of two hundred years per style – some ten styles were deemed necessary to describe architecture of the first three-quarters of the nineteenth century. As architects know, these are Art Nouveau, Art Deco, constructivism, expressionism, Modern or International style, Prairie style, brutalism and neobrutalism, high-tech, postmodernism, and deconstructivism – an average of ten years per style. Since the seventies, however, the postmodern discourse has uttered an orgy of stylistic labels. For example, in *The Language of Post-Modern Architecture*, Charles Jencks introduced or invented as many as sixteen new labels: historicism, revivalism, neovernacular, postmodern classicism, technological and freestyle classicism, rationalism, neorationalism and surrationalism, Rustic Canyon, New Corinthian Order, New Abstractionism, ornamentalism, New Toscanism, radical eclecticism, and contextualism – an average rate of a style a year (Jencks 1984).

Those are only a few examples of historical interpretation. Over the centuries, many others have been offered. An exhaustive list is not required here, because all are bracketed and temporarily suspended.

Bracketing Architectural Doctrines

What remains behind these historical interpretations of architecture is the wide panoply of architectural doctrines. These compose a rather diffuse landscape of various writings that can be grouped in two broad categories: treatises on how to make solid, efficient, and beautiful architecture, and essays on how architecture ought to be understood. Even though one finds a certain amount of overlap between the two categories, it could be said that the first group comprises texts written mainly by practising architects, while the other includes texts by nonpractising architects, and often even by nonarchitects. The lineage of practice-oriented writers starts with Vitruvius, who published his *Ten Books of Architecture* around 23 B.C.,[25] and may well have ended in the middle of the twentieth century with the writings of Le Corbusier and the Bauhaus.[26] And the lineage of criticism-oriented writers may have started with Abbot Suger's writings (circa 1150), and is still thriving; perhaps the last influential text in this category was Charles Jencks's essay on postmodernism, published in 1977.[27] As presented here, these two lineages of architectural doctrine cover only the architecture of the Western world; a similar body of knowledge exists for Oriental architecture. Most of the Occidental architectural theory writings are offspring of the Renaissance and the Enlightenment, when systematic attempts at rationalizing and explaining the world started to be offered. Even though only a few writers have been truly influential – notably Vitruvius, Alberti, Vignola, Palladio, Claude Perrault, Le Corbusier, the Bauhaus group, Robert Venturi, and Jencks – all have made a significant contribution to the present body of opinion. I suggest that here all of them be put in brackets and suspended, irrespective of their importance or significance.

Bracketing of Idées Reçues

Behind the doctrines is found a series of conventional-wisdom statements that are often thrown around by architects who are challenged by our positivistic society to rationalize their intuitive design. Only advertising, it seems, is keener than architecture to produce publicity slogans or self-serving apologia. Perhaps some of the most famous slogans of our trade are worth recalling:

§ "Not all buildings are architecture." The real statement is: "It is very necessary to distinguish between Architecture and Building" (Ruskin 1989, 8).

§ "If it's useless, it's architecture." The real statement is: "Architecture concerns itself only with those characters of an edifice which are above and beyond its common use" (Ruskin 1989, 9).

§ "Nothing that is not practical can be beautiful." (Otto Wagner in Fleming 1991, 473).

§ "Ornament is crime." This was the title of an article that actually read: "Ornament and Crime" (Adolf Loos in Fleming 1991, 273).

§ "Form follows function." (Sullivan 1979, 46).

§ "La maison est une machine à habiter." This slogan has a double meaning: The house is a machine for dwelling, and a machine to live in (Le Corbusier 1958, xxv). Some twenty years earlier, many other French architects used the metaphor of the laboratory to depict a dwelling.

§ "New Architecture." (Walter Gropius at the Bauhaus, 1965).

§ "Less is more." (Mies van der Rohe, ca. 1950).

§ "Less is bore." (Venturi 1966, 23).

§ "I like complexity and contradiction in architecture." (Venturi 1966).

§ "Architecture is a language." (Charles Jencks in Papadakis 1990, 7).

§ "The Yale boxes." (Yale architecture students depicting Modern Architecture buildings, ca. 1955).

§ "Paper architects." (anonymous American architecture students depicting inexperienced postmodern professors of architecture, ca. 1980).

At times, architecture raises passions, and ideological manifestos are proclaimed, such as, for instance, the *De Stijl Manifesto* of 1918:

1. There is an old and a new consciousness of time. The old is connected with the individual. The new is connected with the universal. The struggle of the individual against the universal is revealing itself in the world-war as well as in the art of the present day.

2. The was is destroying the old world with its contents: individual domination in every state.

3. The new art has brought forward what the new consciousness of time contains: a balance between the universal and the individual.

4. The new consciousness is prepared to realise the internal life as well as the external life.

5. Traditions, dogmas and the domination of the individual are opposed to this realisation.

6. The founders of the new plastic art therefore call upon all who believe in the reformation of art and culture to annihilate these obstacles of development, as they have annihilated in the new plastic art (by abolishing natural form) that which prevents the clear expression of art, the utmost consequence of all art notion.

7. The artists of to-day have been driven the whole world over by the same consciousness, and therefore have taken part from an intellectual point of view in this war against the domination of individual despotism. They therefore sympathise with all who work for the formation of an international unity in Life, Art, Culture, either intellectually or materially.

8. The monthly editions of "The Style," founded for that purpose, try to attain the wisdom of life in an exact manner. Co-operation is possible by (signatures): Theo van Doesburg, painter; Robt. van"t Hoff, architect; Vilmos Huszar, painter; Antony Kok, poet; Piet Mondrian, painter; G. Vantongerloo, sculptor; Jan Wills, architect (Jaffäe 1971).

No judgement is passed on these mottoes or manifestos. All of them are inserted in brackets, and temporarily suspended.

REDUCTION:
THE BARE ARCHITECTURAL PHENOMENON

What is not always explicitly noted in architectural writings but always observed in reality is that the architectural phenomenon is about people doing something in a space. Constantly, everywhere, all humans always conduct an activity. This is a universal trait of the architectural phenomenon resulting from the people's symbiosis with the life-world. In fact, the observation extends beyond human beings; it encompasses all living creatures, because to live is, precisely, to be active. Life is nothing but activity in a physical space.

Another characteristic of the same phenomenon can be noted. Inasmuch as the physical space that surrounds human activity is made by a human and becomes an architectural artefact, an apodictic and constant relationship is established between the architectural artefact and the life-world that contains it. Every architectural artefact is always located somewhere, is always an offspring of nature, while remaining a part of our world's ecological reality. As soon as the architectural artefact emerges from the ground it acquires a presence; it is immediately thrown into the relentless course of time. As the architectural artefact can escape neither its cultural dimension, in the sense that it is made by humans for a purpose, nor its spatio-natural condition, in the sense of its natural origin and destination, it cannot escape its temporal condition, in the sense that it necessarily belongs to the evolving present.[28]

Hence, what appears when the architectural phenomenon has been freed from all historical interpretations, all doctrines, and all manifestos and slogans, is the essence of the architectural phenomenon as it presents itself to our consciousness, and as it appears in its universality. It is made of the elements that remain constant when all the variables have been removed.

Perhaps a first formulation of the essence of the architectural phenomenon may be presented as follows. *The architectural phenomenon is a symbiotic whole made of five, and only five, constitutive elements: human beings conducting an activity in a cultural shelter that is inserted in nature and projected through time.*

This is a universal, indubitable, and apodictic statement, based on constant observation, the only and the permanent basic expression of the architectural phenomenon. It transcends all architectural theories. It provides a first description of the noematic structure of the architectural phenomenon. However, in spite of its universality, it is still a description viewed from the outside. As such, it is unsuitable for design, because what is designed is not the phenomenon in its entirety, but only the shelter and part of nature that immediately surrounds it. This is what is called the architectural artefact. A key distinction between the architectural phenomenon and the architectural artefact has to be made: while only the artefact can actually be created and built by the architect, only the architectural phenomenon can exist. An architectural artefact does exist by itself. As soon as it comes into being, it incorporates immediately, spontaneously, the other constituents of the phenomenon, and becomes a fully constituted phenomenon. Hence, in order to design and build an architectural artefact properly, the architect needs to penetrate the architectural phenomenon and seize its inherent characteristics. This is the purpose of the next epochè.

EPOCHÈ OF THE ARCHITECTURAL PHENOMENON

This epochè is called "the unveiling of the architectural phenomenon." The veils are conceptual representations of reality, notions that form the operational noematic structure the phenomenon, organize the constitutive parts of its description, and, as required by the necessities of the architectural design process, integrate input from other disciplines. The identification and specific definition of each veil stem from a careful observation of the urban and architectural reality.

The concept of the veil is useful because it conveys two interconnected and reciprocal ideas. The first is the idea of a reality that is fully dressed, wrapped by several overlapping robes, very rich and mysterious. Such is the sumptuous potential of architecture. The second is the idea of removing one veil after another and discovering the radiant essence of this unveiled reality. What hides under the veil is more luminous than what was apparent at first sight. Such is the luxurious abundance of the architectural phenomenon. The comprehension of the veils" intrinsic composition constitutes the necessary conduit towards grasping the essence of architecture. Although the epochè considers the architectural veils as if they were distinct, successive elements, the actual reality of the phenomenon is different, is, in fact, a whole that cannot exist without the materialization of all its veils in a total symbiosis.

The procedure of this epochè is as follows. The subject selects an architectural artefact. Any architectural thing may do, a simple room, a large city, or even the entire designed environment; but the subject may wish to focus his attention on an object that can be circumscribed. He observes this artefact not as an isolated object, but as a component of a phenomenon, not as an entity outside himself, but as one that encompasses him. Throwing his intentionality on the selected phenomenon, he starts depicting it as he sees it. Having reached the limits of this immediate perception – that is, having absorbed everything that there is to learn at this level – he peels off this first description, he lifts the first veil, and puts it aside in brackets. This gesture is not a rejection of this particular part of the phenomenon, only its temporary suspension; it allows time to probe the veil that lies behind the veil that has just been removed. The same descriptive exercise is repeated for the second veil, and so on, until the subject reaches the foundation of the architectural reality he is experiencing.

Immediately, a few questions come to mind. At the outset of the epochè, how does one know what veil lies behind the veil that has been removed? At this early juncture, no one knows. But by merely conducting the epochè, we discover something, which is simultaneously a part of the essence of the artefact, a part of the essence of the phenomenon as a whole, and a part of the subject's experience within this phenomenon. An example may illustrate this point: Beethoven is composing a symphony. Assuming, for argument's sake, that he is composing the symphony's four movements in their chronological sequence, how does he know the melodic line of the fourth movement after he has finished the first three? Obviously, he does not know before, but only after he has composed it. What happened in between? A certain act of creation, a certain emanation of Beethoven's imagination. What can be said after the fourth movement has been created? One can say that it exists, that it can be described, that it has a sequence of notes that can be read. When played by designated musical instruments, these notes make a series of sounds, structured according to acoustic principles, harmonic ratios, and so on. Finally, one observes that when this melody is played, it creates emotions in the minds and hearts of listeners. Forever, Beethoven's spirit permeates his symphony's essence, an essence grasped and shared by listeners.

The same creative process occurs in the case of the epochè of the architectural phenomenon. The apprehension of each veil implies a certain act of creation, a projection of the subject's imagination. Is there logic in the description of a veil? Of course, just as there is a logical structure behind the melody. As André de Muralt and Suzanne Bachelard have amply demonstrated, this logic is the logic of correlation (de Muralt 1974; Suzanne Bachelard 1968).

If two people conduct their epochè on the same artefact, will they arrive at two different descriptions? The answer to this question depends upon the level of consciousness. Each observer will generate his own description at the level of the artefact's individuality. However, at the level of the universal eidetic concepts of the architectural phenomenon, all observers will generate the same essential framework for a useful comprehension of architecture, simply because the phenomenological epochè brings them naturally towards a comprehensive description of the phenomenon. All music is made of sounds, structured according to harmonic ratios, and played for the purpose of being listened to, and enjoyed by, people; architecture is composed of similar universal elements. In other words, the higher observers rise into the consciousness of the architectural phenomenon, the more universal and transcendental their ideas of this phenomenon become. That is the value of this method: by creating a universal framework that can be modified at will, it accepts and reconciles differences, permits – indeed welcomes and stimulates – an infinity of interpretations without losing its internal, permanent coherence.

Is there a proper sequence of veils in the architectural epochès? No definitive answer to this question appears possible. The only thing that can be said is that five operating principles have directed the conducting of the epochè.

Descartes's suggestion has been followed, and the epochè proceeds from the simplest to the most complex. However, this principle calls for further explanation: although the point of departure might be the simplest in the sense that it is the easiest to perceive, the point of arrival is also the simplest in the sense that it is the most inclusive. Thus, the epochè's movement is from the simplicity of the parts to the simplicity of the whole.

The epochè proceeds from the most immediate view to the most intimate perception of the phenomenon. And once the most intimate perception is described, it suddenly becomes evident. The epochè has this ability to let loose the immanent evidence of the phenomenon's constitutive structure.

The epochè goes from the particular to the universal. Again, posited this way, this principle might be misleading, because the movement from the particular to the universal occurs within each of the veils, as a result of a progression from a direct observation to an eidetic description of the same object.

The epochè moves from individuality, to singularity, to transcendence. And it goes from the more material dimensions of the phenomenon to its more spiritual dimensions.

Is it possible to add or subtract a veil? This particular question has little meaning in a phenomenological query, which is, by definition, comprehensive. In this epochè of an architectural phenomenon, a general rule has been established stating that the ensemble of the veils constitutes the totality of the phenomenological framework leading to the essence of the architectural phenomenon. The process is not an addition of different ingredients, but rather different lighting intensities, or hues of the same illumination. When parts of a phenomenon are put in brackets, the phenomenon is not diminished; it is, rather, enriched by the subject's enlightened consciousness. To ask if a veil has been forgotten is a nonsensical question. It is like asking if there are too many notes in a Mozart symphony, or too many columns in the Parthenon. There is simultaneously one veil and an infinite number of veils, because the essence of a phenomenon constitutes an indivisible whole. Theoretically, it is possible to describe the essence of a phenomenon indistinctly by one word or by an infinite number of words.

Another way of presenting the same idea is to use the metaphor of the pie. The architectural phenomenon is like a pie. In order to taste it, that is, to eat it in order to grasp its essence, one has cut it into twelve pieces. Do the twelve pieces constitute the totality of the pie? Yes, of course. If one eats the twelve pieces, will one have eaten the totality of the pie? Yes. Has a piece been forgotten? No. One may cut the pie into a different number of pieces. But if all the pieces are eaten, the same result is obtained.

To be useful to today's architects who do most of their work where people live – that is, in cities – I suggest that we conduct this epochè at two distinct but integrated levels: the urban and the single-building levels. Another compelling reason for such a double query is this: it is impossible to create urban design without creating architecture, and vice versa. A design for the spaces between a series of buildings – urban design in its simplest connotation – cannot be produced without taking into consideration the design of those buildings – architecture – and, conversely, the design of an individual building is always related to the space around it. When one of these two dimensions is ignored or neglected, the result is always unsatisfactory. By all accounts, one of the most successful urban design projects of all time is Michelangelo's Campidoglio in Rome. This masterpiece could not have been accomplished without a thorough understanding of the necessary relationship between the so-called private buildings and the so-called public areas between them (Webb 1990, 131; Bacon 1976, 118).

Who is observing, describing, and grasping the various dimensions of the architectural phenomenon? This observer is the doubting and thinking architect. Always involved in what he observes, he remains present throughout the epochè. To start the epochè, he looks at the architectural phenomenon emanating from an architectural artefact standing in a city, and focuses his intentionality on its most common manifestation. What does he see?

Veil One: People

Before everything else, he notices people, busy people against a backdrop of buildings, people in their homes, at work, walking in the streets. He sees users of architecture, citizens who are leading their lives in city (or the countryside). If one studies how architecture is described by observers of human affairs who are not architects (but who are themselves users of architecture), if one looks at the works of painters or novelists, one sees that people are shown first, but they are always inhabiting a place. For these observers, the most important element of architecture is the poeple who inhabit it.

Perhaps it is because of their constant movement that people constitute the architectural phenomenon's most conspicuous reality. To borrow phrase from landscape architect Lawrence Halprin, that movement is an urban choreography, a dance of millions of urbanites running, it seems, in all directions, an apparent chaos that nonetheless hides a sophisticated organization. It is not so naïve to point out that cities – and the buildings within them – exist simply to help humans do better. By coming together in great numbers in a relatively small space, people augment their points of contact with one another; they also broaden the range and improve the accessibility of their choices. As urban planner Hans Blumenfeld once said, "breadth of choice is the essence of the metropolis" (Blumenfeld in Piel 1965, 45).

On the final page of his epochal history of the city, Lewis Mumford emphasized the preeminence of human beings in the urban phenomenon with an almost phenomenological discourse. He wrote:

the final mission of the city is to further man's conscious participation in the cosmic and historic process. Through its own complex and enduring structure, the city vastly augments man's ability to interpret these processes and take an active, formative part in them, so that every phase of the drama it stages shall have, to the highest degree possible, the illumination of consciousness, the stamp of purpose, the colour of love. That magnification of all the dimensions of life, through emotional communion, rational communication, technological mastery, and above all, dramatic representation, has been the supreme office of the city in history. And it remains the chief reason for the city's continued existence. (Mumford 1961, 576)

On the urban scale, humans form a crowd. Yet, within it, each human maintains a unique personality and shelters in a distinct place. Urban planning and design imperatives concern the handling of masses; yet the same imperatives are based on a respect for the individual and become building design imperatives. This implies a complex duality that colours all aspects of human existence within city buildings. Roughly six billion humans share the Earth's surface. All are made the same way, yet each is different from the nother. This mysterious duality makes the human condition rich and complex. It also represents a challenge for architects.

Biologists and psychologists agree that all humans are made the same way; even gender differences are subordinate to human sameness (Laborit 1968). Other commentators have said that the complexity of a single human is greater than that of the entire universe. Still, humans manage to form communities, create institutions, share values, and follow similar behavioural patterns. They use different languages, though all languages share the same basic structure (Ruhlen 1997; Piaget 1968; Saussure 1916). They each have a distinct personality, though the same phenomenon of personality applies to all. They each enjoy free will, though freedom is considered a universal value. That is why many humans deprived of freedom are ready to die in order to regain it, even though the will to survive is one of the strongest human imperatives. Common human characteristics are much more fundamental than those that distinguish gender, race, and social group. Humans are even different in the same way: sameness is a characteristic of difference; individualism applies to all. Architecture responds to this shared individualism.

Humans are mysterious, and their destiny unfathomable. Why are some born rich while others can never escape poverty? Why is one daring and creative and another more reflective? How is it that one becomes a pianist, another a chemist, and another a carpenter? Why are some lucky while others are accident prone? Why are siblings often so different? Why is one self-centred and physically well coordinated while another is clumsy, caring, and charming? Why do certain people cheat and others muddle through? Why will this particular man love this particular woman? Why do lovers hurt each other? Why does contradiction rule the human heart, smallness mesh with greatness, and pettiness with formidable generosity? Architecture is made to accommodate all this.

Humans possess seven universal characteristics that embody their organic relationship with the rest of the life-world. First, humans live by absorbing the sun's energy. In his *Biologie et structure*, French biologist Henri Laborit wrote that "any human act, any human thought is nothing but the result of the transformation of solar photonic energy into a more organised form" (Laborit 1968, 75).[29] Moreover, to sustain life, humans absorb and transform the ressources of their environment. They inhale air, drink water and other beverages, and eat food. Even though buildings and cities are energy-consuming machines, they facilitate the energy intake of humans. Second, humans establish contact with their environment through their senses. They see, hear, smell, touch, taste, maintain their equilibrium by perceiving the horizontal and vertical lines established by the Earth's surface and gravitational pull, and orient themselves through rational coordinates and landmarks. A well-designed environment stimulates and enhances human behaviour. Third, humans manipulate data gathered through their senses. Making sense of these multiple environmental perceptions is indeed one of the most difficult challenges confronting modern city dwellers. Most cities today are disorganized contraptions that do nothing but confuse people. Discussing this issue, Kevin Lynch identified a set of basic deficiencies in the urban environment: a burden of overpowering perceptual stress, lack of visible identity, environmental illegibility, and rigidity (Lynch in Piel 1965, 193). Properly cared for, however, cities rapidly become familiar and friendly. Fourth, humans remember, dig roots, and slowly build their cherished urban heritage. The best city is the one we are proud to call home because somewhere within it stands the one special building where we live. Fifth, humans adjust and modify their behaviour. Because they are blessed with a marvellous homeostasis, they are able to maintain their psychological equilibrium within a constantly changing milieu. This is more than a cliché: mediocre neighbourhoods engender barbarism and violence while high-quality ones nurture art and civilized interaction. Sixth, humans possess an effective will. To a certain extent, they enjoy a longterm flexibility, which means that they carry out programmed activities. Conscious of themselves in their environment, they analyse situations and problems, criticize, take initiatives, pass judgements, and draw conclusions. Buildings are like computers in that they enhance a human being's intellectual performance. Seventh and last, humans have feelings. They can be happy or sad, satisfied or frustrated, calm or agitated, serene or angry, full of hope or crushed by despair. Great places inspire great poets.

This is the veil of people, members of the human race, users of the designed environment, and citizens of the community. Further description of them exceeds the scope of this work. At this juncture, the method calls for the veil of people to be put in brackets and temporarily suspended.

What emerges from beneath it is, obviously, the architectural reality minus its first veil; that is, the designed environment without humans. This environment is a set of empty structures of all sorts, still warm from human occupation: lights are on, books are on the shelves, utensils are on the table, and food is in the refrigerator.

Veil Two: Activity Components

The second veil is that of the functional purpose of architecture. The most familiar way to describe a building is to detail its function – what it does or, better, what people do in it. That is why people are looked at first. Removed by the epochè, they leave traces. The imprint humans leave on a building describes that building's functionality, which could be defined as the adaptation of buildings to human needs. "What is this building?" we may ask. The answer always concerns the function of the building: "It is a church"; or, "It is my children's school"; or, "It is my home." Even if we drive into an abandoned town, we can describe its empty buildings by their former usage: the general store, the post office, and so on.

Building functionality is an immanent characteristic of architecture. It is not possible to observe one single building or man-made place that was not built for a purpose. Sometimes, very rarely, the purpose of a building is only spiritual or contemplative. In all other cases, buildings have a so-called practical function: they are places for sleeping, eating, washing, working, praying, meeting other humans, and so on. This consideration of functionality may appear self-evident to most architects. Yet, in many postmodern writings on architectural theory, the idea of functionality is either denied or ignored. What is often proposed is either form for form's sake or a form for transmitting intellectual messages to potential users, messages that are supposed to be clear but are in fact understood only by their authors and a very restricted coterie of the initiated. One example is the "famous" oversized handrail that is supposed to be a metaphor for a horizontal column (Jencks 1984, 67)

Architecture deals not only with the design of places but also with the organization of activities. The English and French languages have a similar expression to depict the symbiosis of activity and place. The English expression, "an activity will take place," immediately conveys this double notion of human interaction in architectural space. The French expression, "une activité aura lieu," carries the same meaning. In both languages, the phrase signifies that the architectural phenomenon might be at the same time universal and immensely simple. "What happens in every place in the city? " we ask. "Always the same event," comes the answer: people doing something at a certain moment. Again, the bare architectural phenomenon appears to the subject's consciousness.

Urban activity components are like the living cells of the urban organism. Each room in each building has one or many functions and hence constitutes an activity component. Each building is simultaneously a cluster of activity components and a single more complex activity component. Each space between each building and each public area is also an activity component. Certain activity components, such as bathrooms or newsstands, may be designed for a programmed activity or a specific function. Others, such as city squares, may be multipurpose activity components and serve many functions, some of them programmed, others fortuitous. Some are consciously designed by someone with a mandate to make them, others are merely appropriated by people. Some activity components are primarily for public functions, others for private use. Through the design of physical structures, the architect's mission is to organize all these activity components in a meaningful, coherent, and functional fashion.

There are many ways of analysing and grouping the activity components of a city. Most planning manuals suggest urban-function typologies and methods for land-use analysis. In an earlier work, I conducted an urban analysis based on American anthropologist Edward T. Hall's theory of culture and proposed a typology of urban activity components subdivided into five broad categories (Hall 1966; Lincourt 1972). Over the years, this typology has proved immensely useful in many urban design projects.

With an aggregate volume of about half of any city's total built volume, residential activity components form the largest category. They are places called home, certainly among the most private places of the city. The popular expression, "My place or yours?" clearly depicts the idea of a personal dwelling where one usually sleeps and keeps one's personal belongings – the milieu of intimacy and privacy. Personal dwellings are among the most used places in a city and, at the same time, constitute the urban *toile de fond*. Unmonumental by definition, they are directly responsive to individual desires. In many countries, their design follows very strict imperatives concerning amount of living space, level of comfort, natural lighting, ventilation, food-preparation facilities, sanitary facilities, and privacy. They respond primarily to the kind of values that are best expressed as personal and private attitudes and desires.

The second category encompasses civic activity components. These are places for social and community functions: city halls, churches, temples, shrines, squares, gardens, hospitals, community halls, cemeteries, and the like. As they cater to common ideologies and the kind of values that buttress collective manifestations, they usually act as the monumental components of the city, and serve as the city's major landmarks or anchors of its tradition.[30]

The third category is education activity components. These are the places where formal knowledge is acquired and transmitted, and therefore perform one of the city's principal civilizing functions. Education activity components range from kindergartens to universities, from continuing-education training rooms to high-tech laboratories. Learning places are indispensable elements of any city; in fact, they appear as soon as a few humans gather somewhere because they are recognized as essential to progress, to the passage from barbarism to civilization, and this is an ongoing concern that permeates all the other functions of the city. With the arrival of the twenty-first century and far-reaching, sophisticated communications technologies, the spatial and functional boundaries between the education activity components and other places, such as homes, offices, and factories, tend to disappear.

The fourth category consists of leisure activity components. These are the places where people entertain themselves, relax, and engage in sports. Some of them are so-called cultural institutions, such as museums, while others are so-called popular joints, such as taverns and bowling alleys. They can be indoor or outdoor, and include cinemas and theatres, stadiums and sport fields, theme and amusement parks, zoos and aquariums, bars and restaurants, golf courses and swimming pools. Leisure establishments are necessary because they respond to deep socializing needs. It is primarily in these places that people identify with their common cultural institutions. More than any other kind of place, leisure establishments serve as social magnets, attracting people and motivating them to pursue positive social endeavours. Another important justification for their presence in the city is this: because they channel the overflow of creative energy, they help defuse tensions and become much-needed instruments of peace. A football game, even though it may draw the odd hooligan, is obviously better than a gang war. As are politics and religion, leisure activities are capable of moving the masses. How does one fill a large stadium? With a political rally, an appearance by the Pope, a championship football game, or a rock concert.

The fifth category is economic activity components. Devoted to the production and management of wealth, these places include all commercial edifices: office towers, industrial plants, and so on. They range from the very small shop to the largest factory, from stores catering to local markets to establishments open to international trade, from very specialized firms to all-inclusive conglomerates, from hotdog stands to stock exchanges, from pawnbrokers"shops to national banks. It is imperative to design and manage efficient urban workplaces because they create the financial means for a decent quality of life in the city. No matter how we define needs and happiness, the latter is always the fulfilment of the former, and this achievement requires means that can only be provided by a healthy economic sector, which in turn necessitates high-quality urban economic activity components. This argument is normally well understood by urban entrepreneurs and business people. Their recurrent mistake, however, is to think that efficient places of business are sufficient to insure a city's well being. As amply demonstrated by the Los Angeles riots, for example, they are not. A healthy city must be healthy in all its parts as well as in its whole.

At the level of the individual building, we find a similar set of activity components. The architect calls the description of these components a brief, or an architectural programme, and it articulates the very purpose of his project. Although the drawing up of architectural programmes is a sine qua non function of the architectural practice for the simple reason that it is the transcription in design terms of the client's needs – and although it is the necessary departure point for any design endeavour and the statement of the problem to be solved – this skill is rarely taught in schools of architecture in a systematic way. As he is when engaging in many other activities of his trade, the architect here is obliged to improvise.

The veil of activity components is the element that best characterizes the architectural phenomenon's contextual, cultural dimension. For example, the design brief for a housing complex in Tunis will be quite different from the brief for one in Edinburgh, although its headings would tend to be similar. And, consequently, the design solution will vary from one place, one culture, to another, even though both projects will seek to house people in the best possible way. Describing these components and their respective performance specifications to their full extent is beyond the scope of this work. Such a task, however, needs to be performed on a constant basis, and architects need to be involved in it.

Let us remove the second veil of the architectural phenomenon, put it in brackets, and observe what lies behind it.

Veil Three: Surroundings

At first sight, the third veil appears to be a vast cluster of nondescript activity components. The specific artefact we wish to describe can easily be lost in this mishmash. Let us recall that the procedure called for a focusing of the observer's intentionality on one phenomenon. Of course, if we observe the totality of the designed environment, a single place and its surroundings become one. In this situation, the characteristics of one place become only qualifications or added dimensions of the complete designed environment syndrome. We maintained this broad perspective in describing the preceding two veils. But the time has come to follow Descartes's advice and break down the designed environment reality into smaller components. To simplify the architectural phenomenon's descriptive process, we must select the place we wish to describe, isolate it from its surroundings, and project our intentionality onto those surroundings. I propose this because it is only by removing the veil of surroundings that we are able to achieve a clearer perception of the selected artefact.

The surroundings of an architectural artefact in this context are all the structures and infrastructures around it, including tamed natural features. The surroundings of a city are its outlying suburbs; of an individual building, its enveloping neighbourhood. Surroundings comprise not only the other architectural areas adjoining the artefact, but also all the roadways, pipes, and wires that emerge from it and contribute to the transformation of our planet into a "global village," to borrow an expression from Marshall McLuhan (McLuhan 1965; Mchuhan and Fiore 1967). In architecture, the conception of an artefact as a terminal plugged into a system of networks constitutes a new approach. So far, few architectural theoreticians have considered this concept. Yet ours is, increasingly, a world of networks of all kinds: institutional, political, communal, management, communication, energy, and transportation. This reality is already recognized by many disciplines close to architecture, namely engineering and urban planning (Dupuy 1991). In these disciplines, network theory and system design has been a bona fide study field for several years. As early as twenty years ago, American planner Charles Tilly, among many others, acknowledged the network character of the designed environment. He said that when we try to sum up "the character of cities, we have our choice of several common metaphors; each of them catches a certain part of the reality. We can call the city a nerve centre, a melting pot, or a hub. I prefer [he said] to think of it as a node in a network (or, strictly speaking, the location of nodes in a great many networks" (Tilly 1974, 5). And, of course, each building is a node in an urban network.

But is the inclusion of surroundings as a necessary entry into the search for the essence of the architectural phenomenon a self-evident gesture? Perhaps. If that is the case, however, how does one explain that the overwhelming majority of buildings considered in architectural magazines are selected not because of their successful integration with their surroundings but, rather, because of their ability to stand out from them? What appears crucial to many architects is to be original, an exigency that must be satisfied at the expense of almost everything else (Harvey 1990). These single-minded, career-driven architects may not be perceiving key dimensions of architecture.

One significant aspect of the idea of surroundings is the concept of spatial influence. A building, and, a fortiori, a city, exerts an influence that is always larger than its immediate physical or functional reality. This influence takes many forms. For instance, a building casts a shadow and creates wind gusts. A structure that is a home triggers strong emotional ties: hence, exile from home is a cruel punishment. A monumental structure acts as a beacon or a symbol of communal recognition. A large city projects its cultural or economic influence onto its extended surroundings. For instance, Paris houses about one-twentieth of France's population and occupies a tiny fraction of the French territory, yet almost all the country's cultural creations are produced in Paris, almost all its television newscasts emerge from Paris-based studios and are manufactured by Parisians, almost all important political decisions, even those affecting the entire French nation, are made in the capital.

Let us bracket the veil of surroundings, and remove it. What remains appears to be an isolated artefact, which is an eidetic concept because isolated architectural artefacts do not actually exist. All buildings in our life-world are, in one fashion or another, a part of their surroundings. From this point of view, the architectural phenomenon is an organic whole that cannot be fragmented. Nonetheless, the epochè requires an eidetic fragmentation. But even this controlled observation may prove to be difficult because something constantly seems to be moving in front of the artefact. What we perceive is a vaporous, ethereal floating veil that partially hides what we wish to observe and hinders the proper focusing of our intentionality. Things, it seems, cannot stop moving, and this movement blurs the observer's perception. Perhaps if we shift our intentionality to this in-between moving veil, we will be able to describe it.

Veil Four: Presence in Evolution

This moving veil is the veil of history. Before the essence of the selected artefact as it stands right now can be deciphered, we have to look at the evolutionary process that has generated it. Because what is observed is always a presence in evolution. The veil of evolution is immensely rich, itself composed of more than one layer. One of these is the long, linear, historical sequence of moments, the parade of days and years that has spun the primary thread of history. Today's designed environment is balanced on the present point in this time line, an elusive spark of reality squeezed between memory and anticipation.

History is not only the linear passing of time. It is also a complex web of influences and coincidences that constantly shapes the economic, political, social, and cultural forces that have allowed for the occurrence of any particular architectural artefact, be it a single building or an entire city (Thuillier 1986, 1990; Carbonell 1991). The evolution of an architectural artefact is also the scenario of events and personal decisions that led to the determination to build this particular structure, on this particular site, for this particular set of purposes, and at this particular moment. The notion of time also covers the artefact's design and construction, activities that took place within a certain duration and influenced the present architectural reality. And after construction was completed, the artefact started a life of its own that continued for several years before reaching the present moment. All architectural artefacts witness the comings and goings of their users, a living process that still influences the present structure. Over the years, the artefact has aged; it may have suffered damage and need renovation or an upgrade. All these factors form the evolution of the present artefact, which I will eventually describe.

History involves change. Henri Laborit wrote that "the passing time that transforms the inert matter which forgets, leaves traces in living matter which remembers" (Laborit 1968, 18).[31] Laborit is partially right, because architectural artefacts also remember. They are not made with inert inert materials, if I may use this odd expression, but by metamorphosed inert materials, materials that have been transformed by the creative impulses of human beings. Once the architectural artefact is built, its inert materials come to resemble living organisms. They age quickly. To stay in proper working condition they require a constant influx of energy. Left to themselves, they soon become obsolete ruins.

Let us remove the veil of presence in evolution, and in so doing freeze the course of time at the present moment. Suddenly, things come into focus and we can clearly see the next veil. It appears to be the artefact that exists now, in its stark material reality.

Veil Five: Materiality

Now we are focusing on one empty artefact that nonetheless displays its purpose, that has been isolated from its surroundings, cut off from the communication links that would normally connect it with the rest of the world, and frozen in time. What we see is a physical entity that can be touched, a structure of some sort, made of materials assembled in a systematic way. To use Le Corbusier's mechanistic words, it is a "stationary machine." Analysing it, one sees a frame, walls, floors, a roof, doors, windows, as well as furniture, equipment, and utensils. Norwegian architect Thomas Thiis-Evensen identified forty building elements in his typology of the architectural material object (Thiis-Evensen 1987). The specification manual of a complex artefact describes hundreds, if not thousands of building components.

But frames or roofs are not what we really see. The objects we perceive are the materials that compose these building elements. We actually see pieces of steel, iron, aluminium, and other metals; we see stones, bricks, and tiles, slabs and blocks of concrete, plates of glass, planks and panels of wood, sheets of plaster and plastic, paint and fabrics. All of these things are the architect's raw materials, like the potter's clay. What he designs is nothing more than a coherent assemblage of them.

This veil illustrates a way of reducing the balkanization of the architectural profession. By recognizing that building materials constitute an essential element of the architectural phenomenon and by putting them at the centre of the theoretical discourse, we begin to establish the framework for a fruitful a cooperation between theoreticians and practitioners.

The journey towards the essence of the architectural phenomenon requires a thorough description of the veil of materiality. But this description, as are those of the other veils, is beyond the scope of this work.

Let us lift the veil and look underneath.

Veil Six: Structuring Systems

What we see is a complex set of raw systems that are meant to connect the various materials and hold them together. Infiltrating the materiality of the artefact, these systems form an organic whole. At first sight, we notice sprawling urban infrastructures, and then, as we focus on a single building, we glimpse the exposed building systems, which are terminals of the larger urban systems. From the simple edifice to the largest city – indeed, to the entire planet and its artificial satellites – everything is laced with overlapping and interconnected networks of organic systems. The word *organic* inspires a human metaphor to describe designed environment systems. Like the human body, the designed environment contains a limited array of systems; in fact, no more than six basic systems uphold it. Its structural frames are like the skeleton; they hold the physical milieu together. The plumbing network, which regulates the flow of fluids, is similar to the cardiovascular system. The electrical network and the communication systems are like the human nervous system; they move electrical power and information. The motorized-movement systems of people and goods can be compared to the muscles; they help carry things and move them faster. And the pedestrian network, in which people socialize, is like the senses; it insures intimate exchange.

The most visible of all architectural systems is the structure. In a way, the physical city is an aggregate of structures, each made of posts, beams, walls, slabs, and joists. No architectural artefact can exist without some sort of a structural frame capable of holding it together. An essential, universal component of the architectural phenomenon, erected structures are the ones that actually make the physical environment; they provide the enclosures, they bear the roofs that shelter us, and they render possible, for example, both underground cities (such as Montreal's) and skyscrapers (such as Manhattan's).

In a city, structures frame the open-space network, which, in turn, largely defines the public domain. In a strange way, the most static of physical systems, the erected-structure system, defines the most dynamic and open-ended of urban organizational systems, the public open-space system. The latter system is a network that delimits the part of the urban environment devoted primarily to public activities, while individual buildings, serving mostly private needs, insert themselves into it. To design a city, and to design the buildings within it, the architect must first lay out the public-domain network; only after that can he implement individual structures. This is how the Ancient Greeks and Romans designed and built their cities (Bacon 1976; Kostof 1991, 1992). They even established a hierarchy of buildings: the temples, the basilica, and other public buildings were positioned first, and only after this were lots for private residences allocated. Private properties were subservient to the public domain; in return, the public domain was conceived to serve private places. That is why it is said that urban design is about the design of constraints while architectural design is about the respect of constraints. All cities display a similar basic organizational framework, although in them the delicate balance between public and private is sometimes disturbed.

The distinction between the public-structuring domain and private structured properties is crucial. Since many public buildings, as well as several private roadways, cohabit with public open space and private structures, it is necessary to underline that this distinction between private and public is larger than its legalistic or even simplistic functional connotation. It relates to the kind of human activity occurring in the city. Private activities frequently occur in public buildings, and, more rarely, public activities take place in private places. A marriage at City Hall is an example of the first kind, and a stroll in a shopping mall is an instance of the second kind. Whether public or private, some activities are very intimate in nature, others very ostentatious, and many others are something in between. For example, sleeping is a very intimate activity, and parading is a very showy one. Humans have designed private and public places to accommodate each kind of activity. Holding a parade in a private place, such as a bedroom, is an absurdity; sleeping in a public place, such as a street, is an anomaly. Only a tiny fraction of citizens sleep in the street by choice. Cities work better when sleeping occurs in bedrooms and parading occurs in the streets; that is, when the complementary roles of each domain are well understood.

The pedestrian-movement system is perhaps the city's most important public network because it encompasses the kind of places where city dwellers become citizens. Public by definition, it nonetheless touches and surrounds all private properties and often penetrates them. This is the network of corridors and stairs, halls and lobbies, sidewalks and pathways, city rooms and squares, malls and arcades, gardens and parks. It not only constitutes the main movement system between activity components, but it is also made up of the principal places for social interaction. Celebrations and revolutions are made in the streets. For the most part, civilization emerges from the billions of human exchanges that happen every day in public places. The charm of European cities rests largely in the quality of their pedestrian networks. Conversely, the failure of many large North American cities is primarily due to their inability to provide adequate places for pedestrians. In America, sidewalks are deserted in city cores outside business hours and are often nonexistent in the suburbs; the most popular gathering places are now private shopping malls.

It is necessary to point out that the pedestrian-movement system exists in all settlements. This is not the case with other types of infrastructure. In its most primitive form, the pedestrian-movement system is merely the space between shelters. Shelters and the pedestrian-movement system are two necessary, complementary, universal urban characteristics. One cannot exist without the other.

The motorized-movement system is the one in which humans use moving machines to transport goods and themselves. It complements the pedestrian-movement system, enhancing an individuals own physical capability. As a rule, this system comprises two basic elements: vehicles and the network of pathways along which they move. Only in the case of escalators and moving sidewalks are pathways also moving elements. Vehicles take many forms: elevator cabins, which move inside vertical shafts; automobiles, motorcycles, trucks, taxis, and buses, which run on roadways. Other vehicles move on rails: trams, metros, and monorails. Yet others are suspended on a steel wire. Some vehicles are private; others are public. The automobile is a piece of private property running on public roadways, while buses are public and taxis fall somewhere in between. It is interesting to note that escalators, elevators, and moving sidewalks can be consigned either to the pedestrian-movement system or to the motorized-movement system because they are motorized systems in which users do not have to give up their role as mingling pedestrians. Another ambiguity exists with bicycles, skateboards, and roller skates. Users of these devices lose some of their pedestrian status because of the speed at which they move, but their vehicles are not propelled by motors. This apparent ambiguity only illustrates the intimate interface between these two main people-movement systems, especially in our complex contemporary cities. Finally, the motorized-movement system includes some rare vehicles that move through the air, vehicles such as helicopters (planes are not yet used for intracity transportation).

The current urban motorized-movement systems that depend on heavy infrastructures to function carry their own internal contradiction. Originally, they were intended to ease the movement of people through urban territory, yet their very presence often renders that movement more difficult. Left to themselves, as they are in primitive settlements, buildings tend to cluster in response to functional or cultural requirements. For example, schools, shops, and churches duster near residences. But, with the rapid growth of cities, not all buildings could be situated near the homes of those they served; an increasing number of residences were built farther and farther away from services and workplaces. To counteract this sprawl, motorized-movement systems were implemented, but these systems required infrastructures that took up more and more space at the centre, and thus displaced activity components to the periphery. In America, where inexpensive automobiles have long been mass-produced, intricate highway networks were built to accommodate the sprawl. Moreover, the mere presence of these transportation systems had an additional impact that compounded the migration towards the periphery: while the new urban highway was meant to serve the existing suburbs, it was, in fact, exploited by those who advocated the creation of new suburbs. Located at ever-greater distances from the centre, these new suburbs required more and larger highways. The vicious circle of urban sprawl was in full swing: fewer and fewer activity components were constructed in the city centre because the space they needed was taken up by the transportation system that was supposed to serve them in the first place; more and more extensive suburbs required more and more highway links, which, in turn, took up more and more room. And a further distortion is introduced by the fact that many activity components tended to locate near transportation nodes as opposed to near their natural neighbours.

The plumbing system transports fluids through a network of pipes, ditches, or canals. It encompasses the water-supply system, the sewer (storm and domestic) system, the oil and gas distribution systems, and, in certain locations, the vapour-distribution network. When urban waterways penetrate a city, they are simultaneously part of the plumbing system and the motorized-movement system.

The power system is that which enhances the power of the human arm. It comprises a network of wires and cables that transport electrical energy to all activity components in the city. Like the water-supply and sewer systems in our modern cities, the electrical system is so efficient, so omnipresent, that it is taken for granted. The act of switching on a lamp, radio, or computer has become an unconscious reflex. It is, however, rendered possible by an immensely complex and sophisticated engineering achievement.

The communications system enhances the human voice. It includes both the cable and the wireless networks: cable and cellular telephone, telefax, computer cables, television and cable television, radio, CD and amateur-radio communications, intercom and paging systems, and security systems. New cities require a communications system that is increasingly elaborate and costly to operate. Such a system is subject to expanding technology and daily innovation.[32]

Two important notions complement the description of urban systems. The first is the recognition that they are vulnerable entities. Although survival in our complex cities is dependent upon the flawless running of these sophisticated networks, they can easily be taken over, sabotaged, or destroyed. Picture for a frightening moment New York without electricity for one year or with poisoned water flowing through its water-supply system. Millions of people would have to be evacuated. That is why, in urban system design, the key objective is to have multiple supply points, control points, and alternative routes; that is, to design systems according to the characteristics of the grid. This is the fundamental reason behind the choice of the grid as the basic organizational principle of most cities (Bacon 1976; Lincourt 1972; Kostof 1991). The grid is an open-ended, efficient spatial form of organization; it allows for a choice of movement. If danger knocks at the front door, escape is possible through the back door. If an accident blocks a street, one can reach the hospital another way. By coincidence, perhaps, the grid is also a democratic form of organization because it has no all-controlling points of convergence and it renders totalitarian police enforcement more difficult. A city on a grid is the antithesis of a panopticon.

The second notion is the idea of servomechanism. Both building systems and urban systems act as servomechanisms for people. A servomechanism is a device that entails a feedback loop and, when applied to machines operated by people, may increase their strength. For instance, if we observe a jetplane pilot in action we notice that, with a gentle push of his finger, he releases a tremendous force that lifts the plane into the air and propels it at a tremendous speed. What the pilot has touched with his finger is a control device that is a servomechanism. A feedback signal tells him whether or not the plane is flying at the proper speed. He can therefore control the movement of his powerful machine the same way he controls the movement of his weak hand. Architectural systems are similarly enhancing devices. For instance, the urban water-supply system that reaches kitchens and bathrooms has replaced the daily activity of carrying water pails, and the telephone carries the human voice all the way to the antipodes. The modern city has transformed citizens into very powerful individuals.

But is this power fundamental to the individual's destiny or is it trivial? Are humans really in control of this vast urban machinery? Perhaps human evolution and the transformation of the designed environment constitute a closed system without an outside regulatory device. Perhaps humans are caught up in this maelstrom and switching on the electric light may be only an illusion of power.

A more detailed description of the designed environment systems is beyond the scope of this work. Such a detailed description is found in numerous planning and engineering textbooks, manuals, and electronic databases.

After being described, the veil of systems is lifted. What remains is, perhaps, the artefact's setting.

Veil Seven: Ecology

This setting may very well infiltrate every pore of the architectural artefact. It is the veil of ecology, living nature. Let us recall that the epochè is probing a specific architectural phenomenon. So far, six veils have been removed, each containing a dimension of the phenomenon, each revealing another dimension. What lies deep under the first six veils is the fact that the architectural phenomenon is but a dimension of the even larger ecological phenomenon, itself a dimension of the life-world.

The life-world ecosystem has been described by many ecologists, notably world-renowned Pierre Dansereau, one of the signatories of the UNESCO Vancouver Declaration on the Survival of Humanity (UNESCO 1989). Dansereau showed that the life-world ecological dimension can be understood as an organism made up of a series of intertwined, largely interpenetrating spheres, each dependant on the others for its own survival and for the survival of the whole. The cosmophere envelopes the Earth and its energy penetrates the planet's successive layers all the way down to the pyrosphere, the Earth's inner fire. Between these extreme spherical layers float and swarm three intermediate spheres: the atmosphere, the hydrosphere, and the lithosphere. Together, these form the biosphere, the fragile domain that sustains life. The biosphere penetrates the atmosphere, the hydrosphere, and the lithosphere, but is incompatible with the cosmosphere and the pyrosphere environments.

The biosphere self-regulating system, explained Dansereau, is a complex ressource-recycling mechanism that includes five elements: the resources that nourish the cyclical process; the agents that trigger the various processes of the metabolism through absorption, transformation, storage, channelling, and transport of resources; the processes themselves through which resources are metabolized: pedogenesis, photosynthesis, predation, and the like; the products that are the output of ecological transformations; and the trophic levels, which relate to the food chain: from minerals, to plants, to animals, to humans (Dansereau 1991).

Humans constitute an intrinsic component of the ecological organism. So do their works. It is not certain that at present humans can control the ecosystem, but they can certainly derail it with the pollution they generate. Pollution is a simple phenomenon. It is not the production of waste, because waste production is a natural function of all living organisms. It is only the excessive production of waste – that is, the production of more waste than can be readily absorbed by the ecological system. Pollution is a by-product of the designed environment. It should be stressed that it is through the making and the operating of the designed environment that humans pollute the ecological world, not by any other means. Many architects retreat from the issue disdainfully, arguing that pollution is not produced by architects, but rather by engineers who made and operate all those dirty machines and industrial plants, and by the military with its frightening bombs and other weapons of mass destruction. This is a weak argument. It serves no purpose to put the blame on others. As I stated before, architects are among the prime designers of the world and, as such, share the collective responsibility; they must contribute to the search for solutions.

Architectural artefacts are nothing but nature transformed. They are made of natural elements, situated in nature, and nourished by nature. Architecture is a part of Earth's environment, a part of our universe. In architecture, nature takes many forms. It is the origin of all materials, the purveyor of all that is necessary to sustain the life of living organisms, including humans, who live in architecture. Nature is also necessary to maintain the existence of architecture itself. It is the site where buildings are built and it is the soil on which they stand. It is the climate: the wind and the heat of the sun, the cycle of warmer days and colder nights, the passing of seasons, the rain and the snow, the hurricanes and the earthquakes that can demolish an architectural structure in a few seconds. Nature is the birds and all the other living creatures that share the environment with humans. It is flowers and trees, manicured lawns and uncultivated vegetation.

Nature is in architecture and architecture is in nature. Nature is part of the essence of architecture and architecture is part of the essence of nature. Having made this primordial statement, we are entitled to ask where ecology is in today's architectural discourse, education, and practice. We may enquire what the postmodern attitude is regarding ecology in architecture and which chapters in Venturi's or Jencks's writings deal with this subject. Yet, seventy-five years ago, the CIAM[33] clearly took an ecological position. Could it be that current avant-garde protagonists are moving backwards on this particular point?

It is relatively easy to probe the ecological dimension of architecture today, because environmental awareness is increasing rapidly. Many scientists and political activists contribute to this new awareness; architects must join the fray.

Let us remove the veil of ecology and observe what lies underneath.

Veil Eight: Form and Space

What we find now is the architectural artefact extracted from its ecological, natural setting – hence, nothing other than an abstraction. Up to this point, the epochè of the architectural phenomenon has remained at the level of the empirical apprehension of its immediately perceivable elements, including its present purpose and its memories. Now, the epochè enters the realm of pure eidetic concepts beyond past or present observable realities. If, through a gesture of the imagination, the observer removes the systems holding together the materiality of the artefact, he or she necessarily sees a form, or a cluster of forms; that is, the abstract contour in three dimensions of the material reality. Form is defined here as the external appearance of a structure, and may be described by geometric shapes: a cube, a sphere, a prism. All architectural artefacts, indeed all physical objects, by the mere reality of their presence, have a form.

Form may be an ambiguous concept, especially in philosophical discourse. Since Plato, the word *form* has sometimes been used as a synonym for *idea*. One may talk of "the ultimate form" to designate the all-encompassing idea of the essence of being. But here, *form* is not used in this way. I employ the term as designers do: to them, it denotes the shape of a thing, or, more precisely, the exterior physical configuration of the thing. Like all designers, architects are form-givers. They cannot practise their trade without an intimate understanding of the language of forms and the laws of geometry.[34] Certain theoreticians of architecture, such as Francis Ching, consider that it is the form and space duality that best defines the architectural reality of a building (Ching 1979, 110–90).

Any architectural artefact description conducted through a phenomenological epochè must include a detailing of form. This dimension of the architectural phenomenon is usually well covered by modern critics because it falls naturally within the contemporary "architecture as art" dialectic. Abstract art is an art of the form. In the eyes of an abstract artist or in the mind of a critic immersed in the world of abstract art, architecture becomes an exercise of forms. Most postmodern architects, in reaction to the "simplistic and univalent forms of modern architecture" (Jencks 1984, 15), have proposed more complex forms with a wide array of historical and linguistic references. For many of these architects, form dominates practice to the extent that several other dimensions of the architectural phenomenon are ignored.

If we penetrate the observed form (or forms), we perceive, we feel, the flip side of that form, the kind of enclosure that architects call "space." Like form, architectural space can be described with geometric shapes, and any artefact may have either one space or a cluster of spaces. Although form and space can be perceived and felt through all of our senses, as anthropologist Edward T. Hall demonstrated (see both Hall 1966 sources), it is mainly through visual perception that they are experienced (Read and Doo 1983). "Solids" and "cavities," to borrow architectural critic Steen Eiler Rasmussen's words, are thus the two complementary visual features of the architectural phenomenon, always in mutual balance, always in tension (Rasmussen 1959). Sometimes, the space dimension seems to disappear from our consciousness, as is the case with the Parthenon. This Greek temple is always presented to us as an essentially external form; we see it emerging from the Propylaea at a thirty-degree angle, a detached object of pure beauty, a white prism under a bright blue sky. Shadows are stark and deep, created by the incisive parallel rays of an omnipotent sun, situated, nonetheless, at the limit of infinity. These are the rules of the cosmic geometry defining architectural forms and playing what Le Corbusier called "the sophisticated, correct and magnificent interplay of volumes assembled under the light" (Le Corbusier 1958, 16).[35]

At other times, the form dimension is the one that is eschewed, as is the case with the Pantheon of Rome. Here, only the interior volume appears significant, an enclosure pierced by a shaft of moving light. Infinity here is a reversed apex located at the centre of the sphere. Caves, unlike even the Pantheon, are almost exclusively space, their form dimension being often reduced to a hole in a cliff. At the other end of the form-and-space-veil spectrum, monumental columns and obelisks are a form without space. Are they still architecture, or have they become sculptures?[36]

Le Corbusier insisted that the architectural plan ought to proceed from the inside out, that the exterior is the result of the interior, indeed that the outside is always a larger inside (Le Corbusier 1958, 146). The movement out of a shelter into the public domain is not a movement into nothingness, only a transfer from one interior to another. For example, in my house in Outremont, I see the space of my dining room and, in it, the form of a table, chairs, and other objects – in sum, I see an interior. When I move out of the house, I see the space of the street, the form of my house, the fence, the houses of my neighbours, and so on; here, also, I see an interior. Form and space are two intertwined dimensions of the same veil.

Let us remove this veil of form and space. What lies behind is perhaps the mysterious means that have made them possible.

Veil Nine: Economy

This is the veil of money. Basically, money is nothing but a tangible means of evaluating and representing the effort required of humans for their own survival and development. To survive and prosper, people need to work. Work is necessary to produce food, make protective garments, construct shelters, and provide services. And the measuring unit of human work is currency. Money serves also as a system for assessing the exchange of services and goods between people, and, as a corollary, as the means by which these same services and goods are acquired. Hence, all objects made in our world and, cynics would add, all human activities, are assessed in terms of money, have a price tag, can be bought and sold. Obviously, the economic reality is somewhat more complex and, especially in the domain of human feelings, many human activities escape the mercantile paradigm. Certain objects, although they cost money to make, acquire a sentimental value and are not for sale.

Making architecture, therefore, costs money. This reality has been well understood since the beginning of civilization by architects and their clients. It is often the first factor discussed when they come together to make a building (Vitruvius 1965, 25; Erlande-Brandenburg 1993, 129–62). Sometimes, this reality is perceived as an opportunity to create innovative, novel solutions. At other times, it is found to be an annoying constraint. On still other occasions, it is taken as evidence that human needs exceed human means; at times such as these, architects cannot implement the best solutions and must instead select the least damaging from an array of unsuitable options. Money, in architecture, always sets the limits and brings the desirable to the level of the possible. In all cases, it profoundly influences all architectural projects. Yet, strangely, this important dimension of the architectural phenomenon is almost never addressed in architecture schools.

The concept of money in architecture covers more than one dimension. First, it relates to a society's general economy. Society and its visible manifestation – the design environment, the city – comprise a structuring public realm into which the private domain inserts itself. The economy follows the same pattern: a public economy, fuelled by taxes and levies of all sorts, complements the more immediate private economic sector. Generally speaking, the public economy supports the implementation and management of public structures and infrastructures, and the private sector generates financing for private properties. There is obviously a wide overlap between both systems of financing and, in many sophisticated developed economies, mutual assistance in the form of subsidy, tax shelter, tax abatement, compensation and the like, has been established. So-called public-private development corporations are visible signs of this collaboration.

Second, the designed environment, which is a product of the previously mentioned double economy, represents by far the largest investment people make. For example, in Canada, the aggregate replacement value of Canadian real assets was assessed in 1989 at approximately 1,100 billion Canadian dollars (Lincourt 1989). This is obviously an abstract figure because a country's total built environment is never actually replaced. What occurs, however, is constant investment in real estate, not only for the erection of new structures but also for the upgrading of existing ones. In developed economies, the construction industry constitutes the largest of all economic sectors. For example, in Canada again, in 1989, the total value of construction work was 100,065 million Canadian dollars, or 15.4 percent of Canada's gross domestic product (Letartre 1992, 33). And that statistic does not take into account the billions of dollars spent maintaining and repairing our environment. If architecture is the prime design activity of the construction industry, then it is a vital part of a very large business indeed.

This introduces the third point. The initial investment in a building is only a fraction of the total investment required during the course of that building's existence. Except for the building's frame and its envelope – if it is made of durable materials such as stone or brick – all other building systems begin to wear out after thirty years, sometimes less. The electromechanical systems, windows, interior finishes, furniture, and roof will then need major repairs. Often full replacement is necessary. Preventive maintenance, when it is implemented, may reduce the total investment in the long term; but still, sustaining a building requires constant investment. The proponents of building-assessment techniques – such as postoccupancy evaluation, building pathology, life-cycle costing, and risk analysis –

have clearly established the point that better management of a building through time will not only preserve its economic value and maintain its performance at a level required by the users but also prevent its decay. Well-built and well-managed buildings may last forever.

Fourth, the specific building-implementation cost is itself a multi-faceted reality. In our modern economies, a typical commercial building-implementation cost is assessed in terms of hard and soft costs. The hard costs normally cover site acquisition and construction – that is, the work performed by the general contractor and the subcontractors – while the soft costs cover everything else – project manager's fee, architect's and engineer's fees, lawyer's or notary's fees, marketing or promotion expenses, interim financing, insurance, and the like. Hence, the cost of the architect's input is only a fraction of the project cost. As far as the construction cost proper is concerned, it may be split into two roughly equal parts: material cost and labour cost. Material cost is itself an aggregate of many components: raw-material-extraction costs, the cost of the various industrial processes that transform the raw materials into usable building products, transportation costs, management and marketing costs, and so on.

Let us remove the veil of economy and observe what lies under it.

Veil Ten: Energy

Underneath, one finds the veil of energy, because money is nothing if not the measurement of energy. Money implies power, the ability to accomplish things, and accomplishing things, including making the architectural artefact, always requires an outlay of energy. Energy, both in its narrowest sense of physical power and in its broadest sense of human creative force, is necessary to create the designed environment and maintain it. Energy is a part of the essence of nature and a part of the essence of the architectural phenomenon. In phenomenological terms, energy is the potentiality of nature.

Architecture cannot exist without the constant injection of energy. An architecture that is outside of living nature and free from the creative interventions of humans cannot even be imagined. Mysteriously, life sprang up on our planet and began to tame energy. Fire was discovered and domesticated (Bachelard 1949). Machines were invented to increase the strength of the human arm. Countless devices, such as the servomechanisms described earlier, were put to work in order to use energy with an ever-increasing efficacy. Architecture is one of the products of the human domestication of energy. Humans had to disburse energy to build their first shelters. This existential condition has never changed. It is a universal attribute of the architectural phenomenon.

But architecture is a demonstration of more than the taming of physical energy. It is proof of the existence of intellectual energy, the kind of creative energy that transformed, for example, a pile of rubble into the Parthenon. A simple example demonstrates this point. Today, many children play with Lego building blocks. Before a child begins to play, she is confronted with a big pile of perhaps a few hundred discreet blocks of several types and shapes. Looking at them, she sees only total randomness, primal chaos. Then she starts to play. With her hands, she mobilizes physical energy in order to lift one block from the pile, then a second block; she plugs the first block onto the second, and so on. A few hours later, the child has built a marvellous castle. What has happened is something more than the harnessing of physical energy, because physical energy would only have generated a random assemblage of blocks. The castle is the product of the child's imagination and creative power. Like Beethoven composing his symphony, the child has harnessed a different type of energy, the energy of her mind (I wanted to use the expression "spiritual energy" but did not because of its religious connotation, which is not implied here). This type of energy is negative entropy, which means that it positively creates works of civilization. Through their respective positions in history, these works become matrices of tradition, creating the eternal memories that form the foundation of knowledge. It is by injecting this intellectual energy into their works that architects introduce order, clarity, continuity, and coherence into the world. And it is their responsibility to do it well.

Let us remove the veil of energy and observe further.

Veil Eleven: Character

What we see now is a more complex abstraction. This is the veil of distinctive sensations generated by the appearance of the architectural artefact. At issue here is the fact that, beyond the architectural artefact's materiality, form, and space – that is, beyond the architectural thing's perceptible configurations – lies another kind of visual dimension that requires a different sort of sensitivity. Three elements interact to form this added dimension: appearance, uniqueness, and distinction. What makes the child's castle so marvellous? Certainly, the fact that it displays a distinctive appearance makes it unique, special. What makes the Parthenon so astounding? Here, too, it is the fact that it displays the same sort of characteristic. This added dimension is what fashion designers call "the look," and what Jacques-François Blondel calls "caractère" (Fichet 1979; Picon 1988).

It is well known in the fashion industry that modelling agencies can represent several young women whose appearance meets very precise specifications in terms of race, complexion, height, weight, hair colour and style. From a certain distance, all these young women look exactly the same, like absolute clones. However, a closer examination will reveal features that distinguish each from the other. And it is possible, also, that one model will stand out, projecting a unique aura. A "top" model is, precisely, one who possesses a truly exceptional look while remaining within the fashion industry's very strict norms. What differentiates a top model from others is character; in this case, we may also use the term *personality*. Similarly, in architecture, distinctive features permit us to distinguish between two, or several, artefacts that have similar geometric characteristics. For example, in a residential subdivision, several houses are built according to the same design, by the same contractor, with the same materials, and within a limited period. Immediately after their construction, all these houses look the same. Some years later, however, we notice that each has evolved according to its own destiny, and strong differences between the various houses have emerged. Each house has acquired its own distinctive character.

These differences create the architectural appearance that exists beyond geometric and material features. They include, but are not limited to, patina of materials, nuance of colour and texture, landscaping, decoration, quality of light, presence of architectural details, signage, furniture and fixtures, and rhythm of secondary elements. For example, at the level of its basic geometry, a large building may have a long façade pierced regularly by numerous similar windows; it may be a bland, anonymous construction.[37] If, however, the windows are adorned with cast-iron railings of varying design, if flower boxes are added, if those windows are also protected by awnings that can take diverse opening and closing positions, then the façade may acquire a personality of its own, a look that is unique – in a word, character.

We need to be prudent with such examples. Because it was necessary to distinguish in order to describe distinction, to point to a unique example in order to show uniqueness, I may have conveyed the impression that "the others" – that is, those artefacts discarded from a particular characterization process – have no character. This could not be further from the truth. Just as each human has his or her own personality, each architectural artefact, from the most humble shed to the most sublime cathedral, has character.

In his *Cours d'architecture*, published between 1771 and 1777, Jacques-François Blondel thoroughly described this notion of architectural character using what he called the "method of definition" (Blondel in Fichet 1979,

410–49). For example, he discussed such traits of character as sublimeness, admirableness, originality, "pyramidality," agreeability, appropriateness, truthfulness, nobility, unity, variety, freedom, abundance, exactness, virility, lightness, femininity, rusticity, naïvety, mystery, greatness, boldness, frivolity, licentiousness, vagueness, futility, sterility, blandness, and poverty.

Let us remove the veil of character and continue to probe the architectural phenomenon.

Veil Twelve: Projection

Behind that of character lies an even more mysterious veil: the veil of human sentiments experienced in architecture. Architecture is more than the sum of everything that has been previously described. The architectural phenomenon is the total lived experience of humans in architecture. The veil of projection is the experiential relationship between a building's users and its physical entity.

Projection is often mistaken for meaning. A projection is the conscious or unconscious attribution to others of one's own thoughts or feelings. In this case, the word *others* means the architectural reality. Buildings are physical, inert things, mere piles of stones. They do not have meanings of their own. They do not speak. Speaking, perceiving, understanding, making sense, are unique human attributes. However, humans send their thoughts and feelings towards their built environment like beams of light or radar sound waves. These rays of sensitivity hit the environment and bounce back to their sender. What humans perceive are not messages emanating from the architectural reality but messages emanating from themselves and reflected by the environment.

A part of what these projections carry is the architect's intentions. In trying to grasp the essence of an architectural phenomenon, it is valid to ask these questions: What was the aim of its designer, and how was it, and is it, understood? Was the architectural artefact the result of a personal conscious will, or did emanate from individual or collective unconsciousness? Or was it a mixture of both?

Another component of these projections is generated by the building users' activities, motivations, and perceptions, which always transform the architect's original intention. Through time and space, architecture provides the missing links between designers' intentions and users' apprehensions and projections.

Architecture also creates continuity through the successive stages of civilization. For instance, a succession of architects designed Greek columns,

Roman vaults, Byzantine mosaics and icons, Gothic stained-glass windows, the medieval city porticoes, Japanese sliding paper walls, Chinese upward-curved roofs, industrial-age cast-iron and glass structures, twentieth-century skyscrapers, to name a few icons, and thus have created an architectural tradition that is part of the human heritage. Even today we admire the masterpieces of the past. They are testimonies to the human quest for wisdom and happiness.

Let us remove the veil of projection, suspend it temporarily with the others, and observe further.

REDUCTION: THE EIDOS OF ARCHITECTURE

We have reached the foundation of the architectural phenomenon. The eidos of architecture may be expressed by an idea that has appeared time and time again during the course of the epochè like a leitmotif. This idea is that the architectural phenomenon is a "shelter housing humans," and a "shelter housing humans" is nothing if not a locale for "dwelling in a place." "A place," wrote Edward Relph, "is a whole phenomenon, consisting of the three intertwined elements of a specific landscape with both built and natural elements, a pattern of social activities that should be adapted to the advantages or virtues of a particular location, and a set of personal and shared meanings." Relph's idea of place is embedded in the concept of the architectural phenomenon as exposed by the removal of the phenomenological veils. A place is, Relph added, "above all a territory of meanings ... [and] what is received from a place includes pleasure or displeasure, loneliness or companionship, a sense of security and danger" (Relph in Seamon 1993, 34).

Dwelling means "being-in-the-world," a vision inspired by Heidegger. For him, place is the context of "things ready-to-hand." In a commentary on Being and Time, Joseph Fell wrote that "the Being of the human being, his essential nature, is Place, the ground and the clearing within which there can be disclosure of beings as what they are ... and, as Heidegger asserted, Dasein names that which should first be experienced, and thence properly thought of, as Place – that is, the locale of the truth of Being" (Fell in Relph in Seamon 1989, 27). Heidegger's idea of dwelling, the locale of the truth of being, is also embedded in Relph's idea of place.

A fortiori, dwelling is truthfully located in a place, a reality emerging from the unveiling of the architectural phenomenon. The dwelling-in-a-place idea is the manifestation of the truth- phenomenon idea as depicted by Heidegger, because ultimately truth is unveiling. In *The Basic Problems of Phenomenology*, the German philosopher wrote that "being-truth means unveiling." He showed that truth is in the *dasein* "unveiled to its own self for itself," and, simultaneously, in the subject's ego performing and experiencing the unveiling. He insisted that "truth and being-truth as unveiledness and unveiling" have the "Dasein's mode of being," and that truth belongs to the ontological constitution of the *dasein* itself. Insofar as *dasein* means being-in-the-world – that is, dwelling in a place – and insofar as "being-true, unveiledness, is the fundamental condition for our being able to be in the way in which we exist as Dasein," then the unveiling of architecture is the truth condition of the architectural phenomenon (Heidegger 1988, 216–21). And the unveiled reality of dwelling in a place is its necessary manifestation. Moreover, insofar as this reality exists in the world as *dasein* itself, design is the apodictic principle of the architectural phenomenon's existence.

It follows that Merleau-Ponty's notion of place, which signifies a passing from "spatialized" space to "spatializing" space, gains not only in validity but also in insight. The unveiling of the architectural phenomenon leads to the awareness of a dynamic, even organic, notion of place, understood as a complex phenomenon apodicticly intertwined with the human condition. Architectural space without the presence of humans is an expression of absurdity, the negation of place, indeed the negation of humanity. Architecture is place, and place is human, as Heidegger asserted. Thinking along the same lines, Christian Norberg-Schulz argued:

architecture is concerned with existential meanings [which] are derived from natural, human and spiritual phenomena, and are experienced as order and character. Architecture translates these meanings into spatial forms [therefore it] ought to be understood in terms of meaningful (symbolic) forms ... place means something more than location, it means having a spirit, and this spirit of the place, this genius loci, presupposes an identification with the environment ... the place is where Man dwells, and he dwells when he is able to concretise the world in buildings and things ... to dwell between heaven and earth means to "settle" in the "multifarious in-between" ... the word "settle" [being] an existential concept which denotes the ability to symbolise meanings. (Norberg-Schulz 1980, 5, 18, 23, 50)

Therefore, architectural artefacts are shelters of the symbolic ability of humans to be in the world. Le Corbusier said that the first gesture of any human being is to take possession of his or her living space, or to dwell in the world. The shelter is the protective, physically constructed aura and the locale of symbols.

Perhaps the most significant summary of the phenomenological understanding of the dwelling-in-a-place idea came from Gaston Bachelard when he spoke of the "intimate immensity" of a house (Bachelard 1964, 168). With two words, Bachelard conveyed both a human feeling and the transcendent and transcendental dimensions of the architectural phenomenon. In places, people do and feel things, which means that they dwell. And this simple notion, also constantly present in the epochè of the architectural phenomenon, means that feeling and doing things conveys the concept of communication, even the communication of ideas or feelings within the subject's self. In a sense, architecture is a materialized reverie, a daydream come true. It can be simple or complex, inhibiting or exhilarating, ugly or beautiful, but it is always truthfully real.

From this, we can formulate the eidos of the architectural phenomenon: *Redraped in its twelve constitutive veils – people, activity components, surroundings, presence in evolution, materiality, structuring systems, ecology, form and space, economy, energy, character, and projection – the eidos of the architectural phenomenon is dwelling in a protective place made for the enhancement of human exchange.*

Demonstrators march in the streets of Paris to demand housing for the homeless

4

VALUES AND DESIGN CRITERIA

Architectural design entails the conscious enactment of a comprehensive decision-making endeavour, which necessitates, on the part of the architect, a never-ending sequence of value judgements. In all cases, the formulation of judgements requires the explicit use of criteria. In this context, a criterion may be understood as a standard by which a thing is assessed. Whether explicitly expressed or not, the validity of the criteria depends upon how well they conform to corresponding human values, which, in turn, underpin judgements. A list of value-based criteria for evaluating places that have already been built and assessing the design of new buildings is the end result of this theoretical epochè and subsequent constitution. This is the answer to the second fundamental question of the theory.

In this epochè, I propose to start with a description of the usual design criteria employed by architects today. Then, by temporarily suspending these criteria, we will uncover a substratum, which could be what a United Nations working paper on housing rights identified as the "entitlements" of housing rights. Here, the word *housing* is understood in its broadest sense as the entire designed environment. After describing the entitlements, we will suspend them as well, and thereby uncover the housing rights themselves. These, in turn, are but a component of human rights, as presented, for instance, in the United Nations Universal Declaration of Human Rights. By bracketing human rights, one discovers that they are grounded in societal values. And, after the values are removed, the telos of the architectural phenomenon is revealed. It is only at this juncture – that is, only when one's consciousness of the essence of architecture can rest on such a universal foundation – that the reverse process becomes possible. It is the constitution aiming at the reconstruction of a richer list of design criteria, validated this time not only by the necessities of the architectural practice but also by the enlightened awareness of our collective values.

Current Design Criteria

As a rule, today, when an architect signs a contract with his client, he pledges to produce an artefact that meets certain simple and well-understood conditions. The first of these is that he must respect the project brief. Although the architect sometimes drafts the brief, it remains a document given to the architect by the client, often as a formal annex to the contract, because it describes the project content. A well-functioning project reflects the architect's respect for the brief, despite the fact that many architectural briefs change as the design process evolves. The second condition is respect for the project budget. Obviously, the budget must conform to the brief and other project constraints. Otherwise, the architect runs the risk of making promises he is not able to keep. The third condition is related to the project site. Several issues are involved, such as soil condition, foundation design, drainage, adequate response to natural factors, and proper connection to utilities. Moreover, quite often, especially in an urban context, historic and social integration requirements are added to the site's problematic. The fourth condition is respect for the law, including full compliance with building codes, zoning bylaws, and other construction regulations. The fifth condition is that the project must be built according to the rules of the construction art; it has to be solidly constructed with judiciously selected materials and systems. The sixth condition is respect for the project schedule, meaning that its implementation must follow a preplanned work programme and be completed within the client's predetermined timetable. And the last condition is that the project must please. This requirement is not always explicitly formulated, although the architect is usually expected to a design a pleasant-looking structure that ensures the users' well being and aesthetic pleasure.

Other design requirements are sometimes added, but, except in rare situations, the seven listed here are the ones that are always present. It follows that the architect feels he has honestly assumed his professional responsibility if his project successfully meets these basic requirements, first in his own mind, but also to his client's and the relevant public authorities' satisfaction. These requirements thus become the criteria for assessing the project's success. However, are these criteria sufficient to guarantee a successful architecture?[38] In order to probe this question further, it becomes necessary to suspend, for a moment, these operational design criteria and look for what may lie underneath.

Under the design rules followed by the architect and the client when they undertake to make an architectural artefact lies a kind of moral contract. By accepting the architect's proposed design solutions, the client – acting, in a way, as a representative of all the project's users – is not agreeing to buy an empty shed. What he or she is actually buying is a dwelling place; the architect has contracted to provide the client with desirable living conditions. In other words, the provision of a new building is always a promise of a better life. Users are entitled to obtain these vessels of improved living conditions and the architect has the obligation to provide them with it. At the project's outset, the prescription for these living conditions may be dictated in the project programme in the form of performance specifications or precise project characteristics. Or, this prescription may take the form of the norms contained in the various building codes that control construction practices. It may also be expressed as the principles outlined in documents produced by institutions that seek to establish the link between architectural standards, living conditions, and human dignity. The United Nations is one of these institutions. In a report entitled *The Right to Adequate Housing* submitted to the United Nations Commission on Human Rights in June 1993, it was noted that "one of the barriers to achieving housing rights has been the long-standing absence of a universally recognised definition of the bundle of entitlements comprising this norm ... [and] viewed in their entirety, these entitlements could constitute the central guarantees which, under international laws, are legally afforded to people possessing housing rights" (Sachar 1993, 13–22). The report suggested seven entitlements:

§ Legal security of tenure: This entitlement stipulates that "all persons should possess a degree of security of tenure which guarantees legal protection against forced eviction, harassment and other threats." Of course, it presupposes that people already occupy a place called home, which they appreciate, and from which they might be evicted or where they may be subject to other kinds of harassment. And this place called home must display the sort of adequate housing characteristics that were depicted earlier in the same report with these words: "Adequate housing is defined in the unanimously adopted Global Strategy [for Shelter to the Year 2000] as meaning: adequate privacy, adequate space, adequate security, adequate lighting and ventilation, adequate basic infrastructure and adequate location with regard to work and basic facilities, all at a reasonable cost."[39]

§ Availability of services, materials, and infrastructures: This entitlement states that "an adequate house must contain certain facilities essential for health, security, comfort and nutrition. All beneficiaries of the right to adequate housing should have sustainable access to natural and common resources, potable drinking water, energy for cooking, heating and lighting, sanitation and washing facilities, food storage, refuse disposal, site drainage and emergency services." Although this entitlement is focused on residential activity components, it implies that the same characteristics apply to other places, such as schools, shops, factories, offices, hospitals, churches, and community and recreational facilities. As formulated, this entitlement concerns several of the architectural veils described earlier: activity components, services, ecology, and energy.

§ Affordability: This entitlement means that a good-quality designed environment must not bear a prohibitive price tag. Obviously, this creates an awesome responsibility for the architect: he has to design an environment that is cost effective.

§ Habitability: This entitlement defines habitability "in terms of providing the inhabitants with adequate space, and protecting them from cold, damp, heat, rain, wind or other threats to health, structural hazards and disease vectors [and the guarantee of the inhabitants'] physical safety."

§ Accessibility: This entitlement states that "adequate housing must be accessible to those entitled to it." The kind of accessibility discussed here is financial, legal, cultural, social, and psychological. It means that, while respecting mutual privacy, housing and all the other components of the designed environment should be accessible to all races, genders, and creeds, as well as "to all disadvantaged groups such as the elderly, children, the physically disabled, the terminally ill, HIV-positive individuals, persons with persistent medical problems, the mentally ill, victims of natural [and other] disasters."

§ Location: This entitlement deals with the other kind of accessibility; that is, the physical accessibility of all activity components, including housing. The UN report states that "adequate housing must be in a location which allows access to employment options, health-care services, schools, child-care centres and other social facilities. This is true both in large cities and in rural areas where the temporal and financial costs of getting to and from the place of work can place excessive demands upon the budget of poor households. Similarly, housing should not be built on polluted sites nor in immediate proximity to pollution sources that threaten the right to health of the inhabitants."

§ Cultural Adequacy: This seventh entitlement stipulates that "the way housing is constructed, the building materials used and the policies supporting these aspects must appropriately enable the expression of cultural identity and diversity." It clearly relates to architectural and urban design.

The UN report on the question of entitlement reached this conclusion: "These extensive entitlements reveal the multi-dimensional nature of the right to adequate housing ... thus, any person, family, household, group or community, living in conditions in which these entitlements are not fully satisfied could reasonably claim that they do not enjoy the rights to adequate housing as enshrined in international human rights law" (Sachar 1993, 19–22). Contributing to the full enjoyment of housing rights is part of the architect's professional mission. Not only should he be aware of these considerations, but also, even more importantly, he should be ready to integrate them into his design.

Let us temporarily suspend these entitlements and observe what lies underneath.

Housing Rights

By all accounts, the foundation of the entitlements is the housing rights themselves. In international human-rights declarations, covenants, and conventions, the right to housing is expressed in at least eight[40] basic agreements: the United Nations Universal Declaration of Human Rights (1948), the UN Convention Relating to the Status of Refugees (1951), the UN Declaration on the Rights of the Child (1959), the UN International Convention on the Elimination of Racial Discrimination (1965), the UN Covenant on Economic, Social and Cultural Rights (1966), the UN Declaration on Social Progress and Development (1969), the Vancouver Declaration on Human Settlements (1976), and the UN International Convention on the Elimination of Discrimination against Women (1979).[41]

All these sources concur: housing is a fundamental human right and it includes more than just the right to basic shelter. "Housing rights" encompass the right to live in a "balanced" community free of discrimination, to enjoy adequate and continuously improving living conditions, to have easy access to social services and medical care, and to enjoy an environment with adequate sanitation, electricity, and water supply, as well as proper transport and communications. To summarize, what this expression of housing rights actually amounts to is that a well-designed twelve-veil environment as described earlier is required.

As all expressions of housing rights are only excerpts of more comprehensive covenants, it becomes imperative to suspend them for a moment and look at what lies underneath and around them.

Human Rights

The right to housing, although comprehensive in its own way, does not stand alone among human rights. It is but a section of a larger body of legal texts, generally called charters of rights. As a rule, these expressions of human rights constitute an essential chapter of most national constitutions, especially those of democratic states. In one fashion or another, they also constitute the basic rationale for most international organizations, agencies, and other groupings of nations, be it on a regional or a worldwide basis. In a compendium of charters of rights published in 1972, thirty international agreements, such as the UN Universal Declaration of Human Rights and the UNESCO Constitution, were cited, as were thirty-three regional texts, such as the treaties creating the European Community and the Organization of American States; 113 national charters of rights or similar texts were cited as well (Torrelli and Baudouin 1972).

Although all of these texts differ from one another according to the particular social, political, historical, and geographic contexts in which they were written, they all proclaim the same basic human rights. The UN Universal Declaration of Human Rights may summarize these various statements. Inspired by England's Magna Carta (1215), the United States of America's Declaration of Independence (1776), the American Constitution (1789) and subsequent amendments, and France's Déclaration des droits de l'homme et du citoyen (1789), the Universal Declaration establishes the preeminence of the human person as the foundation of all human rights – the human person taken both as a distinct individual and as a member of his or her community. It states that all humans are born free and equal and that dignity is inherent to the human condition. It says that every human has the right to life, personal security, and freedom. In this context, freedom is defined as freedom of thought and opinion, freedom of conscience and religion, freedom of movement and place of residence, and freedom of association and peaceful assembly. It says that every human may participate in the affairs of his or her country, has the right to work, to receive an education, and to have social security, implying that he or she has the right to enjoy the full benefit of the economic, social, and cultural rights that are indispensable to his or her human dignity, and to the free development of his or her personality. It stipulates further that every human has the right to privacy, to property, to marry and create a family, meaning that he or she has the right to the kind of place that allows for privacy, and to the kind of infrastructure that allows for free movement and easy access to a place that can facilitate the enjoyment of these rights. It insists that every human has the right to participate freely in the cultural activities of his or her community, to enjoy the arts, and to be involved in, and benefit from, scientific progress. And, included in the UN Universal Declaration, one finds the article that deals specifically with the right to health, well being, and proper housing (UNESCO 1990, article 25.1, 223).

The universal acceptance of these human rights is grounded in two interrelated facts. The first is that the United Nations General Assembly adopted and proclaimed the Universal Declaration on 10 December 1948. This General Assembly includes practically all nations of the world and represents more than 99 percent of the planet's population. It has also endorsed or adopted all the other United Nations covenants, conventions, and related texts. These repeated declarations demonstrate a certain international consensus on the issue of human rights. Of course, a wide gulf persists between the civilizing objectives implied by the charters of rights and the stark reality. Just because the UN has adopted a statement declaring that all humans possess the right to decent housing, it doesn't follow that this right is enjoyed by all. On the contrary: the existing reality, as sketched earlier, is undoubtedly different and rather grim. But this hard reality does not diminish the nobility and the necessity of the objective. It is precisely when the situation is dire that statements of hope become indispensable. The practice of medicine, too, will never cease to be necessary, in spite of the fact that humans continue to fall sick and die.

The second fact that human-rights acceptance is grounded in is that numerous charters of rights have been adopted by many nation-states, not only as a condition of their international activities but also as a set of domestic guiding principles. This attitude of acceptance has penetrated all layers of society's legislation, right down to the level of community regulations.

To promote, control, and apply these human rights, several international, regional, national, and provincial organizations, commissions, tribunals, and courts of law have been put in place. Again, not all is perfect, and discrimination and injustice have not yet been eradicated. But the machinery is in place to improve things. Is there comparable machinery for improving architecture? Let us temporarily suspend these statements of human rights and look further.

Values of Society

Not surprisingly, charters of rights rest on societal values. Values are shared multidimensional principles, always intertwined with one another, situated at the confluence of the physiological, psychological, social, and cultural dimensions of our human reality. They constitute the deep foundation of our collective aspirations, expressing our human telos, or desired destiny. For example, it is because people have agreed that dignity is an attribute cherished by all that it is mentioned in the preamble to the United Nations Universal Declaration of Human Rights.[42]

Closely associated with the values, one always finds the institutions of our society. Such an intimate association exists because institutions are created to protect and facilitate social welfare and are therefore nothing but instruments for realizing people's valued aspirations. For example, the yearning for peace, justice, and freedom – three of the most cherished human values – has prompted the establishment of the institution of democracy, which entails the enactment of a system of laws for protecting and enhancing fundamental human rights – related mainly, in this case, to the desire to live a peaceful life in a free and just society. Each institution is governed by a covenant containing a charter of rights that expresses the kind of values a particular institution wishes to promote and implement. In effect, a statement of rights serves as an institution's guiding principle. Furthermore, as humans are not only spiritual beings but also material entities, their quest to realize valued aspirations necessitates a designed environment; this environment facilitates the management of their institutions and houses their social and personal activities.[43]

First Values

Values emerged over time and were the forces that simultaneously moved our civilization forward and consecrated it.[44] It seems that one of the first values adopted by people was the notion of property. In order to survive and prosper, our early ancestors learned to harness the force of their creative intelligence. They domesticated fire and protected it against intruders (Gaston Bachelard 1949). They made clothes, tools, weapons, and utensils of all sorts. They housed themselves and their belongings in shelters that they fabricated or arranged. Their belongings, as well as their shelters, were hard to make and to maintain, and so immediately became worthy of protection. They had acquired "value." What they had made – or what they could acquire and protect against predators – people determined was theirs. This was the birth of the notion of property as a value. To own property was perceived as both an individual right when it came to certain objects, such as garments, tools, and weapons, and as a communal right when it came to other things, such as the cave, the hut, or the fireplace (Attali 1988).

However, another value was necessary to permit the emergence of the value of property. It was the value that defined the uniqueness of the individual. Only when the distinct individuality of each person within a group was recognized could the right of each person to own things be enacted. Individuality, then, is the sine qua non value underpinning the value of property, and probably the first value to be recognized by humans. These two values are intimately linked to each other because individuality is expressed through the display of belongings and property is always proclaimed by individuals.

Much later – that is, some six thousand years ago – Mesopotamia saw the emergence of the first urban civilization, as we commonly describe it (Mumford 1961; Morris 1989; Kostof 1991, 1992).[45] To manage their communities, the people living between the Tigris and Euphrates Rivers enacted a complex system of laws that was based on an enlarged understanding of the values of individuality and property, encompassing recorded knowledge, specialized economic activities, and real property (Attali 1988, 89–108). They realized that individuals conducting complementary activities in a compact environment require rules for arbitrating incompatible spatial aspirations and a codified system of territoriality. In Mesopotamia, not all activities were permitted in every place, and not all places could belong to everyone. Specific places had to be erected for specific purposes – to store grain, for instance, or to maintain written records, or to worship the gods, or simply to dwell. The value underpinning this spatial fragmentation was privacy, the need of every human, king or slave, to retreat to a secure place where he or she may undertake intimate or specialized activities.

For centuries, these three early values – individuality, property, and privacy – served as our civilization's prime guiding principles. In one fashion or another, they were adopted by all organized societies. Even today, they are still considered prime values: they are shared and treasured by practically all citizens and they form the foundations of many of our laws, including charters of rights.

Values of the Buddha

In 563 B.C., on the banks of the Ganges River, where India meets Nepal, the Buddah was born. He was named Siddhartha Gautama. Seeking a new meaning of life, this son of a noble family and member of the Kshatriya caste rejected his comfortable lifestyle and retreated into an ascetic existence. After six years of isolation and intense meditation, he returned to the world, founded an order of mendicant preachers (male and female), and proposed a radically new way of thinking and behaving. In his first sermon at Varanasi (then called Benares), he suggested "a practical system of spiritual discipline" based on the doctrine of the Four Noble Truths (Suzuki 1972, 162): sorrow is the experience of all men; the cause of sorrow is desire; the removal of sorrow can only come from the removal of desire; and desire can be eliminated by following the Noble Eightfold Path[46] (Carus 1983, 44). If one dutifully follows the noble path, preached Gautama, one may attain a state of illumination or *nirvana* where the *dharma*, or the truth, is perceived in all its bright serenity. Although "precise definitions of Nirvana vary between the different Buddhist schools, it is generally conceived negatively as freedom from ignorance, suffering, and self-interest, and more positively as the achieving of disinterested wisdom and compassion" (Flew 1984, 249).

In his teaching, the Buddha did more than recognize the universal acceptance of the three early societal values of individuality, property, and privacy; he wove them into a code of moral behaviour. Introducing the principle of individual responsibility, he developed a code of ethics. For example, he said that a man choosing freely to follow the Noble Eightfold Path will refuse to desire, let alone steal, other people's property, thus insuring calm, order, and harmony in his community (Suzuki 1972, 162; Carus 1983, 126). Through the process of redefining man's attitude towards himself and society, Gautama articulated three new values. By grounding his doctrine in the idea of truth, itself buttressing the precept of the Four Noble Truths, he acknowledged that the search for truth, the will to travel a long way to find the true meaning of life, the *karma*, was one of humankind's strongest motivations, one of society's stalwart values. But the Buddha also said that man should move beyond consciousness and rise to the level of transcendent humanism. Knowing the truth, he said, entails the responsible adoption altruistic behaviour bolstered by two other values, wisdom and compassion. Wisdom is perceptive, prudent intelligence based on a well-understood experience of self; compassion is discreet, tactful generosity nourished by a well-understood experience of others (Suzuki 1972, 105). In the mind of Gautama, wisdom and compassion are personal attributes with a social dimension; they are what determines a respectful social relationship.

Values of Venerable Master K'ung

Gautama was still a teenager when, at Chu-foo in China's Shantung Province, an exceptional child was born. His name was K'ung. After a solid apprenticeship and a successful career as a public servant, he retired in order to devote his life to studying and teaching the things of the mind. Soon his reputation began to spread beyond his province; to a larger and larger audience he was becoming known as K'ung Fu-tzu, or Venerable Master K'ung. About a thousand years later, the Jesuits Latinized his name to Confucius.

Like the Buddha, but in a different way, Master K'ung proposed a system of ethical precepts that had a profound influence on the evolution of civilization. In his original sayings, the Lun-yii or Analects, he said that social morality is based on three principles: *jen*, or the virtue of humanity, of benevolent love; *yi*, or the virtue of equity; and *li*, or respect for cultural rites and traditions. Similarities can be found between the systems of thought developed by the two Oriental masters. Both were concerned with the welfare of their communities, both emphasized individual responsibility, Master K'ung's notion of *jen* is similar to Gautama's idea of compassion, and both considered wisdom to be one of humankind's most important virtues. Differences can also be distinguished. Master K'ung's system is more communal, more collective, than Gautama's personal, esoteric quest for the truth. Confucianism is, on a basic level, a series of precepts "designed to inspire and preserve the good management of family and society" (*Webster's* 1988); it emphasizes righteousness, decorum, prudent leadership, sincerity, and respect.

Two new values were articulated by Master K'ung. He said that, in an orderly society, the value of compassion is undoubtedly a necessary regulator of harmonious social intercourse, but it is not sufficient. One needs to go beyond individual amenity, transcend the *jen*, and develop collective attitudes. That is why he articulated the values of equity and respect for traditions. Both are values of social stability and perennial continuity; both imply the existence of a sophisticated society.

Ancient Greek Values

At the same time, another system of values was emerging around the Mediterranean Sea. It was developed and codified by the citizen-philosophers of the Hellenic city-states. As we read Plato and Aristotle, for example, we see that the Ancient Greek philosophers recognized the early values of individuality, property, and privacy, articulated values similar to those preached by Gautama and Master K'ung, and added a few more.

The first Greek value was an alternative to brute force for ruling society. The Greek philosophers thought that a more sophisticated and less costly mechanism for establishing and maintaining peace was highly desirable because peace was indispensable to the blossoming of the individual personality and to the protection of property. This desire for peace engendered the political institution of democracy as expressed in Plato's *Republic* and *Laws* and enacted by the ancient Greeks in their practice of government.

It was at this moment, and perhaps because of this unique philosophical context, that another value emerged: the highly civilized notion of human dignity. This noble idea developed because the attainment of peace by democratic means presupposes equal citizens within a community, which, in turn, requires a mutual respect that can only be grounded in a shared dignity. Hence dignity became Classical Greece's second value and immediately constituted the very foundation of the next two values, which were the notions of justice and the common good, two of Plato's main philosophical themes (Lavine 1989, 46–53). A rigorous conception of justice and a generous vision of the common good, Plato wrote, were the prevailing values present in Socrates's rationale for committing suicide, and both values rested on the idea of human dignity. Through his impeccable reasoning, Socrates reached the conclusion that his suicide was necessary not only for preserving his own dignity but also his community's welfare. The idea of an individual giving his or her life for the good of the community is the ultimate expression of human dignity. Moreover, the concept of a community larger than the mathematical sum of its members is another dimension of the common-good value, and it must be understood and accepted as a value if one wishes to live in peace in a just society. In Ancient Greece, the value of the common good tempered the values of individuality, property, and privacy, and this principle still holds today. It is because of the equilibrium generated by these complementary values that the check-and-balance principle is generally accepted in our contemporary systems of law, a principle that ensures the rights of one individual are limited by the rights of others, and the rights of each by the rights of all. Justice, therefore, is the value regulating these competing rights. In modern democracies, this balancing act is maintained by the reciprocal independence of the three constitutional powers: legislative, executive, and judicial – all three necessitating a free flow of information.

The fifth Ancient Greek value was a renewed search for truth, which gave birth to the systems of logic and philosophical dialectic, or the means of acquiring indisputable knowledge through rational reasoning (Blanché 1970). True knowledge is related to wisdom, also a Greek value, because, argued Socrates, knowledge is virtue, and truth must prevail in our system of law. Wisdom, then, is the value required of those called upon to serve on the community's governing council. The proper management of the community's affairs, and the proper administration of justice, said Plato, require a kind of friendly leadership and optimistic humility that manifest themselves through fairness or compassion – that is, through wisdom. Socrates's wise serenity was perhaps the attitude that engendered the emergence of the last two Ancient Greek values: the interrelated concepts of goodness and beauty, the famous notion of kagos kagatos, which integrated the moral code of good behaviour with the aesthetic canon prescribing beauty. Plato argued that the beauty of the outer form emanated from the beauty of the soul. The knowledge of truth tempered by the moral code of behaviour can only be an offspring of wisdom. It seems that these Ancient Greek values, once formulated and demonstrated by the philosophers, were received as immovable notions because they had emerged from a process of coherent rationalization.

As one can see, the early Oriental values were rearticulated by the Greeks. As did the inhabitants of India and China, the Hellenes considered that wisdom was an apodictic feature of civilization and that a civilized society is one defined by the wisdom of its leaders. Gautama's value of compassion is comparable to the goodness of the Greeks, while Master K'ung's idea of equity is similar to the Greek values of justice and common good. The Buddha and the Greek philosophers said that the desire for the truth was one of society's most powerful motivators. What varied was their approach: Gautama looked for the truth through spiritual illumination while the Greek philosophers favoured logical discourse. All sought peace in their communities, but, again, it was the approach that distinguished their systems. Gautama said that social peace is attained mainly through personal responsibility and the absence of desire, Master K'ung said that social peace comes through an equitable social organization in which citizens respect the established rites and elders, and the Greeks argued that social peace is best preserved by an open, public dialogue and a sharing of power. The Greek philosophers were perhaps the first to raise the idea of beauty to the level of social value. And as far as the value of dignity is concerned, it was convincingly illustrated, and with equal potency, by the lives and teachings of Gautama, Master K'ung, and Socrates.

At the same time, in Latium, no more than three sailing weeks west of Athens, seven neighbouring tribes joined forces, subdued the surrounding territories, including Etruria, and started their unstoppable march towards world domination. From 146 to 27 B.C., the Romans conquered Greece and absorbed its system of values.

The Value of Jesus

Rome was at the height of its imperial might when, in Palestine, one of the Eastern provinces of the Empire, people began to pay attention to the revolutionary teachings of Jesus, a young Jewish preacher. For the Roman masters as well as the Jewish Pharisees and scribes, what Jesus was saying was at the same time outrageous and intriguing. Not only did he reaffirm the traditional Judaic belief that there was only one God but he also added that he was the son of that God. The legitimacy of his teachings, he said, came from beyond the world of mortals; it derived from his father, the only, almighty, and benevolent God. Jesus's doctrine was based on one simple, universal thought: love. He proclaimed that God loves people, and to prove this assertion he sacrificed his own life. If, in return, people love God and live according to his teachings, at the end of their lives they will go to Heaven, to his father's kingdom, where they will enjoy eternal happiness. And love is God's precept: love your neighbours, respond to a gesture of hate with a gesture of love, and be charitable.

Although love is a sentiment that has been shared by all human beings since the dawn of civilization, it was Jesus who made it a social force and a principle of life. Since Jesus, love has been a value, and as such transcends religious meanings. Indeed, it is love that best illustrates the marvellous dual human characteristic of sociability/individuality. Love is people's noblest feeling, their most powerful motivator, their richest source of poetic and artistic creation, the energy that fuels their beliefs, and the epitome of their spirituality. No value is more universally acclaimed than love. More than any other value, it raises humans to the domain of God. If, as theists say, it is God who created humans, then the love of God is the ultimate human purpose. Yet if, as atheists say, it is humans who created God as the most perfect model of love, then imitating this model is again the ultimate human purpose.

Love is the noblest of universal sentiments, but it is also the most individualistic, egoistic emotion. Love leads to lovemaking, which generates the greatest self-centred pleasure and, at the same time, guarantees the survival of the human race. The most intimate ritual is also the most cosmic one.

Values of the Medieval World

The values we have discussed so far and their sustaining institutions buttressed Greco-Roman civilization for more than five hundred years – up until the early stages of the medieval world and the establishment of the church as an all-pervasive power. Nurtured in catacombs and secret Druid sanctuaries, a new system of values slowly rose from the ruins of the Roman Empire. Paganism joined its immense mobilizing forces with the newer impulse of Christianity to forge two new values. The first one was hope. Under Roman rule, most humans beings were slaves. Desperately straining for a better destiny, barbarian tribes threw off the yoke of the totalitarian Roman Empire and established their own kingdom. But even with independence, these tribes found that earthly happiness was difficult to attain in such brutal times. That is why the message of the church was so eagerly received. If happiness cannot be secured in this world, said the priests, it can be reached in the Kingdom of God, and they positioned themselves as the only shepherds capable of guiding the flock to Heaven. To this day, the church[47] remains one of civilization's prime institutions and one of society's most important purveyors of hope.

The second medieval value was the quest for the absolute, and it gave birth to the institution of feudalism. The pursuit of absolute perfection is the value that inspired the Arthurian legends: only the purest among the brave Knights of the Round Table could find the Holy Grail and aspire to the ultimate ideal. The notion of the absolute also sustained the "science" of alchemy and the search for the philosophers' stone, the mysterious substance that would not only transform common matter into gold, but would also, more importantly, help to uncover a spirituality hidden in the material underground of the universe. The value of the absolute inspired the Crusades, chivalry, Eleanor of Aquitaine's famous Court of Love, and supported the institution of the omnipotent power, the power of the only God in Heaven and of the only king on Earth. These medieval values did not eliminate the earlier ones; they only cast a shadow upon them for awhile. They were also seen as immovable values, but, contrary to the preceding ones, had emerged from a gesture of faith.

In a world of absolute power, the monarch is all; other humans only exist through and for the monarch. How many acts of torture were committed by absolute rulers in the name of the only God and in pursuit of heavenly happiness? Even laughter was forbidden, because derision could only undermine the sanctity of absolute power. The colour of the Middle Ages was black: the colour of the Great Plague and the smoking ashes of the

Inquisition. Fortunately, the builders of the Gothic cathedrals, ingenious artisans, Dante, and Rabelais kept the lamp of human dignity burning until Greco-Roman values resurged.

Values of Islam

When the Prophet Mohammed began his preaching in 610 A.D., Constantinople and Ch'ang-an were the two largest cities in the world (Morris 1989, 63, 290). By comparison, Mecca and Medina were small settlements. Nonetheless, it was from these Arabian towns that a new religious and social order blew like a desert storm. It would profoundly change the world. Within only a few generations, Muslim armies conquered North Africa and the Middle East and penetrated deep into Europe and Asia. In Western Europe, Frankish ruler Charles Martel stopped them at Poitiers in 732 and, some 760 years later, Ferdinand and Isabelle of Castile expelled them from Spain. In Central Europe, the Ottoman forces took Constantinople in 1453, but were eventually defeated at Lepanto in 1571 and at Vienna in 1529 and 1583. In Asia, Islam extended its influence to India, Pakistan, Indonesia, Malaya, and further.

Beyond its religious dogmas, Islam was, and continues to be, a preeminent force in civilization. Its far-reaching contributions to architecture, mathematics, astronomy, chemistry, poetry, music, and philosophy are indisputable (Glassé 1991). So is its contribution to medicine. For example, as early as the tenth century there were hospitals in Baghdad and most other Muslim cities. Medieval philosophers – such as Ibn Sina Abu Ali al-Husayn, al-Kindi Abu Yusuf, al-Farâbi Abu Nasr, and al-Ghazali Abu Hamid Muhammad – had an intellectual influence that reached far beyond the Islamic world. These thinkers, and many others like them (for example, the Mu'tazilah), studied the Oriental and Greco-Roman masters and attempted to integrate their teachings into Muslim thinking. Like Aquinas in the West and Ch'eng Yi and Chu Hsi of the Rationalist school of neo-Confucianism in the East, they struggled with the difficulty of reconciling theology with philosophy, revelation with rationalization, spirituality with materiality (Flew 1984).

Islam redefined most of the existing values. For instance, the search for peace was deemed so important for Muslims that "Let peace be with you!" became their ritual salutation. The search for the truth was also paramount in the Islamic mentality because it was the foundation of koranic teaching. When the Prophet transmitted the words of Allah, it was understood that he spoke the truth. The act of belief always presupposes the acknowledgement of the truth. The Western medieval values of hope and the absolute were also important values for believers. As Arab scholar Jacques Berque expressed it in his exegetic comments on the Koran, the Islam notion of wisdom is best depicted by an old Arab saying: "Wisdom contains three elements: the elocution of the Arabs, the dexterity of the Chinese, and the reasoning of the Hellenes" (Berque 1990, 758).

In addition, Islam articulated two new values. The first was the idea of fraternity, or brotherhood. What Muslims taught the world was that if you are a member of a community you must look after the other members of your community and, in return, you will be entitled to their care. Certainly Prophet Mohammed was not alone in advocating respect for parents, children, other family members, and neighbours; other teachers did it before him, notably Jesus and Master K'ung. But perhaps more than any other code of ethics Islam made fraternity a social norm. The second Islamic value was the notion of hospitality. For Muslims, visitors are always welcome. Why is this so? Is it because the Prophet declared that believers must help one another? Or is it due to the nomadic lifestyle, in which gathering nightly at the oasis is both a necessity and a pleasure? Or, finally, is it a response to the danger of the land? In the desert, to welcome a traveller is, often, to save that person's life.

Values of the Renaissance and the Enlightenment

While Islam was penetrating India and continuing to prosper in North Africa and the Middle East, while the Ming Dynasty was maintaining an isolationist policy in China – which did not prevent a spectacular flourishing of Chinese arts (architecture, sculpture, painting, and porcelain making) – the Occident was experiencing a social resurrection, a rebirth of the old values. The Renaissance was a refreshing wind of change that issued from Italy and swept through the Christian world. This stimulating breeze did not stop on Europe's western shores; it pushed galleons and caravels across the oceans towards new worlds. In the process, new knowledge was uncovered and new attitudes were established. People were optimistic. They now believed that they possessed the resources to dominate their world.

The Renaissance's new attitude was proclaimed by strong figures, each in his own way redefining the value of individuality. Machiavelli, with his inspired cleverness, showed that the politically weak could also rule and maintain their dignity before the absolute monarch (Machiavelli 1983). Leonardo, Kepler, and Galileo, with their intellectual curiosity, gave new impetus to the search for truth. The erudite Pico della Mirandola presented an "eloquent exposition of human responsibility and dignity" (Flew 1984, 268). And the witty Erasmus reinvented the notion of wisdom and launched the generous idea of humanism, which is nothing if not the idea of tolerance applied to society as a whole. Brunelleschi, Alberti, Michelangelo, and Raphael also gave a new meaning to beauty. But spring is a short season, and even Cervantes and Shakespeare could not contain the reactionary forces. The seventeenth and eighteenth centuries saw the emergence of a new race: the bigots, who thought it necessary to persecute all those who did not think like them. The exhilarating discoveries of the baroque period were constantly overshadowed by religious wars and massacres, such as the Saint Bartholomew's Day killing of three thousand Huguenots in Paris. Perhaps the world was suffering at the hands of too many blind institutions that no longer reflected the values they were created to uphold. Beneath the glitter, this era was a time of filth; hidden under the powdered wigs and stiff lace of the courtiers and courtesans was an obscene corruption; the regime and its intellectual machinery was rotten to the core. Fortunately, human resources are infinite. A new light began to shine through the slime, and it enlightened the world. The Enlightenment's beacons were new giants standing on the shoulders of their Renaissance predecessors. Goethe, Bach, Molière, Mozart, Voltaire, Rousseau, and the Encyclopedists clustered around bright salon hostesses, daring women of merit who encouraged them, along with so many other intellectuals, to develop and exchange their revolutionary ideas. It was while practising the art of conversation that the witty men and women of the Enlightenment shaped the new values of their momentous time.

They began by disengaging the value of the absolute from the value of truth. A key distinction, they said, exists between the two. The search for absolute truth is undoubtedly a legitimate value, they argued, but should remain within the domain of faith, and, to be truly accepted as a value, must embrace freedom of thought. The value of freedom was launched, and it triggered the most monumental period of evolution our civilization has known. It shattered the reign of arbitrariness. The consequence of this rationale was that truth became something different from the dictums of the church or the king. Riding on the crest of a wave of public opinion, a brand-new weapon, the philosophers of the Enlightenment developed the idea of a new kind of truth. If one applies correct reasoning, said Pascal and Descartes, organizes knowledge in a systematic fashion, said Diderot and d'Alembert, and conducts well-controlled experiments, said Newton, scientific knowledge will emerge and engender progress. The awesome idea was born that people, through the mere power of their reason, could change their destiny and improve their living conditions. Fatalism was challenged and the belief in human progress became a new value.

The third value they developed was based on the idea that society was larger than the king's own person. Louis XIV's arrogant quip, "L'état, c'est moi!" ("I am the State!"), was finally contradicted in the eighteenth century. It was perhaps Voltaire, in *Histoire du siècle de Louis XIV*, who first demonstrated that history is more than a record of the actions of one individual, even a king; instead, it is shaped by a collectivity of individuals who share chores, responsibilities, and merits. This idea supported the value of social bonding, the powerful sentiment that created modern nations and gave rise to the principle that society was not dominated by the king, who derived his power from God, but by the nation, which could choose to entrust its governance to the king. A ruler's legitimacy, therefore, depended upon his or her acceptance by the collectivity. The nation-state became the prevailing institution for the enactment of the social-bonding value.

But, claimed the philosophers of the Enlightenment and the mentors of the American and French Revolutions, a nation is made up of citizens, equal in rights and responsibilities: "All men are created equal," and, "Les hommes naissent et demeurent libres et égaux en droit," proclaimed their respective constitutions. The value of equality was deemed so important that the French revolutionaries chose to put it on the same footing as liberty and fraternity.[48] The French Revolution's cry of fraternity, we should remember, was only a new call for the Ancient Greek values of goodness and the common good. The latter, however, was perhaps at the origin of another value that slowly emerged through the eighteenth and nineteenth centuries. It was the belief, now confirmed by scientific evidence, that people's well-being and happiness were linked to good health.[49] Soon, the preoccupation with personal health would be connected to public hygiene. Medical considerations would begin to bear upon the planning and design of cities. All over the world, modern urban infrastructures and modern institutional buildings were created in response to public pressure for more efficient public-hygiene measures. Better water-supply systems, sewers, and sanitary facilities; new designs for housing, hospitals, prisons, and cemeteries; improved street setbacks; and better ventilation: all these were the result of public-health imperatives. Good health, then, became a powerful value, one that profoundly changed the shape of architecture. Today's arguments in favour of housing rights are based largely on the correlation between living conditions in the designed environment and public health.[50]

Values of the Industrial Revolution

In spite of some current postmodern arguments (Lyotard 1984; Jameson 1991; Harvey 1990; Habermas 1990; Rosenau 1992), the Enlightenment project was implemented to a large extent and the Industrial Revolution truly improved the human condition. In our Western world, at least, and in many parts of the Orient, the standard of living increased substantially. The Industrial Revolution brought two new values. The first was the concept of plenty. The modern economy, propped up by increasingly efficient technology, was able to produce goods in enormous quantities. Plenty, or abundance, became, and still is, an important motivator for the capitalist system and the driving force behind the so-called American dream – and those of the rest of the world. Marxism was, after all, nothing more than an attempt by workers to share in this abundance so ostentatiously flaunted by the rich. The second value is directly linked to the idea of plenty. It is because we wish to enjoy an abundance of good things that we have allocated immense resources to technological development. Technology has become a necessity of life. Most people believe that our complex modern society could not exist without its technological infrastructures. People place one overriding demand on technology: it must perform well. Hence, the Industrial Revolution's second value is efficacy. This value is so strong today that it overshadows many other values. The current all-pervading market economy rests on a quasi-religious adherence to the value of efficacy; people fervently hope that if they promote and fulfil this value they will have secured for themselves an abundance of riches.

Late-Twentieth-Century Emerging Values

In the second part of the twentieth century, new values seem to have emerged, counterbalancing the Industrial Revolution's materialistic effects. The double awareness that the Earth's resources are limited and that they are being swallowed in larger and larger portions by technological systems is engendering the value of usefulness. Efficacy is not only a question of high performance but it is also one of strategic choices, priorities, and waste reduction (UNESCO 1989; Dansereau 1991, 1992, 1994). To do more with less, to achieve a high-quality frugality, is a new contemporary value. For example, the sustainable-development idea is nourished by the value of usefulness.

Obviously, the emergence of usefulness as a value is possible only because a set of other behavioural values is also finding its way into people's consciousness. First, the advent of increasingly efficient transportation, communications, and information systems facilitates effective participation in the affairs of the community. By means of the telephone, cable technology, the satellite dish, the fax machine, and e-mail, people can now communicate rapidly and directly with their leaders – and, more importantly, with one another. This eagerness to share information heralds the value of involvement, which takes many active forms: contributing to electronic town-hall meetings, calling talk shows, participating in public-opinion polls, sharing data through the Internet, and joining numerous social and charitable organizations.

People's increasing involvement in this new form of citizen participation may give birth to another value, which could be called the personal sense of collective responsibility. Along with justice, this new value seems to be at the root of major contemporary social changes. These have been reflected in women's-liberation movements and student demonstration – such as the ones against the Vietnam War, the Paris protest of May 1968, and the Tianamen Square uprising of 1989 – as well as demonstrations organized by the proponents numerous ecological movements.

People want to participate in order to assume their collective responsibility in order to fulfil their urge to be in control. This urge is, in fact, yet another value. Many feel that nation-states, international organizations, and modern economic and technological systems have all engendered a bureaucracy and a complex machinery that are beginning to run wild. Plenty, they observe, is not shared equally, and good things may not be so abundant after all. The gulf between the rich and the poor is widening. Marxism may have been discredited by absurd totalitarian regimes, but some of its basic social diagnostics have not been contradicted. Political corruption is rampant and justice today is not the same for all, regardless of the lofty statements contained in charters of rights. And, in spite of the enormous power of the current information and communications systems, truth is not always transmitted and solitude and urban alienation seem to be as pervasive as ever. People, it seems, wish to regain control over their destinies. To be in control is a value that may very well dominate political action during the next century.[51]

Finally, another value seems to be emerging. The old, and still very much alive, value of individuality is taking on a new dimension. Today, people wish to express their personalities and are not afraid to do so creatively. Personalized creative expression is a value that takes the form of alternative lifestyles, music, and fashion. And with a more purposeful domestication of the new computerized technologies, such as interactive television and virtual imagery, the search for new forms of personalized creative expression may move beyond the realm of trivial games; the quest for knowledge is being reinvented (Reich 1970).

Our society is driven by an array of some thirty values, which constitute the foundation of our charters of rights. Let us suspend them and, through them, look for another dimension of the essence of architecture.

REDUCTION: THE TELOS OF ARCHITECTURE

At this juncture, we reach the core of the architectural phenomenon as it wants to be, a vision of the telos of the architectural phenomenon emerging from a phenomenological reduction of human values; that is, the values underpinning design judgements. Facing the task of creating architecture, the architect probes his values and invites other humans, the future users of his architecture, to do the same because the architecture he is about to create is made by a human for humans. So are all architectural works. Why? Why are architects creating architecture for humans sharing the same values? Surely the answer is to satisfy these people, to help them exercise their human rights (which are supported by those shared values), to make them comfortable in the world – in short, to make them happy. How, then, is architecture judged? How is meaningful architecture distinguished from meaningless architecture? How is successful architecture recognized? Perhaps it is by instilling a certain degree of satisfaction in human beings – that is, by exhibiting total relevancy.

Phenomenologically understood, a successful, respectful architecture is a happy architecture. Indeed, if there is a common denominator to all the values outlined earlier it is the constant search for happiness or the realization of a respectful satisfaction. In his essay *Le plaisir*, philosopher Alexander Lowen explained that happiness is the consciousness of growing. And Nobel laureate Albert Szent-Györgyi added that "human activity is dominated by the search for happiness ... happiness, in turn, is essentially self-realisation, a state in which all material and intellectual needs are satisfied"[52] (Szent-Györgyi in Selye 1974, 80). Hence, a thoroughly satisfactory architecture is one that succeeds in satisfying, in a respectful way, all the material and intellectual needs of humans. That is why architects need value-based criteria to design such an architecture. That is also why architects insist that their architecture be judged according to these criteria; it is a method of ensuring that the product is designed to the users' satisfaction. After all, it belongs to those users.

The telos of architecture, then, can be formulated as follows: *Respectfully responding to societal values, the telos of architecture is happily dwelling in a place of satisfaction.*

CONSTITUTION OF DESIGN CRITERIA

It is from the telos of architecture expressed in terms of satisfaction that it is possible to reconstitute a list of respectful, meaningful design criteria.

The structure of this constitution may be compared to a lighthouse. The lighthouse foundation, solidly embedded in the phenomenological rock, is the telos of architecture. The stone tower that rises above the horizon is made of large building blocks, which are values. The spiral staircase is the evolution of civilization, an upward movement towards a more enlightened, respectful world. At the top of the tower is the revolving projector – a complex piece of machinery like a charter of human rights, and like a human institution. It throws out a beam of light that pierces the dark horizon of barbarism. The light itself represents human rights. Depending on its orientation, the light flashes in different ways, sending out different types of beam, different messages: one of them concerns the rights related to satisfactory architecture. Each flicker of the beam of architectural rights is like a distinct design criterion. It is the combination of all these flickers that forms a meaningful message, guiding the architect, lost in the rough sea of environmental mediocrity, to the safe haven of excellence and magnificence.

Applied to architecture, a criterion may be understood as a scale for measuring a design according to the particular reference point that this criterion expresses. What a criterion implies, for example, is that a design that provides the required activity components is assessed higher on this particular scale than a design with deficiencies. Similarly, a design that – according to the architect, the client, and the users – functions in a more efficient fashion than another will score higher than less efficient schemes.

The rationale for introducing each of these design criteria rests on social values. To be valid, a criterion must be grounded in one or many values. Only in this way will it escape arbitrariness and be relevant.

Observing, with the enlightened consciousness generated by the epochè of values, the seven current design criteria described earlier, we notice that these criteria are related to only a fraction of the identified values. For example, the criterion of functionality, in responding to the project brief, finds its validity in the values of efficacy, usefulness, and perhaps property and privacy. Similarly, the criterion related to respect for the schedule is based on the values of efficacy and usefulness. Also, the idea that an architectural artefact must be aesthetically pleasing has been almost entirely eradicated by an architectural discourse that favours a certain type of meaning over visual pleasure. In all, the seven current criteria relate to less than half of the values identified. Moreover, the larger notions of human satisfaction and happiness, ideas that constitute the telos of architecture, are virtually ignored in current theoretical discourse. In fact, a point of view contrary to the desire for human happiness was adopted recently by many radical postmodern architects who argued for an architecture that seeks to disturb rather than satisfy people (Eisenman 1994; Vidler 1992, 69–82).

The values that are consciously enacted in current architectural practice and theoretical discourse are property, individuality, privacy, progress, social bonding, good health, plenty, efficacy, and personalized creative expression. The values that are largely ignored are the search for truth, wisdom, compassion, equity, respect for traditions, the desire for peace, dignity, justice, the common good, goodness, beauty, love, hope, the quest for the absolute, fraternity, hospitality, freedom, usefulness, a personal sense of collective responsibility, and to be in control.

Here I propose a reconstituted list of urban and architectural design criteria. The main, supporting values of each criterion are expressed in parentheses.

1. Presence, complementarity, and reliability of activity components (main related values: dignity, justice, love, fraternity, the common good, hope, and plenty): Architecture is about the provision of places for human activities. Each building or each segment of a city, according to its respective prescribed mission and position in the larger context, must provide certain activity components. And a city as a whole must provide a full set of the kind of activity components society requires: places for residential activities, for protective activities (institutions), for economic activities, for educational activities, and for recreational activities. Urban amenities are a good illustration of this criterion. In order to sustain their daily business in cities, people require a very large set of services, often located in very small buildings called aediculae. These include newsstands, public toilets, bus shelters, public telephone booths, bicycle racks, and the like. Hence, a city with more and better-kept aediculae will be considered of a higher quality than a city that offers fewer, or dilapidated, aediculae. Any one of these service aediculae, taken individually, may not be that important a

factor in a city's overall quality of life; but, taken together, they make an enormous difference.

2. Presence, complementarity, and reliability of building and urban systems (main related values: equity, justice, the common good, plenty, and efficacy): As explained earlier, contemporary architectural artefacts require that six basic systems be present. These are the structure, pedestrian, vehicular, energy, plumbing, and communications systems. This criterion simply allows us to observe and assesses the permanent and constant presence, or absence, of these systems, and to render a judgement.

3. Balance of public/private domains (main related values: property, privacy, peace, the common good, and equality): As all architectural artefacts always touch both domains, it becomes necessary to assess their design according to their position in, and their contribution to, this equilibrium. In fact, a certain complicity is required between the two domains, and each artefact must play a positive role in this relationship.

4. High-performance functionality (main related values: privacy, peace, dignity, efficacy, usefulness, good health, a personal sense of collective responsibility, and to be in control): This is the criterion that we use to assess the spatial organization of the architectural artefact. It is concerned with what Vitruvius called "ordinatio" and Jacques-François Blondel identified as "distribution" (Vitruvius 1965; Blondel 1905). It calls for characteristics such as continuity, clarity, readability, and visibility. It asks for an efficient layout – efficient in the sense that it can respond fluidly to the qualitative and quantitative imperatives of the architectural brief. As several organizational layers may be superimposed, a high-performance functionality often requires a three-dimensional approach.

5. High-performance systems (main related values: plenty, efficacy, usefulness, a personal sense of collective responsibility, and to be in control): All building systems must perform according to predetermined specifications. Reliability and economy are among the required characteristics of those systems. This criterion may seem trivial, but most building or urban systems today are either deficient, or, if they do perform reasonably well, do so at an exorbitant cost. Many also pollute the environment. For example, the private automobile is surely the least cost-effective of all transportation systems for several reasons: it requires an extensive road and parking infrastructure, it sits idle most of the time, it usually carries only a fraction of

the load it was made to accommodate, its propulsion system is not energy efficient, it depletes the planet's resources, it pollutes both the air and the ground, it damages the urban fabric, and it is dangerous to operate.

6. Integration into the natural setting (main related values: property, respect for traditions, the desire for peace, dignity, the common good, beauty, good health, efficacy, usefulness, a personal sense of collective responsibility, and to be in control): This criterion initiates an intimate relationship between the man-made artefact and the site it rests on. When Prince Charles insisted that "we must respect the land," and added that "new buildings can be intrusive or they can be designed and sited so that they fit in," he was calling for the full application of this criterion in urban and architectural design decisions (Wales 1989, 78).

7. Integration into the man-made surroundings (main related values: individuality, property, privacy, equity, respect for traditions, a desire for peace, dignity, justice, fraternity, hospitality, the common good, beauty, social bonding, usefulness, a personal sense of collective responsibility, and to be in control): This criterion compels architectural artefacts to insert themselves harmoniously not only into their natural setting but also into the existing man-made surroundings. Discussing the concept of harmony in urban design, Prince Charles expressed the opinion that "each building that goes beside another has to be in tune with its neighbour" (Wales 1989, 84).

8. Insertion into historic continuity (main related values: the search for truth, wisdom, respect for traditions, love, hope, progress, a personal sense of collective responsibility, and to be in control): One universal truth about the history of architecture is that, since the very first hut was erected, all buildings constitute, in one fashion or another, an addition to an earlier one. This continuous influence of existing buildings on new ones takes many forms. For instance, the very act of designing a building is conducted within another, existing building. Furthermore, all buildings are necessarily the products of their time, which means that they respond to mentalities and emanate from techniques particular to the period in which they are made. Any architect who ignores, negates, or defies the inescapable reality of historic continuity is deluding his clients and himself. This criterion amounts to the full acceptance of the historic presence of architecture.

9. Innovation with respect to historic continuity (main related values: equity, compassion, wisdom, dignity, the search for truth, hope, freedom,

progress, a personal sense of collective responsibility, to be in control, and personalized creative expression): As he is coming to terms with the historic presence of architecture, the architect is also invited to challenge historic determinism and propose design solutions that respond to new issues, aspirations, and needs. The criterion of innovation is a constant challenge to improve upon the last solution.

10. Response to climatic factors (main related values: the search for truth, wisdom, progress, good health, efficacy, usefulness, and a personal sense of collective responsibility): Because it seems to be simple common sense, this criterion is usually taken for granted and ignored by architectural critics. Yet the same modernistic office tower with a central core, curtain walls, and a central air-conditioning system has been constructed in all climates. And the south-facing wall of this office tower displays the same design features and performance characteristics as the north-facing one.

11. Response to social issues (main related values: individuality, property, privacy, wisdom, equity, respect for traditions, the desire for peace, dignity, justice, the common good, goodness, hope, the quest for the absolute, fraternity, hospitality, freedom, progress, social bonding, equality, good health, plenty, usefulness, a personal sense of collective responsibility, and to be in control): This is a multifaceted, complex criterion requiring that a building – or a segment of a city – be more than just a shelter (although this purpose is primordial). A building must be a means of resolving social problems. For example, about one hundred years ago, tuberculosis was rampant in European cities; in response to this problem, better-ventilated residential buildings equipped with adequate sanitary facilities were erected. Architecture thus made a contribution to public hygiene. But what does it do today to curtail crime, violence, alienation, and poverty? How does it help to eradicate current urban diseases?

12. Safety measures within design (main related values: equity, dignity, the common good, and good health): This criterion prompts an architectural design that protects people against accidents. It necessitates the installation of nonslip floors, adequate railings, and proper lighting in public areas, as well as adequate design with respect to fire, floods, landslides, earthquakes, hurricanes, and other natural disasters.

13. Security measures within design (main related values: individuality, property, privacy, equity, the desire for peace, dignity, justice, hope, and to

be in control): This criterion requires design that can protect people against crime. Defensible spaces are needed, and this involves, for instance, the elimination of dead ends in public circulation or the provision of activity-generating places, for day and night, along streets and in other public places. It has been amply demonstrated that urban streets become dangerous at night mainly because they are dark and deserted (Jacobs 1961).

14. Autonomy of systems within systems (main related values: freedom, efficacy, usefulness, a personal sense of collective responsibility, and to be in control): Whether on the individual-building scale or the urban scale, it is absolutely necessary that people be in control of their environmental systems. Their survival depends on it. That is why they require many systems that are simultaneously autonomous and connected to other systems. Numerous autonomous systems are required because if one breaks, others continue to perform. Alternatives must always be provided and their control mechanisms must always be accessible and distinct from the main machinery.

15. Feeling of enclosure (main related values: individuality, property, privacy, and hospitality): This is a comprehensive criterion that may be applied to practically all places, notably private ones. As Vitruvius and Laugier have explained, the primordial concept of architecture, or what distinguishes architecture as a cultural product from the natural environment, is the circle around the fire, the primitive hut, or the basic shelter. To provide shelter for humans is the fundamental purpose of architecture. Hence, the feeling of shelter that an architectural artefact instils – or fails to instil – is the object of this criterion. "One of the great pleasures of architecture," wrote Prince Charles, "is the feeling of well-designed enclosures" (Wales 1989, 86). The enclosure generates both a reality and a feeling of protection and comfort.

16. Positivity of public places (main related values: the common good and social bonding): All public places must be designed as positive, convivial enclosures, not as mere leftovers of the surrounding private properties. In other words, the criterion of the positivity of public places is the transcription into the public domain of the feeling of shelter that had previously been applied mainly to private shelters. Public enclosures can be very small or immense, static or dynamic, monumental or informal, but they should always be vessels of a wide array of public activities. In the domain of human behaviour there is a general principle that architects often overlook:

people go to a place not because of its design interest but because they have business there. Successful architectural places are structures that house needed activities.

17. Respect for bylaws (main related values: equity, compassion, the search for truth, the common good, justice, equality, and good health): This criterion is the assumption that the body of law that regulates the practice of architecture, the development and management of settlements, and the construction industry is there to protect people. It is therefore the architect's professional responsibility and corporate deontology to make projects that respect the law because this demonstrates his respect for the people who experience the artefact.

18. Improvement upon accepted norms (main related values: the search for truth, the common good, progress, efficacy, usefulness, and a personal sense of collective responsibility): The architect cannot reconcile respect for the law with blindness to the countless norms and procedures that regulate the architectural trade and even clutter the construction industry and hinder the management of cities; many are contradictory or obsolete. This criterion requires the architect to exercise his critical judgement with regard to the current ways and means of practising his trade and to improve upon them.

19. Respect for the project budget (main related values: efficacy, usefulness, a personal sense of collective responsibility, and to be in control): This criterion necessitates four actions. First, the architect must ensure that his project budget is realistic, that it meets the requirements of the brief. Second, he must develop the ability to estimate the cost of projects accurately; this skill is not presently taught at most architecture schools. Third, he must take into account the agreed-upon budget in creating his design. Fourth, he must ensure that the cost of construction is properly controlled.

20. Response to higher economic factors through design (main related values: justice, the common good, progress, equality, plenty, usefulness, and a personal sense of collective responsibility): Respect for the project budget, although necessary, is only one of the various economic and financial issues that determine the architectural artefact. Over and above maintaining his respect for the project budget, the architect must understand the larger economic issues and, through his design, contribute to the improvement of society's persistent economic difficulties. For example, one such

issue is that the original investment cost of a building is only a fraction of the entire investment required during that building's active life. The architect's design must recognize this reality.

21. Order (main related values: peace, dignity, justice, the common good, the search for truth, wisdom, respect for traditions, goodness, social bonding, efficacy, usefulness, a personal sense of collective responsibility, and to be in control): Even postmodern architects such as Robert Venturi, who argued for contradiction and ambiguity, acknowledged the necessity of establishing a sense of order in architecture (Venturi 1966). The notion of order is an apodictic sign of human intelligence, one that defines it. It applies equally to the most complex activities – such as controlling air traffic or directing a symphony orchestra – and to the simplest tasks – such as crossing a street. In architecture, for example, achieving order means designing a city in which people do not get lost, designing a kitchen in which the number of physical actions involved in preparing a meal is reduced, or establishing what Prince Charles called a "hierarchy" in our designed environment. "There are two kinds of hierarchy which need concern us here. One is the size of buildings in relation to their public importance. The other is the relative significance of the different elements which make up a building – so we know, for instance, where the front door is" (Wales 1989, 80).

22. Allowance for discontinuity (main related values: individuality, freedom, progress, a personal sense of collective responsibility, and personalized creative expression): Order or harmony in architecture does not mean blandness or boredom. On the contrary, order is the condition that permits the introduction of ambiguous or discontinuous features. And harmony requires counterpoints. The establishment of setbacks, height limits, and other similar urban-design guidelines does not preclude an infinite variety of modulations in building façades. Similarly, control over street signage should not be interpreted as an obligation to have all signs made the same way. This criterion is a call for an orderly disorder or, in other words, for infinite variation within a harmoniously ordered whole.

23. Frugality of means (main related values: equity, wisdom, progress, usefulness, a personal sense of collective responsibility, and to be in control): In a time of diminishing resources, architects need to do more with less. A frugality of means is a sign of quality. It should be viewed not only as a positive response to current economic constraints but also as an indicator

of the architect's understanding of the possibilities of his time. The computer has invaded all facets of our lives; mammoth mainframes have evolved into compact personal computers. Miniaturization is the essence of computer technology. A frugal environment is thus a miniaturized environment. The miniaturized metropolis is no longer a contradiction in terms.

24. Accessibility: psychological and physical (main related values: equity, compassion, justice, the common good, goodness, hope, freedom, equality, plenty, efficacy, and usefulness): At the level of the city, this criterion is a call for easy access. People need to move efficiently from place to place in order to reach the kinds of individuals, services, and products they need to lead their lives. Two kinds of accessibility are discussed here. The first is physical accessibility. It involves the provision of movement infrastructures and the elimination of the so-called architectural barriers that hinder the free movement of handicapped people. The second is psychological accessibility. This is a person's sense that he or she is part of the city and, within the normal and reasonable constraints of privacy, is welcome in all places – especially public places and service centres. Discrimination is the opposite of accessibility. The higher a city's level of accessibility, the better that city is.

25. Control of density (main related values: individuality, property, privacy, equity, the desire for peace, dignity, efficacy, usefulness, and to be in control): Accessibility demands bringing people together, in other words, raising density. But if density becomes too high, people start impinging upon each other's private domains. In this context, proximity means being close to others and promiscuity means being too close.[53] How can people be close without being too close? To what level is it possible to raise density while still maintaining a high quality of environment and life, and while keeping in mind that the quality of environment and life diminishes when density is too low? What is the proper balance? The answer may lie in how much control each individual has over his or her own private environment. Control should always be on the private side. By increasing density, one raises the amount of interface between private and public places. It becomes, therefore, important for the person in the private place to be able to open or close the relationship between the two places. For example, a bedroom is, obviously, a more private place than the street. A window may be a communication device between a given bedroom and the street. The person in the bedroom should be the one who controls this relationship, who decides when and how to look out at the street or be seen from the

street. If density is raised to the point that someone in the street can see into this person's bedroom without the latter's consent, then either the density is too high or the architectural design is flawed. The same reasoning applies to sound. Here, also, a high-quality design is one that offers proximity without promiscuity (Lincourt 1972). Intensity of use requires a proper density, but it is not a synonym for density. It signifies doing more with less, providing places that can accommodate a multiplicity of functions, places vibrant with human life.

26. Human scale (main related values: dignity, wisdom, and beauty): People are the raison d'être of architecture, and so they become, as Prince Charles wrote, the "measure of all things" (Wales 1989, 82). The Renaissance thinkers, who also argued that man was the measure of all things, including architectural objects, no doubt inspired Prince Charles on this question. Human scale is simply the relationship between the size of a building and the size of a human being. To feel comfortable, humans must understand the relative size of the environment surrounding them, and this understanding must be complete with easily recognizable features of human scale, such as steps, railings, doors, windows, storey-defining cornices, fences, and all kinds of decorations. Architectural details provide a human scale. This criterion prompts an architecture that is more than constructed diagrams.

27. Proper use of materials (main related values: efficacy, usefulness, and a personal sense of collective responsibility): The choice of building materials cannot be made in abstraction. These materials must be of excellent quality not only in themselves but also in relation to their use, to their relative position within the various building systems, and to their location in the building. For example, a brick must first of all be a good-quality brick; all architects know that there are ways to measure the technical performance capability of a building product. But the brick must also work well with other materials – the concrete foundation, or the wooden frame, or the insulation. An architect can use the best materials on the market, but his project will not be successful if the assemblage of building materials is inadequate, if that assemblage does not form a coherent and highly efficient set of building systems, or if his detailed design incorporating the best products is badly executed by sloppy contractors or workers. A deep knowledge of building materials and systems is of the utmost importance in producing high-quality architectural work. And there is more: this criterion stipulates, also, that architects find a way to handle materials and

systems that extends beyond mere technical requirements. Again, the brick may be used as an example: if a house is like a shell, then perhaps the best place to put a rough-textured brick is on the outside as a barrier against inclement weather. A rough-textured brick may not be the most appropriate material for an interior bedroom wall. A smoother finish would probably be better. Obviously, exceptions to this rule abound, but they require a rationale.

28. Solidity and perdurability of construction (main related values: property, wisdom, the common good, progress, plenty, efficacy, usefulness, a personal sense of collective responsibility, and to be in control): All structures erected in our world must be well built and made to last.[54] The argument that it is more economical to build cheaply and to demolish a building and replace it with a new one – say after about thirty years – is indefensible. Contemporary American inner cities clearly demonstrate that demolished buildings are not necessarily replaced, even when the demolition is carried out with the best of intentions. Also, demolished buildings always signal a dislocation in the urban fabric and often a displacement of population. It is no coincidence that the people displaced by demolition always belong to the poorest and weakest segment of the population. Demolishing a building because of its internal financial structure may perhaps make sense for the landlord and the bank involved, but it does not make sense if one takes into account the larger economy of the city, or the country, or, indeed, the world. The reason is simple: when financial resources are marshalled to replace cheaply constructed buildings they are not always used to construct new buildings where they are badly needed. Finally, the argument that it is more costly to renovate or upgrade a building than to build a new one is valid only in cases where buildings have been neglected for too long. Well-designed, well-constructed, and well-maintained buildings, in the long run, are highly profitable for both their owners and society as a whole.

29. Proper landscaping (main related values: dignity, the common good, good health, and beauty): Not only should the architectural artefact fit well into its natural setting, but the positive effect of its design should spread to the natural environment that surrounds and penetrates it. Landscaping is an inherent component of architecture and should be treated with the same care, but it requires a different approach, mainly because its basic materials are alive. Landscaping can be done both indoors and out, in all seasons and in all climatic conditions.

30. Proper interior design (main related values: individuality, property, privacy, wisdom, compassion, equity, dignity, beauty, love, fraternity, hospitality, progress, equality, good health, plenty, efficacy, usefulness, a personal sense of collective responsibility, personalized creative expression, and to be in control): It is because mainstream architects have neglected interior design that this criterion is inserted here in an explicit way, while many exterior design elements are left implicit. Interior design is more than the adequate proportioning of each of the spaces of the artefact, although it certainly includes it. It is the finishing of interiors in a way that permits users to conduct their activities within them properly. It covers the finishes, textures, and colours of the floors, walls, and ceilings; as well, it encompasses built-in furniture, various pieces of bathrooms and kitchen equipment, and the harmonious integration of artworks.

31. Proper furniture and utensil design (main related values: individuality, property, privacy, wisdom, equity, dignity, beauty, progress, equality, good health, plenty, efficacy, usefulness, a personal sense of collective responsibility, and personalized creative expression): Linked to interior design is the criterion that addresses the design of furniture and utensils. Civilization means having access to the kinds of objects that permit people to live more interesting and fruitful lives. Architecture provides a vessel of activities that calls for a panoply of equipment, tools, furniture, utensils, and objects of all types. In the home, these things are normally very personal belongings – often heritage items. As people are in daily contact with these objects (for example, they spend one third of their lives in a bed), it is of the utmost importance that they be well designed and well inserted into the architectural vessel. Again, while this may seem a trivial statement it points to a fundamental issue that is almost never dealt with in architecture schools.

32. Good taste (main related values: dignity, respect for traditions, wisdom, beauty, the quest for the absolute, a personal sense of collective responsibility, and personalized creative expression): Architects must strive to design beautiful, pleasant buildings, and they must develop their taste in order to do so. In other words, the search for beauty must become a conscious démarche within the design process, one that permeates all others. The good-taste criterion relates to several dimensions of the notion of beauty. One is the notion of harmony, calling not only for the proper balance of the parts within the whole, as Leon Battista Alberti told us (Alberti 1986), but also, and more importantly, for the proper architectural response

to human feelings. This criterion presupposes that people wish to live in harmony with their architecture, wish to obtain pleasure from their architectural experience, and possess the taste that permits them to appreciate or feel this harmony. The architect's duty is to provide a designed environment that enhances this harmony. Another feature of beauty is proportion. As all physical artefacts have a shape, and as this shape can be measured, it follows that all artefacts have proportions. The architect must learn mathematical proportions and harmonic ratios and apply this knowledge to his design. Beauty in architecture derives not only from harmonious proportion but also from the proper manipulation of architectural elements in order to create the following: rhythm and contrast, continuity and disruption in composition; elements of reassurance and elements of surprise; elements to be seen at a distance and others to be experienced at close proximity; elements disposed in a symmetric equilibrium and elements in a precarious arrangement; a composition of solids and voids that is sometimes under control and sometimes unfinished, sometimes static or solid and sometimes dynamic or fragile, sometimes permanent and sometimes ephemeral, sometimes obvious and sometimes times mysterious. Good taste in architecture also includes the proper use of materials, a judicious juxtaposition of textures, a wide palette of colours, and a magical play of light.

33. Ecological design (main related values: the common good, progress, good health, plenty, efficacy, usefulness, a personal sense of collective responsibility, and to be in control): This is a simple criterion. It stipulates that architecture must not pollute the natural environment. No architectural artefact should pollute the atmosphere as a result of poorly designed electromechanical systems. It should not pollute the ground on which it stands or adjacent water bodies through the careless disposal of wastes, both liquid and solid. It should not cast a shadow over its neighbours (or over itself, as do the tight Haussmannian inner courtyards), a shadow so intrusive that it renders normal life uncomfortable. It should not create gusts that, on certain windy days, could knock down pedestrians bold enough to approach it. In colder countries, the artefact's design should prevent any unreasonable accumulation of snow. It should not be so pretentious and disrespectful of its neighbours that it winds up covered with graffiti. And it should not pollute the visual environment with obtrusive signage.

34. Energy-efficient design (main related values: the common good, efficacy, usefulness, a personal sense of collective responsibility, and to be in control): All buildings should consume energy in a controlled manner.

This, again, is a function of good architectural design (for example, the north façade should not be the same as the south façade; vestibules should be employed in cold climates as air locks; adequate insulation should be used). The design of a building's electromechanical systems and its setting within its surroundings should be responsive to energy-guzzling natural factors such as prevailing winter winds. The architectural design should also facilitate proper building management and proper management of activities in the building.

35. Ease of maintenance (main related values: wisdom, equity, the common good, efficacy, usefulness, a personal sense of collective responsibility, and to be in control): Once built, all architectural artefacts must be maintained, and their maintenance can be easy or difficult, inexpensive or costly. Ease of maintenance should be taken into consideration when the artefact is designed. This is both common sense and wise investment management because neglected buildings deteriorate rapidly.

36. Level of comfort (main related values: dignity, justice, the common good, goodness, beauty, hope, the quest for the absolute, progress, good health, plenty, efficacy, and usefulness): This comprehensive criterion has both physical and psychological aspects. Comfort, of course, contributes to people's well-being. First, this criterion stipulates that the microclimate created inside any architectural artefact must be conducive to a comfortable engagement in prescribed activities. The requirements for this are adequate lighting, ventilation, temperature, insulation, and so on. Second, this criterion refers back to the one discussed earlier dealing with interior, furniture, and utensil design. Third, it involves the notion of conviviality. Architecture, this criterion insists, must be user-friendly.

37. The mysterious criterion (main related values: dignity, the search for truth, respect for traditions, a personal sense of collective responsibility, and social bonding): This criterion is related to the spirit of the place, or what Norberg-Schulz called the "genius loci" (Norberg-Schulz 1980). Although it manifests itself through the physical environment, it is rooted in culture, traditions, and the particular characteristics of a civilization. Being, perhaps, more sensitive than most, artists are the ones who first detect the spirit of a place. Why, after all, did artists come from all corners of the world to gather in turn-of-the-century Paris? What was so special about this city at this moment that drew them like a magnet? Undoubtedly,

this *esprit de Paris* existed before the artistic influx; later, the artists enhanced and propagated the city's ambience in their work. There was a quality then, in Paris, that transcended its inhabitants, that seemed to emerge from its very stones and gardens. The spirit of a city, of a neighbourhood, or of a single house is embedded in its physical reality; in Paris, it may be related to the paved surface of the streets, the beige façades of the buildings, the corridors of plane trees, the cast-iron balconies, the lines of the river banks, the café terraces, the busy boulevards, the noisy metro, the proximity of conviviality and monumentality, and the small rooms tucked under rooftops.

A Non Self-Referential System of Criteria

These are the value-based criteria necessary to buttress the design process and to measure the success of architectural artefacts in terms of human satisfaction. What is proposed here is a non-self-referential system of criteria for evaluating architectural works. It is a system that entails social accountability. It indicates that architecture is made for the purpose of satisfying people in a respectful way and that the expression of this satisfaction comes from the architectural artefact's users, not the architect. And it offers a concrete means of gauging this satisfaction — through criteria that have been extracted from society's professed values. In this endeavour, the architect becomes a privileged facilitator because his creative input is activated for the realization of people's aspirations.

This theory does not attempt to impose these or any other criteria on the architect. It merely points out that these criteria are valid because they are grounded in the values of society. The architect has the freedom to select other criteria, but if he does not construct a rationale similar to the one presented here, a rationale that is drawn from universally shared opinion, he risks being criticized for arbitrariness. This criticism will not only be expressed through explicit remarks concerning his design but it will also be demonstrated by his loss of credibility in society.

Epochès of Three Artefacts

In the next three chapters, epochès of the Palais-Royal, the Fondation Rothschild Workers' Residence, and Outremont are presented. In each case, the method would normally call for the conscious removal of all twelve veils. Here, however, the description of the artefacts has been limited to seven veils: activity components, surroundings, presence in evolution, materiality, form and space, ecology, and character. These are sufficient to demonstrate the applicability of the theory. Also, I believe that all the criteria are not necessary to evaluate the method critically, and so I have selected eight criteria: balance of public realm/private domain; feeling of enclosure; positivity of public places; order; accessibility (physical and psychological); human scale; proper landscaping; and good taste.

5

PALAIS-ROYAL: A PERENNIAL ELEGANCE

You, the reader, are invited to join me on a visit to the Palais-Royal in Paris. I encourage you to observe what you encounter with the inquisitive eye of an architect.

A Regal Place

For those not familiar with French anecdotal history, the Palais-Royal is an urban complex with an ill-chosen name. It was never the royal palace of the Kingdom of France or even one of the king's main residences; these, of course, were the Louvre, the Tuileries Palace, Versailles, and Fontainebleau. Rarely did a king of France even visit it (*Exhibition Catalogue* 1988, 2–35). Yet, it is one of the most regal places in Paris. Construction was started by Cardinal Richelieu in 1624, and the edifice was enlarged and transformed several times; never finished, it has always pulsated with life. The Palais-Royal has continuously played a significant role in the history of Paris, France, and humanity.

In contemporary terms, the Palais-Royal is a multiuse real-estate complex in the centre of Paris. The property of the French government and a multiplicity of private owners, it is managed by a public-private partnership. This sprawling structure was built on a five-hectare site and houses several public and private functions. At the heart of the complex we find one of the better-known and most-cherished public gardens in Paris. With the addition, in 1785, of the three wings surrounding the garden, the Palais-Royal became a residential complex and shopping centre, today comprising some two hundred apartments of all sizes, sixty-eight boutiques, and a few designer studios. It is an institutional building: in the former princely

Leaving the noisy city behind, a young man walks through the galerie d'Orléans portico and emerges into the Palais-Royal garden

residence are situated the two high courts of France, the Conseil d'État and the Conseil Constitutionnel,[55] as well as the Ministry of Culture. As home to two illustrious theatre companies – France's premier company, the Comédie-Française, and the small Théâtre du Palais-Royal – it is also a home for the performing arts. Finally, with its six restaurants and cafés, the Palais-Royal can rightly claim to be a centre for gastronomic pleasure (*Exhibition Catalogue* 1988, 270–86).

Parisians

Broadly speaking, three sorts of people mingle at the Palais-Royal: those who reside or work in the complex; those who come for a definite purpose, such as to attend a theatre performance or buy a gift; and those who come to stroll or sit in the garden for awhile, or just walk through. While out-of-town visitors do come to Palais-Royal, they are in the minority; the overwhelming majority of the complex's patrons, residents, and workers are Parisians, as are the many children who play there every day. Most of the theatre goers are Parisians, although some come from other regions of France or even abroad. When tourists visit the complex, they mingle with the crowds of Parisians who go to the Palais-Royal for a casual purpose. Shopkeepers and restaurateurs will tell you that, on average, tourists rarely account for more than 30 percent of their clientele in the summer and much less over the rest of the year. When all users are taken into account, on a daily basis over a one-year period, Parisians make up about 95 percent of all Palais-Royal users.

Informal Formality

The Palais-Royal complex is a five-storey continuous building with very high ceilings (Champier 1991, 13–432). It forms a long, hollow rectangle, oriented almost perfectly north-south. The former palace occupies the south side of the rectangle and faces place du Palais-Royal. Considered an integral part of the complex, this lively square connects the Palais-Royal to the Louvre and the subway. The other three sides of the rectangle are residential wings; shops are situated on their ground floors. Surrounded and defined by porticoes, three connected open-air public enclosures occupy the rectangle's interior. Behind the south-central wing that houses the Conseil d'État lies the cour d'Honneur, now home to sculptor Daniel Buren's controversial black-and-white truncated columns. A second hard-surfaced courtyard adorned with two fountains boasting movable

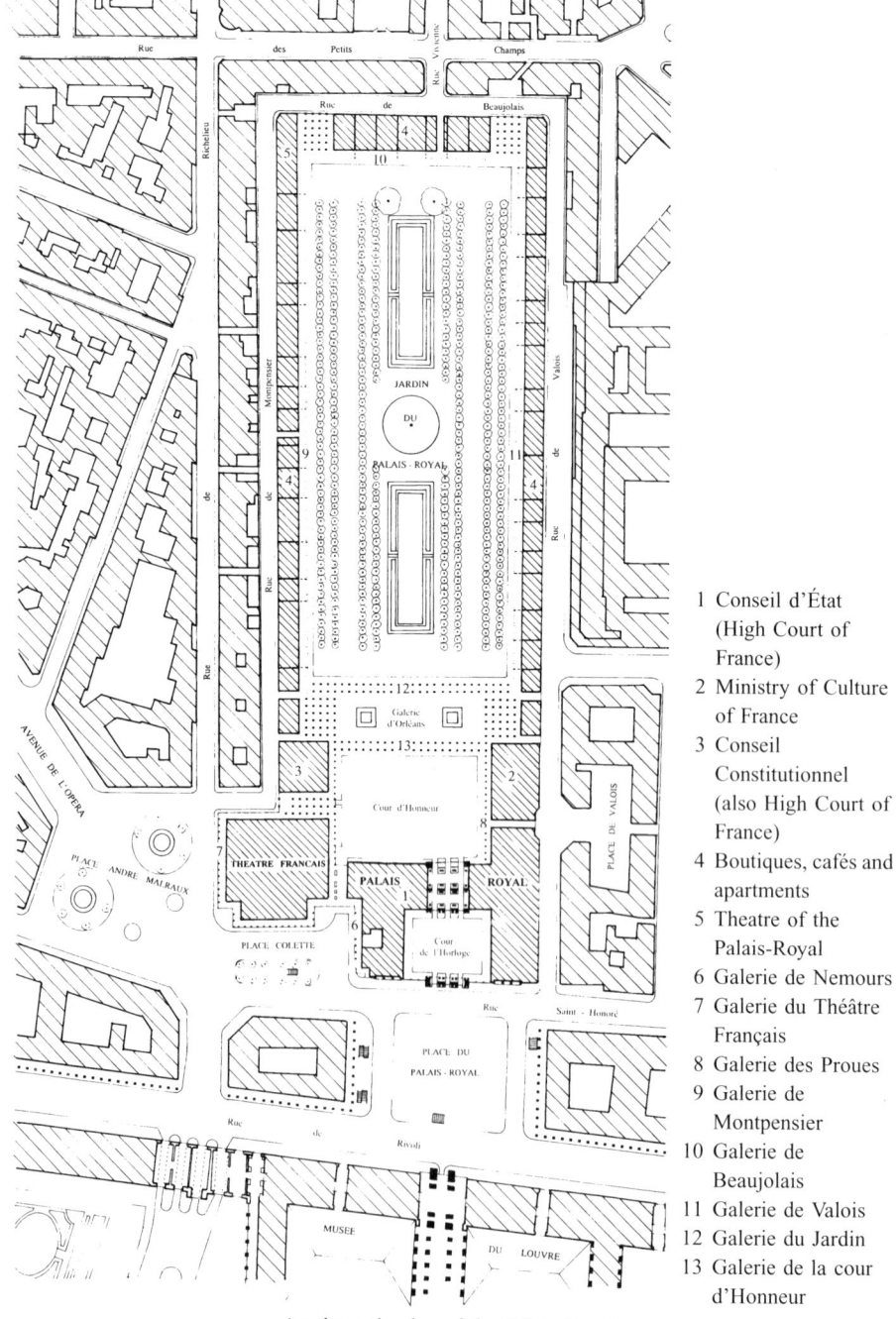

1 Conseil d'État (High Court of France)
2 Ministry of Culture of France
3 Conseil Constitutionnel (also High Court of France)
4 Boutiques, cafés and apartments
5 Theatre of the Palais-Royal
6 Galerie de Nemours
7 Galerie du Théâtre Français
8 Galerie des Proues
9 Galerie de Montpensier
10 Galerie de Beaujolais
11 Galerie de Valois
12 Galerie du Jardin
13 Galerie de la cour d'Honneur

A schematic plan of the Palais-Royal

stainless-steel spheres links the cour d'Honneur with the garden. This courtyard, where a glass-roofed shopping arcade once stood (between 1830 and 1930), is called galerie d'Orléans. And the rectangular garden itself (measuring 228 by 92 metres) has regular rows of well-trimmed chestnut trees, shaded sand alleys, lawns and flowerbeds, a circular pool with a fountain, a few odd antique sculptures, a children's sandbox, chairs and benches, and a miniature canon that is fired every day at noon. The north-south façades on the narrow rue de Valois to the east and rue de Montpensier to the west are, respectively, 377 and 302 metres long, while the north façade on rue de Beaujolais is 120 metres long. Parisians consider the south façade along rue Saint-Honoré to be the Palais-Royal's main façade. It is longer than the north one because the Théâtre-Français wing recedes from the rue Saint-Honoré alignment and protrudes towards the west, forming a set of interconnected squares. More ornate than the others, the south façade embraces Conseil d'État's formal entry way courtyard, called cour de l'Horloge. In its centre opens a decorated porte cochere, which used to admit carriages into cour d'Honneur. From the street side, the porte cochere is aligned on a perfectly – almost – straight axis bisecting cour de l'Horloge, place du Palais-Royal, and, on the south side of rue de Rivoli, the Richelieu passageway of the Louvre; from the courtyard side, however, it is off-centre to the left. This peculiarity illustrates a characteristic of this remarkable network of pedestrian areas: each is simultaneously symmetrical and asymmetrical, formal and informal, in a sort of unruly order.

At the Palais-Royal, formality and perceived symmetry are constantly broken. What appears rectilinear is often slanted, and formal places are used in an informal way. Moving northward from the Louvre's Richelieu gateway, we notice the very formal, rectangular place du Palais-Royal, bordered by the Louvre museum, the Louvre des antiquaires store, the Hôtel du Louvre, and the Conseil d'État edifice. However, this geometric regularity is an illusion: the rectangle is, in fact, a trapezoid, as the façade of the Hotel du Louvre is two portico bays shorter than its counterpart, the façade of the Louvre des antiquaires – that is, it has ten, not twelve, bays. Moreover, in the square, a strong north-south axis, which helps define its monumentality, is broken by one of the metro entrances. Until a few years ago, this formal square served as a very informal parking lot (first for horse-drawn carriages and later for cars); now it is shared by crisscrossing pedestrians, street artists, and roller skaters.

The formal cour de l'Horloge looks rectangular, but is also trapezoidal, and the two seemingly symmetrical side-wing façades facing rue Saint-

The façade of the Conseil d'État wing faces place du Palais-Royal and rue Saint-Honoré; behind the portico is cour de l'Horloge

Honoré are not quite identical. On the west wing we notice a portico, galerie de Nemours, facing place Colette, while such a feature does not exist on the other side, at the corner of rue de Valois and rue Saint-Honoré. Galerie de Chartres, which connects place Colette with Cour d'honneur, is off-centre in the recessed façade that connects the Théâtre-Français wing with the west façade of the Conseil d'état. Similarly, the two elements of galerie du Théâtre-Français, the ones facing place Colette and place André-Malraux, are of unequal length and off-centre with regard to their respective sides of the theatre building itself. Peristyle de Chartres, which connects rue de Richelieu and serves as the entrance porch to the Conseil Constitutionnel wing, is off-centre with respect to both rue de Richelieu and cour d'Honneur. Moreover, it is aligned with neither the rectilinear grid of the Buren columns nor passage de la Cour des Fontaines on the other side of the courtyard. The latter is only a passageway, not a peristyle, although it serves as the entrance porch to the Ministry of Culture. At first sight, passage de la Cour des Fontaines appears to be perpendicular to galerie des Proues or to the Ministry of Culture's rue de Valois façade; in fact, it is at an angle: it is aligned with place de Valois and passage Vérité, on the other side of rue de Valois.

The cour d'Honneur itself looks quite rectangular and formal, but is an irregular area used as a playground. The east and west façades have the same number of bays – eighteen. But the Buren grid is not really aligned with the side bays, though it is perfectly in line with the pilasters of the northern portico. And the back façade of the palace facing the cour d'Honneur is not perpendicular to the side façades.

Galerie d'Orléans is a truly rectilinear and symmetrical place. The two peristyles, de Montpensier et de Valois, are identical and symmetrical; the two stainless-steel fountains are also identical and disposed in a symmetrical way; and the surrounding porticoes are aligned with one another and with the paving-stone pattern. But, like cour d'Honneur, it is a formal place that has been taken over by children.

At first sight, the garden looks formal and symmetrical, but the rectangle may not be perfect. While the two long galeries, de Montpensier and de Valois, each have seventy-one bays, the short galeries do not have the same number of bays: the galerie de Beaujolais has thirty bays while the galerie du Jardin has twenty-nine. The side passageway, connecting rue de Montpensier with the garden, is located almost, but not quite, at the centre of the garden, and is not aligned with the pool. At the north end of the garden, the two side peristyles, de Joinville and de Beaujolais, are symmetrical in relation to each other. The central passageway however, passage du Perron, is off-centre with respect to the garden's longitudinal axis.

A Porous Domain at the Centre

Paris is a spiral of twenty districts, or *arrondissements*. The first arrondissement sits at its centre. And the Palais-Royal occupies the centre of the centre without really being the centre of Paris. If there is a centre to Paris, it is Notre-Dame or the Louvre, definitely not the Palais-Royal. In an ambiguous way that defines its personality, the Palais-Royal is a quasi-centre, or a centre beside the centre. It is a subdued entity within the larger, brasher entity of the city, a multidimensional quarter within a multidimensional capital, a complex of interconnecting places that form a whole within the composite urban fabric of Paris, itself a component of successively larger realms – France, Europe, and the French-speaking international community, called the Francophonie. With its continuous, subtle, off-centre presence in the centre, and, as we have already seen, with its almost magical ability to combine monumentality and conviviality, the Palais-Royal transcends its specific Parisian reality and reaches the world.

The Palais-Royal is perceived as, indeed is, the natural continuation of the surrounding urban fabric, because one can enter its private grounds without leaving the public domain. It is like a porous city portion turned inside out. The only way to enter the Palais-Royal grounds is on foot. Most people enter it at its southeast corner, either through galerie de Nemours connecting with galerie de Chartres, or through peristyle de Chartres, that is, by walking under the porticoes that wrap around the Théâtre-Français wing. These entry routes begin at the urban squares that embrace the main façade of the palace: place du Palais-Royal, which faces the Louvre, and the informal place Colette/place André Malraux dual square, which stands in the foreground of the avenue de l'Opéra vista extending towards Charles Garnier's opera house. One can also access the Palais-Royal courtyards and garden through eleven other passageways. From the north side – that is, coming from rue des Petits-Champs – we may take either rue Vivienne, leading directly to passage du Perron, or, if we move closer to place des Victoires, we may take a narrow passage that cuts through the neighbouring building; this is a kind of public outdoor corridor called passage des Trois Pavillons; here we can buy a newspaper. Emerging from this passage, we descend a few steps, cross rue de Beaujolais, and take peristyle de Beaujolais to reach the garden. Passage du Perron is an inconspicuous corridor, roughly aligned with rue Vivienne; the two side peristyles, de Beaujolais and de Joinville, are more formal spaces; they lead, however, to backstreets. Circling the Palais-Royal, one sees many doors – to apartments, shops, theatres, and so on. Apart from the Conseil d'État's central door on rue Saint-Honoré, facing cour de l'Horloge, in front of place du Palais-Royal, all the other doors look like side doors, even those giving access to such illustrious institutions as the Conseil Constitutionnel or the Ministry of Culture. Even this "front door" has always remained a private one; once it led to the palace, but today it leads to the Conseil d'État. The general public has never used it.[56] From every direction, entering the Palais-Royal grounds requires a circuitous, informal itinerary, illustrating another of the Palais-Royal's fundamental characteristics: it is an urban entity that blends with the surrounding urban milieu in a discrete way.

Many Parisians share novelist Julien Green's opinion that when one enters the Palais-Royal one leaves behind the noise and the stress of the city yet remains in its spirit (Green 1983, 47–51). To promenade at the Palais-Royal is to take a journey into the past without ever leaving the present, to experience a respite from urban activity. In the Palais-Royal, the

One of the main entrances to the Palais-Royal complex is through galerie de Nemours, which is tucked between the Comédie-Française on the left and the Conseil d'État wing on the right

present is never pushed aside by the past since the complex has never ceased to be a lively, contemporary urban place. These overlapping feelings are not inconsistencies or contradictions; they just arise from an abundance of impressions.

History in the Present

It was on 7 September 1624 that Cardinal Richelieu bought, for ninety thousand pounds, a dilapidated mansion called Hôtel Rambouillet in order to reside close to his king's palace, the Louvre. He also wanted a base for managing both affairs of state and private matters. As this mansion was too small to accommodate his abundant needs, he bought up a series of adjacent properties and asked the king to give him some more, including an empty field behind them. Hiring Jacques Le Mercier, Architecte du Roy, he ordered a complete transformation of his new property. And with this commission, Richelieu initiated an organic process of change, demolition, addition, and transformation that would characterize the life of the Palais-Royal for more than three and a half centuries (Champier 1991, 21, 13–34).

King Louis XIII was a suspicious person, and he frowned upon Richelieu's huge expenditure; but being a clever politician, the cardinal had anticipated the king's reaction. He calmed his monarch's apprehensions by signing an agreement with him that the property, known then as the Palais-Cardinal, would revert back to the royal household after Richelieu's death.

Richelieu used the open field behind his mansion to make a garden for his own pleasure and for the enjoyment of the populace. This distinctive characteristic of the Palais-Royal garden – that it is a private place open to the public – has never been altered. The first landscape architect who worked on the Palais-Royal garden was Claude Desgots. He designed it in the fashion of the day, with neat gravel alleys, geometric lawns, and *broderie* flower beds (*Exhibition Catalogue* 1988, 14–15).

Richelieu liked entertaining. In 1635, he undertook an initiative that forever crystallized another distinctive feature of the Palais-Royal. He ordered architect Philippe de Champagne to design a small, six-hundred-seat theatre. Five years later, a second, larger theatre was added, which became the home of Molière's theatre company, the Illustre Théâtre, now the Comédie-Française. In 1663, fire destroyed the larger theatre, but it was quickly rebuilt.

To impress his guests, Richelieu added to his residence what he called "la galerie des hommes illustres," a kind of art gallery with paintings and sculptures glorifying the twenty-five "most illustrious" men in the history of France. (It is interesting to note that there was one woman listed as a famous "man:" Joan of Arc). Richelieu died in 1642 and Louis XIII a few months later. The Palais-Cardinal became part of the royal household and its name was changed to Palais-Royal.

Shortly after the King's death, his widow, Queen Anne of Austria, decided – perhaps because Richelieu's mansion was easier to heat than the Louvre – to settle at the Palais-Royal with her two children, Louis, the future king of France, and Philippe, the future owner of the Palais-Royal. Cardinal Mazarini, who had succeeded Richelieu as prime minister of France, joined them. Their stay at the Palais-Royal was short. An insurrection erupted in January 1649. A mob stormed the Palais-Royal, forcing the queen, her children, and Mazarini to flee, via the back door, into the cold winter night. They came back a few weeks later with an army, but to no avail: a year after their return, a new revolt pushed them out of the Palais-Royal for good. Remembering these events when he took power, young Louis XIV decided that living in Paris was too dangerous and uncomfortable, and ordered that a palace be built for him at Versailles, which was certainly safer but no less uncomfortable. The Palais-Royal was abandoned for ten years before being occupied by Queen Henriette of England.

Louis XIV had four children by his mistress, the beautiful Louise de la Vallière. The first two were boys, born in 1663 and 1665 at the Palais-Royal. The older child was named Charles, and given to a certain Monsieur de Lincour; the younger was named Philippe, and adopted by a certain Monsieur Derssy. I have an ancestor named Michel Desorcis. He was a recruiting agent for the French colony, and he arrived in Quebec at about the time the two children were born – around 1660. The name Lincourt suddenly appeared in my family some one hundred years after Desorcis arrived in Quebec. We may speculate with a smile that perhaps the best way to get rid of the little bastards was to give them to those who were departing for the colonies. There is certainly no connection, but the double coincidence is amusing (Champier 1991, 85).

The king's brother, Philippe, was called "Monsieur." In 1660, Louis XIV persuaded Monsieur, a well-known homosexual and transvestite, to marry Henriette of England. To thank him for his sacrifice, the king gave Monsieur the Palais-Royal as a wedding gift. The gift was officially confirmed in 1692 and the Palais-Royal became one of the private properties of the d'Orléans family, the junior branch of the French monarchy. Henriette died ten years later, Bossuet delivered his memorable sermon, and Philippe quickly remarried, this time choosing one of the most remarkable women of the period, Elizabeth-Charlotte of Bavaria, the famous Princess Palatine. Even well before her marriage, she maintained a lively correspondence with the greatest minds of her time, among them Descartes. Their letters about Seneca's *De Vita Beata*, written in the summer of 1645, are well worth reading. Elizabeth loved her unruly husband in spite of his homosexuality. Monsieur, after all, was a much more interesting personality than his snobbish, arrogant, and sombre older brother.

As soon as he took possession of the Palais-Royal, Monsieur ordered major renovations. Over a period of twenty-five years, the architects Le Pautre, d'Orbay, possibly Jules-Hardouin Mansart, and landscape architect André Le Nôtre modified and modernized the palace, its theatres, and its garden. In 1674, the Princess Palatine gave birth to a son named Philippe, the future regent of France (Champier 1991, 89–125).

Louis XIV finally died in 1710. His great-grandson, Louis XV, was then only five years old and needed a tutor. Philippe d'Orléans elbowed his way into the position of regent of France and, from 1710 to 1723, governed the country from the Palais-Royal. Historians often call this short period the Golden Age of the Palais-Royal (*Exhibition Catalogue* 1988, 61; Champier

1991, 127). After the stuffy, oppressive reign of Louis XIV, the Regency was certainly a breath of fresh air. Michelet said that the regent was not the "best" man in the kingdom (*le meilleur*), but he was the most "good" (*le plus bon*) (Michelet 1966, XI 39). One day, the regent, attempting to reconcile the government budget, cut in half the number of horses allocated to the dauphin. Voltaire said that it would have been better if he had reduced the number of asses who were hanging around the Palais-Royal. The regent thought this was a good joke, but Abbé Dubois, prime minister and "Chief Mackerel," declared that an example must be set. Voltaire was sent to the Bastille. The prime minister's enemies insisted that Abbé Dubois's main function was not only to incarcerate dissidents but also to find beautiful young women for the regent's private orgies – those famous little dinners known as "les petits soupers du régent." Much has been written about these festivities. The regent, on one occasion, invited his private butler to join the frolic. The servant thanked his master but said that he would never debase himself by joining such a corrupt company. The regent laughed. Yet these immoral men were, in fact, intellectually honest. They reintroduced freedom of thought to the kingdom of France and governed with a fair amount of common sense (Touchard-Lafosse 1964, 15–105, 90, 40).

Another innovation of the regency was the twice-weekly masked ball held at the opera of the Palais-Royal or in one of the Palais-Royal theatres transformed into a ballroom. These parties were open to everyone, and it was here that the trick of the double mask was invented. Clever revellers would first put on a realistic wax mask that looked surprisingly like one of several rich and famous court aristocrats; on top of that they would wear a second mask. All night long they would shamelessly plot and flirt, conduct themselves in scandalous ways, and when everyone was half-drunk and the candles had burned down they would remove the second mask and expose the face of a hated aristocrat, deliberately creating much confusion and sparking false rumours. From his private balcony, hidden behind his own mask, the regent would witness it all with a smile while caressing a young masked woman (Champier 1991, 161). The French Revolution was coming.

During the Regency period, constant improvements were made to the Palais-Royal buildings. The principal architects of the time were the two Oppenords. The regent died in 1723. Having reached the age of eighteen, Louis XV was crowned, and the seat of power reverted to Versailles (*Exhibition Catalogue* 1988, 61–78).

The regent's son, Louis-Philippe d'Orléans, did not do much politically, but he diligently worked at restoring the garden and the buildings of the Palais-Royal. In 1730, a landscape architect, also named Desgots (perhaps a grandson of Richelieu's landscape architect), was hired to renovate the garden. This Desgots eliminated the flowerbeds and designed large lawns and two fountains. Apparently, he was also the one who first introduced a major innovation in the development of gardening: the hose. That innovation was considered so extraordinary that Jacques-François Blondel mentioned it in his treatise *Architecture française*.

From 1730 to 1770, several million francs were invested to upgrade the building. Architects Jacques-Sylvain Cartaud, Pierre-Louis Moreau-Desproux, and Pierre Contant (Contant d'Ivry) made fundamental changes to the palace. Cartaud designed the officers' wing facing Fountain Court, the actual place de Valois on the east side. Moreau-Desproux designed the façades of the central building, facing cour de l'Horloge and cour d'Honneur. Contant d'Ivry designed the central hall, the monumental staircase leading to the prince's apartments, and most of the interior of the central building (*Exhibition Catalogue* 180).

In 1763, fire completely destroyed the theatre: only an old harpsichord was saved.[57] Luckily, no one was hurt. The building was immediately rebuilt and the theatre reopened in 1770; Moreau-Desproux was the architect. In 1781, fire destroyed it for the second time. The blaze broke out a few minutes after the public had left the premises. This time, several technicians and actors were trapped inside. The opera company left the Palais-Royal and never returned. Louis-Philippe died in 1785.

Upon the death of Louis-Philippe d'Orléans, his son, Louis-Philippe-Joseph, who would later adopt the name of Philippe-Égalité, took possession of the Palais-Royal and launched the real-estate operation that would radically transform the property. This speculative enterprise has since been named "le grand projet." Philippe-Égalité was a shrewd operator, an energetic and well-educated person, but he constantly outsmarted himself. He had the uncanny ability to transform a spectacular success into a pitiful disaster. Although he was one of the richest people in France, he was always in need of money.

His scheme was to make a huge profit by subdividing the periphery of his garden, and building and selling revenue-producing row houses. The plan was a clever one. Each new owner would take possession of a house that would pay for itself. Philippe-Égalité sold the houses by the arcade; the entire project had 180 arcades. The narrowest house, also the most popular model, had three arcades; a few had as many as eight. The three-arcade house had a basement; three shops with mezzanines facing the portico on the garden side; the owner's apartment, which was located on the first floor; two more storeys with rental flats; and servants' quarters under the roof. By 1790, Philippe-Égalité had sold 166 arcades to 37 buyers; he kept three arcades for himself. Most of the owners were wealthy businessmen – only two were aristocrats. In the space of five years, the Palais-Royal had been transformed into a vast residential complex and lively shopping centre.

The architect of this project was Victor Louis, certainly one of the most talented of his generation. At the time, Louis was a relatively obscure architect, having completed only one significant building, the Bordeaux Theatre. One hundred and twenty years later, a Palais-Royal historian would describe Victor Louis's Palais-Royal composition in these terms:

The architect's skill was evident in the frankness of the scheme and the clearness, sharpness of the composition. No dryness in the silhouettes; no heaviness in the details. The heights of the buildings were admirably calculated and the proportions perfectly correct: if the buildings had been lower, the roofs of the surrounding edifices would have been seen; higher, the garden of the Palais-Royal would have looked like a cloister or a prison. The divisions of the façades, where one admires the harmonious elegance of the pure Louis XV style, the neat curve of the 180 arcades, the finely grooved pilasters, the two storeys and the balustrade hiding the attic, all this retains even to this day a character of majestic and agreeable beauty. (Champier 1991, 243)[58]

Victor Louis was also granted the commission to rebuild the theatre destroyed by fire. It reopened in 1790. He also designed the small Palais-Royal theatre at the north end of the Montpensier wing.

The residential project was barely finished when the French Revolution erupted, and the Palais-Royal was swept into the tempest. Later, Victor Hugo would say that the Palais-Royal was the nucleus of the revolutionary comet. It was at this moment that Philippe d'Orléans, the ultimate aristocrat-cum-speculator, joined the Republicans and changed his name to Philippe-Égalité as a way of demonstrating that he was equal to every other *citoyen*; he also changed the name of his palace to Palais-Égalité. Of course, nobody was convinced, and the name Palais-Royal was never abandoned.

From the moment it opened, the new Palais-Royal was a huge popular success. People flocked to it in great numbers, and there they would eat and drink, cruise and plot, buy and sell, play cards, be solicited by young women of pleasure, swap information, and debate rumours. In those days preceding the revolution the excitement must have been palpable. Sitting in the tranquil Palais-Royal garden of today, I often try to imagine the atmosphere of these historic moments and determine where, exactly,

Camille Desmoulins stood up and called the people of Paris to arms. Perhaps it was at a mid-point of the garden, just outside galerie de Montpensier. On Sunday, 12 July 1789, the brilliant young lawyer/journalist returned to Paris from Versailles with troubling news. The king had adopted a hard line and fired his prime minister, the banker Necker, who wanted to accommodate the Republicans. Camille Desmoulins hurried to the Palais-Royal to join his friends. It was two o"clock in the afternoon. The day was hot and humid, and a jittery crowd was pressing into the Palais-Royal garden. Desmoulins's friends convinced him to address the people. They carried him on a table. He improvised a speech that is now as famous in French history as the Gettysburg Address is in American history: "Citizens, not a moment to loose! I come from Versailles. Mr. Necker has been fired; this signals the massacre of the patriots. Tonight, Swiss and German battalions will march out of the Champs-de-Mars and kill us. Only one solution remains: to arm ourselves, and wear a ribbon as a sign of identification."[59]

An immense roar answered his harangue. The crowd swelled with excitement. Bands of people ran to all corners of Paris calling everyone to arms. Many soldiers joined the revolutionaries. Others did not. Skirmishes erupted. A few people were killed. The body of one soldier was brought back to the Palais-Royal, fuelling the excitement. The Palais-Royal became the Revolution's informal headquarters. Hundreds of people spent the night in the garden.

The following day saw no respite. More fights erupted in the streets. More people were killed, their heads stuck on spears and paraded in the Palais-Royal as morbid trophies. Meetings were called in all the churches of Paris. Most Parisians attended. Every speaker encouraged people to find arms and defend themselves. The next day, the Bastille fell, altering the destiny of France and the world forever.

Philippe-Égalité failed in all his undertakings. In spite of the obvious success of the Palais-Égalité speculation, he was bankrupt. As a member of the National Assembly, he voted in favour of the execution of his cousin the king. A few months later, he was himself decapitated. The Palais-Égalité became the property of the state. To cover his debt, a major part of the immense art collection accumulated at the Palais-Égalité since 1624 was sold in Brussels and London. Camille Desmoulins and several other good citizens who had spent much of their time at the Palais-Royal during the preceding four years were also decapitated.

Under the Directoire and the Empire, the complex was once again officially named Palais-Royal. Its popular appeal never diminished. It was "the" place for Parisians to go. In 1813, a Parisian bourgeois described the Palais-Royal in these terms:

No other place in the world can offer so many delights. Seductions are to be found at every step; pleasures seem to coalesce there. It is a perpetual fair. Every floor has its own use; one finds cafés and restaurants, and numerous salons where the pleasures are as varied as the decor. At any moment of the day, you may ask a tailor to take your measurements and, while you lunch or read a newspaper, make your suit. Peddlers of comestibles can offer the most sought-after things, coming from the most distant lands. As in a catalogue, you may learn about books in a bookstore; here, with the help of an almanac, the gourmet learns about the crops of our fertile gardens and fecund forests; the land and the sea offer the rewards of the rarest catches. In the morning, honest patrons browse in the boutiques while idlers, as they should, start their day at their favourite restaurants. In the afternoon, brokers, caterers, officials and *rentiers* talk loud, debate, and gesticulate. When evening comes, an elegant crowd presses into the luxury shops or hastens to the restaurants. At night come the gamblers, the revellers, and the regular customers of lounges and clubs, theatres and gambling dens, and, mingling with cosmopolitan and ill-matched groups, gallant ladies, peddlers, and pickpockets. Anyone who would depart from Paris without having seen and admired the Palais-Royal would have retained a very incomplete opinion of the capital. Nowhere else in Europe would you find a place like this one. (Champier and Sandoz 1991, 297)[60]

This popularity did not impress Napoléon. In the emperor's scheme of things, the Palais-Royal was not important, even though, it has been said, it was there that he made love to Joséphine for the first time. At one point Napoléon ordered the property to be assessed and put up for sale. The Palais-Royal was valued at 4,411,250 francs. No bid was presented (Champier and Sandoz 1991, 297).

After Waterloo, the complex was given back to the d'Orléans family. Louis-Philippe d'Orléans, the son of Philippe-Égalité, returned from exile, took possession of the Palais-Royal, and ordered a complete renovation of the south end of the property. Architects Percier and Fontaine were hired. Their most spectacular contribution was the monumental stairway of the Montpensier wing.

The Restoration was not a successful regime, to say the least. In the summer of 1830, a short-lived revolution broke out. The three July days of turmoil were called "les trois glorieuses." A friendly mob stormed the Palais-Royal, "kidnapped" the Duc d'Orléans, carried him on its shoulders to City Hall, and proclaimed him the king of the French (as opposed to the king of France, monarch of the former regime). For the first time in history, a d'Orléans was officially king. The Monarchy of July had started. It was to last eighteen years.

On 1 October 1831, a little more than a year after he was appointed king, Louis-Philippe left the Palais-Royal and moved across the square to live at the Tuileries Palace; his sister and advisor, Madame Adélaïde, settled at the Palais-Royal. Little by little, the public infatuation with the Palais-Royal receded. Louis-Philippe ordered the demolition of the wooden galleries and had them replaced with the galerie d'Orléans, an upscale glass-roofed shopping arcade. As a result, some of the most ostentatious brothels and gambling dens were closed. Also, open solicitation was severely policed. The garden was not yet the place of silence it is today, but it was certainly calmer than it had been for forty-five years. Much renovation work was also undertaken in the palace and the residential wings.

The Monarchy of July was no more popular than the Restoration. A new revolution erupted in 1848. This time, the mob was not so friendly. It completely sacked the Palais-Royal. Louis-Philippe was forced to abdicate. Louis-Napoléon Bonaparte, the nephew of Napoléon I, became president of the newly declared republic. Four years later, he proclaimed himself emperor under the name of Napoléon III. The Palais-Royal was again renovated and then occupied by members of the Bonaparte family. In 1864, architect Prosper Chabrol completed the Théatre-Français façades, which we still admire today.

The Second Empire lasted no longer than the Monarchy of July. In 1870, the Germans defeated the French army at Sedan and Louis-Napoléon fled to England. Paris was under siege and its inhabitants were starving to death. Another revolution occurred and the revolutionary proletarian government, called La Commune, took power. It lasted only a few weeks and ended in a bloody repression. The Palais-Royal was burned by the mob. The south-end section was almost completely destroyed. The fire engulfed adjacent buildings and threatened the entire neighbourhood. It was finally extinguished by the heroic intervention of the staff of the nearby Bank of France and some local residents. Once again, the Palais-Royal rose from its ashes and proved itself to be the most extraordinary architectural phoenix.

The period between 1871 and 1998 was much more serene. The two world wars had no direct impact on the fate of the Palais-Royal. A number of renovations were carried out. The theatres were upgraded to meet the changing needs of the theatre companies that used them. The palace itself was transformed into a prestigious office building and occupied by the Conseil d'État, the Conseil Constitutionnel, and the Ministry of Culture.

The galerie d'Orléans shops were closed in 1900 and transformed into government offices; the glass structure was demolished in 1934. Although the residential wings were constantly renovated, their function and exterior appearance were never modified. The shops became more specialized and slowly acquired their present tranquil character. The Palais-Royal porticoes are now known for their stamp and medal shops, their antique and gift boutiques, their cafés and bistros, and the famous gastronomic restaurant the Grand Véfour. The Palais-Royal garden has metamorphosed into a haven of peace.

Stones of Gold

A stroll into the Palais-Royal's material reality is also a promenade into its imaginary realm. Of course the place is a physical structure. We can see it and touch it, yet it triggers dream images. When we observe its façades, caress a column with our hand, and marvel at the sun-and-shadow pas de deux taking place in its courtyards, we may fantasize that this building is made of gold, the material of eternity. If we are to be true to the phenomenological approach, we have to agree with Gaston Bachelard, who wrote, "dream is stronger than experience" (Bachelard 1949, 44). In the description of the phenomenon, imagination complements rational reasoning. When we conduct an epochè on a material entity, we necessarily probe beyond, inside what is perceived through the senses. The search for the essence of a thing is a quest for its origin. In his essay *l'Eau et les rêves*, Bachelard showed that one can establish as "a primordial law of the imagination" that the essence of a matter is both poetic and physical (Bachelard 1973, 16). Before Paul Valéry's poem "Eupalinos ou l'architecte" was published – a poem in which Valéry praised buildings that sing – Bachelard wrote that "imagination is not, as its etymology would lead us to believe, the faculty to form images of reality, but rather the faculty to form images that go beyond reality, that sing reality" (Bachelard 1973, 23).

The entire Palais-Royal complex was constructed of distinctive Parisian honey-coloured limestone. This golden stone dominates all of the other materials used to create the edifice. Here and there, cast-iron railings, fences, balconies, and lanterns join with other secondary materials – the glass of the windows, the canvas awnings and zinc sheathing of the roof – to complete the composition. But the overall impression is made by the early-morning-sun colour of the stone. On certain days, that soft, caressing light, so particular to Paris, turns the building almost pink – it takes on the colour of old gold.

That gold colour also dominates the interiors. The chambers of the Conseil d'État and Conseil Constitutionnel, the monumental staircases and the offices of the Ministry of Culture, boast exquisite gold-and-white woodwork, marble and marquetry floors, bronze and cast-iron railings, crystal chandeliers, rich furniture, and an array of artworks. Technically speaking, the Palais-Royal buildings are simple stone-and-timber structures reinforced here and there with iron rods. Victor Louis introduced the only real technical innovation in 1785 when he used cast iron as a structural material in rebuilding the Comédie-Française. His was one of the very first iron frames in the world. The now-demolished shopping arcade, galerie d'Orléans, designed by Fontaine and Percier and erected in 1830, was also considered one of the finest iron-and-glass structures of its time.[61] The Palais-Royal is like an antique jewel. Its value is more sentimental than real, which means that it is priceless.

Architecture of Respect

When one wants to describe an architectural artefact beyond its materiality, one must detail its form and space, its exterior and interior configurations. As I explained earlier, form applies to a building's exterior shape and space to its interior void. An immediate comprehension of the Palais-Royal's form and space may prove elusive, however, because it is an edifice that hasn't a form but a combination of forms, hasn't a space but a series of spaces, and here the clear distinction between form over space and space within form often disappears. The actual collection of architectural forms and spaces is the result of successive anterior creations of forms and spaces; or, better, its present complex formalistic and spatial symbiosis is the evolutionary offspring of several metamorphoses. Between 1624 and today, the Palais-Royal not only grew by the addition of elements, but it also grew by demolition, drastic transformation, and reconstruction of other elements (Boulet and Gresset, 1984, 1985).

In spite of these complexities, the Palais-Royal has evolved into a simple, unified composition. Simplicity is inherent in its rectangular plan. Unity arises from the homogeneity of the complex's general appearance, from its continuity in space, from its uniform height, and from the use of a single, dominant material. Perhaps unity also comes from the fact that, although the Palais-Royal is a succession of discreet architectural components and details, these were always designed as parts of the whole. While there was never an intention to design a unified masterpiece, there were certainly several successive intentions to design each component as a masterpiece

In the cour d'Honneur of the Palais-Royal are the controversial rows of truncated columns by French sculptor Daniel Buren; while many Parisians are sceptical, children and visitors seem to love them

attached to other masterpieces. If we take the time to scrutinize every detail of every façade and of every room, we see that few corners have been neglected. But, at the same time, no single component tries to dominate the others. The Palais-Royal demonstrates that it is possible to achieve a certain level of quality in one element while respecting the quality of its neighbours. The quality of the present enhances, rather than fights, the quality of the past; it is easier to attain a high level of quality through thoughtful improvements than through cocky improvisations.

At the Palais-Royal, unity transcends perception – it is felt rather than consciously understood. A visitor can never perceive as a whole the numerous shapes of this complex architecture. It takes about one hour to walk around its exterior perimeter, but no one ever undertakes that journey because it leads nowhere. Perhaps scholars can achieve such a comprehensive perception by placing photographs of the various discrete elements of the Palais-Royal before them, side by side – elements such as the rue Saint-Honoré-wing façades designed by Moreau-Desproux in 1753, the Conseil d'État central façade designed by Contant d'Ivry in 1765, the residential-wing garden façade designed by Victor Louis in 1785, and the Comédie-

Française façade designed by Prosper Chabrol in 1865. They are all different, built in different periods by different architects, yet all respect one another, all contribute to the unity of the whole. Architectural details and decorative motifs become visually important in these systematic observations, but in real life they blend into the whole. Well-executed details, well-integrated decorations, and well-studied proportions are to architecture what salt is to soup: when they are not mixed in, the result is bad taste.

The Palais-Royal's forms and spaces defy static or formalistic descriptions because Parisians always perceive them while moving through them, their attention focused on other activities. When they walk through the peristyles, chatting with friends or lost in their daydreams, they unconsciously experience the colonnade's parallax phenomenon and retain from this fixed decor a perception of architectural forms, which is pure movement. When they go to the theatre, they have an artistic or literary experience that is not architecture per se, but that dwells in architecture. Similarly, when they dine at the Grand Véfour and, between courses, admire the restaurant's Art Nouveau mirrors, they have an experience that is more gastronomic than architectural, a moment of personal delight that nonetheless contributes to the overall perception of the Palais-Royal environment.

If we ask what is space and what is form at the Palais-Royal, what is interior and what is exterior, what is inside and what is outside, and, between them, which is the principle and which is the consequence, we may be asking nonsensical questions. We can penetrate the complex and be in its space without moving inside. Many people who say that they have been to the Palais-Royal have never actually entered the building. Perhaps their only experience of an interior space at the Palais-Royal was in a tiny boutique or a café. Similarly, a woman who goes one evening to the Comédie-Française spends several hours inside a major Palais-Royal space without ever having the impression that she is visiting the Palais-Royal itself. In fact, there is no such thing as "the Palais-Royal itself," since the Palais-Royal is a multiplicity of selves. If, the following day, a friend asks the woman where she went the night before, she will answer: "I went to the Comédie-Française." And she might explain further that the Comédie-Française is located at the Palais-Royal only if her friend is a foreigner and expresses an interest in the theatre's location.

At the Palais-Royal, interior and exterior, inside and outside, private and public, space and form, all overlap to create a complex whole. The definition of form as the exterior shape and space as the interior void of the architectural element is irrelevant as soon as architecture becomes urban design, as soon as a building is designed as a part of a larger entity, as soon as the private domain is intimately integrated into the public realm, and as soon as public enclosures for public gatherings and private rooms for private uses complement one another in an organic whole.

The Palais-Royal allows visitors to navigate freely within the interface between the sheltered and the exposed. Around the garden, the porticoes transmit the impression that the walls of the buildings are three metres thick. By ambling inside this perceived thickness, we can experience the edge between form and space at the precise tension point where the "flip-flop" phenomenon occurs, the precise moment when our perception jumps from the enveloping view of the outside form to the enveloped view of the inside space.

The Most Private Public Place

In any city, people conduct their lives by constantly moving from very public places to very private places. Between these extremes, they traverse a wide range of intermediate spaces. A few of these connecting spaces display a complex public/private equilibrium between what they are and what they seem. Such a space is the Palais-Royal, which is public in concrete terms and private in spirit.

Important factors contribute to the unique character of the Palais-Royal. The first is that the complex's main public space, the garden, is a very strong enclosure with very special features. It is a public garden designed as a square; that is, a public place surrounded by shops and restaurants under porticoes. But it is not really a square because it is removed from the street system. It is, however, as accessible as a square. Even though it is a garden, it is not a green or a common, which are distinctive features of the Anglo-Saxon townscape, because the spatial and functional relationship between the activity-generating surrounding buildings and the "floor" of the central area have the sort of immediacy and continuity one finds in Italian medieval piazzas.

Another aspect of the Palais-Royal's uniqueness is that the garden space is too large and the surrounding buildings too low to convey a strong feeling of protection. The garden cross-section ratios – surrounding building height over garden width and length – are $1/5.5$ and $1/13.5$ respectively. But this apparent shortcoming is counteracted by three secondary architectural and landscaping elements that provide their own sense of enclosure. The porticoes offer a first level of enclosure. The small, well-trimmed chestnut trees, aligned like soldiers, provide a second level of protection. Visitors will always experience the enclosed central space through these screens. They will find themselves in a space within a space within a space, their vision hindered by layers of protection that still allow them to experience long vistas and a broad view of the sky.

Yet another distinct Palais-Royal characteristic is that its apartment windows are far enough away to ensure privacy and close enough to permit a reassuring, friendly surveillance. Shortly after Général De Gaulle shouted his famous words, "Vive le Québec libre!" from the balcony of Montreal City Hall, a reporter asked him to define France's policy towards Canada and Quebec. He answered that it was one of noninterference with nonindifference. This formula also describes the relationship between the Palais-Royal apartment dwellers, at their windows, and the public-garden users.

This multidimensional protective sentiment also derives from the Palais-Royal's human scale. In architectural language, the expression *human scale* is much abused, thrown around each time a small, quaint building is being depicted. Human scale has nothing to do with the absolute size of a building. Human scale may or may not be a property of either a large or a small building. It relates the ratio between human-being dimensions and building size. When this ratio is understood by building users through a series of architectural devices that permit them to relate their own dimensions and proportions to the size of the building, then it is said that the building has a "human scale" (Ching 1979, 292–331). The Palais-Royal's human scale is provided by the arcades, the small trees, the garden chairs, the windows, the iron fences, and the lanterns. One is never lost in the Palais-Royal's large space, and at the same time one never loses the feeling of being in a large space.

Another factor that adds to the complex's distinct sense of intimacy is that the garden is a space reserved for pedestrians. In our modern, automobile-oriented cities, such a haven is rarely found in public realms. Automobiles have no access to the garden; they can't even be seen from it. The act of leaving the city and entering the Palais-Royal is made up of a series of well-defined spatial experiences. To enter the garden and interior courtyards the pedestrian has to walk through the building itself, under a roof, into a passageway featuring columns that act as beacons. The act of entering flows effortlessly but still marks a definite transition – a transition from a city of noise into a city of silence.

Convenient Conviviality

Easy access is certainly one of the main reasons for the Palais-Royal's enduring popularity. Up until the invention of the automobile and the construction of the metro, most Parisians walked. The fact that the Palais-

With its lines of trees and surrounding façades, the Palais-Royal garden is a well-balanced enclosure that engenders a feeling of protection

Royal was at the very centre of the city and could be entered from all sides made it a convenient gathering place at all hours of the day and night. The advent of the automobile has not changed the Palais-Royal's basic access pattern. In the centre of Paris, many people still walk, and the Palais-Royal is as permeable and accessible as ever.

Of course, the fact that the Palais-Royal is so close to so many other urban sites increases its accessibility. It is fair to assume that most people come to the Palais-Royal simply because they find it convenient. On an ordinary weekday afternoon, three or four types of people may be found sitting on the garden benches: elementary-school children, lycée and university students, mothers or nannies with small children, gentlemen reading newspapers. When asked why they come to the Palais-Royal, they typically give the same kinds of answers. The children say: "Because it is more pleasant here than in our school yard." How far away is their school? "Oh! Five minutes." Or: "Our school is in the suburbs, but we came here to see a play!" The mothers answer that they come to the Palais-Royal garden because they live in the neighbourhood and the garden is a very nice place to bring the children; they can run and play there in complete safety: "It is

Situated between the cour d'Honneur and the garden, galerie d'Orléans is a popular playground; between 1830 and 1930, an iron and glass vault covered this rectangular area

quiet. When it is too hot, we can sit under the trees. If it rains, we can run under the arcades, there, to that café's terrace, and order a coffee, and a lemonade for the children." One gentleman explains that he has taken to sitting in the garden because it is very nice and quiet and he can read his newspaper in peace: "Because, you see, I am a clerk at the Conseil d'État and my office is right over there, behind that window." The university students reply that the Palais-Royal garden is a good place to study. One boy remarks that the old stones inspire him because he is studying history. His girlfriend adds that she likes observing the children because she is at medical school and thinking of choosing paediatrics as a speciality. The couple look at each other, smile, and say that they just like studying together in a nice, quiet place.

What do all these answers mean? They mean that the success of an urban public place depends on it displaying a few simple characteristics. It must be easy to get to, surrounded by activity-generating functions, close to many other places, pleasant, inviting, protective – in short, very convivial. People must feel that the place belongs to them, that they are welcome to enter and enjoy themselves in it. And the place must provide the basic amenities:

protection from bad weather, places to eat and drink, public toilets, benches, and adequate lighting. The Palais-Royal is just such a place.

The Best Second-Best Place

Everything at the Palais-Royal was designed with a clear purpose in mind. Its original occupant, Cardinal Richelieu, wanted it to be a comfortable residence and a centre of operations. Later, Philippe-Égalité, who only wanted to make money, built the commercial and residential wings as a speculative real-estate venture. Later still, the president of the French Republic wanted to house the Conseil d'État and the Conseil Constitutionnel in a place befitting these most important national institutions and chose the Palais-Royal. In the minds of the decision makers concerned with the Palais-Royal, architectural intentions were always subservient to broad political goals.

In spite of its importance, the Palais-Royal was never intended to be the "best" place in Paris. It was, perhaps, meant to be the second best because it has always been the home of the second most important person or institution in France. The Palais-Royal, then, may be identified as the best second-best building there is. It was Richelieu's residence, and Richelieu was very conscious of the fact that he was second to the king. Later, it was the residence of the d'Orléans family, the junior branch of the monarchy. The palace section of the Palais-Royal was not designed to outshine the main seats of power, which were the Louvre, Versailles, and, later, the National Assembly. Even the Élysée Palace, Hôtel Matignon, and the Luxembourg Palace are more elaborate.[62] But the former Palais-Cardinal was an appropriate seat for the high courts, institutions that are not implicated in the daily exercise of political power.

Richelieu created the public garden as a gesture of goodwill towards the people of Paris. It was to be enjoyed by all. Over the years, the garden has accomplished its mission in a commendable way. But, in the minds of most Parisians, the Palais-Royal garden is neither the most beautiful nor the most popular garden in their city. They will say that Parc Monceau and the Bagatelle rose garden are more beautiful and the Luxembourg garden is more popular. We need only walk from the Luxembourg to the Palais-Royal garden on a beautiful summer afternoon to witness the difference in popularity; compared to the former, the latter is almost empty (Lévesque 1982).

Place du Palais-Royal is certainly one the busiest and better-designed squares in Paris, but it has never been considered one of the jewels of the

French capital. The most sought-after squares are place Vendôme, place de la Concorde, and place des Vosges.

The private residences designed by Victor Louis at the end of the eighteenth century were well-conceived apartments for the bourgeoisie of his time. They were double-orientation flats with a striking view of the garden. Although several layout variations were offered, the typical flat was a three-bay, 93.0 square metre unit with four main rooms. Each flat had two rooms facing the garden, a 34.0 square metre living/dining room, and a 19.5 square metre bedroom; facing the backstreet was the entrance lobby, and service facilities were located in the other two rooms (Boulet and Gresset 1984, 55). Two hundred years later, even though modern amenities have been added, that basic layout has not changed. The garden-side rooms are the same and on the street side, in addition to the entrance lobby, we still find the kitchen, bathroom, toilet, and closets. The original 1784 condominium bylaws, signed by the King of France, Louis XVI, and accepted by his cousin, Philippe-Égalité, still apply.

Since their construction, all of the Palais-Royal flats have been continuously occupied and are still considered some of the most desirable residences in Paris. This unflagging popularity is a convincing demonstration of their design quality. But, in spite of this astonishing occupancy rate, there are many more desirable places to live in Paris. For example, wealthy bourgeois types prefer the lush apartments on avenue Foch, and equally affluent romantics find historical Île Saint-Louis apartments with their views of the Seine more attractive. According to Christian Guéry, real estate columnist for *Le Figaro Magazine*, the Palais-Royal apartments constitute the norm as far as selling prices are concerned. In December 1994, if a Palais-Royal apartment had actually been for sale, it would have gone for 40,000 francs per square metre. By comparison, a recently renovated flat on rue Guénégaud on the Left Bank, a stone's throw from the Pont-Neuf, was sold, unadvertised, for 85,000 francs per square metre (Guéry 1994, 136).

The porticoes surrounding the Palais-Royal garden were designed to create a shopping-centre corridor that would protect patrons from the rain and facilitate mingling. This was, and still is, a successful shopping environment. But more successful retail areas now exist in Paris, such as the Grands Boulevards, the Champs-Élysées, or even the unpretentious but lively rue du Commerce in the fifteenth arrondissement. The Palais-Royal porticoes are famous and exquisitely designed, but, in the minds of most Parisians, they are no match for either the place des Vôsges or rue de Rivoli arcades (Szambien 1992, 33). And the Comédie-Française is certainly not in the same architectural league as the Charles Garnier opera or even the new Bastille opera house. But none of these better-designed or better-known places offer the combination of complementary functions and spaces that the Palais-Royal does, and none have a richer history.

Perdurability

It is perhaps because the Palais-Royal is a survivor that it is distinguished from its contemporaries. Today, most eighteenth-century buildings have either been demolished or institutionalized, transformed into museums or tourist attractions. At the outset, Richelieu determined four basic functions for his Palais-Cardinal: it was to be a princely residence, a government office (his own, as prime minister), a public garden, and a theatre. In 1785, ordinary residences, a second theatre, public porticoes, shops, cafés, and restaurants were added.[63]

Today, eight of the complex's nine traditional functions remain; only the princely residence has disappeared, to be replaced by the headquarters of national institutions. Even in Paris, such a continuity of function and purpose is rare, and it is certainly testimony to the Palais-Royal's success. But, again, which comes first, design or function? Is the Palais-Royal, as an architectural phenomenon, a success because of its continuity of purpose or have its design characteristics prompted a succession of occupants to retain the Palais-Royal's original functions?

The simplicity of the Palais-Royal's basic composition might help explain its perdurability. As I explained earlier, the present Palais-Royal's schematic shape is a simple rectangle resulting from Richelieu's aims: a rectangular public garden behind a princely residence. One hundred and sixty years after it was made, commercial arcades were inserted on the garden's periphery, reducing the garden to its present size, creating the present enclosure, and enhancing the garden's rectangularity. Over the shops and restaurants, four storeys of residential apartments overlook the garden. As we pass through the complex's free-standing porticoes, we witness the garden transforming itself into a series hard-surfaced courtyards that serve mainly as children's playgrounds. The Comédie-Française protrudes into the city as if it were reaching out to its patrons; similarly, the Théâtre du Palais-Royal takes advantage of its location at the north end of galerie Montpensier and displays three façades to the public. The Conseil d'État, being a more private institution than the theatres, recedes and admits its visitors through a front-yard entrance. The Conseil Constitutionnel's and the Ministry of Culture's entrances are inconspicuously located under the side peristyles. The entire place is permeable, allowing a free flow of pedestrians. This simple spatial organization, this almost schematic parti, is perhaps largely responsible for the Palais-Royal's lasting success. One wonders why its obviously well-functioning layout has never – until now – been copied or studied[64] or used as a model for a new inner-city multiuse complex. Is it because it is too simple, too natural, or too evident? Or is it due to the compulsion of many modern and postmodern architects to be different at all costs?

Tradition

When an architectural artefact is permitted to endure, it becomes part of a society's tradition – but only part. When people who are not architects discuss places in a city, they talk mainly about the events that occur in them. This applies to historians writing history books, journalists reporting news stories, and ordinary people expressing their memories. The tradition of the Palais-Royal stems not only from what this place is but also from what it has permitted people to accomplish (*Exhibition Catalogue* 1988, 2–35).

The tradition of theatre at the Palais-Royal illustrates this point of view. Theatre started at the Palais-Royal in 1636 with the first public presentation of Corneille's masterpiece *Le cid*. Molière followed with his Illustre Théâtre; he created many of his masterpieces at the Palais-Royal: *l'École des maris*, *l'École des femmes*, *Tartuffe*, *Le misanthrope*, *l'Avare*, and *Le malade imaginaire*. It is there that the longest, richest, and most famous French theatre tradition was born, and it continues today, as strong as ever. The Palais-Royal as an architectural environment played an important role in this development, but not the major one. The playwrights, the actors, the theatre administrators, and the spectators have always been the major players. Architecture has been essential only in the sense that it has allowed these theatrical events to occur for more than three and a half centuries.

In addition to those of Corneille and Molière, scores of other playwrights' masterpieces were created or played at the Palais-Royal. These include works by Racine (*Andromaque, Britannicus, Phèdre*), Beaumarchais (*Le barbier de Séville, Le mariage de Figaro*), Marivaux (*Le jeu de l'amour et du hasard*), Victor Hugo (*Hernani, Ruy Blas*), Edmond Rostand (*Cyrano de Bergerac*) – just to name the best-known ones. In 1866, Jacques Offenbach created at the Palais-Royal the famous musical *La vie parisienne* based on lyrics by Meilhac and Halévy. This fabulous success followed two earlier ones, *Orphée aux enfers* and *La belle Hélène*. The cancan was created and La Belle Époque began. The Palais-Royal theatre saw the triumphs of some of France's greatest actors and actresses, notably Sarah Bernhardt and Gérard Philippe.

Boutiques

An analysis of the Palais-Royal boutiques may uncover another reason for the complex's lasting success. From the moment the Palais-Royal shopping centre opened in 1789 it was a fabulous commercial bonanza (*Exhibition Catalogue* 1988, 287–308). Overnight, four hundred boutiques sprang up to offer Parisians an immense variety of goods and services. Of these, 266 were jammed into a temporary wooden structure located between the cour d'Honneur and the garden and the other 134 were situated under the porticoes. This amazing popular success may be explained by the fact that these boutiques, as an ensemble, constituted a self-contained universe – the prototype for the modern North American shopping mall. The shops opened onto a public space, the garden, which was a gathering place outside of the ordinary circuits, attached to, yet outside, the city transportation system. It was a new place, not yet claimed by the political ruler. It was private property open to the public, a public place that happened to have a private owner. It belonged to a notorious aristocrat, Philippe d'Orléans, the king's cousin, who was clearly a powerful member of the establishment yet at the same time a self-declared Republican. People did not believe in the purity of Philippe-Égalité's motives, but recognized that he was willing to do business like an ordinary mortal. Parisians immediately perceived the Palais-Royal as exciting and new while still being a safe intermediate ground. Fanatic revolutionaries were not able to criticize their compatriots for going there because they were participating in the most proletarian of experiences, a collective happening enjoyed by the entire population of Paris, including the fanatic revolutionaries themselves. The fanatic reactionaries were also unable to criticize because the shopping centre had been created and was run by one of their own.

Another reason for the Palais-Royal's commercial success was the great diversity, variety, and complementarity of the commercial establishments that congregated there. Even as late as 1836, some fifty years after its opening, following a major clean-up ordered by Philippe d'Orléans that led to the wooden galleries being replaced by the upscale galerie d'Orléans shopping arcades, the list of the shops that remained at the Palais-Royal was still revealing: six reading salons, eleven bookstores, two print shops, eight painter's studios, two music shops, thirty-six jewellers, seventeen fashion boutiques (mostly women's), twenty-two collar, ribbon, and lace

The Palais-Royal's elegant garden is surrounded by elegant shops, cafés, restaurants, and apartments

shops, twenty tailors, eighteen restaurants, thirteen cafés, and other miscellaneous shops. The number of establishments has diminished over the years and the retail mix has changed. Among the stores that may be found at the Palais-Royal today are antique shops, medal and heraldic shops, stamp and lead toy-soldier shops, perfume and jewellery shops, women's apparel boutiques, a music-box shop, interior designers' boutiques, publishers' offices, and antiquarian bookstores. In all, seventy-four shops, cafés, and restaurants make up the present shopping centre.

Although some of these shops carry goods from all corners of the Earth, they have always been typically French in their spirit and attitude. France is a great and powerful nation with a strong, diversified economy. High-quality French products of all sorts abound, but the French have traditionally dominated the market when it comes to food and wine, luxury items, fashion, and cultural products. And, for the past two hundred years, these kinds of products have consistently been offered to Palais-Royal patrons. With regard to culture, democratic institutions, theatre, and gastronomy, the Palais-Royal certainly makes contributions of the highest calibre.

Domesticated Nature

To understand the architectural phenomenon as part of the larger ecological phenomenon, we must take into account two simultaneous and complementary dimensions of this reality: architecture in nature and nature in architecture. Since it was built, the Palais-Royal has been both a positive addition to the world's ecology and a respectful integrator of natural elements.

For Richelieu, the garden was almost as important as the palace itself. It was a central component of his vision. For Parisians of today, the two are impossible to perceive as separate entities. Nature has always been part of the Palais-Royal's architecture. Of course, the kind of nature that exists within the Palais-Royal complex is a domesticated one. The trees are trimmed, the grass is mown, and the roses are carefully nurtured; but this is still done as it has always been done – respectfully.

The Palais-Royal is a gentle object in nature. It does not unduly tax its sustaining power. The current environmental ideology is the so-called sustainable-development philosophy. This ecological attitude permeated the 1992 United Nations Conference on the Environment in Rio de Janeiro, at which a new international environmental blueprint, Agenda 21, was adopted. Based on the sustainable-development philosophy, the agenda stipulates that all physical-development projects on the planet must respect three conditions: they should satisfy the real needs of their users, take into account both short-term objectives and long-term goals, and be implemented in a fashion that fully respects the natural environment. The Palais-Royal is a magnificent example of sustainable development, and it was designed at least two centuries before the advent of environmental movements.

As we discussed earlier, urban pollution takes many forms: air pollution from fumes or dust; soil and water pollution from waste accumulation, dirt, and the depletion of flora or fauna; noise pollution; and visual pollution from, for example, ugly or chaotic signage. The Palais-Royal does not pollute Paris. But this is a negative statement. In fact, the Palais-Royal does more than not pollute its surroundings: it clearly makes a positive contribution to the enhancement of the planetary environment. Due to the Palais-Royal we all live in a better world.

Subtle Proportions

When we walk into the Palais-Royal's enclosures and pay attention to the surrounding architectural shapes, we feel a gentle harmony. Nothing is spectacular. There is no leaning tower as there is in Pisa, no breathtaking vistas as there are at Versailles, and no jewels of iridescent light as there are in the Sainte-Chapelle. The Palais-Royal is simply a well-proportioned, ordinary building.

Because of its size and complexity, the Palais-Royal embodies two kinds of vision: perspective views *en ras-de-façade* and perpendicular views of limited segments of long elevations. Most long façades are perceived on an acute angle. Our spatial experience of the Palais-Royal's circulation spaces, such as the porticoes and the peristyles, is a succession of discoveries. And the various façades – such as the garden façades, which can be fully seen only at the garden's ends where no trees obstruct the view – can be discovered only one at a time. The consequence of this is that it is practically impossible to achieve an overall impression of the Palais-Royal's proportions.

What is possible, however, is to perceive details or segments of façades in succession, and then what we experience are glimpses of proportion. Golden Section proportions and other harmonic ratios appear in many places in overlapping patterns. For example, they are detected on the galerie de Nemours and galerie d'Orléans colonnades, on the eastern façade of the galerie d'Orléans, on the Moreau-Desproux/rue Saint-Honoré façade, and on the garden façades and porticoes of the Victor Louis residential wings.

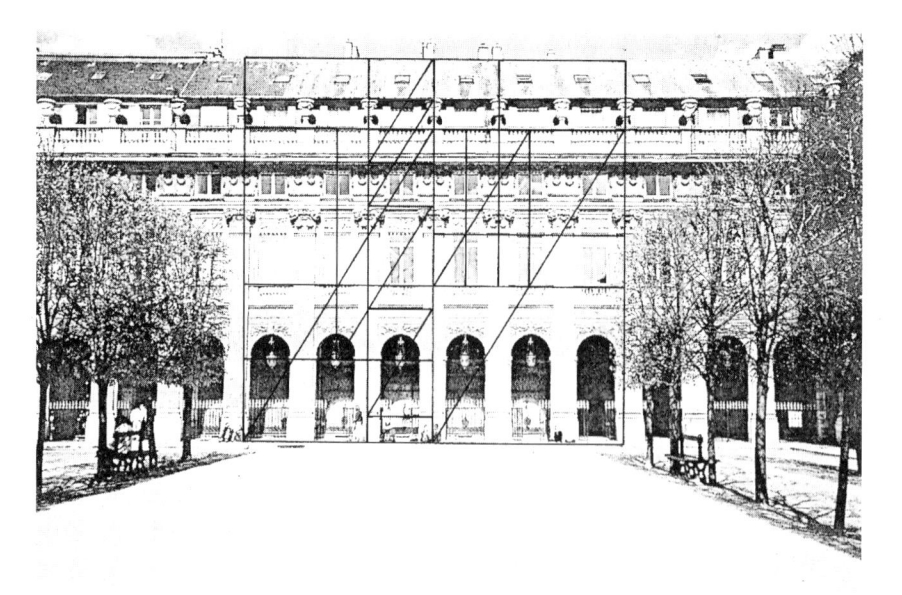

The well-proportioned garden façade of the Palais-Royal was designed by Victor Louis and built between 1785 and 1788, just before the French Revolution

Rectilinearity

The Palais-Royal is the triumph of the straight line and the right angle. It is composed of long, straight horizontal lines interrupted at right angles by shorter straight lines. The garden is composed of straight lines and rectangles. The overall architectural composition is organized according to longitudinal and transversal straight axes (even though few elements actually respect the axial composition). Curved lines appear at the level of the details: the semicircular arches, the round columns, the balusters, the urns, and the decorative floral motifs. But these curvilinear elements are well disciplined and integrated into the larger rectilinear geometry.

The use of the straight line and the right angle to generate a basic spatial organization illustrates, among many other things, what is called "l'esprit logique français"; that is, the desire for clarity through impeccable logic (Fichet 1979, 21). In his essay *Architecture and the Crisis of Modern Science*, Alberto Pérez-Gómez acknowledged and documented the intellectual relationship between Descartes and the seventeenth- and eighteenth-century architectural theoreticians (Pérez-Gómez 1983). In his *Histoire de*

Paris, Pierre Lavedan argued that "Cartesianism was at the basis of Parisian classical urban aesthetic, and that it was in the design of the 17th century *places royales* that it best expressed itself" (Lavedan 1960, 52). Christian Norberg-Schulz, for his part, explained that in seventeenth-century Paris, "it appear[ed] that the world was understood as a series of geometrically ordered extensions" (Norberg-Schulz 1980, 150). Of course, these places and "extensions" were Versailles, Cours-la-Reine, the Louvre, place des Vosges, place Vendôme, and place de la Concorde – artefacts where straight lines dominate. They were the models for the various Palais-Royal architectural compositions,[65] models supported by the ideas of the Enlightenment, articulated by thinkers such as André Félibien, François Blondel, Denis Diderot, and Nicolas Boileau. As secretary of Louis XIV's Academy of Painting, Félibien published a series of treatises on the lives and works of several painters; in them, he claimed that beauty was based on reason. In his *Cours d'architecture*, published between 1675 and 1685, Blondel insisted that, in architectural composition, the exigencies of reason were paramount. Boileau argued for clarity as a condition of beauty (Boileau 1959). In his encyclopedia article on "the beautiful," published in 1750, Diderot wrote that beauty is based on the concept of relationships and that "in beautiful things, we admit only the sort of relationship that a good mind can seize clearly and easily" (Diderot 1946).

Although these were the ideas that influenced the Palais-Royal's architects, no one will claim that the use of the straight line and the pursuit of simplicity and clarity are exclusive to French architecture. Rectilinear architectural masterpieces abound in all civilizations (the Parthenon and the Katsura Villa in Kyoto are two examples among many), and the search for clarity is no more French than are logic, good taste, or gastronomy.

But if clear logic, axial composition, rectilinear spatial organization, straight lines, and right angles are universal features, they are also peculiarly French. Over the centuries, French architects have favoured these features. The Palais-Royal's simple, clear, and easily recognizable frame of reference may therefore serve to explain how the complex's architects were able to adapt to preceding designs and constantly improve upon the ideas of the past.

Discreet Sensuality

In spite of its straight lines, the Palais-Royal gives the impression of being a sensual building. It is like a dignified, chic, mature lady who has known moments of glory and endured periods of turmoil. What she is today is

Depending upon the season or the hour of the day, the Palais-Royal can offer multiple gathering places for those seeking out the sun

determined by what she has been through, and this has engendered in her an attitude of dignified wisdom. The Palais-Royal is a place of tenderness, a place that elicits a gentle smile, a place more feminine than masculine.

Do such sexual metaphors for buildings illustrate collective mentalities and define social peculiarities? We could say that North American skyscrapers are male buildings because of their obvious phallic connotation. We could also argue that because Victorian and North American Anglo architects have shied away from designing public enclosures and have conceived each building as an isolated fortress, they must belong to male-dominated societies. Conversely, we could maintain that the tendency of Italian, French, and Spanish architects to design buildings as parts of a larger enclosure represents the more feminine orientation of their own societies. These debatable ideas were raised by Gaston Bachelard. In his essay on fire, the French philosopher discussed the complementary principles of femininity and masculinity. He wrote, "the feminine principle of things is a principle of surface and envelope, of torso [*giron*], refuge, and warmth. The masculine principle is a principle of centre, a centre of power, active, sudden like the spark and the will. The feminine warmth attacks things from the outside. The masculine fire does it from the inside" (Bachelard 1949, 96).

A gender-based view of architecture is clearly an oversimplification. Nonetheless, because of its enclosing central principle, the Palais-Royal gives the impression of being a feminine place designed by men who loved women and enjoyed the pleasures of life. Richelieu was not always a cold political animal; he had his tender moments (Michelet 1966; Champier 1991). Louis XIV's brother, Monsieur, was a hermaphrodite who devoted his entire life to sensual gratification (Dufresne 1991). The regent was a tolerant, gentle, highly gifted whore. In its glory days after the French Revolution, the Palais-Royal housed more brothels than it is possible to imagine.

Today, the Palais-Royal's playful, pleasure-seeking aspect is more subdued than it was during that hectic period between 1788 and 1830, but it does endure to a certain extent. It seems that the people who have enjoyed the Palais-Royal most are people of refined sensuality, individuals such as Molière, Colette, and Cocteau. If the Palais-Royal is likened, once again, to a mature, sophisticated lady, she is a *grande dame* who has had an adventurous love life and is still very seductive. As she moves through life, she is eternally feminine, like Coco Chanel or Sarah Bernhardt; she answers a compliment with a twinkle of her golden eye, a nod of her head, a graceful gesture of her hand, and a radiant smile.

Situated at the centre of the Palais-Royal garden, the fountain is a favourite resting place

Rhythmic Porticoes

If there is one architectural feature that truly distinguishes the Palais-Royal it is its porticoes. Since the French Revolution, popular images of the Palais-Royal have shown crowds mingling under those porticoes. The same images have been used to praise and to criticize the Palais-Royal as a place for joyful entertainment and a place for sinful cajolery. This is because the porticoes were always at the centre of the action. They played, and still play, many roles simultaneously. They act as intermediate interior-exterior spaces, as main corridors, as a shopping promenade, as a shelter from harsh weather. When they become peristyles they indicate the entrances. When they transform themselves into free-standing porticoes they separate the three interior public spaces. And they establish the rhythm of the entire composition.

At the Palais-Royal, a rhythm is created of continuous, overlapping movements that translate into sounds ranging from a big bass beat to a high, tremulous melodic note. On the long garden façades, two-storey pilasters provide the regular bass line of the composition. Over that runs the softer, more complex rhythm of the trees that stand out from a tranquil background of sand alleys and lawns, adorned here and there by rose bushes and statues. Suddenly, the fountain splashes a counterpoint. Inserted into the pilasters, the semicircular arches furnish the composition's main melodic line; their circular lines link the bass rhythm's straight lines. These arches wrap themselves around the buildings, become pilasters and columns. On the ornate façades of the Conseil d'État, they become a principal decorative element – again semi-circular arches within pilasters or columns. On top of the main melody, the rectangular windows add yet another level of rhythm; here and there, the awnings above them play variations on the main theme. Finally, the small architectural elements, the vertical spears of the iron fences, the decorative floral motifs, the stone urns, and the balusters, all combine to enrich the architectural composition. As I try to describe, perhaps in a clumsy way, the compelling architectural rhythm of the Palais-Royal, Ravel's *Boléro* comes to mind. It is a piece of music in which each increasingly rich layer of rhythm spreads itself over the preceding ones to create, in the end, a fascinating composition.

Character

How does one decipher the character of the Palais-Royal? Is it perceptible in the a manner of a period? Can it be expressed through behaviour? Can it be found in a certain physical attribute?

To link character to the manner of a certain period and describe the Palais-Royal as a neoclassical composition would be pointless because it would neither illuminate the Palais-Royal's physical reality nor explain the perception of its users. In architectural history, style is only a label invented by art historians in order to classify buildings in chronologically visual categories. To say that the Palais-Royal is a neoclassical building does little to explain its enduring love affair with Parisians.

If character is expressed through certain behaviour, then the Palais-Royal attitude might be one of sobriety, of politeness. The Palais-Royal treats people in a courteous way. There is nothing constrictive in its demeanour. It is habitually civilized. The Palais-Royal does not make an effort to be gracious; such comportment comes naturally. Or perhaps it appears to come naturally because it is the result of a long tradition. Buildings are like people, they need to be educated and taught how to behave. Modern buildings are often so crude that they are immediately covered with graffiti. The Palais-Royal respects Parisians and, in return, they respect it. Over the years, the Palais-Royal's owners and designers have treated the complex's users with civility, graciousness, affability, and even gallantry.

If character is to be found in a physical attribute, in appearances, then the Palais-Royal has the subtle character of two of its most illustrious residents, the writers Colette and Jean Cocteau. Colette lived for more than twenty years at 9 rue de Beaujolais. Cocteau depicted the great novelist traversing the Palais-Royal garden with caressing words: "Children are playing police and burglar games in the garden. A queen disturbs their tumultuous adventures. She is Madame Colette, a hat on her shrubby hair, a scarf around the neck, naked feet in her sandals and a cane in her hand. Like those of a lioness, her magnificent eye severely observe those games of war, police and crime" (Cocteau in *Exhibition Catalogue* 1988, 285).[66]

Cocteau himself lived for many years at 36 rue de Montpensier, and wrote this magical description of his Palais-Royal home: "Surrounded by an iron fence and a China wall through which steep staircases lead outside, the Palais-Royal is a small town in a large town. Guarded by cats, this small town has its own ways and uses, and natives like Venetian gondoliers who have never seen a horse or a carriage. Our natives seem to know only the vaults, the lampposts, the alleys, the gold tipped fence, and the labyrinth where discreet shops sell libertine books, stamps and medals" (Cocteau in *Exhibition Catalogue* 1988, 285).[67]

The Palais-Royal's character also comes from the gastronomic restaurant the Grand Véfour. Jean Véfour – who had already bought and transformed the Café de Chartres, situated at the northwest corner of the Palais-Royal garden – created the famous establishment in 1820. It was an immediate success due to the quality of its food and the sumptuousness of its decor. During and after the Second Empire, it became the favourite restaurant of many celebrities such as Victor Hugo; historian and statesman Adolphe Thiers; Marshal Mac-Mahon, the victorious general of the battles of Sebastopol and Magenta; and writer Sainte-Beuve. After World War II, the entire French literary intelligentsia frequented the Grand Véfour. Colette, Malraux, Sacha Guitry, and Elsa Triolet regularly dined at the restaurant, at that point owned by one of the greatest chefs of modern France, Raymond Oliver. In 1983, the restaurant was severely damaged by a terrorist bomb. In typical Palais-Royal fashion, it was immediately reconstructed and emerged as lavish as before.

A Place for All

When the revolutionary Déclaration des droits de l'homme et du citoyen was issued, three words were inscribed forever in the minds and hearts of every French citizen: *liberté, égalité, fraternité*. Within the Palais-Royal, these words are translated into reality. It is there that the Conseil d'État and the Conseil Constitutionnel perform their prime duty, which is to protect these three words, to see that the French Constitution is respected. At the Comédie-Française, all citizens of France share their most profound, their most cherished common cultural treasure, the French language. Language is more important to the French than it is to people of other cultures. For instance, for several years, the most popular television programme in France was *Apostrophe* with Bernard Pivot, a literary talk show. There are two main national institutions that defend and interpret the French language: the Académie française and the Comédie-Française. The former concerns itself with protecting the language while the latter brilliantly illustrates its richness and versatility. Every day at the Palais-Royal a celebration of the French language takes place, a celebration that affects all francophones.

Richelieu, who certainly did not believe in Republican values, created the Palais-Royal under the Ancien Régime. Nonetheless, he incorporated a theatre and a garden as public amenities. The French Revolution found a home at the Palais-Royal in spite of its Old Regime name and its aristocratic owner. This was because the Palais-Royal did not discriminate. All citizens were, and still are, welcome in its garden and porticoes.

Successful Architecture

At the end of our tour, we, the visitors, should reflect on the purpose of the theory we have been working towards in this book: it is a system of thought that is intended to be useful in the practice of architecture. The imperatives of the architect's mission continue to colour our inquiry. However, having adopted a phenomenological attitude, we have enhanced our observation and described without preconception the Palais-Royal as it presents itself to us, because what we are attempting to decipher through this phenomenological probe is the enigma of the Palais-Royal's successful existence. The three questions that we asked frequently during our visit were: Is the architecture of the Palais-Royal successful? If so, why? Could it be a model for a successful architecture elsewhere?

What we discovered was that the Palais-Royal is today a cherished piece of architecture that is well loved and thriving. We observed that people pay large sums of money for the privilege of living there. We were told that no Palais-Royal apartment has ever stood vacant since the residential wings opened in 1785. This demonstration of uninterrupted satisfaction is certainly a sign of success.

At the Palais-Royal, children play in galerie d'Orléans under the windows of the Conseil Constitutionnel, the Comédie-Française, and the Ministry of Culture

The Palais-Royal is a part of the French heritage and, as such, is protected by the community. An architecture that has attained the cultural status of historical timelessness is, by definition, successful.

The architecture of the Palais-Royal is successful because it has never ceased to contribute to its surroundings. It is a positive component of the urban fabric of Paris. Its boutiques strengthen the first arrondissement's retail network; they are a key ingredient of the city's unique quality of life. As a zone primarily for pedestrians, the Palais-Royal offers Parisians a haven of security and serenity. It is an inner-city housing complex in a district that has lost many of its residential units, and as such it has helped to counteract this unfortunate trend.

The architecture of the Palais-Royal is successful because its spaces for intimate meetings and its spaces for communal gatherings have achieved an equilibrium. At the Palais-Royal, private areas blend with public ones; they complement and assist one another. The private places take care of the public places, which, in turn, look after the private places. An architecture has reached its full potential when, as in the Palais-Royal, the individuality of each element balances with the harmonious fusion of them all.

The architecture of the Palais-Royal is successful because the impression of order it gives is punctuated with countless surprising incongruities, because its grandeur is always mitigated by humorous understatement. It is perhaps a serious architecture, but certainly one that does not take itself too seriously. This obvious lack of ostentation is certainly a major factor in its lasting success; people feel comfortable in such places where dignity is enhanced by conviviality. That is why we see children playing every day at the Palais-Royal under the windows of France's supreme courts.

The architecture of the Palais-Royal is successful because it is well-proportioned. The complex has the sort of timeless appearance that pleases children as well as older people. Because the Palais-Royal is at peace with the world people are at peace with it – and in it. With its tranquil beauty and its exquisite serenity, the Palais-Royal respects the people who use it, and they, in return, protect it.

Finally, the architecture of the Palais-Royal is successful because it is architecture within architecture. It is an urban complex at the centre of Paris that is accessible both in the sense that it is easy to get to and in the sense that it is welcoming. And it is connected. It encompasses a wide variety of spaces and functions that serve a rich diversity of human needs, desires, aspirations, and dreams. Even though it is a very large place, the Palais-Royal displays an architecture that is always related to the size of the humans it has been created to serve. Its success stems from the fact that it is an architectural artefact that caters to the most civilized of personal attributes. In a harsh and brutal world, it is a little corner of Heaven on Earth. The Palais-Royal is a place where people can be tender, helpful, and caring towards one another.

Many characteristics underpin the multifaceted quality and mature beauty of the Palais-Royal, and, ultimately, its lasting success. What could be their unifying attribute? If the architect wishes to design a new artefact that displays the same sort of feature that made the Palais-Royal a success, how will he go about it? Obviously an outright copy is not appropriate, because needs and circumstances have changed dramatically overtime. Perhaps what we should explore further are the inherent, phenomenological characteristics of the idea of beauty, because beauty is a dimension of the Palais-Royal's success. And we should also investigate the characteristics of quality because the Palais-Royal's level of quality may also explain its success. In the Palais-Royal, as in all other successful architectural artefacts, the idea of beauty seems inseparable from the idea of quality. If this is true, what we need to discover is a design mechanism that has the power to integrate, in architecture, high quality with great beauty.

Dwelling at the Palais-Royal

Beyond everything else, the architecture of the Palais-Royal is successful because the complex is, fundamentally, a nonrestrictive enclosure that protects and satisfies the people who live in it, work in it, and visit it. It is simultaneously a fortress and a launching pad, a place in which to feel safe and from which to conquer the universe. A sheltering dwelling with a spirit that enhances the human spirit, the Palais-Royal reflects the soul of its users and embodies the unique spirit of Paris. A short text on the Palais-Royal written by Colette beautifully evokes this Parisian spirit:

Our dear Colette was speaking in this way: "By choice, I came and returned to the Palais-Royal. Could one find laziness in this rectangular cloister, haunted by pigeons and cats? I do not believe so. If I had the time, perhaps I would find a certain melancholy in this imprisoned garden. Its interior design is sloppy somewhat, its walls crooked and floors warped, and, behind these beautiful rigid façades, all this ages, deteriorates, plays and changes, and seems to attract busy hosts. My ordinary evenings make less noise than falling leaves, or than the claws of cats scratching the trees' bark. During the day, my deep refuge is not noisy. But I have the luck to be rocked by a muffled vibration, marvellously similar to that of a propeller." (Colette 1987–88)[68]

The many Parisians who gather at the Palais-Royal every day consider its architecture highly successful

The architecture of the Palais-Royal is one that values people more than structures. It is an architecture that has never ceased to be alive. Its excellence and magnificence are undoubtedly due to its physical reality; but, perhaps more importantly, these qualities also stem from the fact that this architecture gives people the opportunity to excel. Architecture is fundamentally a vessel for human activity, a means to an end. Great architecture helps humans to accomplish great things; civilizing architecture encourages civilized attitudes and endeavours. The great accomplishments of civilized peoples are not only such things as the mounting of a revolution, the creation of a theatrical masterpiece, or the preparation and enjoyment of a gastronomic feast, but they are also the simplest daily achievements, activities carried out in a highly civilized way – taking children outdoors to play, reading a book in the sun, or meeting a friend for a cup of coffee. At the Palais-Royal, people live their lives, and the excellent and magnificent environment the complex provides helps them to do this better.

The architecture of the Palais-Royal creates civilization by defying time. It is a place always in the present, riding the crest of the wave of time. French professor of architecture Jacques Boulet wrote that the Palais-Royal is a fragment of a city (Boulet and Gresset 1984). He showed that it is a perpetually unfinished environment, constantly in the making. Today, as always, it vibrates with life, and no doubt will continue to do so as new generations come and go. The architectural present holds memories of past lives and carries with it into the future souvenirs of those being lived today. The lives of people transcend the life of architecture.

The Palais-Royal is a piece of eternity on earth.

6

FONDATION ROTHSCHILD WORKERS' RESIDENCE: AN HONEST ELEGANCE

You are now invited to accompany me to a remarkable residential complex in a traditional working-class neighbourhood of Paris, the twelfth arrondissement.

My first visit there was late on a Thursday afternoon in September 1994. Many more were to follow. I wanted to see a subsidized housing complex that had been brought to my attention by a French colleague.[69] Fortunately, he had provided me with an address – 8, rue de Prague. I could not have found the complex without this information. No exterior features distinguished it from its neighbours. Should foreign visitors be surprised to find that this, a home for less affluent Parisians, does not stand out from those around it that bear no such social stigma? Should they be astonished that this edifice looks even better than many of these surrounding buildings? In the course of our visit to 8 rue de Prague we will discover that this housing complex is, in fact, a remarkable architectural artefact in an exceptional neighbourhood. We will also be reminded that quality of life and quality of architecture are more than a matter of money.

An Inconspicuous Presence

The twelfth arrondissement of Paris is the notorious faubourg Saint-Antoine, where craftsmen have been making wooden furniture since cabinetmaker Jean Cottillon settled there in 1472.[70] Cottillon was the first of the free artisans – that is, free of the corporate control of the cabinet-makers' guild – invited to practise under the protection of a women's abbey, Saint-Antoine-des-Champs, situated outside the Saint-Antoine gate, in full view of the Bastille fortress (Diwo 1984). It is perhaps because of this

Expressive architectural details adorn the Fondation Rothschild Workers' Residence

tradition of freedom that the faubourg's workers took part in all the uprisings that shook Paris over the centuries (Flamand 1989, 20).

During my first encounter with the rue de Prague complex, I just wanted to get the feel of the place. For three hours, I wandered around the complex. What I observed was constant movement – people going in and out of the building through one of its three courtyards, usually greeting one another in a polite manner and often engaging in a little conversation. I saw giggling teenaged girls coming home from school. I witnessed with interest a lady entering the janitor's office, emerging from it, stopping another lady who was crossing the central courtyard, speaking with her, and returning to the janitor's office. She seemed to be on a mission of some sort. I noticed two cooks smoking cigaretts, leaning on the open backdoor of a restaurant kitchen. An older lady with a net bag of groceries, no doubt returning from the nearby food market, greeted a well-dressed young woman with two little children. A group of perhaps twenty small children emerged from what I then thought was a day-care centre – I later learned that it was the annex of an elementary school located across the street – and were picked up by their parents. A gentleman with a folder under his arm rushed out of one of the complex's entrances, followed seconds later by several other people. I then had my first chat with the very amiable head janitor who was at that moment busy painting the iron front gate. In short, what I did was witness a vibrant community functioning in a normal way.

The people I observed were living, working, perhaps visiting, at 8 rue de Prague, a large edifice built in 1909 by a private philanthropic foundation, the Fondation Rothschild (Dumont 1991). Today, the housing complex comprises 297 apartments, 26 shops, and 37 workshops.[71] At the outset, it contained 324 apartments; over the years, small flats were combined to form larger apartments (Hervé 1994). Even by current stringent French social-housing standards,[72] these apartments are small: 50 percent of them are one-room bachelor units with a total area ranging from twenty to thirty square metres; 25 percent are two-room units with a total area of between forty and forty-five square metres; and the remaining three-room units are between fifty and fifty-five square metres.

The edifice is an eight-storey[73] continuous building, on the edge of a 5,630 square metre site, forming an isosceles triangle, its apex pointing east. Rue de Prague runs north-south along the base of the triangle.[74] The triangle's other two sides are bordered by rue Théophile-Roussel (northwest-southeast) and rue Charles-Baudelaire (southwest-northeast). The south apex of the site is slightly truncated by rue Emilio-Castelar. Emerging at right angles from the parts of the edifice that form the short sides of the

The rue de Prague façade of the Fondation Rothschild Workers' Residence displays a rhythmic continuity

triangle, two wings protrude inward creating three interconnected courtyards. These have large gateways opening onto the street.[75] The complex has no corridors, as all apartment doors open onto staircase landings. There are eighteen such staircases, and, except for one, all rise from one of the three courtyards. Recently, the staircases have been renovated and elevators added. Shops and other service centres occupy the ground-floor space, and most face the exterior sidewalks. At the complex's south end there is a wing comprised of what were originally cabinetmaking workshops; today, they are used by other sorts of commercial tenants.

Circling the complex, we notice that its retail and community facilities are of a higher quality, certainly not the kind of establishments we would expect to find in an American subsidized-housing environment. There is a bookstore, an art-supply store, a Vietnamese restaurant, a community restaurant catering mainly to needy senior citizens, an art-book publisher's office, a hi-fi/video shop, a British shoe store, a laundromat, a designer's studio, a printer's workshop, a plumbing-heating contractor's office, and a police station. We also see what appear to be several thriving small businesses occupying the workshop wing, including a dental laboratory, a camera-repair shop employing some forty technicians, an electronic-electrical workshop, a dance and martial-arts school, an advertising agency, and a computer consulting firm. The elementary-school annex occupies another wing. In all, some 700 people live, and about 250 more study or work, in this complex.

A Philanthropic Landlord

The Fondation Rothschild complex is still owned and managed by the same private nonprofit corporation that built it. On 27 June 1904, the three Rothschild brothers, Alphonse, Gustave, and Edmond, announced to the French trade minister their intention to create "a foundation devoted to the improvement of workers' material existence." They were prepared to invest ten million gold francs in the project (Hervé 1994; Dumont 1991, 31–40; Flamand 1989, 112). In those days, this was a colossal sum. Such an unusual philanthropic gesture sent tremors through France's political and financial worlds. It also changed the course of history with respect to social-housing architecture and community planning.

The Rothschild barons were bankers, not industrialists with battalions of workers to care for. Their interest in social housing was indirect, stemming from broad social and political concerns. They sincerely wanted to help the working class (Flamand 1989, 110). Like many well-educated members of

174 IN SEARCH OF ELEGANCE

Schematic ground-floor plan of the Fondation Rothschild Workers' Residence

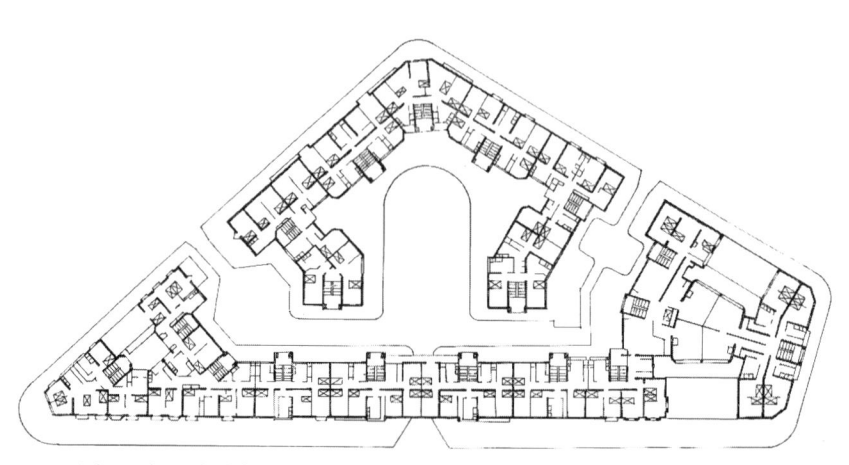

Schematic typical floor plan of the Fondation Rothschild Workers' Residence

France's nineteenth-century bourgeoisie,[76] the Rothschilds were of the opinion that enormous wealth carries with it a social responsibility. It was in order to assume this responsibility in a concrete way that they undertook to establish housing complexes that would embody all the modern social ideas. Influenced by social activists such as Jules Ferry, Émile Cheysson, Georges Picot, Jules Siegfried, and J.B.A. Godin, they believed in the power of education to improve living conditions. The housing complexes they wanted to build would be models of their kind – high-quality residences as well as instruments of social improvement. They felt that a well-housed worker was a happy worker and the best guarantee of political stability. That they chose the tough faubourg Saint-Germain as the site of their flagship project was not a coincidence; it was, rather, the result of a well-thought-out social-engineering strategy.

The formula of employing a private corporation to establish social housing is an interesting one, and, in this case at least, it has proven efficacious for almost a century. According to this formula, a private institution is granted a special status and becomes what is called, in France, a "société reconnue d'intérêt public," – that is, a corporation recognized as serving the public interest. The Fondation Rothschild received this special recognition on 27 July 1904. Three main characteristics define the formula. First, the corporation has to be a non-profit one. Its shareholders, called members, cannot pocket its profits. If a surplus is generated, it is reinvested in the corporation's activities. Second, the corporation has to have a well-defined social mission. In the case of the Fondation Rothschild, it is to build and manage housing for workers. And third, the corporation must submit to strict fiscal control. Between 1907 and 1919, the Fondation Rothschild built five housing complexes, thereby creating 1,125 residential units (Dumont 1991, 168). When acquisitions made after 1980 are added to the list, the foundation's current holdings are 12 buildings housing 1,247 apartments, 1 school, 88 workshops, 81 shops, and 11 parking places (Hervé 1994). Thanks to excellent design, high-quality construction, and, more importantly, constant and meticulous maintenance, all the buildings are in excellent condition. The rue de Prague complex is the most famous of all subsidized housing projects built between 1900 and World War I, and it served as the model not only for the five Fondation Rothschild projects but also for practically all multiunit social-housing projects of that period. At the time of its inauguration, the press called it "the Louvre of social housing" (Quilliot 1989, 76).

This management formula facilitates a very fruitful collaboration between the public and private sectors. A private company with private funds builds privately owned facilities devoted entirely to realizing certain social objectives. The architectural result is a dignified yet convivial private residence with courtyards open to visitors. Unless they wish to go to the shops facing the surrounding sidewalks, residents and visitors alike are invited to pass through the complex's open iron gates and enter the courtyards before penetrating the building itself. As a courtesy, these semipublic – or semiprivate – spaces are impeccably maintained by the private owner. Originally, the complex's community services and many of its shops were for the exclusive use of complex residents; today, the shops cater to the general public and the school annex welcomes children from other residences.

When the complex opened in 1909, some 750 people applied for each of the 324 apartments (Hervé 1994). Since then, vacancies have been extremely rare; if a unit did become available, it was vacant only for as long as it took to clean and repair it. In eighty-five years, practically no tenant has left for negative reasons such as unsatisfactory living conditions or unacceptable management practices. As a rule, people live in their rue de Prague apartments until they die. Often, children take over a flat from their parents. Many current residents were born and raised in the complex. After World War I, although the cost of living had quadrupled during the war, the French government froze residential rents in order to protect tenants – mainly war widows – from eviction. At the entrance to the rue de Prague complex, a marble plaque lists the names of tenants who died during the Great War. Thirty-one names are inscribed; that is, almost 10 percent of the complex's households. The negative side of the rent-freeze legislation was that it meant private foundations such as the Fondation Rothschild would no longer be able to finance the construction of new projects. That is why it reverted to acting exclusively as a property manager. Its original ten-million-franc investment was all it had in its coffers. It is a tribute to the foundation's prudent and rigorous management that, for almost a century, it has been able to finance the maintenance, upgrading, and administration of its properties with its own operating budget – that is, with rental income – alone.

Initially, the monthly rent for a two-room, forty-five square metre flat was thirty-five francs. In 1994, the same flat, renovated and refurbished with a new toilet, bathroom, and kitchen, would have gone for two thousand francs per month, which is the fair market price for a comparable facility in a comparable neighbourhood.[77] However, for the same flat not yet upgraded and occupied for many years by the same tenant, the rent could run as low as 744 francs per month. According to the social-housing laws in France, a landlord cannot evict a tenant who behaves normally. The law further stipulates that tenants cannot be forced to accept upgrades of their flats for the purpose of raising the rent; they may, however, accept an upgrade of their own free will, and, as a result, pay more rent. At rue de Prague today, management gives tenants the choice of accepting an upgrade of their facility and an increased rent or maintaining the status quo. Many longtime tenants choose to remain in their unrenovated flats in order to keep their rent low. As soon as a flat is vacated, however, it is upgraded.

An Intense Neighbourhood

The simplistic, conventional view holds that subsidized housing is necessarily associated with a dilapidated neighbourhood. The rue de Prague complex contradicts this facile assertion, as it lies at the centre of one of the most interesting and lively districts of Paris. Tucked between rue du Faubourg-Saint-Antoine and rue de Charenton, near the Ledru-Rollin metro station, no more than ten minutes from place de la Bastille, it enjoys direct access to a panoply of high-quality urban amenities.

On its northeast side, the residence fronts square Armand-Trousseau,[78] one of the many charming little Parisian parks that were designed according to the same model. These squares often occupy a rectangular city block, three to four times greater in length than in width, and are surrounded by streets. One of their short sides is bordered by a major commercial street. For example, in the fifteenth arrondissement, place du Commerce touches rue du Commerce, and square Adolphe-Chérioux touches rue de Vaugirard. Square Armand-Trousseau is bordered by rue du Faubourg-Saint-Antoine. A community facility of some kind often fronts the parks' other short sides. At place du Commerce, it is a pavilion housing social services; at square Adolphe-Chérioux, it is the fifteenth arrondissement town hall; at square Armand-Trousseau, it is the Fondation Rothschild complex. The two long sides of each of these parks are lined with bourgeois residential buildings that have shops on their ground floors. A band stand invaded by pigeons almost invariably stands at the centre of each park. On each of the two long sides, rows of either plane trees or chestnut trees define the space and provide a sense of enclosure. The ground is usually covered with the golden gravel found throught Paris. Strips of grass or flower beds fringe the sidewalks.

Like the other small parks, square Armand-Trousseau serves as a playground; it is frequently alive with the shouts of children and the chatter of

Schematic plan of the Fondation Rothschild Workers' Residence and its neighbourhood, including square Armand-Trousseau, place d'Aligre and marché de Bauveau

Square Armand-Trousseau, facing the Fondation Rothschild Workers' Residence, is a typical Parisian *square*: a community garden and playground

adults. In the afternoon, we hear the laughter of preschoolers as their mothers or grandmothers (nannies are rare in this proletarian environment) push them on swings. After school, the air is filled with the louder noises of the older children who swarm into the park equipped with footballs. Some kids play ping-pong on cement tables, while others use the bandstand as a roller-skating rink. In the early evenings and on weekends, we may want to linger awhile and try to decipher the strategic remarks of the *pétanque* players. And at any hour of the day, practically every day of the year, we may overhear the softer sounds of the retired citizens who sit on the park benches conversing about their health, the cost of living, politics, and world affairs. Like Diderot's haunt, the d'Argenson bench at the Palais-Royal, these benches are the sort of place where mere mortals become philosophers.

Square Armand-Trousseau is not the neighbourhood's only amenity. Across rue Charles-Baudelaire, in front of the complex, one finds a kindergarten, an elementary school, and a junior high school, Collège Paul-Verlaine. A stone's throw from these, on rue de Cotte, sits a newly constructed municipal day-care centre. Teenagers living at the Fondation

Rothschild complex can choose from more than fifteen different high schools located within a half-hour's walk from rue de Prague. Some of these are public liberal-arts schools, such as Lycée Arago and Lycée Paul Valéry, others are private institutions, such as Lycée et Collège Privés Charles-Péguy, and others, still, are specialized institutions, such as the Lycée Professionnel on rue Ledru-Rollin. Not far away, on rue Pierre-Bourdan, towards place de la Nation, is the famous École Boule, or Lycée Professionnel des Métiers de l'Ameublement,[79] named in honour of the great seventeenth-century cabinetmaker, an institution that keeps the neighbourhood's cabinetmaking tradition alive. Two major hospitals, Hôpital des Quinze-Vingts[80] and Hôpital Saint-Antoine, are less than ten minutes (for pedestrians) from the rue de Prague complex. The latter occupies the site where the abbey of Saint-Antoine-des-Champs once stood.

Leaving the Fondation Rothschild complex and walking east on either rue Théophile-Rousseau or rue Emilio-Castelar, we reach in less than two minutes the famous semicircular place d'Aligre and the adjacent covered market, Marché de Bauveau. I say "famous" because this food marketplace is rich in history; even those Parisians who have never visited the Marché Bauveau know of it. In 1776, the abbess of Notre-Dame-des-Champs[81] gave a small corner of the abbey's land to a certain Monsieur de Cerville on the understanding that he would build a new straw and hay market there. The new facility was to replace the traditional market, which, for more than four centuries, had been set up in front of the abbey gate, in the middle of the road that would later become rue du Faubourg-Saint-Antoine. A victim of its own success, the market created traffic congestion, blocking the abbey's front door. It was in order to solve this problem that the abbess initiated the building of a new facility. The timber structure of the new market was designed by the architect Lenoir and erected within two years. In 1778, the straw and hay market settled into its new quarters and began to flourish. Eleven years later, on 14 July 1789, revolutionaries on their way to the Bastille ransacked it. They needed the straw to set the fortress on fire. In 1843, the market was rebuilt, and a small service building with a clock tower was constructed in the middle of the plaza (Hillairet 1957, 74). Over the years, produce other than straw and hay was sold, and, during the twentieth century, with the disappearance of the horse-drawn carriage as a mode of transportation, this other produce totally replaced the initial commodities. After World War II, some of the older buildings forming the square's semicircular border were demolished and replaced by ordinary-looking modern structures. Fortunately, on market days, these buildings disappear behind the tightly packed stands that jam the square.

The Marché de Bauveau and the place d'Aligre food market are a two-minute walk from the Fondation Rothschild Workers' Residence

Today, the place d'Aligre market is as popular as ever. It spreads beyond the covered structure and the square; stalls overflow into the adjoining rue d'Aligre. The market continues to offer not only the widest variety of high-quality farm produce, but also flowers, garments, and secondhand objects of all kinds. The French call this kind of bric-a-brac commerce "la brocante." Open every day of the week except Monday, the market undoubtedly constitutes one of the main features of the neighbourhood's exceptional quality of life. Living one block away from the market, residents of the Fondation Rothschild are close enough to enjoy the market regularly, yet far enough away to be shielded from its clamour.

The d'Aligre market is not, by any means, the only shopping centre in the faubourg. Scores of commercial establishments line most of the streets, notably rue du Faubourg-Saint-Antoine, rue de Charenton, avenue Ledru-Rollin, and the newly renovated avenue Daumesnil. The latter is the site of one of the most interesting urban-design projects Paris has seen in years. Located five minutes from the Fondation Rothschild complex, it substantially increases the neighbourhood's already exceptional quality of life. An abandoned elevated rail line, which runs alongside avenue Daumesnil and, further east, rue de Charenton, has been transformed into a green promenade linking place de la Bastille with Bois de Vincennes. The promenade's western segment is a 1.4-kilometre-long stone structure that extends from the Bastille opera house to the rue Mongallet crossing. It looks like a Roman aqueduct, comprising sixty semicircular arches. A pedestrian walkway runs along the top of the linear structure, about twelve metres above the regular sidewalk. Shops and other facilities are installed inside the arches. The project also includes four hundred new housing units. This linear park complements the two major green spaces of the neighbourhood, both located within fifteen minutes of rue de Prague: the Arsenal Basin, which links the Seine with place de la Bastille, and the newly designed Parc de Bercy. Fondation Rothschild residents can also walk to two railway stations, Gare de Lyon and Gare d'Austerlitz, and, of course, to place de la Bastille, with its opera house, cafés, and the unique FNAC music store.[82]

It is all of these amenities, as well as the cabinetmaking factories, warehouses, offices, stores, and residential buildings, that form the faubourg Saint-Antoine of today. It is an intense, accessible, and convivial place. The rue de Prague residents, as do other residents of the neighbourhood, benefit from this rich environment. As we visit the district, it becomes very clear that architecture is first and foremost a vessel of human life, and successful architecture is both a condition and a consequence of this success. At the close of the twentieth century, life is not always easy for many Parisian blue-collar workers. For them, the cost of living is high, wages are low, flats are small, and unemployment is rampant. Yet human fraternity, a revered French value since the Revolution, is perceptible in the faubourg Saint-Antoine; it is tangible, for instance, at the restaurant located in the Fondation Rothschild complex that is dedicated to serving needy senior citizens.[83] Housing complexes with social consciences and easy access to facilities buttress such mutual-assistance establishments. Almost a century ago, the Rothschild brothers wanted to do their part to solve what the French today call the "problème de l'exclusion," the terrible social disease that transforms good citizens into homeless, marginalized nonentities. In its day, the rue de Prague complex embodied an attempt to eradicate social exclusion. The project has succeeded on many levels.

A Solid Structure

From a technical point of view, the rue de Prague building was carefully designed and built. It is a traditional masonry construction. Set on stone foundations, brick and stone walls support timber floor structures and a

Designed at the beginning of the twentieth century, the Fondation Rothschild Workers' Residence possesses a timeless dignity

timber-framed, slate-covered sloping roof. Reinforced cast-in-place concrete was used for the staircases and for the workshop wing, which required longer spans and stronger load-bearing floors. Most of the complex's large, traditional French windows are adorned with wrought-iron railings.

Ten years after construction, and because of the rent-control legislation, the foundation found itself in a financial straitjacket. Between 1920 and 1950, its limited revenue was used almost exclusively to cover the mortgage, and what little remained went into everyday maintenance and administration. As no money was available for renovating or upgrading, the building was left untouched for thirty years. Still, it has aged beautifully and was in relatively good condition when, in 1950, the first series of renovations, which mainly involved the plumbing and heating systems, was carried out. Between 1960 and 1965, the brick and stone façades were cleaned by sand blasting. This abrasive technique caused serious damage to the brick, and further repairs had to be undertaken. In 1974, an extensive upgrading programme was launched. It started with the renovation of the staircases and the installation of elevators. In staircase lobbies, artworks in the form of mosaic panels depicting the different trades that still flourish in the faubourg Saint-Antoine were added.

As I explained earlier, when this work was carried out, management asked residents if they would agree to have their flats refurbished and pay a higher rent. In the case of those tenants who declined, the work was postponed until the flats were vacated. Bricks had to be replaced in a few places on the courtyard façades. With the arrival of new tenants, the workshops were also renovated. Parts of the roof and windows were repaired. And the places where water was leaking from the courtyard floors into the basement were patched (Hervé 1994).

Sidewalks and Courtyards

Like the Palais-Royal building, the Fondation Rothschild edifice is a sophisticated arrangement of multiple shapes. From the surrounding sidewalks, we perceive the solid form of a continuous yet extremely variegated wall. We enter the complex at the centre of the rue de Prague façade, through a formal porte cochere, and penetrate the central courtyard, called "le square" or "la grande cour." At this precise moment, as in the Palais-Royal peristyles, we are inside the building without having left the outside. Proceeding into the central courtyard, we enter a powerful enclosure. Here, we are definitely inside the place yet still outdoors. As we stand within the two intertwined spaces, the enclosure appears simultaneously static and dynamic. For example, emerging from the porte cochere, we stand in the central courtyard and also in a walkway, running perpendicular to the entrance axis, alongside the interior long façade and leading into two side courtyards. The same feeling of spatial duality stays with us as we move towards either of the lateral courtyards. We experience the odd yet comfortable sensation of being able to choose, of being able to stay here or leave if we so desire; the feeling of protective freedom prevails.

The side courtyards are smaller than the central square. On the right is the Baudelaire courtyard, more linear than its counterpart, with skylights that bring natural light into the section of the basement where the communal baths, showers, and laundry facilities used to be located. The lobby that fronts the workshops opens onto this courtyard. On the left is the wider Roussel courtyard, with its irregular pentagonal shape. We can only understand its pentagon dimensions if we study the ground-floor plan of the complex. The courtyard is actually a dynamic space, more or less diamond-shaped, at a forty-five-degree angle in relation to the long façade, and with two sides missing.

At first sight, our impression of these connecting courtyards is one of verticality, of tightness. The interior space appears greater in height than in width, and, in some instances, it is. But, after observing more carefully and at greater length, we realize that this powerful sense of enclosure is not constricting. All the interior spaces are linked to the exterior by the porte cochere and the wide iron gates. While it is true that the ends of the protruding wings come close to the long north-south interior façade, these are still narrow segments that form wider spaces on both sides. Even in the interior courtyards, all the apartment windows admit abundant natural light and from them the vistas are surprisingly long.

What adds to the sense of openness in this strong enclosure is the fact that the courtyard forms are simultaneously simple and complex. The central courtyard appears to be a symmetrical rectangle, yet nothing in it is symmetrical. The porte cochere is off-centre to the left, and the courtyard's basic floor plan, which is semicircular at the end opposite the entrance, is off-centre with respect to the building's façades. Moreover, this seemingly rectangular courtyard is not rectangular at all because the side façades open away at an angle of almost forty-five degrees, forming a quasi-square area superimposed on the quasi-rectangle. And this square, which is more like an irregular diamond, is off-centre in relation to the porte cochere. The side courtyards have similarly complicated, dynamic forms, laid out, nonetheless, according to a strong formalistic spatial organization. In this classical composition on a triangular site, few angles are right angles, yet the

In autumn, the trees in the central courtyard of the Fondation Rothschild Workers' Residence take on a warm, golden colour

building's overall geometric pattern is rectilinear. The edifice is simultaneously inward and outward looking. Positive spaces are created on both sides of it. The shops and other facilities open onto sidewalks lined with trees (on rue de Prague) and the exterior façades are punctuated with windows that overlook the street or, in one instance, the small park.

Undoubtedly, such spatial complexity comes from the delicate equilibrium of multiple constraints, notably the irregular triangular site, the natural-light and ventilation imperatives, the need to have multiple staircases and entrances opening into interior courtyards, the need to open the courtyards to the streets, a double orientation for the flats, and, in addition to all of these, the financial requirement of providing as many flats as possible. The result is a dynamic, open enclosure that instigates a sophisticated play of opposing characteristics. If "a man's home is his castle," then the rue de Prague complex is a friendly castle that protects its residents and respects its neighbours.

Public-Hygiene Consciousness

One century before it became popular, the rue de Prague project put into practice the sustainable-development concept so dear to today's environmentalists. In the truest sense of the word, the project was, still is, an ecological one, the product of two centuries of public-health awareness, culminating, in 1905, in a momentous architectural competition. The competition was the Fondation Rothschild's first public initiative, and its impact has been profound (Dumont 1991; Flamand 1989). The winning entries were projects that embodied all the ecological ideas that had been percolating in France since the Regency.

Like the Paris of today, the French capital of the eighteenth century was a crowded commercial and industrial town, a metropolis where people came to make their fortune or simply to improve their lot. Although some ten thousand new residential buildings were erected in Paris between 1758 and 1788, and although the living conditions of most Parisians were improving, most eighteenth-century Parisians lived in small, overcrowded, damp, and filthy rented flats with no sanitary facilities. They were forced to use public places as their main living and working spaces. In the eighteenth century, the streets of Paris were no more than dark, narrow, muddy, congested alleys, the site of smelly, noisy, and dirty activities, dangerous but vibrant social arteries. Traffic snarls and accidents were frequent, and most streets were open sewers where deadly diseases were spread.

For eighteenth-century Parisians – with the exception of a few very rich ones – life was a constant struggle (Lavedan 1960). Drinking water was scarce and expensive. In many districts, it had to be distributed by water carriers. At public fountains and wells, people shared water with horses, stray dogs, and other animals. Washing was a major undertaking. Even sleeping was dangerous, because numerous tenements were built on rotten foundations over old quarries; many collapssed. In 1780, an inner-city mass grave caved in, filling the air with putrid smells. The flow of the Seine was not controlled, and major floods occurred regularly. The riverbanks were muddy, squalid areas; workers who toiled along them became sick just by inhaling the polluted air. If it wasn't water, then it was fire that brought destruction. Because most streets were not illuminated at night, people carried torches and abandoned them, still burning, everywhere. Fires were frequent. In 1718, a conflagration destroyed many buildings on Île de la Cité. As a consequence, the derelict little structures that were cluttering the Notre-Dame cathedral were demolished. For the first time since the church's construction, the side façades could be admired from a distance. In 1772, another fire destroyed one of the wings of the Hôtel-Dieu hospital. To improve fire fighting and prevention, fire pumps were installed in many districts of Paris.

During the eighteenth century, in spite of having to endure two wars and a corrupt regime, Paris expanded and French society as a whole became more affluent. New industries were created, some employing up to four hundred workers. Textile and paper mills settled in the faubourg Saint-Marcel, and glass, china, and wallpaper (such as Réveillon) factories sprang up in the faubourg Saint-Antoine to complement the furniture workshops (Lavedan 1960, 52). Like the streets and the riverbanks, the factories were desperately unhealthy places. Although the major plagues that decimated Europe in earlier centuries were no longer a threat, epidemics still broke out regularly, especially in Paris. With every new epidemic, it became more apparent that the dirty streets, open sewers and dumps, insalubrious factories, overcrowded prisons, hospitals, and cemeteries, were generators of disease (Fortier et al. 1975).

Eighteenth-century French society reacted the way all do societies under similar circumstances. As it got richer, it developed higher expectations and demanded better living conditions. Stumbling about in filth became more and more intolerable. Slowly, the issue of public hygiene gained credibility, and finally there was a call for more efficient management of public affairs. At the beginning of the eighteenth century, under the Ancien Régime, Paris was administered by three complementary authorities. The first was the superintendent of buildings, who supervized construction. This was one of the most important positions in the royal government. Under Louis XIV, the powerful minister of finance, Colbert, retained it himself. Under Louis XV, the job was given to Marigny, Madame de Pompadour's brother. The second authority was the lieutenant of police, who was responsible for keeping order in the capital and seeing that all community regulations were respected, including public-hygiene edicts. This also ranked among the most powerful of government positions. The third authority was the provost of the merchants, the equivalent of London's lord mayor, who was simultaneously appointed by the king and elected for two years by the city council. It was a post for a nonaristocrat in good standing with the monarch. His responsibility was to maintain the public domain: streets, squares, ports, bridges, fountains, and sewers, where they existed.

It was due to the joint efforts of these three authorities, and those of many enterprising citizens, that the major urban changes that eventually shaped the Paris of today were initiated. During this period, urban bylaws were first instituted in Paris. Soon, they were being applied systematically. For example, it was now mandatory to align streets and buildings. Building height was also regulated: sixty feet was the limit in 1783. The width of streets was controlled: in 1783, all new streets had to be at least thirty feet wide (Lavedan 1960, 49). At the beginning of the eighteenth century, street lighting was almost nonexistent. Responsibility for it fell to a designated leading citizen in each district. By the end of the century, it was in much wider use and its management was centralized under the lieutenant of police's authority (Fortier et al. 1975, 302).

The concept of public realm versus private property was increasingly recognized and the distinction became an inherent factor in urban regulations. While the police controlled public places, they respected private property. The municipal police, for instance, did not have access to the Palais-Royal, which helps to explain not only the complex's astonishing popularity but also the fact that revolutionaries could plot there with impunity. However, this respect for private property was not absolute. The police entered private homes when their services were requested. A few municipal bylaws dealing with behaviour in private establishments were instituted. On 28 October 1796, a police edict forbidding the raising of pigs and rabbits inside residences was issued.

During the eighteenth century, numerous major urban-planning measures and urban-development projects were initiated. It was then that Paris's first main underground sewer conduit was built on the Right Bank. Most of the abandoned quarries beneath buildings were filled. To deal with the capricious flow of the Seine, a flood-control master plan was developed by the municipality's chief architect, Pierre-Louis Moreau-Desproux, and riverbank work – including the erection of port structures – was carried out, notably near place des Grèves and Île des Cygnes. In 1782, a grain harbour designed by engineer Lespinasse was built. In 1765, architect Pierre Patte conceived a transportation master plan, known as the "Plan pour faciliter l'accès de Paris." Such a plan had become necessary because the construction of new streets was now out of control. A district-by-district strategy for beautifying Paris was also conceived and activated. In 1728, street names were inscribed at every corner (which implied that most people now knew if not how to read fluently then at least how to decipher a street sign). Starting in 1765, oil lampposts appeared along the streets of Paris. In 1782, sidewalks were installed as both a security and a hygiene measure. A 1786 municipal edict obliged Parisians to sweep the street in front of their house every morning. Private companies were created and awarded monopolies over the provision of some services: supplying water, selling life insurance, slaughtering animals, and cleaning cesspools.

A cleaner city and antiseptic hospitals became major preoccupations of many prominent eighteenth-century Parisians. Progress in medicine, awareness of individual rights, and a new understanding of the relationship between urban design and public health contributed to a dramatic evolution in these areas. In their thoroughly documented study, Bruno Fortier and his colleagues explained that commissions were created to tackle the problem of insalubrity in the city and its hospitals (Fortier et al. 1975). Various academies and societies were called upon to give their advice. The reports of the Academy of Sciences and the Academy of Architecture, created by Colbert in 1666 and 1671 respectively, and the Academy of Medicine, created a century later, reflected a consensus on important urban-design measures. If contagious diseases were to be eradicated, the academies argued, then the city had to be clean and properly maintained. Sanitary facilities had to be installed in residential buildings. Cleaner, larger, better-ventilated hospitals had to be built outside the city walls. Methods for designing better hospitals became a topic of study in schools of architecture. Hospital-design competitions were organized and prototypical concepts proposed. Most architects suggested a rectangular grid pattern with isolated pavilions, like the design that had been used to construct the Hôpital des Invalides. Architect Bernard Poyet proposed a circular plan for an eight-thousand-bed hospital. As a result of these initiatives, two new hospitals based on the rectangular-grid concept were built on the outskirts of

Paris: the Sainte-Anne and the de la Roquette. They were to influence hospital design for almost two centuries.

The academies called for the elimination of open sewers. They proclaimed that the practice of throwing garbage out of the window into the street must be stopped. Filthy places such as muddy riverbanks, swamps, garbage dumps, and damp buildings (for example, those constructed on bridges) should also be sanitized or eliminated. New buildings should have large windows capable of admitting generous quantities of natural light and fresh air. Polluting industries should be severely policed; they should be sited and designed to prevent the contamination of residential quarters. Like hospitals, cemeteries and prisons should be moved out of the city and their design radically improved.

In the wake of the French Revolution, public-health management was transferred from the police to the civil administration. Hospitals were also passed over to civil authorities. The culmination of these administrative changes came in 1802, when Napoléon created health committees, or "conseils de salubrité," which undertook to clean up Paris. The emperor also implemented major water-supply systems in the French capital. At last, potable water could be distributed to many districts in abundant quantities.

The Hygienists

Public-hygiene awareness continued throughout the nineteenth century, bolstering larger public-works programmes. In 1824, Paris had 37 kilometres of sewers; by 1850, the network had increased to 130 kilometres; and, by 1871, after renowned prefect of Paris Baron Haussmann had made his enormous contribution, 560 kilometres of sewers crisscrossed the Paris underground (Flamand 1989, 53). The city's first public toilets were installed in 1840; public fountains multiplied, reaching a total of 1,837 by 1850.

Around 1820, the idea that a person's health had a bearing on the public interest started to be promoted by a group of activists who became known as the Hygienists. In 1829, in order to disseminate their ideas, they launched a publication entitled the *Annales d'hygiène publique et de médecine légale*.[84] Like their predecessors in the academies, they asserted that urban-planning principles were based on public-hygiene necessities. For them, a good city was a city inhabited by citizens who were not plagued by recurrent diseases resulting from unsanitary facilities, miasmic water, stagnant air, and insufficient natural light. To be healthy, they argued, people require pure water, clean air, and abundant sunlight. They added that in order to be pure, water and air must circulate freely; and in order to be effective, sunlight must penetrate all dark interiors. Hence, wider streets and buildings with larger windows had to be built to facilitate air movement and the admission of natural light. Water-supply and sewer systems had to go beyond merely fulfilling a communal-distribution function in public places and service every building in the city. The goal of good health for all citizens also made the establishment of efficient public institutions dedicated to these tasks necessary.

Initially, the Hygienists' ideas concerned general urban-planning principles and the creation of more adequate infrastructures and other kinds of public facilities, but the group soon began to focus on housing conditions. They were well aware, however, that in spite of the wide dissemination of their ideas and the erection of a certain number of better-equipped residential buildings, workers' living conditions in Paris had still not improved substantially. In 1832, a cholera epidemic swept through France and killed 18,602 people in Paris alone. According to a doctor's report published in 1840, most workers' dwellings in Paris were overcrowded, had no chimneys, and were not equipped with sanitary facilities.

A new determination to solve the problem arose during the last quarter of the nineteenth century. Two international conferences on public hygiene and housing were held in Paris, one in 1878 and the other in 1889. Simultaneously, several experts' reports on the subject of public hygiene and workers' living conditions were submitted to the National Assembly; they called for new political and legislative measures. The 1889 conference was organized in the wake of the Paris International Exhibition, which had been held to celebrate the French Revolution's first centennial. Meeting in the shadow of the newly erected Eiffel Tower – a structure glorifying industrial progress and the power of the machine – delegates to the International Conference on Workers' Housing arrived at three basic conclusions. First, they stated that the solution to workers' housing problems could only come from private initiatives. Second, they declared that workers' residences must be clean. Third, they announced that these accommodations must be affordable (Flamand 1989, 79). The following year, the conference's leading figures, Jules Simon, Jules Siegfried, Georges Picot, and Émile Cheysson, along with their junior partners, created the Société des HBM,[85] the first private corporation devoted to the task of providing affordable and healthy housing for workers. The term *worker* was understood by these gentlemen in its broadest sense; it referred to all people of modest means, including, of course, blue-collar workers, artisans, and white-collar employees alike.

Such corporations undertook to implement housing projects, but soon it became apparent that the problem was greater than their ability to solve it. The Hygienists needed richer, more powerful allies. In 1894, in order to recruit new adepts and reach a larger audience, they organized, in Paris, another international conference on the same topic. This time, numerous architects, rich philanthropists, and senior civil servants joined the Hygienists in their quest for innovative answers to the workers' -housing dilemma. Cheysson, Picot, and Siegfried again took centre stage. Two reports presented at the conference outlined the magnitude of the problem and fired the imaginations of the participants. In giving the first of these reports, Jacques Bertillon, a medical doctor working with the Statistics Bureau of Paris, informed delegates that 600,000 Parisians were living in substandard accommodations. This meant that 24 percent of Paris's population was inadequately housed. The second report came from Paul Juillerat, head of the Municipal Bureau of Sanitation. For ten years, this diligent civil servant had accumulated statistics on the sanitary condition of eighty thousand of the city's buildings. He pointed to a strong correlation between living conditions and tuberculosis. At this time, twelve thousand Parisians were dying of tuberculosis every year. Juillerat indicated that while the average tuberculosis mortality rate in Paris was 1.8 percent per city block, it jumped to 8.5 percent on blocks where substandard living conditions prevailed, and to 20 percent in tenements. In certain buildings, a person was sure to die of tuberculosis within ten years of moving in. Juillerat added that the tuberculosis mortality rate was linked to the number of storeys a building had: the higher the building, the higher the rate. It was also linked to the floor one lived on: the closer one was to the sun, the smaller the likelihood of catching the disease. The number of windows a dwelling had was a factor, as well: fewer windows meant a greater incidence of tuberculosis. And, finally, the tuberculosis mortality rate was correlated with density: crowded flats nurtured tuberculosis (Dumont 1991, 35–39). Although Juillerat's method was later challenged, his conclusions had a major impact on the conference, which ultimately endorsed six architectural recommendations:

1. Whenever possible, urban streets should be oriented north-south; apartments that traverse the buildings that front on these streets will therefore be well-lit at both ends.
2. Urban streets should not be narrower than the height of the buildings that front on them; a similar proportion should be applied to courtyards.

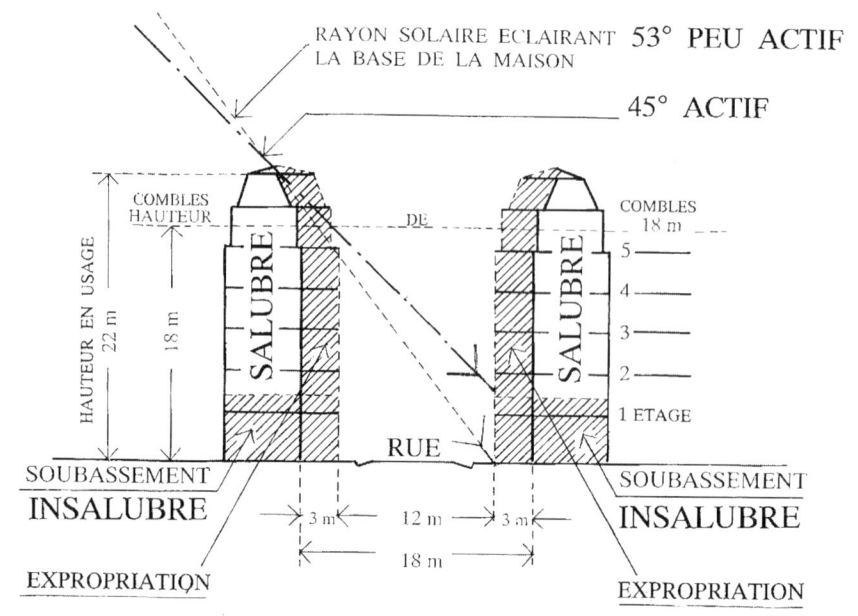

Translation: *rayon solaire éclairant la base de la maison*, sun ray reaching the building base; *actif*, active; *peu actif*, not very active; *salubre*, salubrious; *insalubre*, insalubrious; *combles*, attic; *hauteur*, height; *expropriation*, expropriation; *soubassement*, building base; *hauteur en usage*, usable height.

An urban-design diagram inspired by the studies of the Hygienists: to be salubrious, a street must allow for abundant sunlight; it must be therefore at least as wide as the buildings facing it are high

3. Courtyards should be larger than those designed according to Haussmannian principles and, if possible, open to the street.
4. Windows should be as large as possible and have lintels as close to the interior ceilings as possible.
5. In residential flats, the kitchen should be considered a habitable room, not an appendix to the living room.
6. Apartment buildings should be designed to permit all rooms of all flats to receive as much natural light as possible.

An Architectural Competition

It was in this social context that the Rothschild brothers decided to create their foundation. Its first executive board included the three of them, their three respective sons and designated successors, and four leading Hygienists:

Siegfried, Cheysson, Picot, and a railroad executive named Griolet. With the initial Rothschild donation of ten million francs at their disposal, the Hygienists were finally in command of a powerful instrument for the implementation of their ideas.

After acquiring land, including the large triangular site in the faubourg Saint-Antoine, the foundation invited architects to participate in an architectural competition. The rules of the competition, drafted by a technical committee composed of Siegfried, Cheysson, Picot, and the foundation's newly appointed chief architect, Henri-Paul Nénot, were unorthodox. A two-tiered competition was proposed. The winner was given no guarantee that his project would be implemented; however, generous cash prizes were offered. No explicit programme was provided, only vague recommendations that nonetheless reflected the committee's well-known ecological and social philosophy. It was simply requested that submitted designs be for a multistorey building located on the problematic, triangular rue de Prague site in the restless faubourg Saint-Antoine. Furthermore, it was stipulated that the building should not be like, or look like, an army barracks, as many earlier subsidized housing projects did.[86] Interior corridors should be avoided, because they were seen as dark, unhealthy, and dangerous places where a communist revolution might be fomented. Competitors were asked to provide a construction-cost estimate and a financial study that would demonstrate a 3 to 4 percent return on the investment. They were also invited to take into account the tastes, needs, and aspirations of the neighbourhood's residents, the project's future users. The most modern electro-mechanical services as well as the most progressive community amenities could be included in their schemes.

In March 1905, 127 anonymous competitors handed in their drawings, which were immediately exhibited at the Paris city hall. The press commented on the event enthusiastically. Twenty-five entries were selected to move on to the second stage; and, eventually, seven projects received prizes. Designed by a young, unknown architect, Augustin Rey, the winning entry was unanimously acclaimed by both the jury and the press as the obvious first choice. Rey's scheme distinguished itself by having a very clear concept, a flawless rationale, a seductive aesthetic, and many innovative elements. In his project, the building's residential wings created three large, well-lit, well-ventilated courtyards that opened to the streets. The central courtyard was, in fact, a real square. The flats were larger than the norm of the time and designed for family life. All were well ventilated and many even had cross-ventilation. Large double-hung-type windows with prismatic glass in their upper sections allowed 40 percent more light into a room than the average window at that time. The kitchens were well equipped and were always a discrete room. All flats had generous storage space. All staircases served only two flats per landing; each was well lit and ventilated by large windows. These staircases were designed with curved steps, narrower on the sides and wider in the centre, permitting an easy climb for children on the sides and for adults in the centre. Two handrails were to be installed on each staircase, one at the normal height and the other at a lower height for children.

Rey's project encompassed a wide array of common services and facilities. The basement contained common baths and showers, a communal laundry, storage areas for the shops and the flats, and a coal furnace fuelling a central hot-water heating system. On the ground floor, in addition to the shops, there were bicycle-parking rooms, a "health food" restaurant, a small library with a writing room, and a small meeting room. Workshops were grouped in one area; some were located at ground level, facilitating the supervision of children playing in the central courtyard. On the top floor, in addition to bachelors' rooms, well-ventilated drying spaces behind claustra and a sun deck for tuberculosis convalescents were proposed.

Aesthetically, Rey's project pleased everyone. What he had achieved was a very convivial architecture. Covered with white stucco, the exterior walls were punctuated by large windows that opened onto balconies generously adorned with flower boxes. The overall impression was one of cleanliness and health, exactly what would be expected of an ecological scheme. Another young architect, Henri Provensal, who had also proposed a very sophisticated scheme, won second prize. His project was considered too monumental to warrant first prize.

The Fondation Rothschild immediately hired Rey and Provensal. Their role was to be the design architects of an in-house architectural firm under the general direction of Chief Architect Nénot. They combined their talents to design and build the foundation's first two projects, situated on Popincourt and Belleville streets. Meanwhile, Ray's original rue de Prague scheme had sunk into financial difficulties. After careful analysis and some painful soul-searching, the foundation decided not to implement it because it was too expensive. For two years, Rey tried to modify the plan, but Nénot rejected both of his new proposals for the same reason: they were still too costly. In view of this situation, and because he was becoming more interested in his new career as a conference speaker than his career as a practising architect, Rey left the foundation.

The project that was eventually built on rue de Prague was the work of Nénot, assisted by Provensal and the other foundation architects. The

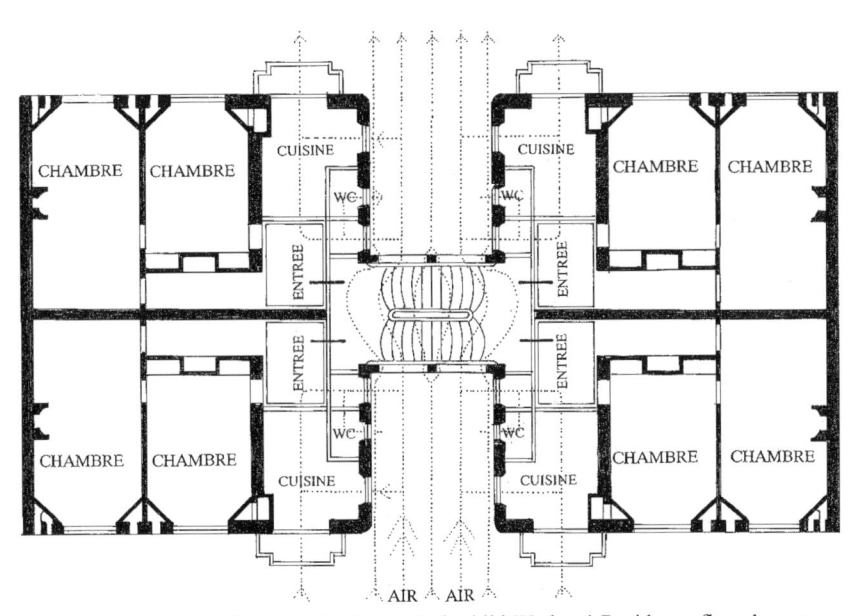

Schematic floor plan of typical Fondation Rothschild Workers' Residence flats; here, two double-orientation flats open onto the well-lit landing of an equally well-lit staircase; the dotted lines illustrate the flow of cross ventilation

ecological spirit of the original scheme was preserved. Many of its community facilities were also maintained. However, to make the project financially feasible, the area of the flats was reduced. When the complex opened in 1909, it boasted 324 flats as well as a spectacular array of the most avant-garde equipment and social amenities. People had seen similar schemes on paper, but this time it was for real, and they were impressed. Here is a full list of the project's features:

1. Thirty-six workshops for cabinetmaking artisans stacked on six floors and equipped with electrical power and an elevator.
2. Shops occupying the complex's ground floor. These were part of a "food cooperative" and catered mainly to the needs of the building's residents; they included a bakery, a butchershop, and a fruit and vegetable shop. No wine shop was allowed, because alcoholism was considered a social disease that must be aggressively curbed; according to the complex's rules, any tenant caught drunk would automatically be expelled.
3. A communal laundry. As it was forbidden, for sanitary reasons, to wash clothing inside the apartments, a laundry equipped with the best and most

modern equipment available was provided; residents were encouraged to wash their clothing frequently.

4. Common showers and baths. In 1909, the flats had no bathrooms, only toilets. All residents had to use the common facility and were encouraged to wash daily; this was not the usual practice in those days.

5. A mortuary room.

6. A dispensary supplying the essentials for ordinary health care and preventive medicine.

7. A day-care centre accommodating three- to six-year-old children.

8. A supplementary school (*une école de garde*) to take care of children after school and on Thursdays, when school was closed. Part of this project's mission was to look after children while their parents worked.

9. A home-economics school for women. Here, everything there was to know about running a household was taught.

10. A communal kitchen, attached to the home-economics school. Hot, healthy meals were prepared here twice daily by the women of the complex; these were sold and eaten at home (Dumont 1991, 84–90).

Today, all these common services have been replaced by amenities better adapted to the contemporary lifestyle and an improved standard of living. Small bathrooms have been installed in the apartments, rendering the common facilities obsolete. The same sort of services that were originally offered only to the complex's residents are now provided in the neighbourhood by the municipality or the state for the population at large.

Ordinary Charm

It is both difficult and easy to describe the rue de Prague complex's aesthetic. It is difficult because the project displays none of the usual characteristics of what our culture considers a beautiful architectural artefact. It does not have the serene charm of the Palais-Royal, or the impeccable proportions of Gabriel's Petit Trianon, or the mystic radiance of the Sainte-Chapelle, or Notre-Dame's grandiose sublimity, or even the perfectly balanced composition of Paris's notable seventeenth-century *hôtels particuliers* – for instance, Pierre Rousseau's Hôtel de Salm. Conversely, it is easy to articulate the complex's aesthetic because it has, simply, the noble beauty of an honest, mature worker.

The residence's composition is both straightforward and immensely subtle. It is an enormous structure adorned with tiny details; its broad, extensive façades have been broken up into smaller segments. As observers, we are caught up in the intriguing interplay between a stable general appearance that integrates everything into a static whole and a dynamic general appearance that features very little repetition. On these façades, many details belonging to the same architectonic language are used in a wide variety of ways and in many different places. In traditional Haussmannian fashion, the street façades contain strong horizontal lines formed by the window alignments, the wrought-iron balconies, and a succession of cornices. Balancing these horizontalities that accentuate the street perspective is a large vertical rhythm that is established by protruding vertical elements; different types of overhang emerge at different levels. Four or five tonalities of pinkish-yellow brick alternate with greyish-gold stonework. Another, finer rhythm is created by several cornice, window, and balcony details assembled in different ways and in different places. On the fifth floor, a single balcony adorned with colonnettes supporting a basket arch protrudes above an already protruding element, thus creating a deeper platform and a deeper shadow. The same motif is repeated four times on the sixth floor. In certain places, the iron railing of a balcony is no wider than a single window; in other places, it links several windows. Sometimes, on the higher storeys, the balcony railing wraps around the corner of the building. In a few odd places, small triangular balconies are found. Some are set in the stone, others in the brick. The roof starts at the seventh floor in certain places; in others, it starts at the eighth floor.

While a strong horizontal composition was maintained on the street façades, verticality was accentuated on the courtyard façades. The latter façades are broken into narrow vertical bands, some protruding, others receding, some displaying wide windows, others narrower ones; these windows sometimes belong to apartments and other times to staircases. All apartment windows are individual openings set in the masonry; they feature folding vertical shutters and most have vertical rectangular proportions. The workshop windows, however, form a continuous horizontal band, resting on the exposed reinforced concrete slab. This thoroughly modern motif preceded Le Corbusier's renowned design vocabulary by a full generation.

These façades reflect the lives conducted behind them. Red canvas awnings protect some particularly sunny windows while flower boxes garnished many balconies. The central courtyard is a charming little garden with a bubbling circular fountain at its centre. Eight chestnut trees dominate an arrangement of smaller trees, bushes, and flowers and define the space around the fountain, creating a more intimate enclosure within the walls of the building. Four benches illuminated by four lampposts invite residents or visitors to sit while waiting for a friend or for the children in

The stone and brick façades of Fondation Rothschild Workers' Residence have varied tall windows, balconies, and cast-iron railings

the school annex. Elsewhere in the courtyards, large flowerpots supply touches of colour. The entrances to the ground-floor apartments of the two assistant janitors, which are situated near the iron gates on rue Théophile-Roussel and rue Charles-Baudelaire, are decorated with flowerpots. In most places, courtyard floors are covered with yellow tiles. The entire place is impeccably clean.

Admittedly, this complex is not ostentatious. It is just thoughtfully and tastefully constructed and maintained. Designed with maintenance requirements in mind, it has aged extremely well. Softened by the patina of time, it has acquired the status of a cultural artefact. It is neither chic nor tacky; neither flashy nor timid. It does not try to imitate anything else, to be either falsely avant-garde or falsely nostalgic, to be either bourgeois or proletarian. It only tries to remain true to itself. It succeeds admirably. The rue de Prague complex is an amiable, solid, serious, diligent, honest worker. Rarely has a nobler architecture been produced.

Demonstration of Satisfaction

With the permission and help of the Fondation Rothschild management, I distributed a questionnaire to the rue de Prague complex residents. The survey was conducted between 15 and 21 November 1994. Its purpose was to assess the residents' level of satisfaction and to identify the reasons for their satisfaction or dissatisfaction. It contained six questions. At that point, the complex housed 323 tenants; 297 were apartment residents and 26 were shop or workshop occupants.[87] The complex had 323 mailboxes, and so 323 questionnaires were distributed, even though the survey was addressed mainly to the residents, not the shop or workshop occupants. The survey was conducted anonymously, but a few respondents chose to sign their names. (A sample of the questionnaire is reproduced in the appendix to this book.)

Seventy-two questionnaires were completed and returned. Only residents answered (that is, shop and workshop occupants did not). The response rate was 22.3 percent based on the number of questionnaires distributed; based on the number of residents, the rate was 24.2 percent.[88] The questions were as follows:

1. *How long have you resided here?* Twenty-four residents (33.8 percent) answered ten years or less, twenty-one (29.5 percent) said between eleven and thirty years, fifteen (21.2 percent) said between thirty-one and fifty years, seven (9.9 percent) said between fifty-one and eighty years, and four

(5.6 percent) said eighty-one years or more (one respondent did not answer). The longest residency period was eighty-five years; it was claimed by a lady who had been residing at the rue de Prague complex since its opening in 1909. The shortest residency was claimed by a young family that had moved in three months earlier. The duration of the average residency was 27.3 years. These figures clearly indicate a certain stability.

2. *Taking into account the amount of rent you are paying, are you satisfied with your residency here?* The answer was extremely positive: 97 percent of respondents said they were either satisfied or very satisfied. The breakdown was: forty-four (61 percent) said "very satisfied," twenty-six (36 percent) said "satisfied," one (1.5 percent) said "dissatisfied," and one said "very dissatisfied." These answers confirmed this epochè's findings.

3. *If you are very satisfied or satisfied, please list, in order of importance, the three main reasons for your satisfaction.* Several answers were provided. These were grouped into four categories. First, there were the replies related to the architectural quality of the complex, such as comfort, good design, and quietness. This category was the largest: there were thirty first-priority answers, twenty-eight second-priority answers, and fourteen third-priority answers, for a total of seventy-two. Second, there were the replies related to the quality of the neighbourhood: sixteen first-priority answers, seventeen second-priority answers, and seventeen third-priority answers, for a total of fifty. Third, there were the replies related to the management of the complex: eight first-priority answers, thirteen second-priority answers, and twenty-six third-priority answers, for a total of forty-seven. Fourth, there were the replies related to the value-for-money ratio. Many said that at the Fondation Rothschild complex they obtained the best value for money: sixteen first-priority answers, five second-priority answers, and five third-priority answers, for a total of twenty-six.

Respondents reported that some of the factors that contributed to their level of satisfaction included (at random): the quietness and politeness of residents, the civility of residents, good maintenance, serious management, reasonable rent, the kindness and amicability of the janitors and other personnel, good security, comfortable accommodation, good lighting, balconies, easy access to elevators, the upgrading of the apartments, the cleanliness of the facilities, the outdoor plants and flowers, the trees, the courtyard's small garden, the quietness of the surrounding neighbourhood, the central location, the proximity of retail facilities, the proximity of transportation. These answers also confirmed the epochè's findings.

4. *If you are not satisfied, indicate, in order of importance, the reasons for your dissatisfaction.* The two residents who did express displeasure said

that their apartments were insufficiently insulated against noise, that building security was not adequate, that there were problems with the plumbing, that their windows did not open properly, and that they were having difficulty integrating into the community of the complex. The one person who answered "dissatisfied" had been living in the complex for fourteen years; the one person who said "very dissatisfied" had been there since 1945. A few of the respondents who expressed their satisfaction also offered suggestions for improving some of the complex's physical aspects. The issue of acoustic insulation was raised six times; upgrading plumbing and windows was also mentioned, as was tightening up security.

5. *Are you satisfied with the neighbourhood?* The responses were unanimously positive, although two respondents did not answer.

6. *What are, in order of importance, the main reasons for your satisfaction or dissatisfaction with the neighbourhood?* Several reasons were given, and these were grouped under two themes of equal importance: conviviality and accessibility. Under conviviality was cited the neighbourhood's general quality: its simultaneously residential and commercial aspect, its typical Parisian flavour, its rich history, the fact that it was calm yet lively, friendly, quiet at night, popular, and reasonably secure. Under accessibility was cited the neighbourhood's central location: the fact that the complex was within walking distance of numerous shops and services; the proximity of place d'Aligre and Marché de Beauvau; the proximity of a metro station, bus stops, and access points to other types of public transportation; the proximity of hospitals; the proximity of square Trousseau.

Respondents were also invited to write down any additional comments, and thirty-eight did. Here is a representative sampling: "We are lucky to live here"; "Let's hope it lasts"; "Thank you Fondation Rothschild"; "Places as nice as this one should exist elsewhere"; "Increase lighting in the entrance portals"; "There is no doubt that the trees contribute to the conviviality and the quality of the complex"; "I congratulate the gardener"; "In spite of its good points, the neighbourhood was better twenty to twenty-five years ago"; "May I move to a larger unit within the complex when one becomes available?"; "Even here old people feel lonely"; "I like it here, my neighbours are very nice people"; "The acoustic insulation should be improved"; "There is the square nearby that allows children to play"; "Old people also frequent the square, which is nice"; "Architects, developers, and the City of Paris should use our residence as a model for more adequate housing conditions for people, and for a more reasonable maintenance of public places!"

Although the Fondation Rothschild Workers' Residence is a dense residential complex, its courtyards do not feel constricted

Successful Architecture

All the characteristics of successful architecture evident at the Palais-Royal may be found at the Fondation Rothschild Workers' Residence. The complex embraces a sophisticated balance of public and private domains, both in its physical manifestation and its intellectual organization. Whether we stand in the complex's central courtyard, in its side courtyards, in the surrounding streets, or at the place d'Aligre market, we sense the positive nature of the public places in and around rue de Prague very strongly. This environment is composed of a series of well-ordered, easily recognizable places rich in manifestations of individual life. Located in the middle of a convivial neighbourhood where services of all kinds are immediately accessible, the residence is itself a welcoming yet protective enclosure. Although the rue de Prague complex is a large, dense architectural artefact, it maintains its human scale. We sense this in the proportioning of the public and semipublic spaces and in the fine orchestration of architectural details. The product of two centuries of public-hygiene awareness, this subsidized housing residence is an environment that has domesticated nature in a simple, respectful way. For almost a century now, its outward appearance has responded positively to the tastes of its users. Its aesthetic characteristics transcend short-lived styles or fashion trends; they form a part of the distinctive look of Paris. With this timeless aesthetic, the rue de Prague complex belongs to the cultural mainstream.

We have discovered that the Fondation Rothschild Workers' Residence is a place of high quality and great beauty. Its success is as spectacular as that of the Palais-Royal, but in a totally different way. Both places are cherished pieces of the common cultural heritage. They satisfy their users. And, ultimately our aim in this phenomenological probe is to uncover not so much what differentiates one artefact from another but, rather, what their common, essential attributes are.

Dwelling with Respect

More than anything else, perhaps, what the rue de Prague complex illustrates is that a successful architecture is an architecture of respect. This residence was conceived with respect for workers, and, in return it has earned their respect for almost a century. No graffiti has ever appeared on its walls. Particularly in the late nineteenth century and the early twentieth century, respect for workers implied social promotion. The Fondation Rothschild residence is a real-estate undertaking with a social agenda. Although the discourse of the nineteenth-century Hygienists sounds paternalistic and politically biased by today's standards, it did issue from a genuine social concern. Of course, the motivations of France's Fourth Republic bourgeoisie were multifaceted. It was in their own interest for them to quell social agitation, defeat the anarchists, and curb the rise of socialism and communism. These people wanted to preserve the social order because they believed – and, we have to admit, with some validity – that chaos would inevitably bring ruin to everyone, including themselves and the proletariat. In the face of worker unrest, these social leaders could have adopted a repressive attitude, as many others had done. But they chose, instead, to show respect for the working class and to treat it with dignity. Of course, again, a total eradication of social and economic disparities was unattainable. Only a demagogue could promise such a utopian result. The Rothschild brothers were not demagogues. As financiers and men of action, they did not make promises they could not keep, and the workers were grateful for their candour. Everyone knew that a vast gulf existed between the workers' living conditions, even at the progressive rue de Prague complex, and the lifestyle of the Rothschild's. What the Fondation Rothschild

At the Fondation Rothschild Workers' Residence, two women walk by one of the three janitor's lodges; this one faces rue Théophile-Roussel

promised and delivered was the best possible workers' residence for the price, located in the centre of the workers' own world – a residence in line with the workers' tastes and aspirations. The Rothschild brothers put forward an honest proposition. The fact that the workers who have inhabited the residence over the years have responded to that proposition in a consistently positive fashion proves that they have always understood the spirit behind it.

The rue de Prague residence is a no-frills project, but it is not a simplistic one. The complex demonstrates its respect for its residents by communicating several things simultaneously. It proclaims that workers may be uneducated, but not unintelligent, and can be educated if the proper facilities are made available to them. That is why the complex was made into an instrument of education. The project implies, further, that quality is not limited to certain social classes at the expense of others. Just because a residential complex is made for workers it should not be stripped of ornamentation and made to look like a factory. The rationale is simple: if it is inappropriate for the residence of a factory owner to look like a factory, then it is also inappropriate for the residence of factory workers to resemble a factory. Modern architects, practising later, forgot this common-sense attitude. It took postmodern practitioners to recapture it.

To show respect for a group of people is to welcome them into the social mainstream. At the rue de Prague residence, workers live as other, more privileged people do; their sensitivities, desires, and needs are accommodated. What workers want is what everybody else wants: an affordable, comfortable home that is part of a secure, pleasant environment; and respectful and amiable neighbours. They want to live in a decent neighbourhood where they can enjoy access to commercial, recreational, educational, religious, health, and other social amenities. They also want to be able to travel to their place of work, and elsewhere, on an efficient transportation system. The Fondation Rothschild Workers' Residence has offered all of this to its residents for more than eighty-five years.

Seen here closing the perspective of avenue Laurier, Mont-Royal is an important and highly visible component of Outremont's landscape

7

OUTREMONT: A CONVIVIAL ELEGANCE

Now for our third phenomenological journey. I invite you to Montreal, where we will stroll through the municipality of Outremont, my home.

Outremont is a small community tucked into northern flank of Mont-Royal. The mountain is at the geographic centre of Montreal, a large island on the Saint Lawrence River. To say the least, Montreal is a place of very sharp climatic contrasts. Summers in Outremont can be surprisingly hot, springs and autumns always seem too short, and winters are bitterly cold.[89] But all the seasons have their pleasant days. The summer of 1993 was particularly felicitous. Mild mornings were followed by warm afternoons; bright blue skies were adorned here and there with puffy white clouds. The evenings were soft, and they enticed Outremontais out of their cosy homes for a walk under the tall Norway maple trees. Crowded sidewalk cafés turned away disappointed patrons, while energetic tennis players waited in line for a court. People commented on the weather with a smile. During this memorable summer, it seems that Montrealers, in particular those living in Outremont, had forgotten for a brief moment the severe recession and the never-ending political gloom.

Four months later, the winter of 1994 brought the coldest weather in living memory. When they needed to venture outdoors after the temperature had hit thirty below zero, Outremontais walked briskly, pulling their heads down, leaning into the biting wind. But even during this winter the weather was not always unbearable. Certain days were glorious, especially those following a snowstorm, when the world seemed immaculate. Then, Outremontais enjoyed a walk under the vault of tall maple trees hung with garlands of frozen crystals that glimmered in the sun. They may have wished that the ice diamonds were real and could be invested to fight the

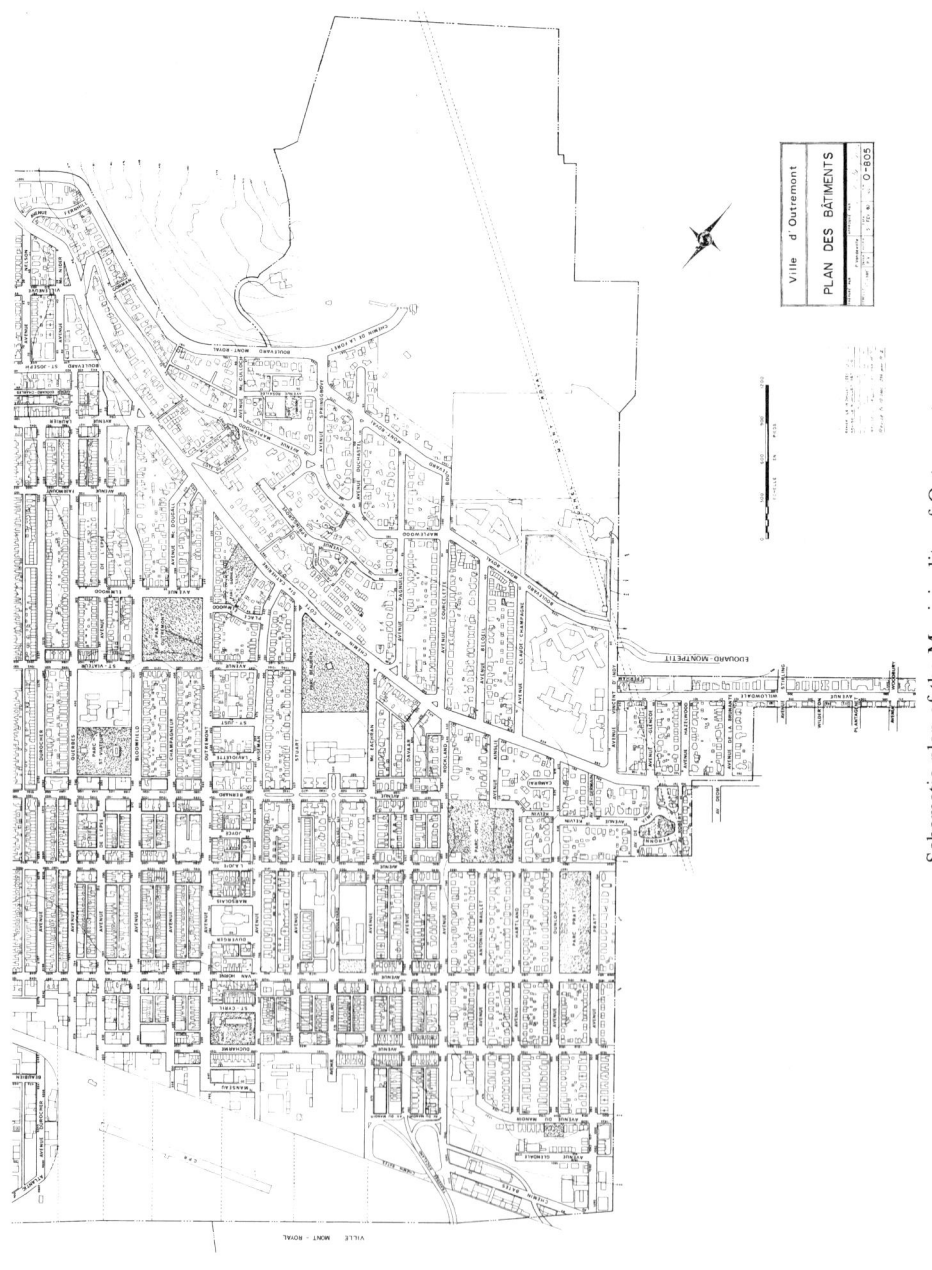

Schematic plan of the Municipality of Outremont

recession and alleviate political tension. They commented that winter could be beautiful but was definitely too long. If only spring would come! And, of course, it did, as always, and accomplished its recurrent miracle.

A City within a City

In Outremont, signs are necessary to indicate the administrative limits of the city. Walking north[90] on Hutchison Street, for instance, we need help to understand that the buildings on the right-hand side are in the City of Montreal while those on the left are in Outremont. Outremont is an autonomous municipality almost entirely surrounded by the City of Montreal. Only a short segment at the western end of its northern border touches another municipality, Ville Mont-Royal. On the Island of Montreal, twenty-nine such autonomous municipalities join the City of Montreal proper to form the Montreal Urban Community.[91]

This city-within-a-city situation has created a permanent ambiguity that both helps and hinders Outremont's development. Because of the central position of their city with respect to Montreal, Outremontais live near most places of interest. They perceive this as a great advantage. But this geographical bonus has led Outremontais to feel that they have no need to establish, within their own municipal area, the sort of urban amenities one finds in comparable cities, such as a cultural centre or a central communal plaza. This is viewed by many as a disadvantage; they say it undermines the community spirit.

The People of Outremont

In Outremont, most conversations are conducted in French (Bisson 1993, 44; Stats Can). It is the dominant language, and so it is heard in the streets, in shops and cafés, and at City Hall. Official statistics show that the mother tongue of 67 percent of the municipality's 23,000 residents is French. Another 20 percent speak French as their second language. And it is fair to say that the rest of the population understands enough French to be able to conduct daily activities in the community without undue difficulty. Also, 75 percent of Outremontais speak English, which makes Outremont a bilingual town. Several other languages are also spoken in Outremont: Greek, Yiddish, Arabic, Spanish, and Italian, to name only the most prevalent ones. We have to remember that Montreal is a large, cosmopolitan city where more than a hundred languages are spoken daily. With its 23,000 residents, Outremont is a microcosm of the Greater Montreal Region, which is home to 2,750,000 people.

Two-thirds of Outremont's citizens are of French ethnic origin, and the other third is divided into three almost equal parts: Jewish, Greek, and that vague denomination called "others." As a city is basically a marketplace of ideas, goods, and services, most Outremontais will not dispute the assertion that the cultural diversity within their community augments the richness of exchanges. Being liberal at heart, they will argue that a community that welcomes a multiplicity of ethnic groups strengthens itself. But ethnic diversity also engenders communication problems. For example, the cultural interface between French Canadians and Hassidic Jews in Outremont is not always harmonious, due to differing traditions and cultural shyness. Yet, good faith prevails most of the time, and efforts are made on both sides to open up channels of communication between those who have been in Quebec for three hundred years and those who arrived more recently.

In Quebec, the common perception of Outremont is that it is a very affluent community. This is false. While not poor, Outremont does not even rank among Montreal's wealthiest neighbourhoods. For instance, the average income in Outremont in 1993 was $20,900. In the community of Nun's Island it was $36,000.[92] In Westmount, which is the traditional anglo counterpart to franco Outremont, it was $34,000 in the sector north of Sherbrooke Street, and $26,900 in the less affluent sector situated south of that artery. It could be said that poor Westmounters are still wealthier than Outremontais. For comparison's sake, the average Canadian income is $19,300; in the province of Quebec it is $17,800, and in Greater Montreal it is $18,800 (Stats Can).

In Outremont, among a majority of citizens who are of modest means there are a few millionaires. Most of them reside on the hill that rises from the south side of chemin de la Côte-Sainte-Catherine. Certainly, wealth is not frowned upon in Outremont, but it is not one of the most important criteria Outremontais use for judging their neighbours. Lifestyle and personal behaviour are. People of all means are welcome in Outremont, but they are expected to maintain their homes properly.

Outremont's flair could perhaps be characterized by what movie director Luis Buñuel called "the discreet charm of the bourgeoisie."[93] Even newly affluent Outremontais are discreet; they make a point of not looking nouveau riche. Like Outremontais of longer tenure, they are genuinely proud of their older homes and take meticulous care of them. A few years ago, they were caricatured as the *bourgeoisie décapante* because, apparently, the

The twin houses of Outremont in the bright winter light

only thing they could talk about at cocktail parties was the long hours they had spent removing the old varnish from the woodwork of their houses. In French, the verb *décaper* means to expose the natural grain of wood; but it has another connotation. A *décapante* attitude is an abrasive one – an attitude that tends to temper amorous initiatives. Outremontais, of course, would take exception to this caricature.

Three factors explain the mythical image of an affluent Outremont. The first is that the citizens of Outremont are well educated; 50 percent of them have attended university. The second is that this well-schooled community is extremely active politically, not only at its own municipal level but also on larger stages. It is said that Outremont harbours more politicians per square metre than any other city in the world. For instance, in 1994, the premier of Quebec, Jacques Parizeau; the leader of the opposition, Daniel Johnson; and two former premiers, Daniel Johnson's brother Pierre-Marc and Robert Bourassa, were all living in Outremont, as were many other politicians. The third factor is that many Outremontais are artists, intellectuals, and celebrities. Their individual reputations indirectly add to Outremont's fame.

A Residential Neighbourhood

What strikes us as we stroll along the tranquil streets of Outremont is how many well-maintained residences there are. Other sorts of buildings are relatively rare. Outremont is, fundamentally, a residential district. City officials would tell us that, if we had the patience to count them, we would find 3,624 main buildings. Other small structures, such as sheds or garages, would not be included in this count. Of these main buildings, 94 percent are residential structures; this figure represents a grand total of 10,059 residential units (City of Outremont 1993).

Some residences are very modest, while others are mansions, imposing and sometimes even ostentatious. From an architectural viewpoint, many of them are quite remarkable. For example, on chemin de la Côte-Sainte-Catherine is the present City Hall, the oldest house in the city of Outremont. This small, well-proportioned white house was built for the Bagg family in 1817 and used, at one time, as a warehouse for the Hudson's Bay Company. Nearby, just around the corner on avenue McDougall, the beautiful, white Ferme Outremont emerges from a canopy of deep-green maple trees. This farmhouse was built in 1838 for L. T. Bouthillier, but could have been designed by the most daring postmodern architect. It is the property that inspired the city's name. Further west on chemin de la Côte-Sainte-Catherine stands the symmetrical Ozias-Lamoureux house, designed in 1912 by architects Doucet and Morissette (*Continuité* 1991).

When we climb the hill south of chemin de la Côte-Sainte-Catherine, we see mansions interspersed with religious and educational institutions. Some are large but ordinary-looking modern bungalows built after World War II, such as the Parent residence, designed by Roland Dumais in 1949. Others – for instance, the Sévère-Godin mansion, designed by R. C. Betts in 1935 – are akin to small castles. Others, still, are charming old gentleman-farmers' cottages hidden under deep foliage, such as the Maher residence on avenue Maplewood, built in 1906.

But it is when we walk downhill, cross chemin de la Côte-Sainte-Catherine, and explore the straight north-south avenues that we sense the spirit of residential Outremont. There, behind corridors of tall maples, we discover a series of red brick houses with white wooden porches – a sight that is unique to Outremont. What is remarkable is not so much this or that specific house but the combination of them, the residential assemblages.[94] Many streets are lined with densely packed, free-standing cottages or twin houses. On other streets – for instance, avenue Durocher or avenue Querbes

Practically all Outremont houses have a front porch

– the residences are contiguous, forming a wall of two-storey row houses or three-storey walk-up triplexes.

Taking a closer look, we see that it is possible to construct a wide variety of residential buildings while maintaining a strong sense of continuity. At the level of their generic features, all Outremont houses can be assigned to one of no more than five categories: the free-standing two-storey cottage; the twin or semidetached house (two cottages joined by a common wall), such as my own house on avenue Kelvin; the two-storey row house; the row triplex; and the multiple-unit, four-or-five-storey residential building. Also, almost every Outremont house is made of brick, has a flat roof, a wooden front porch, at least one balcony, and cornices. Yet, at the detailed-design level, practically every building is distinguished in some way. Often, developers have asked architects to design not one house but a pair or a series of houses. The architects have responded by designing similar yet different buildings. Pairs of houses have been designed asymmetrically, duplexes with the same basic floor plan have been adorned with different features – here a bow window, there a larger porch.

Three Commercial Avenues

Of course, all cities need nonresidential buildings as well. In this respect, the situation that prevails in Outremont is ambiguous. Even a very perspicacious pedestrian will have to search long and hard to find a real industrial plant in Outremont, or even an office building. Perhaps he or she will discover a paint plant on chemin Bates[95] or an obscure two-storey brick building housing professional offices, but that will be about all.

Retail establishments are highly visible, however, and concentrated on three east-west avenues: Van Horne, Bernard, and Laurier. For historical reasons, these commercial establishments are located on Outremont's east side, close to the Island of Montreal's populous centre. They cater almost exclusively to the daily needs of Outremontais. While a piano or a car cannot be purchased in Outremont, grocery stores, bookstores, bakeries, pastry shops, and boutiques of all kinds abound, and are generally excellent. This unique condition – what does exist is of exceptional quality, but major components of a normal city are nonexistent – would be a serious shortcoming if Outremont were either an isolated municipality or a suburb. Due, however, to Outremont's central location, this lack of urban activity components does not constitute a problem for Outremontais because what does not exist on its territory is easily accessible nearby.

In Outremont, what is called avenue Van Horne is just the central segment of a very long commercial street that runs through several residential areas of Montreal. East of Outremont, it becomes boulevard Rosemont, the main commercial east-west axis of this district. West of Outremont, it passes through the Côte-des-Neiges district before becoming chemin Fleet in Hampstead. The stores on the section of avenue Van Horne that traverses are no different from those that line this thoroughfare in the other districts. However, the American-style strip malls that clutter avenue Van Horne in the Côte-des-Neiges area are not to be found in Outremont. One distinguishing characteristic of the Outremont segment of avenue Van Horne is that a major college, Collège Stanislas, stands next to it; the institution's students and professors patronize the local shops.

While avenue Van Horne is not especially renowned, Outremont's other two commercial avenues are quite well known throughout Montreal. Avenue Bernard is famous for its cafés and restaurants, its ice-cream parlour, Le bilboquet, and, of course, its "cinema," Théâtre Outremont. Some say that this soon-to-be-restored movie palace is the only truly historical monument in Outremont and one of the best Art Deco artefacts in North America. Avenue Laurier is even more popular. This distinctive shopping street is crammed with expensive boutiques, exclusive food stores, and high-quality restaurants. And in the middle of this chic environment sits the ultimate proletarian restaurant: Bar-B-Q Laurier is a culinary institution in Quebec, the original Montreal-style grilled-chicken eatery.[96]

Distinctiveness in Continuity

Although, as I mentioned, we must rely on signs to identify the exact administrative limits of Outremont, we perceive subtle differences in the urban fabric when we actually penetrate it. As a geographic entity, Outremont has both strong edges with clear entry points and invisible borders. The northern edge is formed by the impassable Canadian Pacific rail yard and tracks. This very large site is the last undeveloped land in Outremont. Over the past twenty-five years, numerous urban-design studies have been conducted in an effort to develop this land, which is probably the most desirable piece of real estate in Montreal.[97] Because of the barrier created by the rail yard, pedestrians who do try to enter Outremont from the north encounter difficulties because the only access route is via a steep overpass over the railyard. The southern edge of Outremont, on the high end of the slope, is equally impassable but much more agreeable. It is formed by boulevard Mont-Royal. This artery skirts Parc Mont-Royal (which is part of the City of Montreal's territory) and the Mont-Royal cemetery.

While Outremont's north and south edges are well defined, its east and west sides are porous. Coming from the Côte-des-Neiges neighbourhood, we enter Outremont by taking either chemin de la Côte-Sainte-Catherine or avenue Van Horne. The arrival point is almost imperceptible. Suddenly we feel that we are in Outremont, but we are not really aware of the exact moment we crossed the border. From the east, the interface between Montreal and Outremont is even subtler because there are eleven east-west streets that connect Outremont to avenue du Parc, an important Montreal north-south thoroughfare. Two notable eastern entry points are avenue Van Horne and avenue Laurier. And the main axis penetrating Outremont from the southeast, and also one of its main landmarks, is chemin de la Côte-Sainte-Catherine, the former Indian pathway that circled the mountain and linked the north and south banks of the island.

Surface routes are not the only ones connecting Outremont to the rest of the world. Travelling on the metro, we may emerge in Outremont from one of two stations. And, obviously, Outremont is part of the worldwide network of cables and high-tech wires that human ingenuity has invented to transform the planet into a global village. Outremont is not an egocentric city. The strong cultural identification that characterizes Quebeckers and French Canadians, enhanced by their high level of education, gives the citizens of Outremont an assurance that makes them citizens of the world.

A Twentieth-Century City

Present-day Outremont was built almost entirely during the first half of the twentieth century. Before 1895 it was an agricultural settlement, and before the arrival of French settlers in the middle of the seventeenth century a forest. According to some historians, after Jacques Cartier had explored this part of the island in September 1535 he reported seeing a small Iroquois settlement (Tessier 1954, Beaugrand-Champagne 1993). This Native village was located where the section of avenue Maplewood that runs between avenues Pagnuelo and McCulloch is now found. In this particular location, the mountain forms a terrace and a small brook emerges; this may be the reason the Iroquois chose the site for their settlement. Today, this clear-water spring, largely channelled through underground pipes, is still visible at its source in the Mont-Royal cemetery.

A century later, in 1642, when Sieur de Maisonneuve founded Ville-Marie, no Indian settlement was found anywhere on the northern flank of

Mont-Royal (Biggar 1993). As every Montrealer knows, the French town was built on the banks of the Saint-Laurent where the Old Montreal historic district sits today. In those early days of the colony, Outremont was no more than a beautiful, dark wood, bisected only by a narrow Indian path.

In the aftermath of the founding of Ville-Marie, the king of France gave the Island of Montreal to a religious order, the Sulpicians. Soon after wards, the order began to survey and subdivide their vast domain, allocating farmland to French settlers. These subdivisions were called *côtes* because they resembled ribs; a main access road formed the spine. That is why Montreal has several neighbourhoods that bear this appellation: Côte-des-Neiges, Côte-Vertu, Côte-Saint-Antoine, and Côte-Saint-Luc.

The Côte-Sainte-Catherine subdivision was created in 1694, and six farms covering approximately three-quarters of the actual area of Outremont were allocated by Monsieur Dollier de Casson, the Sulpicians' superior, to Jean-Baptiste Tessier dit Lavigne, Jacques Tessier dit Lavigne, Charles Gervais, Louis Gervais, Jean Tessier dit Lavigne, and Nicolas Gervais. These French farmers were the real founders of Outremont. Each farm was a long, north-south rectangle, 175 metres wide and 1,754 metres long (Bisson 1993); together they were to define the permanent street pattern of Outremont.[98] The former Indian path circling the mountain connected Ville-Marie with the new settlement and was soon enlarged; it became chemin de la Côte-Sainte-Catherine, the "road" to the Côte-Sainte-Catherine subdivision. It cut diagonally through the south end of the farms.

In the following years, a few more farms were added to the original group. The 1731 census indicated that ten farms, covering almost the entire territory of Outremont, formed the Côte-Sainte-Catherine subdivision. On this land, eight farmhouses as well as a few secondary structures were built (Bisson 1993, 25). That was how it stood when the British defeated the French and took over the colony in 1763. During the following century, affluent English and Scottish gentlemen bought up the subdivision's best farms and became gentlemen farmers.

On 23 February 1875, the Côte-Sainte-Catherine subdivision obtained its first municipal charter from the Quebec Legislature and the Village of Outre-Mont was created. Save rare exceptions, such as Docteur Beaubien, all the main landowners of the new village were Anglo-Saxon: Cook, Pearson, Gibb, Dunlop, Thornbury, Taylor, Wiseman, McDougall, Bloomfield, Pratt, Nolan, and so on. At the time of its creation, the Village of Outre-Mont had a population of some 250 people living in 40 houses; 80 percent of the population was of Anglo-Saxon origin.

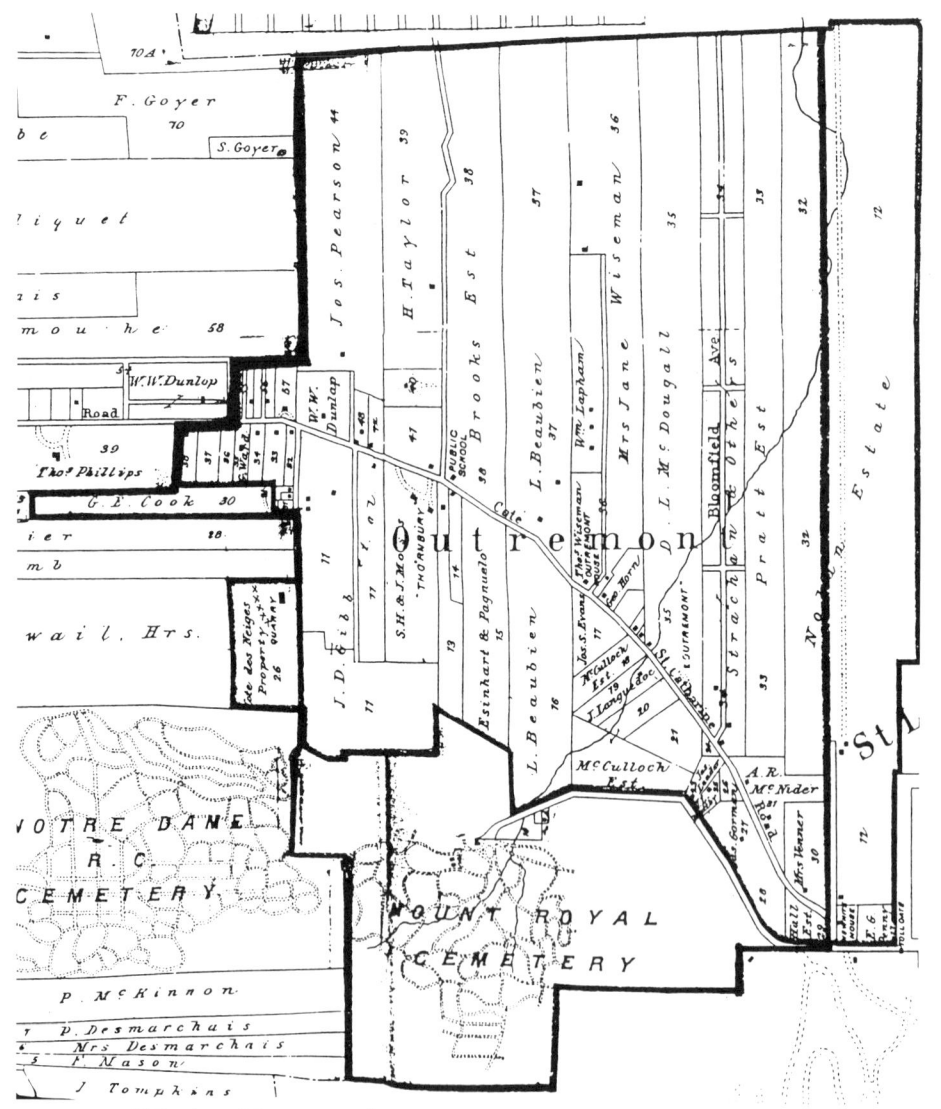

This plan of Outremont, circa 1875, shows the original farm subdivisions

In 1895, the Village of Outre-Mont transformed itself into the City of Outremont, and William Dunlop became the first mayor elected in the new municipality (Rumilly 1975).

The Outremont of today was built between 1900 and 1950 (Bisson 1993, 78–130; Rumilly 1975). In the twentieth century, the population rose steadily: from 1,150 inhabitants in 1901 to a peak of 30,750 in 1941, followed by a stable period until 1961, and a decline to the present-day level of 23,000. It seems that the population decline has now ended and that the city is entering a second stable period.

In the period just preceding World War I, a subtle turnaround occurred in Outremont's demographic trend. Little by little, French Canadians moved back to Outremont and regained their majority position. Joseph Beaubien, heir of one of Outremont's founding families, succeeded Alfred Joyce and Timothy Gordon to become, in 1910, Outremont's first French Canadian mayor. He retained this position for thirty-nine years.

About 1890, the first subdivision plans for the City of Outremont were presented to the municipal council. Joseph-Émile Vanier, a capable man who combined the professions of architect, civil engineer, and surveyor, drew up one of these plans. He proposed new north-south streets following the farm property lines. Vanier's plan was approved, and work began on creating the new subdivisions. In 1911, City Engineer Duchastel drew a map of Outremont that showed a pattern of properties almost identical to what it is today.

Year after year during the first half of the twentieth century, new streets were created, new lots put up for sale and bought, and new houses built. Simultaneously, modern infrastructures were installed. Electricity, gas streetlights and a telephone system quickly followed water-supply and sewer systems. As early as 1896, electric tramways ran along chemin de la Côte-Sainte-Catherine. In 1914, Outremont became the first Canadian city to replace its gas-streetlight system with the new electric tungsten-filament technology.

At the turn of the century, Outremont authorities undertook to beautify their city. They were influenced by the City Beautiful movement that came out of the 1893 Chicago Columbian Exhibition and by Sir Ebenezer Howard's Garden City concept. Such new town-planning ideas did not dictate the Outremont urban grid, however, because, as we have already seen, it had been established earlier by historical, geographical, and cultural circumstances; yet the town planners did positively influence the way this grid was developed. For example, as early as 1911, Outremont started to plant trees on both sides of its streets, creating the urban forest that we admire so much today.

Walking to Places

One reason cities are created is to increase access to goods and services. A city in which such accessibility is difficult is undoubtedly a city that has failed. Outremont has succeeded. From their position at the centre of Montreal, Outremontais can easily reach a wide range of urban services. But accessibility is not only related to the proximity of places of interest and the absence of physical barriers; it is also very much a question of feeling welcome in the places that one needs to frequent. In this respect, Outremont is highly convivial. No fences have ever been erected to hide private residences. Parks and squares are accessible at all times. During business hours, the doors to public buildings are kept open and visitors are generally greeted with a smile. In stores, cafés, and restaurants, we sense a civility that adds to the neighbourhood's friendly atmosphere.

When asked why they have chosen to live in Outremont, residents usually give answers that are related to accessibility: "Because it is like a village in the city"; "Because it is a very nice place with peaceful streets"; "Because it is close to good schools, to Collège Jean-de-Brébeuf, to the Université de Montréal, because it is close to ... everything." Indeed, a great variety of educational institutions are found in Outremont: elementary schools such as École Saint-Germain, Collège Stanislas, anglophone and francophone public high schools, some private boarding schools, a few units of the Université de Montréal, such as the very famous Vincent-d'Indy music school, and many others.[99]

In Outremont, most students walk to school, and they are not the only pedestrians to be seen. Most Outremontais walk, either in the course of conducting their business or to shop. They find walking very pleasant, except, of course, on extremely cold, windy winter days. They enjoy walking in Outremont for two reasons: distances are short and the environment is pleasing. It is possible, for example, to reach City Hall on foot from anywhere in the city in less than thirty minutes. As most sidewalks are lined with charming, well-groomed properties, the walk can be a pleasant experience. Some pedestrians will choose to follow a path that cuts across one or two parks, making the walk even more delightful. During the past few years, Outremontais have taken up cycling and roller skating in growing number. With this simple, almost simplistic, characteristic – that is, being a tightly packed, inner-city, pedestrian-oriented neighbourhood – Outremont distinguishes itself from most middle-class North American residential districts, which are disjointed, car-oriented suburbs on the outskirts of cities.[100]

In Outremont, institutional buildings blend into the residential fabric

The Parking Issue

No severe traffic problems are experienced in Outremont. Its street grid blends effortlessly into the Montreal network. In spite of its hard north and south edges, Outremont's grid is an open one, with no more than five dead-end streets. During rush hours, traffic is heavy only on the main axes;[101] the rest of the time, it is fluid. Except where traffic lights are necessary, stop signs have been installed on the four corners of every intersection, making circulation extremely safe. In any discussion of driving in their city, Outremontais are only likely to complain about one thing: the parking situation. They say that it is the shortage of parking space that is forcing them to park on their front lawns – more precisely, on that part of the front lawn that belongs to the municipality, where the mature maples grow. This is against municipal regulations, and those who do it risk the censure of their law-abiding neighbours and city-imposed fines. Where to park the car is a large existential question in Outremont. Still, it is difficult to embark on a philosophical discussion of this topic without smiling. The Outremont transportation problem is more aesthetic than functional: what many Outremontais resent is the sight of cars parked in front of residences. In 1993, the Municipal Council decreed that residences could no longer have garage doors on their street façades. Citizens who want to upgrade their houses and build indoor garages now have to find a way to bring cars in either from the back or from the side. This, of course, is impossible in certain instances.

A successful city must have all its urban systems functioning optimally. Even given today's elevated level of technological expectation, the performance of the urban systems of Outremont is very high. Pure water always flows out of Outremont faucets; supplies are abundant. Natural gas, piped in from Western Canada, is available everywhere. Electricity is cheap in Quebec, and its delivery reliable. Severe winter weather may cause the occasional power failure; but service is restored quickly. The telephone network works well and connects Outremontais efficiently to the rest of the world. Cable television, telefax, and electronic mail are readily available. But technology is not the entire picture. The simplicity of the urban grid and the tightness of the urban fabric facilitate the functioning of the urban systems. Through its layout, Outremont demonstrates that expensive technology is not the only way of obtaining high-performance urban systems. Intelligent design can work, as well. For example, by definition, an urban street system is a means of getting easily to various places in the city. If we enjoy a street system that allows us to walk to most places of interest in a pleasant environment rather than forcing us to drive through an ugly no-man's-land, then perhaps we do not need all those space-guzzling urban highways that create deep trenches in the urban landscape and that siphon traffic out of the existing grid, creating more traffic jams.

Red Brick and White Woodwork

I have already mentioned that most of Outremont's buildings were erected during the first half of the twentieth century. More precisely, 1 percent of the city's existing structures were built before 1900, 86 percent between 1900 and 1950, 12 percent between 1950 and 1980, and 1 percent since 1980 (Bisson 1993, 145). This is a remarkable amount of construction in a short span of time; and it may be the main reason that Outremont's buildings display such uniformity in construction materials and techniques. These buildings do, however, as a whole, provide an interesting demonstration of the architectural taste and design styles of this period.

While in the minds of many Outremont architects stone was a noble material to be reserved for institutions and churches, red clay brick was the most appropriate material for residences. Almost every house in Outremont

The main elements of Outremont's street archetype are rows of two-storey houses, flat roofs, red-clay brick, white woodwork, front porches, well-maintained lawns, bushes and flowers, and tall Norway maple trees

is made of brick. The most common construction technique for the exterior wall of a residence is to install three layers of brick with, on the inside, a wooden lath, a metal mesh, plaster and paint. Some houses have wooden frames covered with brick. A few of the more modern houses have stucco exterior finishes. Most roofs are flat and have inside drains. Exterior architectural features are made of wood: stairs, porches, balconies, columns, cornices, and miscellaneous ornaments. Some houses, however, have metal detailing; some porches have brick columns. Contrasting with the deep red of the clay brick, most exterior woodwork is painted white or off-white. Many houses, even the most humble ones, have fine oak or maple interior woodwork, oak floors, and fireplaces with oak mantels. The interior ceilings are much higher than the postwar norm, which is odd because today people are taller than their grandparents were.[102]

Vaulted Street Space

As we experience, one by one, the residential streets of Outremont, we notice only one basic form: a straight alignment of cubes. It is this perspective of

The vaulted street space distinguishes Outremont

positive street space that triggers our strongest visual impression of Outremont. Exploring the city's residential thoroughfares, we walk under a vault created by towering Norway maple trees, a pleasantly proportioned natural enclosure that has an air of serenity, enhanced in summer by dappled sunlight and in winter by dark branches that strive to pierce clouds laden with snow.

The cross section of a typical residential street in Outremont may be described as follows: the asphalt pavement is 10.0 metres wide. On both sides, the sidewalks are 1.5 metres wide and made of concrete. The red brick houses are 12.0 metre high two-storey cottages or twin houses with a flat roofs hidden behind cornices and parapets. The houses are set back 10.0 metres from the sidewalk. The entrance to each house is through a white wooden front porch. The interior ground-floor level of each house is some 1.5 metres above outdoor ground level. This ensures that, in such a cold climate, the house sits on a foundation lying below the frost line, deeper than 1.25 metres. Taking advantage of their excavation holes, Outremont houses have basements, and these are relatively well-lit spaces. The presence of such basements explains the high level of the interior ground floor. This is especially advantageous in winter, when some two metres of snow cover front lawns. As no fences are allowed in front of houses, individual front lawns combine to form a green strip that runs alongside the sidewalks. The first three metres of this continuous lawn, measured from the sidewalk edge, belong to the city, but are maintained by each homeowner. In the middle of this city-owned lawn, planted every fifteen metres, stand the majestic Norway maples that form the vault over the street and a canopy over the entrance to each house. Flowerbeds, small bushes, and vines complete the front-lawn landscaping. The vaulted street space is the first urban-design feature that signals to visitors that they have arrived in Outremont; they now occupy a space of discreet charm.

In a world of diminishing resources, intelligent urban design involves doing more, and better, with less. One way to accomplish this would be to construct public places that are multipurpose. Outremont has taken this initiative. Here, a street is simultaneously a vehicular-trafic artery, a parking space, and an esplanade for pedestrians. It is a positive space that enhances the community spirit of its residents, a place to meet and greet neighbours; it can even be a place to hold children's parties. In Outremont, a functional relationship has been established between the façades of houses and the street proper. It is possible, from the front door and windows of a house, to see and talk to people on the sidewalk; this creates a very secure environment. Although Outremont's residential streets are public places that welcome visitors, they truly "belong" to their residents.

All cities in the world are structured the same way: private properties are inserted into the public realm. Equilibrium between the two is difficult to achieve. For example, in most North American suburbs the balance is tipped in favour of private places. Public areas are often nothing but undistinguished wastelands where the only activity is the movement of cars. Little social interaction occurs in these vague spaces. Outremont is exemplary, because a rare complicity between the public and private realms has been achieved. When we walk along its streets, we admire lawns, flowerbeds, trees, and bushes. Some of them belong to the city; others to private owners. We cannot determine which is which. The public authority trusts private owners to maintain public grounds; and private owners trust the public authority to the extent that they will plant flowers on the city-owned strip of lawn that extends all the way to the well-travelled public sidewalk.

Dwellings are made to shelter people, and cities are built to protect communities. In Outremont, the psychological feeling of belonging to the community is quite strong and it manifests itself in numerous ways. Residences are cosy, agreeable, protective, and yet open to the exterior world. Streets are secure places where people meet. Parks are never far away, accessible to all at all times. Shopkeepers are amiable. Certainly, this sense of community is experienced differently by French Canadian residents than by those of other ethnic groups, but the fact that all Outremontais have freely chosen to live there indicates that they feel an attachment to their home community.

The harmonious continuity of the residential street space is counterpointed here and there by institutional buildings: churches, synagogues, temples, schools, and colleges. Although Outremont's three commercial street spaces appear less protective than its green, vaulted residential corridors, they display the same human scale. Continuity is stronger than distinctiveness on Outremont's residential streets; but the opposite is true on the city's commercial thoroughfares. There, harmonious features, such as the tall trees, the continuous front lawn, and the meticulous landscaping, have been replaced by smaller trees, wider sidewalks, flower boxes, sidewalk cafés, a panoply of street furniture, and a multiplicity of commercial signs – devices that strengthen difference at the expense of congruity.

Easy Orientation

Practically all of the 3,624 buildings in Outremont are distributed over a rectangular grid of long north-south rectilinear city blocks covering an area of 382 hectares. There are eighty-one streets in Outremont. The city is a network of 41.8 kilometres of streets, 11.9 kilometres of back alleys, and 72.5 kilometres of sidewalks. North of chemin de la Côte-Sainte-Catherine, where the terrain is relatively flat, the grid maintains its rectilinearity. In the southern section, it is twisted by the hilly terrain. Boulevard Mont-Royal and avenues Fernhill, Maplewood, and Springgrove bend to follow the contours of the slope.

In Outremont, strong, distinctive urban features facilitate orientation. Its street grid is the continuation of the Montreal rectilinear grid; as a consequence, 74 percent of all Outremont city blocks are perfectly rectangular. Chemin de la Côte-Sainte-Catherine, which is the main access route to the central business district of Montreal, cuts diagonally across this rectilinear grid. While the commercial avenues run east-west, all the long sides of the city blocks, which are predominantly residential, are oriented north-south. In places where the grid is deformed, the slope of the hill helps us to orient ourselves. We know that chemin de la Côte-Sainte-Catherine is at the bottom of the slope.

In Outremont, landmarks such as churches, colleges, and parks are easily identifiable. On most streets, the backs and fronts of buildings are clearly differentiated. Except in the case of a few residences and institutions perched on the hill, front doors and addresses are clearly visible from the street. And street names are posted at every corner.

Outremont was designed according to simple principles. Enhanced by the influence of the City Beautiful and Garden City movements, the basic rectangular layout became a relatively dense urban environment. The typical Outremont city block is a long rectangle oriented north-south with a back alley following its longitudinal axis. This back alley does not extend all the way to the avenues along the short ends of the rectangle. It stops behind the lots facing these avenues and, there, is met at right angles by two other back alleys that reach the avenues fronting the long sides of the block. This configuration permits a continuous façade on the east-west avenues, where most commercial and institutional facilities are located.

Today, all parts of the city, except for the Canadian Pacific Railroad marshalling yard, are fully developed. Hence, urban planning and design have become more a question of preserving and improving the existing environment than of creating a new one. The Outremont Architectural and Planning Commission spends long hours dealing painstakingly with an array of details. The city's larger urban-design policies are largely unspoken and based on a set of widely accepted values. Heated discussions erupt every week at the commission, as they should, but a large cultural consensus assures that the debate stays under control.

In the mid-seventies, the government of the Province of Quebec initiated an urban-renewal programme. Grants and incentives of many kinds were offered to homeowners to support the upgrading of their properties. An enormous number of Outremontais, in close collaboration with city authorities, took advantage of this fiscal incentive. However, this initiative is not the most important factor contributing to the excellent quality of Outremont's current building stock. Perhaps the dominant factor is the overall quality of the original construction. The city's pre-World War II houses, even the most humble ones, were well built with top-quality materials. For example, my own house, built in 1919, is still in excellent condition. The brick joints have never been touched and look like they will last for another century. Another factor that explains the quality of Outremont's constructed environment is that architects were commissioned to design most of the houses. Their success is a tribute to the entire profession – as it was practised in Montreal during the first half of the twentieth century. Yet another factor is that Outremont residences are constantly renovated and upgraded in order to fight the ravages of time. And, finally, Outremont's buildings and grounds are, as a rule, carefully maintained on a daily basis. Every day, Outremontais battle obsolescence and decay in small but effective ways.

Intense Community

As a spatial organization, Outremont has been functioning extremely well for almost a century. Compared to the North American norm, it is tightly packed. Its density is higher than the Montreal average, which, in turn, is higher than that of most North American cities. Outremont's overall density is 60.2 people per hectare, while the City of Montreal's is 57.5, and the Montreal Urban Community's is 40.5 (City of Outremont 1994). (In the United States, these figures would be converted to 24.4, 23.2, and 16.4 people per acre, respectively.) Such density indicates an intense land use and is a sign of frugality and efficient land management. While most North American cities are plagued by a disjointed urban sprawl, land is not wasted in Outremont. Vacant lots and those areas that the French call terrains vagues have been almost entirely eliminated from the Outremont landscape. Few neighbourhoods in North America can make such a claim. Those that are able to include Back Bay and Beacon Hill in Boston, Society Hill in Philadelphia, and San Francisco's inner-city residential districts. No doubt these are high-quality places equal to Outremont in many respects, but the cost of living in them is much higher than it is in Outremont.

Especially in the eastern section of Outremont, the streets are lined with continuous façades of three-storey row houses

Though it is a city with no industrial base to funnel large sums of money into its coffers, Outremont maintains a municipal tax rate lower than that of Montreal. This is certainly due to a century of excellent management. In the 1930s, during the Great Depression, Outremont was constantly cited as one of the best-run public administrations in the Province of Quebec (Bisson 1993, 115). Its efficient management was due, in part, to careful political monitoring on the part of the citizenry. Also, the city has functioned well because beyond the work done by the city's elected representatives and their civil servants are the efforts of the people who manage its private utilities, such as telephone, natural gas, and cable television. Furthermore, there are the contributions made by the city's private commercial establishments and even its individual households. A city needs to be well managed at all levels by all parties, because things are always interconnected and interdependent. Bankrupt households do not pay taxes, and this reflects negatively on the quality of municipal services. And, obviously, boarded-up shops reduce the attractiveness of commercial areas and undermine the efforts of those who try to establish a healthy business climate.

Not everything is perfect in Outremont. Homeowners and shopkeepers are still struggling to cope with the recession.[103] But Outremontais admit that the impact is less severe in their city than in most other parts of the Montreal region. They understand, also, that the current recession distorts most economic assessments, even in Outremont. The residential real-estate market has always been active in Outremont. There have always been plenty of houses for sale in the city; today, they just remain on the market longer than they did a few years ago. Compared to 1989, the commercial value of private property has fallen by about 10 to 15 percent. This trend is occurring in many parts of Canada. Outremont's properties, however, have maintained their value relative to other municipalities and are still considered very desirable places to live. For comparable accommodation, prices in Outremont are somewhat higher than they are in other inner-city districts of Montreal but considerably lower than in more affluent communities, such as Westmount or Nun's Island. In the commercial sector, empty facilities exist but are relatively rare.

Nature Given, Nature Enhanced

For a century now, Outremont's God-given natural environment has been enhanced by millions of respectful interventions that have transformed the city into a vast urban garden.

The omnipresent Mont-Royal is the dominant geographical feature of Outremont. The "mountain" is a gentle hill large enough to make its presence felt, yet low enough that older residents of boulevard Mont-Royal or avenue Maplewood can walk back to their homes without overexerting themselves after shopping on avenue Laurier. *La montagne*, as Mont-Royal is customarily called, is part of Outremont's decor. Strolling along avenue Laurier, we see clearly that the mountain forms the street space's western back wall, closing the perspective. It looks like a vertical green wall, as high as the surrounding buildings. However, in spite of the strong presence of the mountain in the city, no major mountainside public park is located in Outremont. The vast Parc Mont-Royal, designed by Frederick Law Olmstead and located a few steps away, is actually within City of Montreal territory. The only two mountainside spaces in Outremont territory are a cemetery and a wooded knoll adjacent to it, tucked in behind the Vincent-d'Indy music school.

The editors of the Quebec cultural magazine *Continuité*, in their special 1991 issue on Outremont, called this cemetery one of the most beautiful

Raw nature: this knoll is located on Mont-Royal next to a cemetery

"parks" in the Province of Quebec. Opened in 1852, the well-planned Mont-Royal cemetery has always been meticulously developed and maintained. Rare species of trees were planted there and the terrain smoothed to form gently rolling lawns. Today it is also a lively bird sanctuary. A few celebrities rest there, under the foliage: former Prime Minister of Canada John C. Abbott; and Anna Leonowens, the governess of the King of Siam, who inspired the musical comedy *The King and I*. When we retreat a few steps from the cemetery lawn and venture into the dense wood behind the music school, we experience one of Outremont's most amazing features. Here, no more than a ten-minutes walk from the busy city, we discover an untamed wilderness. No manmade construction has ever stood among these trees and bushes. This terrain remains as it was when de Maisonneuve founded Montreal in 1642.

According to the official count, there are some eighteen open spaces in Outremont: parks, sports fields, playgrounds, and minisquares. Among these, five very beautiful parks, well distributed through the city's central section, stand out: Joyce, Pratt, Saint-Viateur, Outremont, and Beaubien.

Access to the parks of Outremont is not hindered by fences

Together with the architecturally harmonious residences and the vaulted street spaces that surround them, these parks place Outremont above most other municipalities in terms of environmental quality ("Parcs" 1991).

Parc Joyce is the former property of Alfred Joyce, who was, briefly, mayor of Outremont in 1906. In 1926, he gave his property to the city, instructing that it be transformed into a public park. In addition to undulating lawns, generous trees, and "secret hiding places" created by natural rock formations, the park contains a well-used tennis club and a playground.

About five minutes to the west lies perhaps the most beautiful park in Outremont, Parc Pratt. Acquired in 1929 by the municipality, this property was at first considered too small to be an urban park. Nonetheless, the city manager at the time, Émile Lacroix, teamed up with architect Aristide Beaugrand-Champagne and horticulturist Thomas Barnes to create a jewel of urban landscaping. Despite the truism that a committee cannot design, it is hard to deny that in this case a triumvirate of very talented individuals was able to produce a remarkable urban oasis. As a tribute to its beauty, wedding parties invade Parc Pratt every Saturday of the fair season to conduct photo sessions.

At about the same time, Beaugrand-Champagne also designed another magnificent little park, Parc Saint-Viateur. Two steps north of commercial avenue Bernard and three steps away from Théâtre Outremont, this park is distinguished by its annular pond; a white pavilion dominates its central island. In winter, the frozen pond becomes a skating rink. In fact, Parc Saint-Viateur is but one of the elements that makes this particular city block an interesting campus. Complementing the park itself are public tennis courts; a meeting house for teenagers; Outremont's francophone public high school and its sports fields; two large residences belonging to the Clercs de Saint-Viateur, a religious order that played a major role in the city's development; two apartment buildings; and a miniplaza linking the park with avenue Bernard.

Parc Outremont is perhaps the most dignified and formal of the five parks. It has been in the public domain since 1898. Here, also, in the middle of a magnificent lawn, we discover a pond with a charming fountain. Its flowerbeds display spectacular tobacco flowers. In this serene location, Outremont erected its war monument.

Parc Beaubien is the youngest and largest park of the group. It was designed and built in 1961. Its north side faces chemin de la Côte-Sainte-Catherine, and its south edge touches the anglophone high-school's sports field. A fountain with a soaring water jet, installed on the park's north edge, has become a well-known Outremont landmark. This park also boasts a large playground, a small hill that becomes a toboggan slide in winter, as well as exquisite lawns, bushes, and flowers.

These five parks share some strong attributes. Each has a rectangular outer rim defined by the street grid. However, within its rectangle, each was designed according to curvilinear English-Garden landscaping principles. The parks are small enough to facilitate personal security, yet large enough to allow visitors to experience a relative solitude. Their edges are soft and porous; access to them is not hindered by fences or gates. Together, the five rectangles have a total of twenty sides; that is, there are twenty linear interfaces between the parks proper and the rest of the urban fabric. Sidewalks border sixteen of the twenty park sides; two other sides touch high-school properties, one more backs onto some private properties, and the last opens onto a commercial street through a minisquare. Where park lawns border the sidewalk, there are no interruptions or obstacles.

Another common attribute is the fact that these parks are all multiusage areas. Each has particular uses that distinguish it from the others, but all share a common function: they serve as relaxing promenades. In all of them, vegetation is varied, but soft green lawns dominate. Water is part of the landscaping in four of them. In winter, these green spaces become white playgrounds featuring skating rinks, toboggan slides, and open snowfields for skiing and snowshoeing. All of the parks, like every other public place in Outremont, are carefully maintained. We sense a strong and intimate bond between the residences encircling the parks and the parks themselves.

Outremont is a residential neighbourhood hidden under a forest. Statistically speaking, Outremont has less green space than the North American norm, certainly less than many other Quebec municipalities, but this apparent shortcoming is amply compensated for by the fact that every private front lawn and every backyard is, in itself, a little garden. Because the front yards are contiguous, because Outremont is tightly and fully built, these thousand little pieces of garden play a vital rôle in the formation of the urban landscape. The City Hall computer will show that in 1994 the city owned 5,263 trees along its streets, and 1,400 more in its parks. Given that the city's population is 23,000, the ratio of trees per person is 0.29; this outstrips Montreal (0.25), Laval (0.21), and Quebec City (0.11). The computer will further show that if we add in the trees on private properties and those in the Mont-Royal cemetery, we will obtain a very respectable ratio of 0.70 trees per citizen.

The city's towering Norway maple trees are very old; most of them were planted over sixty-five years ago. In an urban setting, the average life expectancy of this species is fifty years. There is a constant danger that one day a disease – like Dutch elm disease, which decimated so many trees some years ago – will wipe out these glorious maples. Or that a severe ice storm will destroy them in one night. In response to this very real possibility, Outremont authorities have instituted an aggressive reforestation programme: with the help of the city's powerful computer, the trees are monitored, nurtured, and pruned with love and care. As a rule, a tree that dies is immediately replaced by one of a different species in order to eliminate the risk of having a disease kill all the trees on a single street at once.

Frugality

Outremont is a frugal town. Energy is not wasted there. In a northern climate, row houses or even duplexes are more energy efficient than detached houses; compact cottages are also more energy efficient than sprawling bungalows. These considerations have influenced the city's architectural design. Outremontais often choose to walk rather than drive, or they opt to use the bus or the metro, thus conserving energy (Guenet 1992). The energy-conservation programmes recently initiated by the province's utility companies, Hydro-Québec and Gaz Métropolitain, have persuaded home owners to improve the insulation of their homes, mainly under flat roofs, and transform their old oil-heating systems into more efficient, cogenerating electricity/natural-gas systems. The brick walls of most Outremont residences were built before World War II at a time when energy conservation was not an issue, and are often difficult to retrofit. Cold air continues to filter through them. During the past ten years, heat pumps have been installed extensively, but they are noisy and cause neighbours to complain.

Another energy factor comes into play in every urban setting: human energy. Perhaps because they inhabit a northern climate where the seasons change constantly, Outremontais always seem to be working on their properties. In winter, they shovel snow and combat the ice; in spring, they clean, nurture awakening lawns and budding bushes, and plant new flowers; in summer, they repair and paint houses, and mow lawns; and in fall, they rake up millions of fallen leaves. Always, however, the first snow catches them by surprise. Because they miss the opportunity to remove the last of the dead leaves, they fear that the foliage will rot under the snow and damage their lawns. But nature has a way of surprising everyone, and every spring the flora emerges as lush as ever.

Distinctive Look

Visitors to Outremont always agree with residents that the city has character. Its unique look is a product of the continuity of the urban fabric, the green-vaulted, straight residential streets, the harmonious succession of residential façades, the red clay brick, the white woodwork, the front porches, the cornices and balconies, and the parks. All this creates an aesthetic of gentle rhythms, of diversity within a strong unity, and of an intimate relationship between architecture and landscape design. In fact, its structures aside, Outremont is a glorification of the art of gardening. In Outremont, citizens have been inspired to re-create, every spring, a garden city in the harsh Canadian climate; this constitutes a tribute to the civilizing power of the flower.

One very interesting aspect of Outremont's character is the fact that it has no distinctive architectural style of its own – or, perhaps, that it displays a random combination of thirty different styles (Bisson 1993, 172). The issue of whether to adopt a so-called conservative aesthetic or a so-called avant-

Located at the corner of chemin de la Côte-Sainte-Catherine and avenue Dunlop, this Outremont house was built in 1890; the design of its façade is timeless

garde aesthetic is rarely discussed in this city; it has never really been considered relevant in matters of urban design. Even though architects designed most Outremont buildings, it seems that styles, fashions, and architectural ideologies were never dominating features of the constructed landscape. These things have always been subordinate to larger community concerns. It is fair to assume that the many architects who designed Outremont wanted to please their clients. It seems that their ideas were formulated out of private considerations and, consequently, were rarely disseminated.[104]

Locus of Values

By the mere fact of living in a place, people create an ambience and, in return, are influenced by it. What is the significance of Outremont for Outremont residents? Is it only a series of buildings? Or a tranquil neighbourhood in an exciting city? Or a place to live? Or is it also the locus of their values? If Outremont demonstrates anything, it is that there is always a strong relationship between the quality of the designed environment and the quality of life. Like the Palais-Royal and the Fondation Rothschild Workers' Residence, Outremont is a civilized place that is conducive to civilized behaviour. Or perhaps the opposite is true: civil, respectful people require a civil, respectful environment. I have had numerous conversations with many residents of Outremont over a period of more than twenty years and have taken on several consulting assignments with the city; from this experience I have gained the clear impression that Outremontais love their city and would not live anywhere else in the Montreal region.[105] By and large, the people of Outremont are well-educated, articulate citizens, aware of their values, and, to a large extent, in control of their municipal destiny. They want to maintain what they have chosen to be a part of: a respectful community and a high-quality environment.

Because of the close relationship that exists between "ordinary" citizens and their leaders, politics in Outremont is a family affair. It is a dynamic networking that transcends all political ideologies. When it comes to municipal affairs, it matters little if one is conservative, liberal, separatist, or federalist. Everyone talks to everyone else, including to the many important, and not so important, politicians of every stripe who live in Outremont.

A few years ago, under a previous administration, a political incident occurred that illustrates the intimate involvement Outremontais have with the political process. When the first warm days of spring arrive, as soon as the ground is dry enough, many younger citizens rush to the parks. Living in apartments without backyards of their own, they settle onto the

In Outremont, the environment is secure and convivial; private properties complement the public domain

grass to work on an early suntan. Some take exception to this ritual, calling it an indecent display of flesh. They phone City Hall and voice their complaints. Usually, by the time the issue comes up for discussion, the arrival of fall has rendered it irrelevant. But, this particular spring, a retired French Canadian judge, two or three Hassidic rabbis, and few elderly ladies convinced the city administration to act swiftly. An edict banning the "wearing of bathing suits and bikinis" in the parks of Outremont was passed. Of course, this measure immediately triggered a hilarious uproar. The next day, Montreal's leading newspaper, *La Presse*, published a cartoon showing two plump middle-aged ladies in a graceful Outremont park; both were nearly naked except for their straw hats, jewellery, and high heels; they were busy expressing to an equally naked and equally plump mayor their appreciation – they were very pleased that the bikini had finally been banned from the city's parks. The new bylaw permitted men to jog wearing only a pair of shorts but forbade women to wear a bikini top with shorts. Many joked that they agreed with City Hall: bare-breasted jogging women were preferable to those wearing tops. In the heat of this "crisis," a meeting of the Municipal Council was convened. That day, the weather was gorgeous, and practically all of Outremont decided to exercise their democratic rights: the meeting turned into a social gathering. Neighbours and friends who had not seen one another for a long time took advantage of the assembly to catch up with one another. The council chamber was too small to accommodate such a crowd, and spontaneous debates erupted on the sidewalk. Arguments developed based on concerns ranging from protecting the innocence of children to promoting equal rights for women. Contradictory opinions were humorously, if not forcefully, presented. During the meeting I asked the mayor, a lawyer, a former Quebec minister of justice, and a longtime personal friend, if he had obtained a legal opinion regarding this bylaw. He said: "Of course!" and added that he was "on safe ground." This assurance given, he struck the desk with his gavel and the bylaw was ratified. Many citizens shook their heads, anticipating that this measure would be nothing but *un coup d'épée dans l'eau*, "a useless gesture." Sure enough, a few weeks later, a young, aggressive Outremont lawyer – a jogger – perhaps prompted by his girlfriend, challenged the bylaw in court. The city lost on the grounds that the bylaw violated certain provisions of the Canadian and Quebec charters of rights. And that was the end of the Outremont bikini crisis.

    This incident serves as a demonstration of how democracy works in Outremont. Extremely sensitive, as it is, to the little whims of the citizenry, the Municipal Council sometimes goes too far and adopts ridiculous measures. But most of the time prudence and common sense prevail. The incident also shows that Outremontais can quickly mobilize themselves to participate directly in the affairs of their city. Finally, it shows that in Outremont information flows freely, political debates are public, and people care.

Successful Architecture

As we conclude our Outremont promenade, we can repeat almost word for word the remarks with which we were able to summarize our first two journeys. The architecture of Outremont is as successful as that of both the Palais-Royal and the Fondation Rothschild Workers' Residence, and for the same reasons: it displays an equilibrium of the public and the private realms, a sense of enclosure, a positivity in its public spaces, an order that still embraces innumerable variations in a complex harmony, a convivial accessibility, detailed architectural features that maintain a human scale, exquisite landscaping in both its public and private areas that fully respects the environment, and a restrained, nonostentatious beauty that responds to its users' tastes. And, as are the other two places, Outremont is a neighbourhood where people have chosen to live, a neighbourhood that provides its residents with ongoing satisfaction and delight.

In short, Outremont is a place of high quality and great beauty. In a totally different way, its success is as profound as that of the Palais-Royal or the Fondation Rothschild Workers' Residence.

To Dwell in Outremont

A dimension of the essence of architecture is dwelling. Above everything else, to dwell is to be able to live at home. Outremont demonstrates this idea in a fundamental way, because it contains excellent and magnificent dwellings adapted to the needs of the community. As we have confirmed, successful residential architecture implies that each and every person is provided with a dwelling they can call home. This is not an abstract concept, but, rather, a deeply felt reality constructed from physical materials, a place that enhances human dignity – your home and my home. All dwellings are dwelling, all homes are home, as universally unique as people themselves.

Outremont has shown that to dwell is to have a secure place in a secure environment, to benefit from several overlapping shelters, to care about matters of the heart as well as concerns of the mind. It is to live in an

This fountain located in Parc Outremont is an Outremont landmark

environment where respect for individuality is magnified by respect for the community. It is to live in concordance with the seasons and to enjoy the sun and the rain, the dandelions and the snowflakes, the squirrels and the sparrows. It is to realize that a fruitful, harmonious order is one that emerges from an acceptance of diversity rather than an imposed sameness. To dwell is to know and be known, to welcome and be welcomed, to have a propitious community environment to share.

To stroll in the garden of the Palais-Royal is to indulge in a moment of peace

8

REVEILING ARCHITECTURE

The preceding epochès and constitution were attempts to grasp the essence of architecture. Using three examples, we explored the symbiotic idea of high quality and great beauty as the necessary conditions for producing an architecture of satisfaction. But our inquiry is not yet finished. We have not taken the final step of the epochès. This step might involve a fuller formulation of the essence of architecture and lead to a respectful, successful design. And we have developed only one constitution; more are required.

At this juncture, it might be worth recalling what we have accomplished so far:

a. A theoretical framework based on phenomenology has been developed; it provides a method for describing, assessing, and making architecture.
b. Architectural theories have been bracketed and temporarily suspended for the purpose of asserting a first utterance of the universal idea of the architectural phenomenon as it presents itself to our consciousness.
c. A further phenomenological reduction of the architectural phenomenon has led to the identification and temporary removal of the twelve veils that constitute its intrinsic reality; its eidos in terms of the composite idea of dwelling and place have thereby been uncovered.
d. Another epochè has been conducted. It has unveiled the social values that buttress the housing rights expressed in universal charters of rights. It has resulted in a formulation of the telos of architecture in terms of people's satisfaction. This reduction has permitted the constitution of a series of thirty-seven value-based design criteria; these constitute a basis

for assessing design schemes, as well as existing places, and for facilitating the making of a satisfactory architecture.

e. The phenomenological method of inquiry, both factual and judgemental, has been applied to three enduring and successful architectural artefacts in order to uncover the reasons for their lasting success; many have now been discovered and formulated.

All of these accomplishments combine to create a rich array of deconstructed elements, each of which constitutes, in one fashion or another, either a piece of the architectural phenomenon or an element in the process of designing architectural things. Perhaps they provide a solid-enough justification for continuing the constitution procedure initiated by the formulation of criteria. Perhaps an approach to making a more satisfactory architecture could be constituted at this point. This double "perhaps" is an expression of caution, an architect's reflex. If the deconstructed phenomenon, resulting from the epochè, can be compared to the architectural brief, which expresses discrete programmatic requirements, and if the coming phenomenological constitution can be associated with design, then prudence is justified. All experienced architects know that architectural programmes tend to evolve during the design phase. It is therefore prudent to wait until the project is finished, until the programme's final utterance is crystallized. Here, also, it might be conceivable that the consciousness of the essence of architecture might be modified, even enhanced, as the means of making it are developed. The formulation of the essence of architecture may have to wait awhile longer, until more constitutions have been developed.

A DESIGN STRATEGY

The task of reassembling the scattered ingredients constituting the architectural phenomenon requires a means, some sort of conceptual instrument, to reconstruct what has been deconstructed. This constitution is conducted in order to complement the answer to the third fundamental question of the theory: "How do we make a more satisfactory architecture?" Raised earlier by the constitution of the value-based design criteria, this constitution continues with the elaboration of an urban- and architectural-design strategy.

What I propose is a phenomenological, action-oriented, prescriptive approach that considers it more efficient to start constructing the kind of future that we want now than to try to predict the kind of mediocre future that will inevitably be imposed upon us if we do not intervene. This approach also suggests that rather than designing isolated and unrelated buildings in this uncertain world it might be more productive to integrate individual buildings into a coherent environmental whole that reflects the values of the community. While it is difficult to construct a world, it is easy to build a building. Many little buildings, made in a coherent way, may facilitate the construction of a more coherent world. Such coherence is needed both in design intent and in the resulting reality; a coherent design will produce a coherent product and a coherent theory will bolster a coherent practice.

At the level of operational structure, the design strategy presents itself as a general process. However, at the level of application, it allows for infinite variation. Its enactment does not presuppose any particular ideology. For instance, an architect who advocates the Modern Architecture viewpoint could apply it with as much efficacy as an architect who argues for postmodernism.[106] The strategy is, basically, an urban-design strategy, one that encompasses at one of its stages a more precise architectural-design process. As we shall see, the notion of the architectural scheme is presented in the strategy as a "desired future." In this sense, human satisfaction is the ultimate goal and central principle of the strategy. It is a goal that can be obtained only through a constant dialogue with people and through the mobilization of the non-self-referential, value-based design criteria.

Although the strategy is described in a linear fashion, it is not, in fact, linear. Rather, it is a never-ending procedure that must be reviewed constantly and requiring, as Lyotard said, a permanent "radical rebeginning" (Lyotard 1991, 132). Everywhere and at any given moment, several of these procedures are being conducted, each influencing the others, each being improved or distorted by the others.

As intentionality is the consciousness of something else, design is an intentional procedure that targets the object to be designed. This seemingly obvious statement aims at reasserting that the making of the designed environment starts with a proactive knowledge of the work. Let me repeat that it is impossible to design an unknown object. Furthermore, it is impossible to achieve excellence and magnificence in architectural design without acquiring the most intimate knowledge of the object to be made, without a thorough understanding of its inner structuring, its outer configuration, and its ramifications for its surroundings.

The strategy contains seven steps. It could be presented in a "time-quality/beauty" Cartesian orthogonal double-axis diagram. The grid's ordinate is the axis of the symbiotic concept of quality and beauty (Q/B). It is a vertical, upward-pointing arrow that indicates levels of quality and beauty, taken as a unified attribute: the higher the arrow points on the scale,

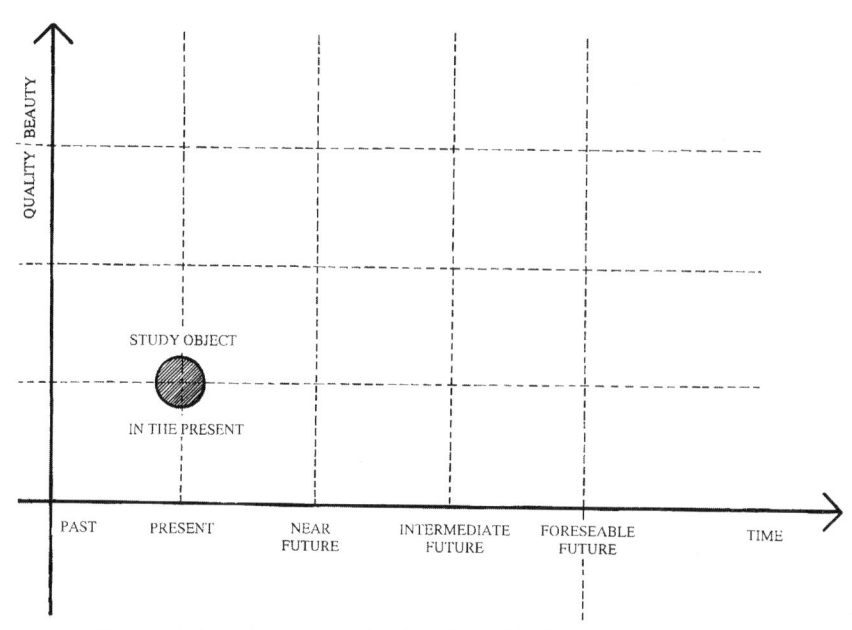

Design strategy diagram: on the Cartesian grid, phase one of the strategy

the higher the quality/beauty of the object is. During the implementation of the strategy, this scale is used to compare existing artefacts, or a design scheme with what it seeks to replace. In order for a design object to rank higher on the scale, both its quality and beauty have to increase; if only one dimension of one of that object's attributes is poor, then it will descend on the scale. The grid's abscissa represents the course of time [T]. It is an arrow pointing to the right, or to a future that is foreseeable.

On the diagram, the object to be designed is represented by a circle. At the outset of the strategy, this circle is placed over the moment designated as "Present" and at an arbitrarily selected level of quality and beauty. It is arbitrary because, in this matter, no absolute scale can be established. The scale is nothing but an abstract measuring device, which will eventually be defined by society in light of its accepted values. The arbitrary coordinates of the existing object serve as the departure point of the strategy. From that point on, a series of steps will be taken to raise the object's level of quality/beauty as it progresses through time. A horizontal line, passing through the centre of the circle that represents the object, forms its baseline.

In this strategy, the object to be designed is defined by a universal feature: a material entity to be transformed. This always implies a site.[107] An empty site is not nothingness: it is an object to be changed by design interventions. The strategy calls for the replacement of the "present" physical situation with an improved "future" physical situation. Two examples may be used to illustrate this point: now and here, there is an empty lot and later, but still here, through an architectural intervention, it will be filled with a residential building; a dilapidated neighbourhood is upgraded through a series of urban-design and architectural interventions. In both cases, indeed in all cases, the existing reality of the site is replaced by a new reality. The challenge is to engineer a change for the better. The architectural project is the prescriptive activity through which this positive metamorphosis occurs. It always entails an understanding of the reality to be changed, the creation and representation of the scheme to be implemented before it becomes reality, the expressed will to implement it, and the actual construction. The architect's mandate is to ensure the coherent conduct of this activity.

Step One: Description of the Actual Situation

The first step of the strategy is the careful, painstaking description of the reality to be transformed by the project – a description of the place where the project is to happen. This description, necessarily synchronic, is something well beyond what is normally understood as site analysis, but includes it. It comprises all relevant data related to the site and the anticipated scheme.[108] It involves the systematic description of eleven of the twelve veils of this particular architectural phenomenon. Only eleven veils are activated here, because the twelfth one, the veil of history, is spread over the course of time towards the past. We will deal with it later, in the second step of the strategy.

This study starts with the phenomenological description of the people affected by both the existing situation and the future scheme. Hard information such as demographic and social data, as well as softer, more diffuse behavioural insights are provided. Questions such as these are asked: What are the unwritten or unspoken cultural patterns of the area? What are the prevailing ideologies? What are the mobilizing motivations? What is the informal power structure? Moreover, all the activity components that exist on the site, as well as the elements that comprise the site's surroundings, its materiality, and its structuring systems, are described. The natural factors that influence the site, from soil type to climatic conditions, are added. A detailed description of the existing reality's visible features – shapes, exterior forms, interior spaces – is carried out. The description includes a thorough understanding of the economic, budgetary, and financial questions related to both the existing reality and the future project; it covers, as well, an estimate of the amount of energy already embedded in the existing reality and of the amount required to create and build the project. Finally, each existing situation has a character and carries with it an array of meanings and symbolic dimensions; these must be understood by the architect to the fullest extent possible, and described.

Far from being exclusively factual, the phenomenological description of the existing situation is also judgemental. The value-based criteria outlined in chapter 4 are called upon to support the assessment of the existing reality under scrutiny and to complement its description. The description cites the existing reality's positive and negative attributes; the problems the latter pose are to be investigated.

With the aid of this multifaceted factual and judgemental description an image of the study object – as it appears today, before the scheme is conceived – can be drawn. Graphically, on the Cartesian diagram, this image takes the form of a poché filling the circle located over "present." In practice, at this juncture, extensive study reports are drafted. Step one is complete.

Step Two: Historical Description

Reflecting on the existing situation in which he must intervene, the architect is compelled to ask how it has occurred. What is the genesis of this reality? Of course, such questioning, prompting a diachronic description of the study object, presupposes a certain deterministic view of the architectural phenomenon. While the architect may accept that determinism is not absolute and that fate always distorts the best-conceived plans, he cannot negate that his own trade is deterministic to a large extent. By definition, design is making things happen, and thus involves manipulating evolution. By his design action the architect becomes an agent of change. If he accepts the deterministic dimension of his own action, he has to accept the similarly deterministic dimension of builders' or other architects' actions. Because, without exception, all buildings that have ever existed were designed; they were, and are, the result of a deterministic creative action.

The existing situation is rolled back, and this produces several descriptions of the same reality at different moments of the past. We now have a

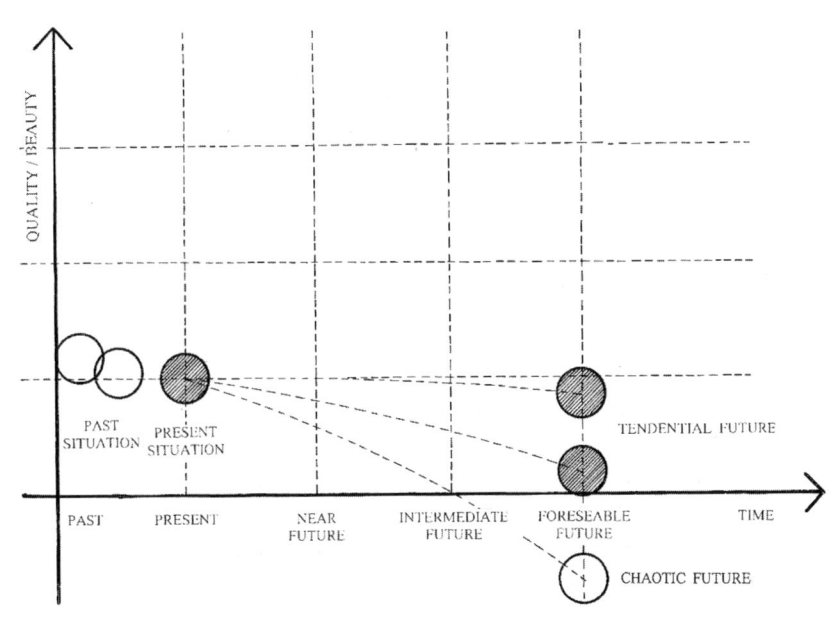

Design strategy diagram: phases one, two, and three of the strategy

sequence of at least two images of the same reality, one from a distant past and one from a near past, that illustrates an evolution culminating in the present study object, which as already been described in the preceding step.

Such a return to the past is necessary for more than one reason. A study of the past helps us to understand the present, uncover a meaningful inspiration for the future, and trace evolutionary curves. At least two moments in time are necessary to trace the trajectory of a trend. Without a knowledge of the past with which to anchor the curve, a projection into the future is not possible.

Like the description of the present situation, the description of past situations comprises the eleven veils, complemented by the veil of history, and activates, again, the value-based criteria. While the veils remain constant through time, criteria may not, and this raises a problem. Which criteria should be used in this reflection on the past? Should one utilize criteria supported by values as they were perceived in the past, or criteria based on values as they are currently interpreted? I would suggest that we employ the latter criteria for two compelling reasons. The first is that we live in the present and the act of making the project exists in the present, transforming a current situation. It is no consolation to people who today suffer from a situation created in the past that it was created with the best of intentions. If today's judgement is that a certain environmental situation is unacceptable, then one needs to understand how this particular situation has occurred. The second reason is, simply, that no other course of action is possible. In matters of environmental assessment, cultural behaviour, social interaction, and political determination, hindsight is unavoidable. The phenomenological template that we used to describe the present situation must be used in the course of our historical studies if we are to compare the past and the present.

With this method of comparative description, we may identify meaningful trends and chart the evolution of the study object. When this is done, images of the same study object – but this time depicting its past situations – will be symbolized on the diagram and positioned at their respective moments in the past.

The first delicate gesture of the strategy now occurs. It is time to compare the present and past situations and pass a value judgement as to their quality/beauty levels. What is the basic trend? Has the quality/beauty level of the study object gone up during the past several years or has it slid down? As a rule, though – and because the client has hired an architect – we may assume that improvement is needed, at least in the opinion of the client. At best, the existing situation is assessed as unsatisfactory, at worst as problem-ridden. The architect and the client do not make this assessment alone. Three other parties may be (indeed, should be) involved because they are directly concerned with the product of the architectural undertaking. These are: the users of the future artefact (when they can be identified), the relevant political authorities, and the general public. In this group – encompassing architect, client, users, authorities, general public – only the architect has the ability to view the situation as a future design. He has the responsibility of validating the views of the other parties, which are largely empirical, to give them a design substance, and to help raise them to the level of a professional undertaking. From this assessment, the basic historical trend of the study object is charted. It is either horizontal, ascending, or descending. If the trend is ascending or even horizontal and the present situation is judged satisfactory, the exercise may stop here. All other outcomes warrant intervention, and the strategy may proceed.

Step Three: Projection of Future Trends

The third task of the strategy is to probe the future – always a frustrating job. Various statistical models exist to simulate urban evolution and project trends with a certain degree of accuracy (Wegener 1994), but these models are efficient on the macro scale and as a means of isolaing trends that feature repetitive patterns and hard, verifiable data. Architecture, however, is always on the micro scale; it always deals with the most minute and intimate details. Of course, any study of an architectural phenomenon will contain many macro-scale elements, such as demographic trends, economic or financial cycles, market tendencies, fiscal patterns, transportation analyses, and weather information; it will also contain numerous projections related to such social issues as crime or public health. Statistics exist on most aspects of our collective life. Still, the same architectural phenomenon also has many dimensions that defy repetitive patterns. In spite of obvious methodological difficulties, these unquantifiable, largely unpredictable dimensions must also be included in the trend-spotting exercise.

The projection of future trends, like the return to the past, is an intellectual journey through time. As I said earlier, in our individual as well as our collective lives, in our houses as well as our cities, the course of time involves more than the passing of the hours. It includes predictable patterns and unpredictable events. We can, perhaps, predict the cycle of life (birth, growth, ageing, and death), the process of decay (of biological and material objects), the acquisition of experience, the permanence and failure of memory, and the cycles of nature. We can also predict that there will be moments of joy and moments of sorrow, easy and difficult times, and that people – should they so decide and up to a certain point – can influence the course of history. Individual as well as collective initiatives create opportunities. For instance, at the level of individual destiny, suffering through our school years will most likely help us to obtain a better job later on. An illustration of collective initiative is found in the tradition of *la corvée*, still flourishing in many rural communities. When a house or a barn burns down, villagers gather to help their unfortunate neighbour. Working together, they may rebuild the structure in a single weekend. While the men are busy with their hammers and saws, the women prepare food and serve wine and beer. A sad event is transformed into a festive happening, a demonstration of social solidarity. Such collective action influences the destiny of the village, making it a better place to live. Institutions, *cadre de vie*, and built forms do not only evolve through time according to their own cosmic destinies; they are also influenced by human interventions. This particular aspect of our evolution can be predicted.

What can not be predicted is the specific occurrence of events within general patterns. Individual efforts may flounder, projects launched with the best of intentions may abort, and armed conflicts may destroy years of construction in a single day. Positive unforeseen events happen, as well.

But whether they are positive or negative, events hide most of their motivating dimensions and many of the reasons for their occurrence. What can hardly be known in advance are the depth, richness, and power of the individual and the collective unconsciousness that triggers events. Love, hate, fear, insecurity, ambition, creativity, generosity, and a sense of responsibility are all elements of human nature that profoundly, but mysteriously, influence our destiny and the way our designed environment is built through time.

In the strategy we are now developing, such a limitation of our ability to predict the future is not crucial because it is a part of the exercise that does not directly determine the final outcome of the strategy. We must remember that the essential purpose of the strategy is not to predict the future with absolute certainty (we know the limitations of the exercise too well to believe that this is possible), but to invent and then construct the sort of future people want. Nonetheless, and in spite of its imprecision, the trend-spotting exercise is necessary if we are to document in a diachronic way the weaknesses and strengths of the current situation: are things likely to improve or deteriorate? It is also indispensable for establishing future quality/beauty levels. In other words, the projection of future trends helps us to demonstrate the severity of the problem and the urgency of the task.

Past trends are already charted on the diagram. Now they have to move ahead of the present moment and penetrate the future. How will the study object behave if the same evolutionary patterns persist? Left to its own evolutionary forces, will that object maintain its overall quality/beauty level, slip downward, or move upward? If the future trend is upward, then perhaps this particular object's evolution should not be disturbed; may be it should be allowed to run its natural course; that is, the project stops here. If it remains at the same level of quality/beauty, and if this level is presently acceptable, then perhaps our resources should be channelled into more problematic areas. Again, the project may stop here. If, however, the situation deteriorates, then intervention may become necessary. Like living creatures, manmade objects age and decay. Constant maintenance is necessary to maintain their physical integrity and performance capability. Also, as users' needs evolve, unattended objects become obsolete and rapidly sink below their original, intended quality/beauty level.

How far into the unknown future will we be able track these trends? In fact, the same question should have been asked with respect to the historical study. In both cases, the answer relates to the specificity of the project at hand. As a rule, the past and future horizons should be placed far enough away from one another to allow enough time for a meaningful change to occur and near enough to be manageable. A horizon established at too great a distance into the future or the past engenders too many distortions. For example, if we were, today, to rebuild East Lake Meadows (the Atlanta housing project described in chapter 2), we might well have to look at how things were in that part of the world some fifty years before the project was constructed. If we wanted to understand how such a horrible environment could have been created, we would certainly have to study the social, political, and economic situation of Afro-Americans since World War II. We would have to examine, for instance, the impact of the GI Bill, the civil-rights movement in the South, and the federal subsidized-housing programme. A projection some fifty years into the future might also be necessary. The actual reconstruction period would probably last no more than about ten of the fifty years our projection would cover, but beyond that first ten-year period the community would continue to live and changes would occur. Three successive generations might have to come into being before the kind of community and environment people now want is realized. It took longer than that for the Fondation Rothschild Workers' Residence to reach the high quality/beauty level it currently enjoys.

On the diagram, the horizon takes the form of a second vertical axis, similar to the first one, and located on the far-right side. It is on this second quality/beauty ordinate that the end results of the future trends are depicted. What is described is a series of images of our study object at a certain future moment if the present trends continue and if no architectural interventions occur in the meantime. In addition, this trend projecting does not take into account major catastrophes, such as an earthquake, a war, or a major epidemic, which defy prediction.

A series of quality/beauty levels defining different environmental states for the future, or simply different futures, are inscribed on this second axis. From top to bottom, these different futures are:

1. Utopian future. This future is situated outside the diagram proper, above any normal architectural schemes. In architecture, the creation of utopian concepts is a necessary exercise and an integral part of architectural knowledge development, but should occur outside the scope of this particular procedure. It falls under the headings of research and philosophical speculation. While fulfilling a mandate for a client, the architect may look at utopian images but not propose them. It is a question of professional integrity. Utopia is always beyond reach. In architectural practice, the proposal of unreachable goals wrapped in seemingly buildable images is nothing but demagoguery.

2. Desired future. This is the model, or the goal to attain, or the architectural scheme. In fact, for any project, there might be not just one desired future but a cluster of several alternative ones.

3. Probable future. This is the future that occurs if this procedure is enacted. On the quality/beauty scale of the future, the probable future is lower than the desired future because, in any project, compromises are inevitable and the original scheme is rarely implemented as originally proposed, especially in the case of large-scale multiyear projects. This is neither surprising nor frustrating. The desired future sets very high standards of quality/beauty, proposes an ambitious goal, and stands as an exciting model. It is by setting such lofty objectives that a lower yet still elevated quality/beauty probable future is achieved. But this probable future is substantially higher on the quality/beauty scale than the future that inevitably occurs if no architectural interventions are implemented.

4. Tendential future. This future, projected according to tendencies, is the result of the trend-spotting exercise conducted in the third step of the strategy.

5. Chaotic future. This is the unthinkable future, resulting from either a major catastrophe or gross, persistent neglect and mismanagement. Like the utopian future, the chaotic future is situated outside the diagram proper, well below both the baseline and the horizontal time axis.

The second delicate gesture of the strategy occurs here: again, a broad value judgement is made. Is the tendential future lower on the quality/beauty scale than the present situation, or is it higher? In other words, if no one intervenes and the present situation follows its normal evolution, does it degenerate, stay at the same quality/beauty level, or improve by itself? This means that there is, in fact, a sixth future. The tendential future may transform itself into an unacceptable future. Do people accept this transformed Tendential future? If they do, then this future is called acceptable, and the procedure stops here. If they do not, then it becomes unacceptable and triggers further action. The project moves on to the next step, in which an architectural scheme is designed, submitted, and discussed.

Step Four: Design of Desired Futures

Perhaps another name for these futures could be willed futures. As I have already said, the creation of an architectural scheme is a voluntary act. Of

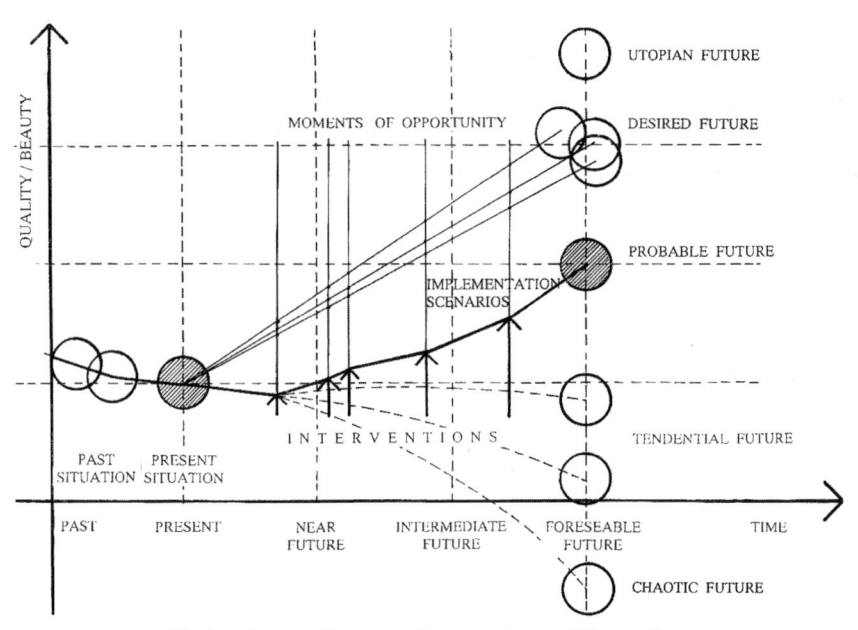

Design strategy diagram: all seven phases of the strategy

all the tasks in this procedure, the making of desired futures is simultaneously the most exciting and the most difficult. It involves the design of the architectural scheme, the creation of what is intended to become an architectural artefact, itself a fundamental ingredient of the architectural phenomenon, a place where people will live. In phenomenological terms, to make a desired future is to enact the architectural phenomenon reveiling process. This process calls for the proposal of more than one design option based on different but complementary requirements. These alternatives are discussed with the client, the users, and other relevant authorities before the preferred option is selected and implemented.

In all cases, be it the simplest project, such as the building of an ice-cream stand in a park, or the most complex one, such as the transformation of Tokyo's financial district,[109] what we are endeavouring to do is conduct an architectural project that will result in one or many architectural schemes.[110] As Peter Rowe showed in his essay *Design Thinking*, there is no single process for making an architectural scheme; there are at least four. Rowe called them "positions": functionalist, populist, conventionist, and formalist (Rowe 1987, 124). As he pointed out, however, they all share common characteristics. They are all problem-solving endeavours. They all require that decisions be made, which, in turn, means that tools are needed for making these decisions, hence the value-based criteria. They all deal with the making of material things, implying their construction. Furthermore, as these things are constructed, they acquire a shape, raising the problem of their appearance. All these positions concern the transformation of a site. In short, in all cases, to conduct an architectural project is to reconstitute what has been dismantled by the preceding epochès – that is, to reveil what has been unveiled. This is design.

If we are to grasp what act of making an architectural project truly entails, we should observe an architect in action and relate his design gestures to the various veils of the descriptive epochè. In a different way, this sort of critical observation has been attempted and described by Peter Rowe in his study. Discussing the merits of "procedural aspects of design thinking," he wrote: "By contrast, in the use of bottom-up or hierarchical decomposition-recomposition methods, the aim is to provide a complete, or at least extensive, description of the inherent structure of a problem space from the outset by explicitly breaking down – decomposing – the problem as given and understood into its most fundamental components ... the relations among these components are then systematically identified, allowing recombination into a coherent picture of the problem-space structure" (Rowe 1987, 71).

The studies the architect conducts during the first three steps of the strategy will nourish his architectural-design undertaking. They will provide him with a good knowledge of the object he is to design.

As a rule, the architect's design endeavour starts when he tries to understand the problem posed by the client's brief. An in-depth probe into human needs and aspirations is the first design gesture an architect makes and the necessary foundation of any successful design. Thus, the design constitution is initiated by the unfolding of the first veil of the architectural phenomenon. The architect may find it necessary to take into account not only the specific requirement of the users but also the broader, more universal dimensions of this particular set of people. The study of the human condition is, of course, an unquantifiably immense multidisciplinary task. In the specific case of an architectural project, it incorporates physiological and psychological issues, social and cultural dimensions, and economic and financial inputs. The architect, who obviously does not possess universal knowledge, must rely on the contributions of those who work in other disciplines.

The second design gesture is attempting to understand the future scheme's functionality, and it necessitates unfolding the second veil over the first one. During this particular part of the design process, the architect always asks some very simple questions: What exactly is the purpose of this scheme I am trying to design? What are its activity components? What are their basic characteristics? How are they related to one another? What is the problem I was hired to solve? At this juncture, functional diagrams and schematic plans may be produced.

The third design gesture is tackling the project budget. The veil of economy is the architectural phenomenon's undergarment. Although most of the time unseen, it is unavoidable. If not properly draped, it shows through the other veils. Throughout the reveiling process, money considerations will come into play. The architect may wish to incorporate this constraint into the process as early as possible in order to avoid unpleasant surprises later on.

The fourth design gesture – which is sometimes made earlier – is a study of the project site. The architect must be familiar with the site's environmental characteristics. Here, he deals with two veils simultaneously: surroundings and ecology. To solve the problem adequately, he has to do more than merely study the distinctive features of the site. He needs to investigate the project's broader ecological implications. He must determine whether his scheme will pollute the surrounding environment. And he should also exceed his basic obligation and ask himself whether the project makes a positive contribution to the establishment of an ecologically sustainable development, as recommended, for instance, by the UN's Agenda 21.

Site analysis also takes into account the imperatives of the surroundings. By advocating an international style or linguistic, metaphorical considerations at the expense of contextual or environmental imperatives, many modern and postmodern architectural projects have neglected this aspect. A phenomenological-minded architect will find it necessary to ensure that his project's surroundings become an essential dimension of the architectural phenomenon, a veil that is not left in the linen chest. This veil implies the acknowledgement that every building should always be situated at the confluence of a multitude of networks. This network of networks extends beyond the geographical limits of a given neighbourhood and delves into the fabric of the first veil, into matters of culture, belief, ethics, social issues, and political considerations.

The unfolding of the previous veils has provided the architect with an enlightened understanding of the problem; he is now anxious to take the next step and start looking for formalistic design solutions. Here, also, he unfolds more than one veil. Over those already redraped, he layers the veils of materiality, structuring systems, and form and space. An experienced architect will understand the formation of these veils and manipulate them simultaneously, playing one against another, using one to enhance another. By doing so, he will obtain a proper symbiosis of discrete elements that takes into consideration the project's budget and other financial and economic matters. It is largely through the design manipulation of these three veils that a building is given its sense of order and its constitutive spatial structure. It is here that the input of such disciplines as tridimensional geometry, space syntax, and behavioural science become useful; these fields of study offer an array of systematic methods for dealing with complicated design imperatives.

The architect has so far ignored the veil of presence in evolution. Although he is forwarding design solutions, he has only an intuitive idea of the evolutionary process that has led to his project. This is a mistake. He should have integrated historical considerations earlier in the design process, certainly before the search for appropriate forms and spaces was initiated. He needs to investigate the project's specific background, the history of the community to be served by the project, and the larger forces that shape the human condition. In other words, as the placing of the project in the life-world occurs simultaneously in space and time, the architect must complement site analysis with evolution analysis.

It is at this point in the design undertaking that all the veils begin to wrap the future project in a coherent, phenomenologically meaningful solution. As spaces and forms are being shaped, an image of the project emerges. The veil of character, invisible until now, becomes more and more apparent, demanding attention. While trying to define the character of his scheme, the architect activates his judgement of taste and addresses the issue of beauty.

Throughout the design undertaking, the architect is acutely aware of the creative difficulties of his endeavour. At the end of an intense design session he is intellectually exhausted, having expended copious amounts of energy. Tedious, mundane considerations such as energy consumption, the transport of materials, and soil weaknesses constantly undermine the pleasing forms he would propose. The veil of energy is omnipresent, in the spirit of the architect as well as in the process of the scheme. A sensitive architect will recognize this complex veil and manipulate it to his project's advantage.

The architect is conscientious and wants to do more than just provide a well-built, functional, pleasant-looking building. He wants his scheme to make a useful contribution to civilization; he wants it to stand as a positive statement that comes from him as a designer, from the future building's users, and from the community at large. Therefore, he introduces into the design process the veil of projection. He truly desires to design a building that will reflect what is best in the community. Great designers create works that achieve a positive symbiosis of their own intentions and the aspirations of the community.

Finally, the architect wants the people who will use his work to be satisfied with it. It is fair to assume that all architects and most builders pursue this objective. However, the fact that many fail to attain it is made evident in the published criticism of such diverse observers as French novelist Nicole Buron, Prince Charles, Charles Jencks, and various postoccupancy specialists. Not all architects, in a conscious fashion, wrap their proposed designs in the twelve veils of the architectural phenomenon. Many forget certain veils; others deal with some of them in an empirical or even unconscious way. Others, again, choose to ignore certain veils either because they are too troublesome or too difficult to handle. Much later, when the building has acquired a life of its own, and phenomenologists decide to conduct an epochè of it, what will they find? At the level of the artefact's factual reality, they will certainly discover all twelve veils. Whether thoroughly conducted in a conscious way or not, design always implies the complete reveiling process, and the resulting artefact always contains the twelve veils, because these veils constitute the apodictic constitutive elements of the artefact's architectural reality. However, at the level of critical assessment, in light of the thirty-seven criteria outlined earlier, will the investigating phenomenologists see a respectful, successful architecture like that of the Palais-Royal, the Fondation Rothschild Workers' Residence, or Outremont, or will they witness a disturbing, mediocre reality? It is fair to assume that these phenomenologists will find in the artefact no more than what has been put into it.

The strategy calls for the design of more than one option. Each of these alternative schemes are new images of the reality that was described in the previous steps, a reality that is be transformed in order to satisfy human desires. After being endorsed by the client, the future users, and the community, the schemes become objectives. On the diagram, architectural schemes become a cluster of circles, images of the desired future, and, after their desired final implementation date is determined, they are placed on the Q/B ordinate at a level below utopia and above the tendential future. It is part of the architect's responsibility to propose to the client, the future users, and the community at large the proper level of quality/beauty for his schemes. But the decision to endorse a particular set of desired futures at a certain quality/beauty level falls to others, not the architect. What this process stipulates is that the architect, by the very nature of his actions, recognizes the social- and cultural-accountability dimension of his action and incorporates it into the design process in a positive way.

Step Five: Tracing Implementation Scenarios

This step works best backwards: from the accepted schemes that constitute the desired futures we trace the lines that link them with the existing situation. These lines represent scenarios. Their purpose is to help transform the present situation into the situation described by the desired futures. In other words, these scenarios chart the positive interventions needed to move the study object towards a higher level of quality/beauty. In the case of a simple architectural project, the transformation may be accomplished in one step over a short period. However, the implementation of large-scale schemes takes a long time and is accomplished by small increments. The strategy is to situate these increments in a coherent framework, each enhancing the others, as was done for the Palais-Royal.

A scenario is an organized sequence of events and decisions that allows us to proceed successfully from a departure point to an arrival point. It requires coherent policies in line with the imperatives of the desired futures, manageable and practical programmes of action, efficient management, and adequate financial resources. A scenario also identifies opportunities, sensitive moments in time when interventions are not only easier to make, but also more likely to produce meaningful results with a minimum of disturbance. For instance, in Paris, the first centennial of the French Revolution presented the opportunity to give the Eiffel Tower to the world. In Montreal, Expo '67 was a means of celebrating the Canadian Confederation's first centennial; it became an opportunity to build a subway system, a network of highways, the performing-arts centre Place des Arts, and many other public facilities. As such opportunities are unfortunately all too rare, their full potential must be exploited. That is why the procedure proposed here is relentlessly opportunist; it is constant process of analysing and criticizing existing situations, designing and building new artefacts. That is also why it is of the utmost importance that all these discrete interventions cease to be disjointed occurrences and become ingredients of a larger enterprise: the construction of a better future for the community. This enterprise must be a public one; it has to involve the community because architectural design entails not only the making of places but also the programming of activities. In his book *A Vision of Britain*, Prince Charles argues convincingly for this principle of community involvement in architecture (Wales 1989). People must involve themselves in all phases of the procedure, including the implementation phase, because it is during this phase that the many details that clutter architectural schemes are ironed out. These details affect the daily lives of users as much as broad conceptual solutions do. As they are related to the users' intimate cultural requirements, these practical details, if badly managed, often destroy the best-conceived schemes.

Planning is paramount and fully justifies the old saying "Failing to plan is planning to fail." On the diagram, vertical lines placed at their respective moments in time, and cutting through both the curves of the future trends and the path of the scenarios, represent the opportunities.

Step Six: Implementation of Interventions

Up to this point in the strategy, only intellectual work has been performed. Now the time has come to start constructing pieces of the various schemes that were designed, discussed, and approved. It is at this moment that massive sums of money are invested to transform the existing reality into a desired one. Many types of intervention are necessary and should be structured in such a way that each complements the others. For instance, as illustrated by the Fondation Rothschild Workers' Residence, the desired future may require not only the construction of inner-city residential buildings but also the enactment of the kinds of social and educational programmes that can make a complex affordable and accessible. Similarly, the required architectural innovation does necessitate a comparable financial creativity.

In the diagram, the implementation of interventions may be represented by a series of upward-pointing arrows, superimposed on the lines of opportunity. They touch the tendential trends at key moments of opportunity suggested by the scenarios and bend them upward, generating an improvement of the situation, pushing the existing reality towards the realization of the proposed schemes, towards the attainment of the desired future, which resides at a higher quality/beauty level. After several interventions aimed at the betterment of the designed environment, the future that will be obtained will probably not be as high as the desired future is on the quality/beauty scale; it will, though, be better than the existing situation, and certainly better than the situation that would have occurred if no intervention had taken place.

Step Seven: Evaluation

If the architect is sure of one thing, it is that the designed environment can always be improved. The last step of the strategy is an evaluation task, which feeds back into the design undertaking. This constant process of assessment mobilizes the value-based criteria.

THE IDEA OF ELEGANCE

The previous constitution raises two issues. The first relates to the architect's obligation to succeed. His mission is not only to make architecture, but also, and more importantly, to make successful architecture. The reveiling procedure depicted earlier suggests a way to proceed. If the architect chooses to follow it and consciously drapes his design with the twelve veils, he increases his chances of producing a more comprehensive and coherent design. Moreover, if he opts for a rigorous, critical, one could even say phenomenological attitude towards his own creation, involves people in his design endeavour, and passes his schemes through the critical screening process that the thirty-seven value-based design criteria constitute, he also increases his chances of producing a more pertinent architecture. But, at both levels, the element of chance remains. What if the architect follows the procedure, and, precisely because he investigates the situation thoroughly before rendering his critical judgement, comes to the conclusion that his work is unsatisfactory? Is it simply because he lacks talent? Or is it because he is proceeding without a guiding beacon? Instilling talent in an architect is beyond the capability of any theory; but providing him with guidelines may be both feasible and useful.

The second issue raised by the previous constitution is that the Q/B scale of the design strategy implies that the double concept of quality and beauty can be appreciated, or, in one fashion or another, be an object of critical judgement. The hypothesis here is that the two following statements have a decipherable meaning: "This artefact is better than the other artefact"; and, "This artefact is more beautiful than the other artefact." To say that the first judgement emerges from a rational procedure and the second from an emotional one may not be sufficient. To say, also, that both such judgements are often intertwined, each helping or distorting the other, may not add much either. To say, further, that people, in conducting their daily affairs, continually make both gestures may still be insufficient.[111] In daily life as in architectural design, rational judgements sometimes precede emotional ones; at other times, they follow them; on still other occasions, both judgements are made simultaneously. In certain instances, one type of judgement seems to disappear from the decision-making process. In some experimental science procedures conscious emotional judgements are – almost – eliminated; and in some artistic design happenings conscious rational judgements are also – almost – put aside. However, in designing an architectural object – in making a purposeful artefact that has an appearance – both types of judgement always cohabit. Yet this assertion may still fall short of fulfilling the architect's need. For him, it is imperative to move beyond merely distinguishing between better and worse, and between more beautiful and less beautiful, and embark on the journey of making excellent and magnificent architecture.

To resolve these issues, we must elaborate a multifaceted, multilevel constitution:

1. The first level deals with the idea of quality, which leads to the idea of quality assessment, implying the concept of measurement, nourished by some of the value-based criteria outlined earlier. Since quality can be measured, we can establish levels of quality from mediocrity to excellence. Hence, the architect's goal is to produce an artefact that reaches the level of excellence. The principle of excellence is satisfaction.
2. The second level of the constitution develops the idea of beauty, which leads to the idea of beauty appreciation, implying the concept of taste, also nourished by some of the previously outlined value-based criteria. Since beauty can be appreciated, we can establish levels of beauty from ugliness to magnificence. Hence, the architect's goal is to produce an artefact that reaches the level of magnificence. The principle of magnificence is aesthetic pleasure.
3. In architecture, things are necessarily connected in a symbiotic whole; veils are intertwined to form the architectural artefact, which is subsequently embedded in the architectural phenomenon. The notion of beauty is part of the definition of quality, and vice versa. The symbiosis of the idea of excellence and the idea of magnificence forms the idea of elegance, which is the ultimate attribute of all architectural works. Elegance, however, is more than a compound of excellence and magnificence.
4. Furthermore, the idea of measurement, in matters of quality, generates the concept of degrees of excellence. And the parallel idea of appreciation, in matters of beauty, generates the concept of examples of magnificence.
5. Finally, the symbiosis of degree and example in matters of architecture engenders the idea of archetype. An architectural device, the portico, is an example of an architectural archetype. Architectural-design beacons are,

precisely, archetypes of elegance; they may emerge from the examples of successful architecture described by the epochès of the Palais-Royal, the Fondation Rothschild Workers' Residence, and Outremont.

Quality and Excellence

As it is commonly understood, the idea of quality carries two basic meanings and both are always present in architectural discourse. The first is that *quality* is a synonym of *attribute*, or *characteristic*, or *property*. For example, if a structure is solid, we say that solidity is a quality of that structure. The second meaning is the notion of value,[112] or worth. It is in this sense that we speak of good quality or bad quality. The so-called quality/price ratio, which is so prevalent in marketing today, relates to this second meaning of quality. Getting the most for the money is a ongoing topic of discussion between the architect and his clients. A thing always has a set of qualities that establish its worth in the mind of the person assessing it. In *Webster's* dictionary, quality is defined by this idea of measurement. *Quality* is "a grade, a degree of excellence, like goods of first quality" (*Webster's* 1988). Things that have the highest quality reach the level of excellence.

The related ideas of quality and excellence, applied to a manmade object, a fortiori to an architectural artefact, could also be understood this way: designed objects, from the smallest to the largest, will reach excellence if they have a full measure of five particular characteristics. Put differently, excellence in a designed object is the integrated result of five complementary and fully satisfied concerns or characteristics. To illustrate these characteristics I will use the example of a universally acclaimed high-quality object, an object that has acquired the status of excellent: the Montblanc pen.

The first characteristic of quality is a clear purpose; an object must show that its designers had a genuine understanding of its users. The purpose of the Montblanc pen is to write, and, according to practically everyone who owns one, it does so very well indeed. It is well balanced in the hand and moves smoothly on the page. The ink flows smoothly to its tip and on to the paper. Its designers have recognized that the most important component of the pen is the tip, and so they have covered it with either silver, gold, or platinum, the most precious of metals. The tip is also finely engraved, with a touch of subtle humour. It is inscribed with the number 4,810 and this puzzles new owners until they are told that the figure is, in metres, the altitude of the Mont Blanc summit. The little white star on top of the pen's cap represents a snowflake, or the eternal snow at the top of the highest peak in the Alps; it distinguishes authentic Montblanc pens from counterfeits. The white star and the inscribed number lend a touch of informality to this very serious-looking object. Writing with this pen is a serious business, but it can also be fun. The Montblanc pen is an instrument that accomplishes what it was designed to do gracefully and efficiently. The person who buys one is not cheated; the pen's designers care about their customers.

The second characteristic of quality is perdurability. The Montblanc pen is sturdy, made with the most durable of materials: lacquered resin, solid plastic, stainless steel, silver, gold, and platinum. With reasonable care and simple maintenance, it will last a lifetime. In this sense, the designer's of the Montblanc pen respect not only their customers but also their own product.

The third characteristic of quality is ongoing improvement. The pen's designers know that high quality is never achieved overnight; it always comes out of extensive research and meticulous probing. In the seventeenth century, French philosopher Nicolas Boileau proposed a simple formula for attaining quality in literature and, for that matter, in all things. This formula is known today by all francophone schoolchildren: "Hâtez-vous lentement ... Avant donc que d'écrire, apprenez à penser ... Ce que l'on conçoit bien s'énonce clairement, et les mots pour le dire arrivent aisément ... Vingt fois sur le métier remettez votre ouvrage ... Polissez le sans cesse et le repolissez" (Boileau 1959, 41). This precept of hastening slowly, of thinking before writing, of putting one's work back on the worktable twenty times, and of polishing and repolishing one's work until it is satisfactory, has been a recipe for success for artists and scientists, writers and actors, designers and philosophers, since Demosthenes practiced diction with stones in his mouth. The Montblanc pen embodies the wisdom of this dictum. The models on the market today are the result of countless improvements over the years; the next generation of models will be improved versions of these. The pen uses an old substance – liquid ink – in a very high-tech fashion. Manufactured by the most advanced, computer-assisted, precision machine tools, the pen's discrete parts are finely crafted and combined neatly into a refined whole. Concerned with the long term, the Montblanc pen's designers understand that today's success is based on meticulous past efforts and future success is based on work performed today. In the past, they have constructed their future, which is the present success, and they continue to do so.

The fourth characteristic is focus. The pen's designers are not trying to make all things for all people. The theme of their business is writing.

Montblanc puts a limited number of models on the market, along with a few ancillary accessories such as inkwells, desktop stands, blotters, writing paper, and leather diaries. The basic pen models are offered in two colours, black and burgundy, and all have the same distinctive shape and the same mechanism.[113] Such focus helps Montblanc to achieve the highest level of sustained quality.

The fifth characteristic is appearance. The object displays aesthetic characteristics that are accepted by most people and that can survive the erosions of time. Excellent objects are made to seem beautiful not only today but also tomorrow, next year, and next century. The Montblanc pen's shape, form, and proportions are beyond fashions. The writing implement looks simultaneously old-fashioned and thoroughly modern. Its look appeals to the most avant-garde artist and to the most conservative politician. It is because the Montblanc pen's designers have succeeded in giving their product a universal and timeless look that it has become a status symbol: the Meisterstück 149 is the pen most often used for signing international treaties.

As it is presented here, beauty appears to be an element of the quality paradigm. However, this aesthetic characteristic does not apply equally to all designed products. It relates mainly to those that are visible. A hidden valve, or a computer chip, for example, is not asked to be visually pleasing, only to perform at the highest level of efficacy. However, many high-quality products made for an exclusively functional purpose, such as machine tools or surgical instruments, have an inherent beauty that is recognized by the art establishment.

In architectural theory today, postmodern and deconstructionist discourses largely ignore the idea of quality (Venturi 1966; Jencks 1984; Harvey 1990; Vidler 1992), although it is fair to assume that most architects honestly strive for excellence in their work. Even beyond the realm of architecture, the production of high-quality objects is a recognized necessity, in practice as well as in theory. In the fields of opera and classical music, for instance, success requires excellence, and it only comes to those who train long and hard. In the industrial world, it was an American theoretician who taught the Japanese that they must strive for excellence. His principles became the basis for Japan's remarkable economic success. As early as 1945, Edwards Deming proposed an industrial strategy based on excellence and reinforced by these precepts: "introduce quality throughout the manufacturing process; become competitive; develop a relation of trust with your suppliers and customers; constantly improve the quality of your product, as well as your corporate planning, and service to your clients; work in teams; eliminate barriers between the technical, marketing and after-sale service people; replace production quotas by leadership; make workers proud of their products; and put in place a program of continuing education" (Deming 1991).

It took American businesspeople more than four decades to rediscover the necessity of excellence and apply similar principles. They were spurred on by several provocative books. Today, in the management section of any bookstore, several best-sellers may be found that describe the implementation procedure for what is called the total-quality concept. The Japanese and the Europeans, these books' authors insist, have demonstrated that the production of excellent products and the provision of excellent services are indispensable to competing successfully in today's global markets. The books illustrate this axiom by relating success stories as well as horror stories. Practical advice for becoming successful is also offered. Tom Peters, in *Thriving on Chaos*, told his readers – mainly corporate managers – to "specialize, create niches, differentiate, provide top quality as perceived by the customer, provide superior service, emphasize the intangibles, achieve extraordinary responsiveness, be an internationalist, create uniqueness, become obsessed with listening, achieve flexibility, innovate, simplify." (Peters 1987).

What I am advocating here is the application to architecture of the idea of quality similar to that which Deming and Peters advocated. What we require is an idea of quality that is simultaneously an artefact's attribute, an expression of its worth, and a synthesis of the five characteristics just outlined: purposeful concern for users, perdurability, constant improvement, concentration, and a timeless aesthetic.

Quality Assessment: Measurement and Degree

As quality is a value that has a variable worth, a scale for measuring quality can be established. Strictly speaking, measuring a thing implies determining its magnitude, extent, or degree in relation to some standard. Philosopher S. S. Stevens put forward a theory of measurement that distinguishes four levels of measurement, or four types of scale. The first is the nominal scale; it shows whether two things are identical or different. The second is the ordinal scale; taking two nonidentical things, it shows that one is "more something" than the other. This scale defines an order of things. The third is the scale of intervals; it permits us to determine whether the difference between two things is different from the difference between two other things. The fourth is a scale of intervals in which the origin is defined

(Stevens in Auroux 1990, 1605). In the theory of architecture presented here, the second scale is used.

Can quality in architecture be measured? To the extent that architecture is a manufactured product that people buy, the answer is "Yes." In line with *Webster's* pointed definition and Stevens's scales is Tom Peters's argument concerning the notion of quality measurement. Such a measurement is made by establishing performance standards. High-quality products are therefore products that continuously meet high standards, and excellent products, such as the Montblanc pen, are those that achieve the highest standards possible. Peters was emphatic: "Quality is measured. Measurement is the heart of any improvement process. If it cannot be measured, it cannot be improved ... you must start by measuring the 'poor-quality-cost,' precisely and in detail ... measurement must begin at the outset of the program ... measurement should be visible ... measurement must be done by the participants: that is[,] by the natural work group ... quality is rewarded ... when quality goes up, costs go down ... and quality improvement is a never-ending journey" (Peters 1987, 90). Peters insisted that in order to make successfull high-quality products, one needs both an efficient system of quality control and a passionate commitment to its application. This, no doubt, is good advice for architects, as well.

Principle of Quality: Satisfaction

In architecture, as in other industrial fields, only the highest-quality standards are acceptable. The needs of the individual and the imperative of general economic prosperity demand it. The value-based criteria sketched earlier constitute an extensive list of these standards as they relate to architecture. But what is their principle? Peters posed the same question to the business world:

Quality is not just an inspector ... it's not just in the product ... but what is it? ... how do we define it so that we can get a handle on it, and cope with it? ... I asked [said Peters] about 50 methods editors [in industry] to help me define quality in terms of the key element they work with: specifications ... here are some of the answers I received: 'a specification is a minimum requirement to which we produce a product ... [it] tells the manufacturing plant what to produce ... [it] tells a salesperson what he'll be selling ... [it] spells out the limits within which we can produce a satisfactory product' ... these were all very interesting, I told them ... but nobody picked up on the fundamental reason we have specs in the first place, and that is: 'specifications should define what it takes to satisfy the customer.'

Period. This is what quality is all about: the customer's perception of excellence. And quality is our response to that perception. (Peters 1987, 101)

This should also be the case in the domain of architecture.

People express their satisfaction. In a democracy, this expression can take the form of an election. In the business world, it is highlighted by the motto "The customer is always right." The architectural product is more complex than a single-purpose consumer good, and the architectural customer is more than a single individual. Simply because the pursuit of excellence, based on the principle of satisfaction, is a vital undertaking, it does not mean that the architect's only role is to give clients what they want. If his mission starts with a focus on clients satisfaction, it continues with concern for client welfare and ends with involvement in society's larger concerns. The architect acts like a medical doctor in this respect. Within the context of his deontology, he must develop the kind of knowledge that will allow him to advise his clients about issues that reach beyond their initial demands. After all, the architect is the expert in architecture, accountable to society, and has the duty to inform his clients, who may not understand the complexity of architecture or the consequences of their own demands.

Beauty and Magnificence

Beauty is usually defined as "the sensible condition of aesthetic excellence considered to arouse the keenest pleasure" (Flew 1984, 39). Accepting that beauty is related to pleasure, eighteenth-century French philosopher Denis Diderot asked the obvious question: "Is this thing beautiful because it pleases me, or does it please me because it is beautiful?" (Diderot 1946, 1106). And his answer was that he agreed with Saint Augustine, who said that the second option is the valid one. Undoubtedly, the majority of architects would agree with Saint Augustine and Diderot, because they try to make beautiful buildings.[114] For at least three millennia, the architect's training and practice have presupposed that there is an attribute called beauty, that architectural artefacts displaying this attribute can be produced, and, consequently, that beautiful artefacts please those who experience them.

This position is based on authorities dating back as far as Plato, who believed that beauty is "an intrinsic property of objects, measurable in reference to, for example, purity, integrity, harmony, or perfection" (Flew 1984, 39). It is interesting to note that, according to Antony Flew, at least,

On the golden sand of the Palais-Royal garden the sun traces a pattern of intricate beauty

beauty, like quality, can be measured. For the ancient Greeks, supreme beauty merged with supreme good: this conviction was the source of their famous dictum, *kagos kagatos*, or "beauty/goodness." Perhaps they formulated the original concept of elegance – also the merging of supreme good, which may be associated with excellence, with supreme beauty, which is magnificence. Another way of presenting the same concept is to say that beauty is the splendor of good and truth.

Vitruvius's architectural treatise was written some three centuries after Plato's time. Rome had already become a proud, immensely powerful society that had digested the ancient Greek aesthetic canon. In this world dominated by military might, beauty had become subservient to practicality. It is therefore not surprising that Vitruvius's discussion of beauty passes through notions of quality. In the preface to his memorable French translation of Vitruvius's *De architectura*, Claude Perrault wrote that Vitruvius enunciated the three necessary qualities of a building: solidity, utility, and elegance. He said that the order of these qualities illustrates the spirit of the Roman architect, who was primarily a no-nonsense builder. According to Vitruvius, Perreault added, the composition of a building is the first work, and the principal work, of an architect; today we would say that design better fits this description. This composition is conducted according to a two-step procedure. The first step is *l'ordonnance* (in Latin, "ordinatio"), which is combining the various parts of the work to achieve the dimensions that will satisfy programmatic needs.[115] The second step is *la disposition* (in Latin, "dispositio"), which is studying the details necessary to establish the forms. To be satisfactory, said Perrault, *ordonnance* and *disposition* must follow the letter and spirit of several rules of harmony based on the notions of proportion; appropriateness (*convenance*), which implies respect for the conditions of the site; climate and usage; and distribution, which is defined as a virtue of economy generated by the proper choice of materials and respect for the budget (Perreault 1965).

During the Renaissance, Leon Battista Alberti also addressed the idea of beauty in architecture, saying that "Beauty, Majesty, Gracefulness, and the like Charms, consist in those Particulars which, if you alter or take them away, the Whole would be made homely and disagreeable." He added that beauty is obtained through the proper manipulation of what he called three "Things": number, which is proportion, congruity, which is the manner in which architectural elements are assembled, and collocation, which is the equivalent of the modern term *craftsmanship*. It is by means of these things, argued Alberti, that the architectural artefact obtains its "Beauty, Dignity, and Value" (Alberti 1986, 195). Beauty is more than an aggregate of ornaments. Ornament is "a kind of additional brightness and improvement to Beauty. Beauty is something lovely which is proper and innate and diffused throughout the whole, whilst Ornament is something added and fastened on, rather than proper and innate" (Alberti in Wittkower 1988, 41). Thus, according to Alberti, beauty is a harmony inherent in the building, a harmony that, as he subsequently explained, does not result from personal fancy, but from objective reasoning.

If the concept of harmony was used in the Renaissance to define beauty, then what is harmony? Rudolf Wittkower informed us that Alberti defined it as "the essence of beauty ... it consists ... in the relationship of the parts to each other and to the whole." Alberti recommended simple ratios. As Wittkower explained, "the whole façade of S. Maria Novella can be exactly circumscribed in a square" (Wittkower 1988, 50).

Inspired by the writings of Alberti, Vignola, Perrault, and François Blondel, Jacques-François Blondel said that in matters of architectural composition architects must rely on a set of principles and, in their works, try to reconcile suitability, proportion, symmetry, ordering, and harmony (Blondel 1905). For Blondel, writing in the eighteenth century, the first architectural attribute is *convenance*, which is suitability or appropriateness. Blondel's definition of *convenance* varies somewhat from that of Vitruvius. For Blondel, appropriateness relates to the choice of materials and the disposition of spaces in a plan. It is what imports the proper sense of spatial organization to a building; it gives the structure its dignity and its character. In the context of a building, the qualities of simplicity and richness are both related to the idea of appropriateness. Functional characteristics related to the idea of quality, such as spatial organization, are, in Blondel's mind, intimately related to aesthetic considerations, such as dignity. Blondel's second attribute is *la proportion*; this underpins the architectural orders. Proportion provides "la manière de bâtir," or, "the proper manner of a building." According to this manner, solidity is the Doric order, adequacy (*moyenne*) is the Ionic order, and delicacy is the Corinthian order. For Blondel, mastery of proportion is a part of the science of architecture, and proportion is what gives beauty to a building – to each of its parts and its totality.

Blondel's idea of symmetry is the ratio of heights, lengths, widths, and depths in all the measurements of a building. Today, the same notion is what is called the proportions, plural. According to Blondel, the making of beauty implies elements that are measured. He argued that symmetry is based on the proportions of the human body. Blondel's fourth architectural attribute is *l'ordonnance*, or ordering, or arrangement. Such a literal

English translation of the word *ordonnance* reveals only a part of its meaning. *L'ordonnance* also means the proper selection of the architectural Order. This Order is what imparts the character of a Greek temple to a structure: Doric for the temples of Mars, Ionic for those of Apollo, and Corinthian for those of Venus. Blondel added that arrangement is the attribute that permits elegance to be introduced into a rustic building. Finally, he concluded that harmony is both the interrelationships among all the parts of a building and the equilibrium of the various design principles.

In *Critique of Judgement*, Blondel's contemporary, German philosopher Immanuel Kant, offered a set of definitions for the beautiful, and, in so doing, established a distinction between free and dependent beauty. Such a distinction is pertinent to the theory presented in this book because architecture entails both symbolic and functional dimensions. Kant insisted that the first kind of beauty "presupposes no concept of what the object should be; the second does not presuppose such a concept and, with it, an answering perfection of the object." To illustrate each of the two kinds of beauty, Kant explained that "flowers ... and designs *à la grecque*, foliage for framework or on wall-papers" are examples of free beauty; but the "beauty of man (including under this head[ing] that of a man, woman, or child), the beauty of a horse, or of a building (such as a church, palace, arsenal, or summer-house), presupposes a concept of the end that defines what the thing has to be, and consequently a concept of its perfection; and is therefore merely appendant beauty" (Kant 1985, 185, 186).

Both kinds of beauty are supported by Kant's conception of the beautiful. Kant argued that the beautiful contains four "moments." They are complementary; together, they define the beautiful. First, the beautiful is apprehended by a judgement of taste; it is aesthetic. This means that such a judgement is neither cognitive nor logical. It involves the "faculty of estimating an object ... by means of a delight or aversion apart from any interest [and] the object of such a delight is called beautiful." Second, the beautiful is "what pleases ... universally." Third, the beautiful contains "the form of finality in an object." Fourth, "the beautiful is that which ... is cognised as object of a necessary delight" (Kant 1985, 161–96).

Kant's four notions – of disinterested emotional delight, universality, finality, and necessity – are present in Le Corbusier's aesthetic discourse. In his Modern Architecture manifesto, *Vers une architecture*, the Franco-Swiss architect accepted Kant's distinction of free and dependent beauty, but linked both kinds of beauty within one demonstration (Le Corbusier 1958). Le Corbusier's argument unfolded as follows: Beauty in certain objects moves us. Those objects that move us are the ones characterized by pure, simple forms that we can read clearly. Thus, in order to move us – that is, in order to be beautiful – buildings must have pure, simple forms. Furthermore, Le Corbusier said, buildings must also serve a purpose; they must respond to human habitation needs. Architects must follow the example of engineers. Not only have engineers learned to respond efficiently to human needs with their buildings and other structures, but they have also succeeded in giving them pure and simple forms.

The sort of Modern aesthetics Le Corbusier proposed for architecture went further than Kant's view that a building was only capable of displaying dependant beauty. Le Corbusier said that a Modern building has both kinds of beauty. As pure geometric forms, Modern buildings are demonstrations of free beauty because, he said, they clearly satisfy our aesthetic judgement; their simplicity delights us. As functional, mass-produced "machines," Modern buildings possess dependent beauty because, he added, they clearly display their finality.

Le Corbusier developed his argument with classical logic. He said that the engineer's aesthetics and the architect's aesthetics are interdependent, although one (the engineer's) is blooming while the other is regressing. The engineer puts us in contact with the laws of the universe and thus achieves harmony. Through his activity, the architect makes forms that are pure creations of his spirit. These forms touch our senses and trigger profound feelings. When these forms have an order in harmony with the order of the world, we feel beauty. Eyes are made to see, Le Corbusier claimed, and what they see are forms under the light. Primary forms are beautiful because they can be read clearly. Like engineers, architects should make simple forms governed by geometry and mathematics.

To answer the problems of the world, Le Corbusier continued, architects and engineers make volumes defined by surfaces and generated by "the plan." Without the plan, there is disorder and arbitrariness. The plan carries with it order and the essence of feeling. The plan proceeds from the inside out: the outside is the result of the inside. The *ordonnance* implies a hierarchy of goals and a classification of intentions.

According to Le Corbusier, order is necessary, not only in the plan but also in the design of the forms. Guiding patterns (*tracés régulateurs*) are required to establish aesthetic order. These patterns guard against arbitrariness, but they are ultimately just a means of assisting architectural creation. Architectural styles are to be eliminated because they are lies. Unlike buildings subjected to styles, planes, automobiles, and ocean liners are truthful and beautiful because they are the answer to well-stated problems. The problem of human habitation should be posed in a similar fashion so that people's real needs are addressed. The answer is to make a house like a mass-produced machine using industrial machinery; this accords with the new spirit that the industrial age has brought us. Thus, the house is a machine for dwelling, or a machine to live in.

Le Corbusier concluded that this new industrial-age spirit, *l'esprit nouveau*, calls for new standards. To reach perfection, he insisted, we must establish standards that are the product of scrupulous logic and of a rigorous analysis of well-stated problems. The Parthenon conforms to a set of standards, and it moves us. Like the Parthenon, architecture implies the initiation of an emotional relationship with raw materials. Architecture goes beyond utilitarian things. Architecture is plastic art, spirit of order, and unity of intention. Architecture is the sort of passion that transforms inert stones into life. Finally, Le Corbusier asserted that people require this new spirit in architecture. Either it is given, or revolution will erupt. The choice is either Modern Architecture or revolution. Naturally, Le Corbusier would opt for architecture (Le Corbusier 1958).

This thesis has profoundly influenced architecture for half a century and for at least three reasons. The first reason is that it simultaneously proposed a bold new vision and a return to the Enlightenment's *esprit de système*, a spirit that brougt glory to Western civilization. What Le Corbusier implied was that the Beaux Arts model of architecture deviated from the original architectural system of order and discipline. Like the great masters of the Renaissance and the classical period, Modern architects – such as, of course, Le Corbusier – went back to Ancient Greece and Rome and rediscovered the secrets of absolute beauty. At the same time, Modern architects proposed a bold vision for the future. They said that it was easy to identify the problems: it was only necessary to listen to people as they expressed their needs. The technological and scientific means of solving their problems were now at hand. With Le Corbusier as their spokesman, they proposed that a new attitude be adopted that would bring humanity into a new world, a progressive world where problems could be solved in an efficient way – hence, a world of beautiful architecture. In fact, Le Corbusier appealed to reason with an emotional argument and, at the same time, to emotion with a rational argument.

The second reason for the success of his thesis was that he succeeded in linking free beauty and dependent beauty. Efficient, functional, and economic architecture need not be ugly; beautiful architecture need not be useless. In fact, Le Corbusier said, existing Beaux Arts buildings were both inefficient and ugly because their plans were arbitrary and their forms too complicated. Efficient architecture is architecture that follows the principles of Descartes and the other Enlightenment philosophers, principles that call for solving problems in a clear way. And beautiful architecture is architecture that respects the Enlightenment's precepts of measure, clarity, and dignified sobriety (Fichet 1979). Beautiful architecture will also be efficient architecture if architects design it the way engineers design planes.

The third reason Le Corbusier's thesis wielded such influence is that the definition of the beautiful it contains is inclusive; that is, it encompasses Kant's four constitutive notions. When Le Corbusier said that architecture went beyond the utilitarian, that it was a matter of emotion and pure beauty, he was talking about Kant's idea of disinterested emotional delight. When he said that beauty occurs when architecture accords with the laws of the universe, he was referring to Kant's notion of universality in aesthetic judgement. When he argued that the great problems of society were resolved by means of well-planned architecture – architecture such as that designed by engineers – he was bringing into his definition of the beautiful the notion of finality, which Kant associated with dependent beauty. And when he claimed that the choice was either architecture or revolution because people demanded a new spirit, he was clearly referencing the notion of necessity that Kant introduced in his own discussion of the beautiful.

Perhaps the only discrepancy between Kant's approach and Le Corbusier's argument has to do with what constitutes free beauty. Kant's examples are the flower, designs *à la grecque*, and foliage on wallpaper. Le Corbusier's view of free beauty is the pure geometric form. On what philosophical authority did Le Corbusier adopt such a view. And, more importantly, what gave him credibility in responding to this particular question? Perhaps it was in Hegel that Le Corbusier found his inspiration. In the French translation of Hegel's *Aesthetics*, entitled *Introduction à l'esthétique/L'idée du beau*, we read that art "is made to awaken in us the feeling of the beautiful." We also learn that "a work of art must contain only what is essentially at the service of the expression of its content; it must contain nothing superfluous nor useless." Furthermore, beauty in things made by humankind, beauty in "abstraction," has a form that displays such characteristics as regularity, symmetry, and harmony. Therefore, Hegel said, the fact that "the abstract purity of matter in terms of its form, colour, sound, etc., constitutes the essential component [of a work of art] ... [L]ines precisely traced, running in a uniform fashion, without deviating to the right or to the left, smooth surfaces, etc., satisfy us because of this solid precision and uniformed unity" (Hegel 1979, 64, 79, 196).[116] This, it seems, describes Le Corbusier's aesthetic approach.

An entrance gate at Outremont's Royal cemetery is resplendent in winter

This discrepancy is the main weakness of Le Corbusier's Modern Architecture theory. His entire aesthetic argument rests on the assumption that all people enjoy an architecture composed of simple, geometric forms, as described by Hegel. But what if people, instead, wanted a busy, flowery, decorated architecture? What if this responded to their social and functional needs? Half a century later, the postmodern critics recognized this shortcoming in the aesthetic position of the Modern Architects and articulated a new aesthetic, one that did away with the geometric purity and simplicity of Modern Architecture.

What I am suggesting here, however, is that we rise above the modern/postmodern debate and explore the idea of beauty in other discourses. One of the philosophers to have discussed beauty as an attribute of a thing most convincingly is George Santayana. In his book *The Sense of Beauty*, originally published in 1896 and based on a series of lectures delivered at Harvard University, he wrote:

Beauty is an emotional element, a pleasure of ours, which nevertheless we regard as a quality of things ... we have now reached our definition of beauty, which, in the terms of our successive analysis and narrowing of the conception, is value positive, intrinsic, and objectified. Or, in less technical language, Beauty is pleasure as the quality of a thing ... this definition [of beauty] is intended to sum up a variety of distinctions and identifications which should perhaps be here more explicitly set down. Beauty is a value, that is, it is not a perception of a matter of fact or of a relation: it is an emotion, an affection of our volitional and appreciative nature. An object cannot be beautiful if it can give pleasure to nobody: a beauty to which all men were forever indifferent is a contradiction in terms. In the second place, this value is positive, it is the sense of the presence of something good, or (in the case of ugliness) of its absence. It is never the perception of a positive evil, it is never a negative value. That we are endowed with the sense of beauty is a pure gain, which brings no evil with it. When the ugly ceases to be amusing or merely uninteresting and becomes disgusting, it becomes indeed a positive evil: but a moral and practical, not an aesthetic one. In aesthetics that saying is true – often so disingenuous in ethics – that evil is nothing but the absence of good: for even the tedium and vulgarity of an existence without beauty is not itself ugly so much as lamentable and degrading ... Beauty is therefore a positive value that is intrinsic: it is a pleasure ... Morality has to do with the avoidance of evil and the pursuit of good: aesthetics only with enjoyment. (Santayana 1955, 32)

The notion of beauty pertinent to architecture, and suggested by this theory, incorporates the dimensions that Santayana outlined. Beauty is a worthy value intrinsic to a thing, a positive, emotional attribute generating pleasure in the humans who experience it. Beauty encompasses elements such as perceived truth, symmetry, measure, equilibrium, appropriateness (*convenance*), harmony, rhythm, contrast, colour, texture, light and shadow, and order. It can be both free (the beauty of a rose) and dependent (the beauty of a Japanese sabre). It can imply purity and simplicity and still incorporate ornament or decoration. Beauty is joyful and respectful. Beauty cannot be created solely through a design process based on deductive or inductive reasoning. Sensitivity comes into play, because to attain beauty we must penetrate the realm of the unexplainable. And beauty depends upon the tasteful manipulation of proportions.

Magnificence is great beauty. The various notions of beauty are also the constitutive elements of magnificence – only raised to their highest levels. Hence, magnificence in an architectural artefact results from the material reality's greatest aesthetic attributes. This point is fundamental: an architectural artefact is a three-dimensional material reality, and, consequently, magnificence will emerge from this reality if it generates the greatest aesthetic pleasure. As a three-dimensional shape, the architectural artefact has a succession of lengths, widths, heights, and depths; it has a shape that can be measured. Therefore, all architectural artefacts have proportions. This is a universal, indubitable, and apodictic characteristic of the architectural artefact. It is this shape, perceived by people, that engenders the first order of aesthetic pleasure. Before all other aesthetic attributes can be activated to instil pleasure, the architectural artefact must exist; it has to acquire its shape and display its proportions. The creation of beauty in architecture, then, starts with the actual creation of the artefact, implying the proper manipulation of proportions or harmonic ratios. The preeminence of proportion in matters of architectural aesthetic pleasure has been recognized by practically all theoreticians of architecture, except those who now embrace postmodernism. Indeed, virtually all recognized architectural masterpieces display harmonious proportions. This is why they were designated as masterpieces in the first place.

Over the centuries, architects disagreed as to what constitutes a proper manipulation of proportions, but they never went so far as to ignore all systems of proportion – until today. Even Le Corbusier felt compelled to study proportion. He devised the modular system of proportion and systematically applied it to his projects (Le Corbusier 1948, 1955). But, as Le Corbusier himself said, a system of proportion is like a well-tuned piano: no matter what state the instrument is in, it is always up to the pianist to play well. Perhaps some of today's postmodern architects are trying to make music without an instrument at all. This is the view presented by such contemporary critics of architecture as Prince Charles and Rob Krier. In his book *Architectural Composition*, Krier laments what he calls the sorry state of architecture today, and strongly advocates the study of proportions (Wales 1989; Krier 1989).

In his memorable *Cours d'architecture*, written between 1675 and 1685, François Blondel discussed extensively the problem of making very beautiful architectural objects. Using what he called reasoning by induction, he showed that beauty, indeed magnificence, in architecture can be found in good proportions. Blondel began his argument by saying that architecture is not like mathematics, a science that permits clear demonstrations. Contradictory sentiments regarding beauty in architecture are often expressed; Blondel knew this, but would nonetheless try to reason by induction and convince others that beauty in architecture derives from harmonious proportions.

First, Blondel explained, we must look at experimental science – for instance, the problem of equilibrium. If we put two different masses on a stick that is positioned on a support, we can place the two masses in relation to the length of the stick in such a way that the entire system achieves a balance. The longer arm with the smaller mass compensates for the shorter arm with the larger mass. We can calculate this equilibrium and formulate for its behaviour constant, stable, and indubitable principles. Second, Blondel said that we can apply inductive reasoning to the problem of optics. Here, also, we can calculate the angles of perception and reflection of light. As it was with the problem of equilibrium, it is possible to formulate in optics constant, stable, and indubitable principles. Third, Blondel proposed a study of music. Beauty in music is produced by the harmonic ratios of sounds. These ratios are well known. Musicians cannot produce beautiful, harmonious music if they do not adhere to the laws of harmony. These are also constant, stable, and indubitable principles. Having performed these three demonstrations, Blondel returned to the problem of beauty in architecture. Over the years, he remarked, we have observed that many pleasant-looking buildings have been erected. The most pleasant-looking ones are those displaying a respect for well-established harmonic proportions. In architecture, as in music, that which we find beautiful is respectful of harmonic ratios.

From these four instances of inductive reasoning, based on four sets of observations, Blondel formulated his conclusion. Beauty or magnificence in architecture is a question of equilibrium, and equilibrium is regulated by constant, stable, and indubitable principles. Beauty in architecture is perceived visually by the observer, and thus activates the laws of optics, which are, in turn, regulated by constant, stable, and indubitable principles. Beauty in architecture is experienced through perceptions, which are similar to perceptions of music; music is based on respect for well-observed harmonic ratios, ratios that are also constant, stable, and indubitable principles. Therefore, since the three constitutive elements of architecture are regulated by constant, stable, and indubitable principles, and since we observe that the beauty of a building is also related to good proportions, it follows that, in architecture, beauty based on good proportions is also regulated by constant, stable, and indubitable principles. And, of course, Blondel went on to specify what good architectural proportions ought to be if beautiful buildings are our goal (Blondel 1979).

Beauty Assessment: Taste and Example

The double idea of beauty and magnificence establishes a hierarchy in matters of aesthetic judgement. It implies that certain things have a greater beauty than others and that magnificence is the highest of all possible levels of beauty. It further implies that to select these various levels of beauty is to exercise taste. The beauty/magnificence notion also encompasses the idea that if we wish to design a magnificent building we have to manipulate a series of aesthetic devices; the most important of these (and perhaps the only apodictic one) is the proper manipulation of harmonic proportions. It is because the architect's taste is the result of intensive training that he can choose the "best" proportions for a given artefact. But are we sure that such aesthetic hierarchizing is possible? The answer is that it is not only possible, but it is also carried out every day in the course of a variety of human activities. People can distinguish between a thing that is more beautiful and another thing that is less beautiful; if they could not, an event such as a beauty contest could never be organized. How is Miss World selected if not through an exercise of judgement guided by taste? The same sort of aesthetic judgement is made each time a music competition is held. When, for example, Van Cliburn won the Tchaikovsky Competition some years ago, he was the beneficiary of a judgement of taste rendered by the jurors, an aesthetic assessment that ranked the competing pianists. Similarly, all graphic-art competitions involve taste-centred judgements; entries are compared and one is declared the most beautiful. When Chef Joël Robuchon of Paris prepares a gastronomic feast, it is not only a dazzling display of chemistry and culinary savoir faire, but also, and more importantly, an expression of exquisite taste. How does he approve each dish if not by tasting it? How does he select the proper wine to accompany a dish if not, again, by making a judgement based on taste? And what architect will argue that aesthetic considerations do not play a paramount role in architectural competitions?

Kant was not the only thinker to insist that a judgment regarding beauty, or an appreciation of aesthetics, is taste. Diderot, François Blondel, Jacques-François Blondel, and Montesquieu, among many others, concurred. For them, taste is discernment in matters that cannot be explained. François Blondel insisted that taste, in spite of the fact that it might be coloured by localized cultural influences, can be acquired and developed, but only through long practice, solid experience, and good education.[117]

One of the most interesting works ever written on taste is Montesquieu's *Essai sur le goût*, or *Essay on Taste*. According to the author of *Lettres persanes* and *De l'esprit des lois*, taste is what permits us to experience the pleasures of the soul. After distinguishing natural taste from acquired taste, Montesquieu wrote that it is desirable to know the source of the pleasures of which taste is the measure, and added that the most general definition of taste, without considering whether it is good or bad taste, is what ties us to a thing by a feeling.

His definition of taste applies equally to the things perceived by the senses and matters of the mind. He explained that we sense things, even the most intellectual ones. But we need a certain discernment to assess properly the things we sense with our feelings, and this discernment is broader than taste; it is *l'esprit*. Montesquieu defined *l'esprit* by indicating that it is a generic concept incorporating many options, such as genius, common sense, discrimination, correctness or appropriateness, talent, and taste. *Avoir de l'esprit*, or having this subtle discernment, means having the proper attitude regarding the things to which it is applied. If these things are clearly circumscribed, having discernment is called talent. If these things are of interest to educated people, such as, for instance, architects, having discernment is called taste. And if these things are the traits of an entire people, having discernment is called *l'esprit*. Taste necessitates intellectual curiosity. It is motivated by the pleasure derived from the perception of a rich variety of well-ordered things, and includes the pleasure of perceiving symmetry and contrasts.

For Montesquieu, taste is also the ability to deal with surprise. In making aesthetic judgements, what we see may sometimes surprise us because our particular perception of a thing can differ from out common-sense understanding of it. Montesquieu used an architectural example to illustrate this point. He explained that the dome of Saint Peter's Cathedral in Rome is immense. We know, said Montesquieu, that Michelangelo wanted to build a dome as big as the Pantheon and raise it up into the air. He set this gigantic mass on large pilasters, and the result is that we perceive a mountain that we know to be very heavy but that somehow looks very light. Hence, said Montesquieu, we remain in doubt, torn between what we know and what we see. Taste is therefore the ability to discern between knowledge and perception (Montesquieu 1993).

Jacques-François Blondel's discussion of taste follows a similar line of thought. For him, taste is the judgements we make concerning matters that cannot be governed by the rules of certainty or demonstrated rationally. It is easier to formulate what is not good taste than what is, and to depict it with images rather than metaphysical definitions. It would help to explain the notion of taste, Blondel asserted, if we could define it, but taste is one of those elusive things that constantly defy human understanding. For him, taste is the means of achieving beauty, which, in turn, constitutes the principal end of architectural design. It implies the symbiotic manipulation of commodity, solidity, and beauty. Blondel warned of two mistakes we might make, both of which result in bad taste: connecting the heavy with the delicate and using too many ornaments in creating a simple architecture.

It was in the context of this discussion that Blondel criticized certain architects of his time for rejecting the teachings of the masters of previous periods. He insisted that these architects were abondoning rules that had amply demonstrated their validity and were relying exclusively on their imaginations. Such architects were displaying bad taste by merely following the fashion of the day, and a fashion always looks ridiculous after it has been replaced. Blondel added that intervention and ingenuity are necessary, but must always be controlled by principles (Blondel 1905). On this particular point, Montesquieu's position was that rules are necessary, but a person of taste knows how and when to break them in order to achieve a higher quality of art. The licence to break the rules to satisfy the demands of taste should never be confused with the rejection of all rules, because this leads to the justification of ignorance, amateurishness, improvisation, and, inevitably, to mediocrity.

In architecture, therefore, good taste is the ability to pass educated aesthetic judgements. Such judgements are based on social values. Every person passes them on a daily basis as he or she experience architecture, and they are always made in the same way: by comparing two artefacts. An artefact is declared beautiful when it evokes the same sort of pleasure that was experienced in another, similar circumstance. This "other, similar circumstance" could be either another artefact or a composite model.

A judgement based on taste is not made in the same way a rational assessment is. If a given thing can be quantified, then a judgement of it is rendered either by comparing it to another thing or to a common standard. These two methods apply equally to a factual assessment and a judgement of quality.[118] In matters of quality in architecture, judgements are made either by comparing or by using a standard of measurement.

However, when it comes to measuring beauty in architecture, a common yardstick does not exist. Only comparison is possible. That is why the concept of example becomes critical in the conduct of aesthetic judgement. Plato, and later Plotinus, recognized this issue when, in different ways, they compared the greatest beauty with that of God. Plato talked also about comparison with nature. The comparison of the illuminated Gothic cathedrals with celestial Jerusalem is yet another example (Michel 1906). When Kant used the rose as an illustration of free beauty and Le Corbusier employed the Parthenon as an example of his conception of beauty, both were recognizing the preeminence of the example in matters of aesthetic judgement.

Principle of Beauty: Pleasure

In his book *The Phenomenology of Aesthetic Experience*, philosopher Mikel Dufrenne explained that "it is not we who decide what is beautiful. The object itself decides, and it does so by manifesting itself. The aesthetic judgement is passed from within the object rather than within us" (Dufrenne 1973, lxii). How, then, do we ascertain whether an architectural artefact manifests itself as beautiful or magnificent? Taste is the means, but how is this means activated? In architecture, aesthetic appreciation is not primarily the domain of architects, but, rather, that of the artefact's users and of the general community. The making of beautiful, magnificent artefacts is the true domain of the architect.

It follows that if the architect is to be successful he must make artefacts in such a way that they will prompt an aesthetic response in the minds and hearts of the world community. The architect has the aesthetic duty to design artefacts that please. Pleasure, therefore, is the principle of beauty, and great pleasure is the principle of magnificence. This pleasure could be either individual, contextual, social, or universal, depending upon the sort of artefact and the level of perception. It could also be several of these simultaneously. While the aesthetic pleasure inherent in one's own living room is individual, indeed secretive, the aesthetic pleasure of a public monument is societal, although experienced by distinct individuals. A masterpiece is a masterpiece precisely because it evokes universal, or at least widely shared, aesthetic pleasure. In all cases, those who determine the source of beauty and magnificence in an architectural artefact are not the architects.

Now it is time to blend together the notions of excellence and magnificence.

The Notion of Elegance

In the context of this theory, elegance is defined as the symbiosis of excellence and magnificence and the ultimate attribute of any design process or creative endeavour.

Perhaps a generosity of feeling towards people and the world in general, and the architectural work in particular, is the point of departure for making an elegant architecture. It could be argued that an architect cannot design an elegant artefact if he does not comprehend elegance, indeed if he is not elegant in his behaviour and manners. Politeness is the first external manifestation of an elegant attitude. A person cannot display real politeness towards others without having an honest respect for them and for their

This Outremont street demonstrates that an architecture of elegance is also an architecture of respect and satisfaction feelings. An elegant design, therefore, is polite and respectful. Conversely, an egotistic design attitude may lead to a very elaborate solution, or to an exorbitant one, but arrogance will always transpire. However, this does not mean that elegance is an ethical position. It is, more accurately, an attitude. Sloppiness is not, in itself, unethical. But if one claims to be an architect, that is, if one seeks the awesome responsibility of designing and building people's most intimate environments and manipulating their largest investments, then it is one's duty to be thorough and strive relentlessly for excellence and magnificence in one's work.

French poet Sully Prudhomme (1839–1907) wrote a remarkable piece on elegance. Although largely forgotten today, he was not a minor literary figure in his time. He has the distinction of having received, in 1901, the first Nobel Prize for literature. He was a member of the Parnasse group. In mid-nineteenth-century France, the Parnasse was the name adopted by a group of writers who had positioned themselves against Romanticism. In addition to Sully Prudhomme, this coterie included such literary celebrities as Théophile Gautier, Théodore de Banville, Leconte de Lisle, José-Maria Heredia, François Coppée, Paul Verlaine, and Stephane Mallarmée. Their philosophical foundation was the cult of "impossible art," or art for art's sake. It is said of Sully Prudhomme that his Parnassian inspiration was tinged with *intimisme*. When he was still a young man, he wrote in his personal diary – on 4 July 1868 – a thoughtful page on elegance. He was commenting on a lady whom he had met a few days earlier:

Elle est élégante. Je ne parle pas seulement de cette élégance de second ordre qui n'est autre chose chez la femme que l'instinct de la toilette qui lui sied. Quelle femme ne possède à quelque degré le souci et le don de se parer selon sa personne? J'entends une élégance plus relevée, celle qui sait assortir les manières à la finesse et à la fierté de l'esprit, plutôt que le vêtement au corps; ceci est donné par surcroît. L'aisance est signe de supériorité comme l'assurance présomptueuse est marque de médiocrité. Mais il faut que cette aisance soit faite de grâce pour se faire agréer, c'est-à-dire qu'elle doit être naturelle. L'élégance est aisée, elle est le geste d'une âme d'élite. Elle ne s'apprend pas, elle est spontanée, toutefois elle se connaît, et en cela elle confine au goût. Aussi n'y a-t-il pas loin de l'élégance à la recherche. La recherche peut encore être élégante, mais où commence l'affectation, l'élégance finit. Combien toutes ces nuances, en apparence subtiles, se saisissent bien dans la femme! Dans celle dont je m'occupe ici, je crois trouver la pure élégance; c'est la moitié de sa beauté. Sa toilette est pleine d'invention et dénuée de prétention; elle croirait, j'en suis convaincu, commettre une faute grave envers elle-même, si elle se rendait remarquable par quelque chose dans sa tenue; elle sait qu'il ne s'agit pas

The main gate of the Fondation Rothschild Workers' Residence illustrates that a discreet environment is a condition of elegance

d'être remarquée, mais d'être bien distinguée, qu'il faut ne ressembler à aucun autre, mais en restant soi. Or on est en soi par toute sa personne, non par l'exagération d'un détail, car tout se tient en nous et par conséquent tout doit s'harmoniser dans nos dehors. L'élégance dans les petites choses est simplement de la grâce; dans les grandes, c'est de la dignité, mais ce doit toujours être de l'esprit. Cette qualité exerce sur moi une séduction extraordinaire, bien que souvent elle m'humilie un peu. Oh! que je voudrais faire un vers qui lui ressemblât! (Sully Prudhomme 1960, 158)[119]

Just as that one sentence by Descartes, quoted earlier, defined the architect's role, this page by Sully Prudhomme presents a series of notions that define elegance. Sully Prudhomme began his elegant text by stating that elegance is much deeper than surface appearance. For him, true elegance is grounded in the *esprit* of a person, meaning, of course, subtle intelligence and sensitivity. By making a distinction between elegance of the first order, related to the subtleties of the mind, and elegance of the second order, related to material reality, he confirmed that degrees of elegance can be perceived, even though elegance sits at the pinnacle of aesthetic and quality perception. He established a hierarchy: the spiritual beauty of the woman he was admiring was more important than her physical appearance. He did not, however, negate the importance of the latter.

By using the rare verb *seoir* to indicate that any woman has the instinct to groom and adorn herself appropriatly (or, at least with "some degree" of "talent") – "qui lui sied" – he introduced the classical notion of *convenance*, or appropriateness, into the idea of elegance. Ease, *aisance*, is a sign of superiority, while presumptuous self-assurance is the mark of mediocrity. By asserting this, he was advocating honesty and humility. To design an artefact that looks natural, that seems evident, that is not constricted or arrogant, is perhaps what is required of the architect. To be accepted, Sully Prudhomme said, ease must entail natural grace. As it is used here, the word *natural* does not mean "related to nature," the opposite of *artificial*. Rather, it means the sort of grace that flows effortlessly. How many buildings display an effortless grace? The Palais-Royal is one.

By saying that elegance is a gesture of the noblest soul, *d'une âme d'élite*, that it is spontaneously known rather than acquired, and as such proceeds from taste, Sully Prudhomme was not negating education. On the contrary. What he meant was that elegance is not solely a question of rational understanding; it is also a question of sensitivity. Scientific knowledge can be taught through logical demonstration. In this sense, elegance cannot be taught. Aesthetic knowledge can only be shown through example.

This small house in Outremont demonstrates that elegance is the opposite of ostentation

Recherche is not far from elegance, said Sully Prudhomme. As it is used here, the word *recherche* does not mean the quest for scientific truth. It connotes, rather, a studied attitude, a desire not only to be excellent in all things, but also to be refined, subtle, polite – in a word, civilized. Although elegance is close to this sense of *recherche*, Sully Prudhomme advocated prudence: if *recherche* becomes affectation, elegance disappears. He explained that a truly elegant woman knows that it would be a grave mistake to try to stand out. An elegant woman must simply be distinguished. She must not look like anyone else and remain true to herself. She remains true to herself by allowing her entire personality to shine forth, not by exaggerating one detail. Every aspect of her is related to all her other aspects, and, consequently, all parts of her must be harmonized in her appearance. In other words, Sully Prudhomme was advocating a harmonious appearance in harmony with the soul.

Sully Prudhomme summarized his thesis on elegance by stating that elegance in small things is simply grace, while true elegance is dignity in great things. But, he added, such grace and dignity must always be the result of intelligence and sensitivity – that is, of *l'esprit*. We could infer from this that it is the mandate of the architect to design a dignified world containing graceful cities, and dignified cities containing graceful buildings, and dignified buildings containing graceful details. Sully Prudhomme concluded his reflexion with two ideas. First, he claimed that elegance was teaching him humility; if only he could write a single verse as elegant as this elegant woman. Second, he implied that elegance was to be the ultimate attribute of his poetic work.

A Phenomenological View of Elegance

Mobilizing the phenomenological approach depicted earlier, we will describe the idea of elegance by listing its essential features. Elegance is a universal eidetic concept. Under the scrutiny of our intentionality, its noematic structure appears, and it is the active symbiotic confluence of the idea of excellence with the idea of magnificence. It is only when these two ideas mesh that elegance emerges. It follows that elegance is an apodictic dimension of the architectural phenomenon's eidos when it has fulfilled its telos. A nonelegant architecture, therefore, is an incomplete architecture because it has not yet reached its full potential. According to this definition, most architectural artefacts are phenomenologically incomplete; this explains the current level of environmental mediocrity and related social dissatisfaction. Hence, an elegant architecture is a satisfactory architecture

Children at play in the Palais-Royal garden demonstrate that elegant architecture allows convivial activities to take place in a beautiful setting

because it fully responds to people's needs. And it follows that an elegant architecture is an architecture of respect because to attempt to meet people's aspirations is to show respect for their values. Elegance is the premier attribute of architecture because it is the one that acknowledges its eidos and carries it to its telos.

Elegance is a generic notion, a universal that relates to people, attitudes, objects, buildings, art, science, problem solving, and practically all human endeavours. Elegance requires maturity because it is the product of patient searching. Education is necessary for acquiring and producing elegance. In his *Dictionnaire philosophique*, Voltaire insisted that although elegance looks easy, everything that is facile and natural is not necessarily elegant. To understand the distinction, hinted Voltaire, one must embark on a patient search.

Elegance can only be acquired through an intentional projection towards others. As a consequence, an elegant architecture is organically related to the people living in it. It is the truest demonstration that their habitation problems have been satisfied. As it finds its validity in the polite and positive recognition of people's shared values, an elegant architecture is not self-referential. Hence, elegance does not proclaim itself. Self-proclaimed elegance would be a contradiction in terms because it would be ostentation, and elegance is the opposite of ostentation. Since "others" are those who proclaim the elegance of a thing, they form a necessary dimension of its essential reality.

Deeper than surface appearance, elegance is the emanation of the full being. It finds its soul in the spirit of a being. Elegance is not an afterthought, it cannot be added after a work is finished, it cannot be painted on, and it cannot be faked. Elegance requires truth, because elegance necessitates appropriateness, an attribute that opposes falsity. An architectural artefact that is not properly organized, not appropriately located or inserted into its social and cultural fabric, cannot be elegant because it is imposed or constricted. Elegance is the contrary of constriction. Because elegance responds to complexity, it incorporates subtlety in creation and refinement in development. Jean Cocteau was certainly in agreement with Sully Prudhomme when he wrote that "l'élégance consiste à ne pas étonner"; or, elegance means that one should not astonish. Elegance is neither frivolous, elitist, nor snobbish.

In contemporary architectural discourse, the concept of elegance – either as one design attribute or as the ultimate design attribute – has never, until now, been discussed. What I am putting forward here as the ultimate attribute of architectural design is the search for a meaningful meaning, if such a tautology is allowed. Perhaps it is even impossible to design a meaningful contribution to the enhancement of our civilization without elegance. Perhaps elegance is a necessary vehicle for human evolution, emancipation, and development. Elegance has appeared in all civilizations. In each instance, the creators of elegant works, whether in architecture, art, science, or literature, have always taken a rigorous approach to their work and demonstrated a depth of thought capable of producing rich, positive meanings.

Is elegance the same thing as perfection? If perfection cannot be achieved in our imperfect world, it remains, nonetheless, a goal to pursue. Elegance, then, may be the attribute that brings things close to perfection. Elegance may not be synonymous with perfection, but it may be the last step leading up to it.

Illustrations of Elegance

A few examples may serve to complement this description of elegance. In Imperial Rome, Petronius was Nero's hired writer and confidant. Tacitus was a contemporary historian. In his *Annals*, Tacitus called Petronius an *elegantiae arbiter*, "a judge of taste" or an "arbiter of elegances," plural. The arbiter of elegances was considered to be the most important authority on a wide range of questions that all required judgements based on taste.

The Corinthian Order is an example of architectural elegance. The Tholos of Epidaurus is one of the finest examples of this Order. Some two thousand years after its construction, Palladio, a down-to-earth practitioner, risked a qualitative judgement and categorically stated that the Corinthian Order was more elegant than the others (Palladio 1965, 21). Palladio actually used the word *elegant* and, in his admirable work, revealed himself to be a man of exquisite taste. We could say that the Corinthian Order is the weakest of the three Orders; or, conversely, argue that it is the most refined of the three, that it would have been impossible to design the Corinthian Order before the other two, that this Order was, in fact, the third generation of this architectural design. In other words, the Corinthian Order that was declared elegant by Palladio might be the product of successive improvements. If, indeed, it is an improvement on the preceding versions, then it represents excellence on excellence, magnificence on magnificence.

Architect Arthur Stratton wrote, "the most perfect Greek Ionic capital is from the Erechtheum ... and the Ionic Order as a whole is of exquisite refinement" (Stratton 1986, 8). Like Palladio, Stratton was passing a quality and aesthetic judgement on a structure several centuries after it had been designed and built. Can we infer from this judgement that the expression "exquisite refinement" is a synonym of elegance, and that elegance is a notion that defies time?

The Attic amphorae were artefacts created by the same race of designers who made Classical Greek architecture. Today, these vases are still considered to be extremely beautiful, even elegant. Like the Greek temples, they were designed according to a very strict system of proportion. In his meticulous study of harmonic ratios in nature, art, and architecture, György Doczi also cited as examples of very beautiful objects the Minoan kantharos, the Cretan krater, the Lung Chuan vase of the Sung Dynasty, and the Pueblo earthenware pot (Doczi 1981). Do we infer from this that elegant objects are always designed according to harmonic ratios?

During the thirteenth century, the Sainte-Chapelle is Paris was designed by architect-mastermason Pierre de Montreuil under the sponsorship of Saint Louis. For more than seven hundred years, there has been a general consensus that this little Gothic chapel is a pure jewel, one of the most elegant buildings that ever existed. In his monumental *Histoire de l'art*, published in 1906, French historian André Michel criticized some of the

The Corinthian capital of the Tholos of Epidaurus
is an example of perennial elegance in architecture

colour included in the chapel's stained-glass windows, but added that this defect was minor and could only be perceived by the specialist: "the eye that does not analyse remains under the charm ... this stained glass, depicting a celestial Jerusalem with precious stones, will always remain for the general public the most beautiful of the Middle Ages" (Michel 1906, 2: 381). Today, the *Michelin Guide* calls it a "masterpiece of the High Gothic" (*Michelin France* 1995, 192).

Another example of elegance that emerged from the Middle Ages is the book *Les très riches heures du Duc de Berry*. A richly illustrated prayer manuscript, written and designed in the first half of the fifteenth century, the book is held at the Musée Condé in Chantilly, France. It contains exquisite miniatures, many with architectural illustrations. In a recent publication, three museum curators, eminent art critics, and historians, called this work a "summit of the history of painting" (Samaran 1969). These sources associate elegant objects with such ideas as Heaven and a "summit." Do we infer, therefore, that elegance is close to perfection?

In his book *Baroque Architecture*, architectural historian Henry Millon said of the Petit Trianon at Versailles that it was the most beautiful of all the residences designed by Gabriel. He declared that this building succeeded in integrating a "calm dignity" with the "most elegant and harmonious proportions" (Millon 1965). Another architectural historian, Christian Otto, in his book on Balthasar Neumann's baroque churches, talked about "the elegant force of [Neumann's] architecture, matching human scale with monumentality, the pleasure of familial things with grandeur" (Otto 1979). In both aesthetic judgements, the word *elegant* is used to describe an undisputed architectural masterpiece. Do we infer from this that elegance is a necessary condition of an architectural masterpiece?

Similarly, Botticelli's allegory of spring, *Primavera*, is generally considered an expression of grace and gentle rhythms; it depicts a wistful Venus representing divine beauty and divine love. Botticelli was perhaps a fashion designer without knowing it. His finely draped robes adorned with flowers can be compared to a garment described by Marcel Proust in *À la recherche du temps perdu*: "Mrs. Swann would appear, spreading around herself an always different toilet, a large parasol of a subtle shade that matched the scattered petals adorning her dress ... smiling, pleased with the weather ... assured that her toilet was the most elegant of all" (Proust 1954, 636).[120] This link between Botticelli and Proust is intriguing. What, in Botticelli's and Proust's minds, was the secret of elegance? Proust's vision of elegance in a woman is very close to Sully Prudhomme's, as well. Do we infer from this that the same concept of elegance spans centuries, countries, and civilizations?

Proust's view of elegance may trigger memories of another famous French text on architecture, Paul Valéry's *Eupalinos ou l'architecte*. In this poetic essay on architecture, the French poet wonders: "Tell me (since you are so sensitive to the effect of architecture), did you not observe, strolling in this city, that, among the buildings that inhabit it, some are mute, and others speak; and others again, which are the rarest, sing?" (Valéry 1944, 35).[121] Do we infer from Valéry's text that the architect's task is clear? If he designs buildings that sing, will he be designing elegant buildings?

Most of these examples relate to society's privileged segment. Does this mean that money is necessary to achieve elegance? Certainly not; numerous examples of inexpensive yet elegant artefacts may be found. For instance, what could be more elegant than chopsticks? Indeed, in Japan, on the streets and in ordinary bookstores, stationery stores, grocery stores, fan shops – that is, in shops where ordinary goods are bought and sold by ordinary people – there are countless examples of pure elegance. The standard method of tying onions or radishes together, the technique of fashioning two bamboo sticks into a crutch to support a branch of an old tree:

Seen in a Chinese market, this display of vegetables shows that
elegance can be an attribute of an unpretentious artefact

these things are elegant. In every modest sushi bar, the sushi pieces are not just thrown onto a plate; they are disposed in a meticulous way; flavours are enhanced by a harmony of colours. In China, simple objects such as baskets, straw hats, or brushes are designed in the most elegant manner. Such elegance has nothing to do with wealth. It has to do with taste and civilization.

More famous examples of elegant objects designed by ordinary people for ordinary people are manufactured by the Shakers. Visitors to Hancock Shaker Village in the Berkshire Mountains of western Massachusetts learn how members of the Shaker community, about one hundred years ago, designed and constructed for their own use buildings, chairs, brooms, boxes, garments, and elegant objects of all kinds including a particular style of woman's cloak. This cloak was an immediate and immense fashion success. Well-dressed women from Boston and New York ordered them not only because they found them comfortable and warm, but also because of their elegance. One century later, Shaker objects and furniture are still considered elegant. They are marketed all over the world. Shaker design is an example of elegance that has defied time. In her study of Shaker culture,

At the end of the nineteenth century this Shaker cloak, called the Dorothy (after its designer Dorothy Ann Durgin) became the epitome of elegance; intended as practical garment for Shaker women, it was also adopted by chic and affluent New York and Boston ladies

June Sprigg said that the most appealing quality of Shaker design is its optimism. She wrote that "those who would lavish care on a chair, a basket, a clothes hanger, or a wheelbarrow clearly believe that life is worthwhile. And the use of every material – iron, wood, silk, tin, wool, stone – reveals the same grace, as if the artisans were linked in their collective endeavour in ways that transcend understanding. It is no exaggeration to call Shaker design *other* worldly. In freeing themselves from worldly taste, the Shakers created a purity of design that endures" (Sprigg 1986, 22). The Shakers raised frugal elegance to a level of pure delight.

The Elegance of the Studied Artefacts

The obvious question that is raised by all these descriptions of elegance is whether the three architectural artefacts studied in this work are examples of an elegant architecture. The answer is "yes," and for the following reasons.

The Palais-Royal, the Fondation Rothschild Workers' Residence, and Outremont are all inhabited, multiuse urban entities. Their residents have never ceased to want to live in them; these are extremely pleasant places to live and to visit. Residents insist that these places have become a part of their heritage. They protect them against all degradation and constantly upgrade them. Moreover, these artefacts are praised by a wide variety of observers who are not theoreticians of architecture. Yet, so far, critics of architecture have ignored them.

Because of their residential components, these three places are alive at all hours of the day, every day of the week. They are much more than self-contained, isolated objects: they constitute dense fragments of city. All three simultaneously generate a strong sense of enclosure and an equally strong web of connections to their surroundings. Each stands as a telling demonstration of the necessary symbiosis between urban design and architecture proper. Each offers a balance between the public and private domains. Over the years, these places have prospered because of their own merits and benefited from the attributes of their neighbours.

All three places give preference to the pedestrian and encourage social encounter. They are examples of efficient management. Over the years, they have maintained an intelligent relationship between the private and public economic sectors. Although created by private entrepreneurs, they were designed to fulfil larger goals than immediate financial and practical objectives. They were built to answer people's social needs in the context of a broad political agenda. Each has acquired a cultural heritage and become a living testimonial to the history and modernity of its community.

These three sites constitute a positive acknowledgement of their natural surroundings. In them, nature is largely domesticated, but always in a respectful way; and it is constantly nurtured. Landscaping was an important element of their original designs and is still perceived as such by their contemporary users.

The success of these places comes equally from the quality of their intrinsic reality as structures and from the quality of the human activities they facilitate. In different ways, all three artefacts display a strong sense of order at the level of overall space organization and a wide diversity at the level of detail. Composed of multiple layers of harmonious rhythm, they feature a unity of materials, colours, and textures. All are well-proportioned on the human scale. None show any technological prowess to speak of. However, all are solidly built structures made with durable materials that have aged well; the patina of time has enhanced their aesthetic qualities.

Each of these examples demonstrates that the success of an urban place depends largely on whether it is well used by people; a successful architecture is, after all, respectful, convivial, and accessible. The Palais-Royal illustrates, further, that conviviality can be compatible with monumentality. All three entities exemplify a frugal architecture, which does not mean an austere or dull architecture, but one that evinces a joyful serenity. If a place can be defined negatively, then none of these are ostentatious, arrogant, or pretentious.

Now, at a time when architects tend to be marginalized, it is interesting to note than they played a central role in the making of all three places. These entities are not the works of a single master but, rather, the products of a succession of sensitive and polite architects, each respecting the intentions and designs of his predecessors. While all of these architects were undoubtedly talented and competent professionals, none were the stars of their time. Perhaps their lack of fame is explained by the fact that they were more interested in designing solid and beautiful buildings that responded to their clients' needs than in garnering public acclaim. Their names rarely appear in architectural-history books.

This trio of artefacts convincingly illustrates Relph's and Norbert-Schulz's definitions of place and Heidegger's concept of dwelling. Each loudly proclaims that, in a world that is becoming more and more brutal, people desire places where even little children and the elderly can feel comfortable. People want an architecture that respects them; in return, they will cherish it, as indeed they have always done at the Palais-Royal, the Fondation Rothschild Workers' Residence, and Outremont.

THE IDEA OF ARCHETYPE

Architects require an operational concept that can encompass the idea of measurement in matters of architectural quality and the idea of example in matters of architectural beauty. This concept, I am suggesting here, is the archetype.

The word *archetype* is a combination of two Greek words: *arkè*, or "beginning," and *tupos*, or "form." Hence, *archetype* means "first form," or original model, something that serves as the foundation for subsequent variations and combinations. In a family of types, the archetype acts both as a generic departure point and as the noematic structure's underpinnings; that is, as both the principle of the process (of knowing a thing, for instance) and as the principle of the product (the cause of the known thing). To be effective, an archetype must respect two conditions. The first is the formal condition, which stipulates that the archetype's appearance, one of its possible forms, maintains the characteristics displayed by the original model. In other words, a type belongs to an archetype if it is the manifestation of the archetype's essence. The second condition is the intellectual one, which stipulates that the type's specific description is inscribed in the archetype's generic description (Auroux et al. 1990, 1:149).

In the twentieth century, a certain number of architectural writers have touched upon the concept of archetype, notably Norwegian architect Thomas Thiis-Evensen and myself, more than twenty years ago (Thiis-Evensen 1987; Lincourt 1972). In *Archetypes in Architecture*, published in 1987, Thiis-Evensen put forward the same definition of archetype as the one I have just outlined, and discussed in detail some forty architectural archetypes grouped under the architectural shelter's three basic delimiting elements: the floor, the wall, and the roof. Fifteen years earlier, in *Le mésodesign*, I adopted the classical definition of archetype and offered a series of urban-design archetypes. In both cases, the theoretical development of the concept of archetype was limited. Here, I am attempting to carry it further.

The current definition of archetype was formulated by Swiss psychiatrist and psychologist Carl Gustav Jung (1875–1961). Analysing his patients' dreams and probing the idea of a personal unconscious, Jung made a fascinating discovery. He found that deep in the minds of all humans lay "a much bigger entity than the personal unconscious, which he termed the collective unconscious" (Robertson 1987, 85). This led Jung to define the concept of archetype as follows: "there exists a second psychic system of a collective, universal, and impersonal nature which is identical in all individuals ... this collective unconscious does not develop individually, but is inherited ... it consists of pre-existent forms, the archetypes" (Jung in Robertson 1987, 85).

Psychologist and mathematician Robin Robertson explained, in his book *C. G. Jung and the Archetypes of the Collective Unconscious*, that Jung insisted that the archetype (from the collective unconscious) and the instinct (from the personal unconscious) were two sides of the same coin. Jung went on to state that "there is good reason for supposing that the archetypes are the unconscious images of the instincts themselves; in other words, that they are patterns of instinctual behaviors ... the hypothesis of the collective unconscious is, therefore, no more daring than to assume there are instincts ... the question is simply this: are there or are there not unconscious, universal forms of this kind? If they exist, then there is a region of the psyche which one can call the collective unconscious" (Jung in Robertson 1987, 86). And, explained Robertson, Jung claimed that he had reached the scientific certainty that the collective unconscious, and thus the archetype, existed.

Robertson brought a precision to Jung's position by establishing a distinction between the archetype itself and the image it projects. He argued, "it [was] understandable that [Jung] originally thought of the archetypes as 'primordial images,' since it was the symbolic images that he encountered in the dreams of his patients. But he came to realize that the images were personal or cultural, and that we could make no conclusions about the structure of the archetypes themselves." Robertson cited Jung again: "an archetype in its quiescent, unprojected state has no exactly determinable form, but is in itself an indefinite structure which can assume definite forms only in projection" (Jung in Robertson 1987, 102). In Robertson's words, "the best way to express the situation seems to be that the archetype comes first, but it is empty until the actual experience gives it form. Of course, in saying this, we are merely saying that the actual structure of archetypes in the unconscious is beyond human observation" (Robertson 1987, 102).

Referring to a critical perception of the world achieved through comparative assessment, Robertson wrote, "we experience the world rationally and ... the archetypes are activated in many, perhaps all, human situations. As we personally experience the world through the archetypes, the archetypes are given a particular, highly personal form. Eventually the world is almost entirely encountered through our personal memories; the archetypes lie deep within ... thus archetypes are activated when necessary, and accumulate personal memories around themselves to form complexes [a grouping of memories]. However, an additional element enters the picture to enormously broaden possibilities, and that element is unconsciousness" (Robertson 1987, 105). It follows that, insofar as archetypes embedded in the collective unconscious exist, they can be perceived through the formulation of images.

This is Jung's concept of archetype: it is a mental construct. That being said, we may ask what the relation is between the concept of archetype described by Jung and a concept of archetype that may be relevant to architecture. One the one hand, mental archetypes are related to the collective unconscious and are an integral part of human brain activity. They contain, or may be composed of, groups of memories, and are triggered when human beings move through life and interact with the rest of the universe. But these expressions of the perceived experience of the world emerge, first, from the buried unconscious, and only afterwards do they percolate up to the conscious level. On the other hand, the architectural archetype always take the form of a physical, built, three-dimensional entity. What its observers perceive are not the archetypes themselves, but an emanation of them – that is, a type. It is to this or that particular type, rather than to the archetype, that those who are experiencing architecture respond. Nonetheless, architectural archetypes sit outside the human mind, and, though types, are perceived by it. The experience of these artefacts is a conscious phenomenon that operates on two levels simultaneously. The first is direct perception: we are in this room, we perceive its walls, indeed we are a part of this spatial phenomenon. The second is the emergence of feelings: we feel comfortable, we like or dislike it. These feelings are coloured by groups of memories coming from the unconscious; that is, from mental archetypes, as defined by Jung.

Strictly speaking, and according to Jung's definition, the archetype has nothing to do with architecture per se and everything to do with the human mind experiencing architecture. But we have to go further: we must jump the frontier between the mind and the built environment and project the concept of archetype onto the physical environment. By doing so, we will come to recognize that groups of architectural forms and spaces may constitute an architectural archetype just as groups of memories may form a mental archetype. In this case, the architectural archetype is a metaphor for the mental archetype.

We have to treat architectural archetypes with prudence. We cannot correlate a human meaning or feeling with an architectural artefact. All the theoreticians of architecture who have tried to accomplish this feat have failed. Moreover, to associate a set of complex psychological images emerging from the unconscious with a complex group of architectural forms is to compound the difficulty. To avoid the problems inherent in formulating a psychological interpretation of architecture, we have to avoid claiming that an architecture can hold the same meaning or trigger the same feeling for all people in all circumstances. In other words, to play its role to the fullest extent, the architectural archetypes has only to be a model for architectural composition. And each individual is allowed his or her own feelings towards each concrete emanation of that archetype which has been used as a model.

In her book *Archetype, Architecture, and the Writer*, Bettina Knapp studied ten writers who developed a human archetype based on an architectural metaphor.[122] She began her argument by explaining that the inventor of the concept of archetype, Jung, built his own home, Tower House, on the shores of Lake Zurich: "Surrounded by a moat, the tower acted as both a retreat and a protection from the outer world. It could be said that Jung's emotive roots were embedded in this architectural monument: it was a sacred space where the inner riches lying buried within his collective

This portico at the Palais-Royal illustrates the idea of architectural archetype

unconscious nourished him continuously. By organising or shaping space, Jung articulated the mysteries existing inchoate within him in a visual language" (Knapp 1986, vi). According to Knapp, the architectural experience played a role in Jung's development of the concept of archetype.

"Architecture as a spatial creation," she continued, "is the outer garment of a secretive and vital system; it is a non-verbal manifestation of a preconscious condition ... archetype is an elusive concept that cannot really be fully defined ... archetypes, perceived in the form of primordial images, are present in dreams, legends, fairy tales, myths, religions and cultural notions, and modes of behavior the world over ... when the words archetype and architecture are juxtaposed – as in archetypal architecture – the concept may be looked upon as a line, shape, or depth perception that manifests itself as an autonomous, a priori image in the collective unconscious" (Knapp 1986, vi). Thiis-Evensen spoke of archetypes in a similar way: "archetypes may be understood as images in relation to ... architectural form, function and technology" (Thiis-Evensen 1987, 17).

Following her introductory remarks, Knapp offered a definition of architectural archetype: it "is a physical representation of the psychological and functional condition of an individual, culture, class, and period. It is a composite of opposites: rhythmic yet static, subjective yet objective, timely yet eternal, affecting the senses of those who create it, live in it, and look at it in its own day, and also the generations to come, who are likewise exposed to its beauty or ugliness, to all the factors projected upon it. It is a microcosm of the macrocosm" (Knapp 1986, vii). This is the idea of architectural archetype that I have adopted in presenting my theory.

The Portico as an Architectural Archetype

The portico is a device that may be called upon to illustrate the idea of archetype in architecture. To describe it we must begin by recognizing three notions. First, humans share certain characteristics. Second, these generate universal needs, which may be met by architecture. Third, the architectural response to a human universal need depends, in part, on the architectural archetype. The portico encompasses these points. It was invented in response to a universal human need: the need to conduct private activities and public ones, and to establish a buffer between the two. As the portico is a generic concept that may take an infinity of built forms, it is truly an archetype.

People need privacy primarily because they need to rest. Neurologists and physiologists tell us that the brain and body function essentially the same way in all humans (Laborit 1968, 1970, 1974). Both the brain and the body expend energy in order to function, which means that they get tired. This is one of their universal traits. The human range is short: the wakeful period lasts no more than a few hours and is followed by a period of sleep. Every night humans pass from the state of consciousness into the state of unconsciousness. These two states are so closely interrelated that one is always defined by the absence of the other: to be awake is to be not asleep, and vice versa. Humans who cannot sleep die. We spend about one third of our lives asleep.

In architectural terms, this universal human need to rest imposes a requirement on all residences. The design response to this need is the bedroom – a private, quiet, comfortable space where humans lie horizontally on a flat surface, which is usually called a bed or a couch, and where they fall into a state of unconsciousness. A good bedroom is one that allows for privacy, quietness, and comfort. These notions are relative, of course; in certain societies, many people sleep together in not-so-cosy places. Yet this reality does not contradict the general argument. Given the choice, most people would choose to retire to a secluded place to sleep. The fact that, in certain circumstances a human need is not satisfied does not negate its existence. Often, cultural behaviour patterns – such as sleeping in groups on the floor – are prompted by a lack of financial means. It is like walking barefoot. Many people do, but as soon as they can afford to, they buy shoes.

If sleeping is a basic human need requiring a private place, then eating is a need that necessitates venturing out in public. To survive, humans must leave their protective shelters and gather food. In today's urbanized society, this involves shopping.[123] Outlets for this activity are either in the public domain or directly connected to the public domain; they must be easily accessible. Contrary to a private place, where inhabitants control usage, a public place is one in which each person has to share control with many others. This shared control is a maintained through a communal code of behaviour.

The need to rest and the need to eat engender a duality: all humans are involved, at some time, in activities that are related to the private side of their being and, at other times, in communal activities. Sleeping is an activity that humans consider very private and for which they require private spaces. At the other end of the spectrum, communal activities, such as the selling and buying of food, require special architectural public places, such as markets. Also, by default, the spaces between private structures are public. As humans are sometimes in one kind of space and sometimes in an other, they must constantly shuttle from very private to very public spaces, and vice versa. Soon, the abrupt passage between the two types of space proves to be uncomfortable and the need arises for buffer or intermediate spaces.

Analysing the evolution of intermediate spaces, we discover that one of the very first interior divisions in a primitive hut was between the community quarters and the nuclear-family quarters; that is, between the more public and the less public areas. Later, the nuclear-family areas were further divided to create the very private place for women to deliver children and the less private place for the family to gather. Later still, the dwelling was divided according to basic functions requiring different levels of privacy: cooking, eating, entertaining, and working in less private spaces; and sleeping, lovemaking, and child delivering in more private spaces. Coming from the outside or from the communal quarters, visitors and family members would enter the dwelling by passing into the less private quarters; family members would proceed to the sleeping area; visitors would rarely go into the very private rooms.

In fact, this sequence of rooms was nothing more than a common-sense spatial organization related to basic privacy requirements. In order to establish levels of privacy, different sorts of buffer space were invented: vestibules, lobbies, entrance halls, and anterooms. They have appeared in all civilizations, in all periods, and take countless shapes. For instance, in a traditional Muslim courtyard house, visitors are invited first into a ceremonial court and from there proceed to a guest room; never are they allowed into the women's quarters. In a traditional Chinese house, visitors walk through the same sequence of semipublic/semiprivate spaces: first they enter a visitors' courtyard and then they are admitted into a second, more private courtyard; afterwards, they are asked to step up to a veranda and from there they are shown to a guest room. A similar sequence exists in Occidental contemporary dwellings. For example, in my house in Outremont, the sequence of intermediate spaces from the street includes the front walkway, a short staircase leading up to the front porch, a vestibule, and a hall opening into the living room.

The portico is one of those intermediate spaces that acts as a buffer. It is an outdoor, protected, linear space situated in front of, or around, a building and delimited by a row of columns. It sits at the interior/exterior, inside/outside, private/public interface and is the transition between the two.

Simultaneously private and public, the portico is a usable, functional area that faces another public place, such as a sidewalk, a street, a square, or a garden. This definition of *portico* applies equally to a single building and to a row of adjacent buildings (Szambien 1992).

Sometimes called an arcade or a colonnade, the portico is neither of these, even though it always incorporates a row of columns that delimits its inside/exterior public space from the adjacent outside/exterior public space. An arcade is merely a succession of arches. One was built in Medieval Genoa to delimit the harbour area from the rest of the town. Here, the arches were set side by side, forming a kind of freestanding wall punctuated by arched openings. When arches are perpendicular to a pedestrian thorough fare, they form an archway, which is yet another synonym of arcade. This kind of arcade is sometimes located inside a building or between two solid walls (Fleming 1991, 15). The word *arcade* also designates a shopping centre in the form of a covered passage with shops on one or both sides, such as the magnificent Burlington Arcade in London, or those noisy places where people flock to play video games or feed slot machines.

A colonnade is a series of columns, and should not be confused with a portico. Freestanding colonnades were used in Ancient Rome to define public areas. The remains of such colonnades can be found in Palmyra, in present-day Syria. A colonnade set in front of a building's façade, inaccessible to the public and serving only as a decoration, is not the kind of portico discussed here; Perrault's colonnade on the east façade of the Louvre would be an example.

Another version of the portico is the monumental porch. For instance, the porches of Andrea Palladio's Villa Rotunda are referred to as porticoes (Wundram 1989). The more convivial residential front porch, such as that found in Outremont, serves some of the same functions as the portico but is not a bona-fide portico. The Greek architectural device called *stoa* and the Italian medieval-city device called *loggia* are natural extensions of the portico. The *stoa*, a standard feature of Classical Greece's public places, was a market structure. It served the same purpose as the portico and was often located in front of shops. The *loggia*, an innovation of Italian medieval city designers, was a short, enlarged portico, generally a little more monumental than other porticoes, and situated on important squares. It was also used in the same way as regular porticoes were.

Ambiguity is a major part of the portico's interest. Legally, does it belong to the public or the private domain? Perhaps it belongs to both. Spatially, is it a private space given to the public, or an incursion of public space into private territory? Again, it may be both. Is it an extended sidewalk along which pedestrian traffic flows parallel to a building's façade, or is it the building's entrance porch through which pedestrians move perpendicular to the façade? Yet again, it is simultaneously both. Is it a space for movement, or for stationary activity? Surely it is both.

The need to protect pedestrians from the rain and the sun was the first motivation for designing porticoes. Other devices, too, accomplish that task: the awning, the canopy, and the marquee. The difference is that while the portico is a space carved out of the building mass, these devices are external features tagged onto the building. Theoretically, we can rip a marquee from a building without undermining its solidity or structural integrity. If we try to eliminate the portico's columns, however, the entire façade will crumble. Moreover, the basic character of the sidewalk is not altered when an awning or a canopy protrudes over it. In this respect, the portico is different. When the sidewalk penetrates the building's façade and becomes the portico's floor, it acquires a new dimension. Retaining its public-right-of-way status, that sidewalk also becomes an outdoor lobby of the building. For these reasons, awnings, canopies, and marquees are not porticoes.

What is this ambiguous space? What are the constitutive elements of the portico? These may be presented as follows:

a. The carved space. This is a long, horizontal, and linear prismlike space. In cross section, it often takes the shape of a rectangle, or a square, or a rectangle surmounted by an arch.

b. The floor. Under a portico there is always a hard-surfaced directional floor that runs parallel to the building's facade. The directional character of the portico's floor is established mainly by the space. Sometimes, however, a floor pattern adds to the directional quality, offering counterpoints to the main direction; it may also indicate such things as the location of entrance doors to the building, major exits leading to the adjacent public space, or an interface with another portico. Most often, the portico floor's texture or material is related to the building's texture or material rather than to that of the public floor it skirts. The portico's pavement belongs to the building; it is clearly a part of its architecture.

c. The ceiling. Most of the time the ceiling of the portico is flat and horizontal. Sometimes it is a barrel vault; more rarely it is a gable or a series of groined vaults. In the case of the Greek *stoa*, it is slanted on one side. The ceiling's material and texture always belong to the building.

This rue de Rivoli portico facing place du Palais-Royal is an architectural device that could enhance conviviality in any city square

d. The back wall. This wall plays an important role in the portico's success. If it is blank, then the portico may be relegated to acting as a conduit for pedestrian traffic only. In that case, the portico loses most of its usefulness and relevancy as an architectural device. A stronger management of the portico's space may then be needed to use the space fully and to compensate for the reduction in spontaneous activity caused by the blankness of the back wall. An active back wall is one with many holes: windows and storefronts, doors and passageways. Behind these holes, we often find the kind of facilities that generate activity: stores, restaurants, pubs, cafés, artisans' workshops, community-service centres, entrance halls, lobbies, portes cocheres, passageways leading to interior courtyards, gardens, and so on. The activity they produce spills over into the portico space.

e. The colonnade or the arcade. A row of columns or pilasters forms the portico's front wall. This constitutes an important part of the device because it defines its spirit. A great measure of the portico's success derives from the equilibrium between the spaces on both sides of the colonnade. If the columns are too flimsy and placed too far apart, then the portico will be too open and will not offer sufficient psychological protection and intimacy for the private side of the space to function properly. The opposite is equally true: closely placed fat columns will darken the portico and make it uninviting. People will hesitate to venture inside this space and may perceive it to be dangerous. Indeed, Spiro Kostof remarked that throughout history porticoes were eliminated because they had become too dangerous (and also too dirty). He said that "in the late 15th century, King Ferrante of Aragon, King of Naples, counselled Pope Sixtus IV to follow his example by tearing down porticoes and widening the streets" (Kostof 1992, 217).

To be fully used and appreciated, a portico must be perceived simultaneously as both an interior and exterior space. This ambiguity must be maintained if the portico's success as an urban amenity is to be ensured. As the activities most likely to be conducted there are precisely those that belong on the private/public meeting ground, this in-between character must be preserved. A café under a portico illustrates this point. The owner must feel that this café space belongs to her, that it is part of her establishment. She must not hesitate to invade it and set up tables there. At the same time, the café's patrons must note that these tables are on the sidewalk, understand the implicit invitation, and feel welcome to walk in, sit down with a friend, and order a glass of wine. And the pedestrians strolling under the portico must not be intimidated by the presence of the tables; they must understand that these tables are in the public domain. Then the synergy will be complete, because the fun of sitting on a café's terrace is watching passers by and the fun of walking by a café's terrace is looking at the people who are sitting here. This urban spectacle all takes place under the portico's protection.

Seen from the public area in front of the portico, the colonnade defines the aesthetic character of both the building as a whole and the portico as a distinct feature of this whole. From within the portico, it establishes a rhythm of openings that frame the view towards the outside world. Those inside can choose to be completely or partially hidden, or to be fully seen by the outside world. Under the portico, we are in an ambiguous semiprivate/semipublic space, a space more private than the outside world and more public than the building's interior. The portico brings a certain level of privacy to the public realm – not enough to be discriminatory, just enough to play with. This kind of complicity between the private space and the public realm exists at the Palais-Royal, and its visitors experience it with considerable delight.

f. The steps. Sometimes, the floor of the portico is a few steps higher than the floor of the adjacent public space. This minor difference of level helps define the portico space and enhance its stagelike character. When there are two or three steps outside the column line, a dimension is added to the public/private interface. The steps are almost a part of the entirely public space, but not quite; they are not "protected," but neither are they "dangerous." They are like the high-diver's platform, a place to hesitate for a moment before jumping into the unknown, a place from which to look up at a cloudy sky and decide whether to open an umbrella or hail a taxi. When the portico runs along a street, quite often the single step constitutes the sidewalk curb, as it does on rue de Rivoli in Paris. Often, also, there is a change of texture in the floor from the lower, public surface (the street's asphalt) to the portico floor's more refined texture (stone paving), or from concrete to stone, or from coarse stone to polished stone, or from grass to brick paving, and so on.

g. The light fixtures and furniture. Nowadays, porticoes are lighted with electric fixtures. Since early times, they have always been lighted by one means or another because they have always been heavily used, even at night. Over the centuries, porticoes have been lit by resin torches, oil lamps and lanterns, and gaslights. Light fixtures have been hung from the ceiling in the portico's axis, or between columns in line with the columns' axis, or attached to the columns, or attached to the back wall.

Other minor architectural elements are often added to the portico. An iron grid may prevent pedestrians from venturing into hazardous areas, flower boxes may help define the space further, benches may indicate that a portico is not only a passageway but also a rest area. Business has always been conducted on such benches. The concept of the modern bank was developed on a bench, a *banco*, apparently under one of medieval Florence's porticoes. The "banker" would install his bench, invite his client to sit with him, discuss his financial problems, and offer advice or a loan. The early Florentine banker was a strange mixture of godfather, psychoanalyst, shrewd businessman, politician, and patron of the arts. The portico was his court.

A portico is an outdoor, public, pedestrian-circulation space under the protection of a private building. We can come close to the building, experience an aspect of it, yet remain on the public thoroughfare. We can use the portico even if we have no business to conduct within the building.

For many interior spaces that require an immediate and close relationship with the exterior – a shop, for instance – the portico eliminates the need for a vestibule. The portico is a place for business. Merchants display their wares beneath the shelter of its roof, where prospective clients stroll and browse. Commerce can go on even on a rainy day or a day when the sun is blazing. Commerce always takes place at the private/public interface. The client – the public figure – comes from the public domain and enters the private domain of the merchant. In order to attract the client, the merchant displays, in full public view, his merchandise, yet keeps a tight control over it. Until a product is sold, it remains in the merchant's private domain, exposed to the public. After the sale, it disappears into the client's own private domain. The portico, an architectural device designed to be at the private/public interface, is particularly well suited to the private/public act of commercial exchange.

When porticoes face public squares or major arteries, they often become places where important activities occur. In the Italian medieval cities, prominent families built *loggias* to house civic functions. Kostof describes the Florentine *loggias* this way: "[they] served as the site of family ceremonies like marriages and funerals, and the signing of important documents. In 1470 there were still 17 of these aristocratic loggias in existence, among them that of the Rucellai, which is described by a member of the family as being 'per honore della nostra famiglia, per aoperarla per le

The portico is to be found in lesser-known architectural artefacts; here one protects students from the rain at a school in La Robertsau, near Strasbourg, France

letitie e per le tristitie' (for the honour of our family, to use on joyful and sad occasions)" (Kostof 1992, 218). Significant private family activities were conducted in public. We witness here, again, the same private/public ambiguity: a decidedly private affair, say a marriage, is performed in full view of the public; the portico, the ambiguous private/public device, becomes the proper place to hold such an event.

The conditions a portico must meet to be successful are very simple. It must be a public place facing another public place. It must display a proper balance between its openness and its closeness. It must have a back wall that generates or, at least, permits activities other than just walking, although this activity is an essential part of the portico's function and should in no way be neglected. It must maintain the marvellous ambiguity that resides between its private aspect and its public appearance. And, if the portico is also well proportioned, it may become a very beautiful and positive addition to a city's architectural heritage.

The portico is an architectural archetype. Its noematic structure is defined by the invariant components I have just outlined. Over the centuries, all over the world, in all climates, and in all civilizations, the portico

Andrea Palladio's basilica in Vicenza illustrates both the idea of the portico and the concept of an architecture of elegance; it is undoubtedly a masterpiece

has been used as a buffer between two places requiring different levels of privacy. It has taken an infinite variety of shapes, but in all cases it has retained its essential characteristics.

The Archetype of Elegance Idea

Two central ideas of the theory have been constituted: elegance and archetype. I now propose to combine them in order to generate the operational idea of an archetype of elegance, or a useful design model.

A wedding party gathers in Outremont's Parc Pratt for a photo session; a moment of happiness in an architecture of satisfaction

9

ARCHETYPES OF ELEGANCE

Archetypes of elegance are created with the sole purpose of helping the architect in his design endeavours. They provide design models for him to follow. They are only suggestions, not rules. The architect and his client are free to accept or reject them. However, if they do accept them, they increase their chances of obtaining the kind of architecture to which they aspire. My argument is this: as these archetypes are inspired by places that are elegant and successful, they are likely to produce an elegant architecture.

Artefacts that result from a design process buttressed by archetypes are simultaneously universal and unique: universal due to their filiation to the archetype and unique due to their grounding in a specific site. Insofar as both the archetype and the resulting types respond to the values presented earlier, they will find validity in a social consensus and be relevant.

The idea of architectural archetypes of elegance may be described using three examples: an inner-city residential unit inspired mainly by the Fondation Rothschild Workers' Residence, a park similar to those found in Outremont, and a public square like place du Palais-Royal. Although inspired by components of the three sites we explored earlier, the archetypes of elegance I will now present are not copies of these places. They are originals adapted to the present times, models that introduce new features without losing the original spirit. Since they are abstract constructs, they are necessarily schematic and presented in terms of spatial configuration and functional characteristics. They are not destined to be built as they are schematically described. On the contrary, they are open to an infinite range of applications, depending upon the peculiarities of the site, the moment in time, the client's specific requirements, the community's cultural traits, and the architect's creative talent. Also, they are not meant to be re-created throughout an entire city. What engenders monotony is not adherence to a set of archetypes but the slavish repetition of a type.

The suggested archetypes are only examples of what the theory I have been building can produce. More archetypes may be derived from the studied artefacts. The Palais-Royal garden may generate a garden archetype, the streets around the Fondation Rothschild Workers' Residence may support the elaboration of a high-density urban-street archetype, and the residences of Outremont may inspire at least two residential archetypes. Further phenomenological investigation of other successful artefacts may produce other meaningful models.

In the following presentation of the three archetypes, some space measurements are introduced. This is simply done to make the descriptions more precise. Measurements are given in metres, from centre wall to centre wall, and from finished floor to finished floor.

WHERE PEOPLE RESIDE

Among the millions of activity components that coalesce in a given city are the very special ones people call home. These are no ordinary places. They are what American psychologist Richard Lang called "the intimate hollow ... carved out of the anonymous, the alien." Home is where "the commerce of strange and familiar, which forms a central dialectic of human existence," takes place (Lang in Seamon 1989, 201). As Edward Relph explained, "an individual is not distinct from his place; he is that place" (Relph 1976, 43). The need to appropriate one's own place is deeply entrenched. It is often expressed in popular language. English-speaking people refer with affection to the spaces they inhabit as "my place" or "your place"; this locale is wholly unique because it belongs to me, or to you; it is our ultimate refuge and the bastion of our privacy. French-speaking people do not even talk about a geographic location when they mention their places of residence. They name it by referring only to themselves: "le chez-moi," "le chez-toi," "le chez-soi." Remembering Gaston Bachelard's marvellous formula, we can identify home as the locus of intimate immensity where the miniature becomes infinite. Home is the protective castle, the comfortable place in which to entertain, the cosy nest in which to rest, a vessel for sadness and happiness, and a casket of love (Bachelard 1964, 140–90).

The residential archetype suggested here is a popular residential unit located in a high-density urban neighbourhood. It illustrates what could be an elegant, affordable dwelling for the next few generations, what could be a dignified place for people to reside.

Archetypes of Elegance

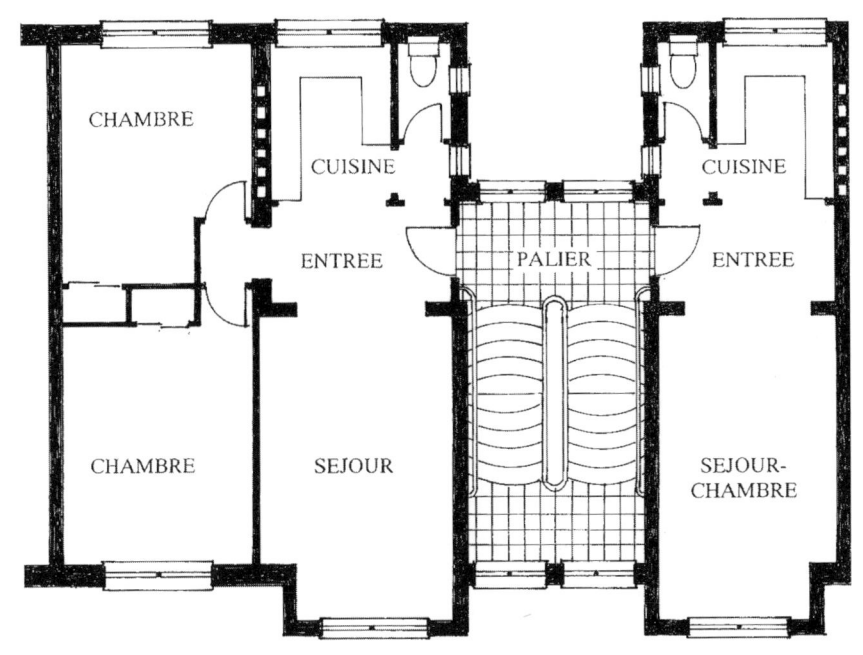

The inspiration for a residential archetype of elegance: schematic plan of a typical flat at the Fondation Rothschild Workers' Residence

Inspiration from the Fondation Rothschild Workers' Residence

The rue de Prague residence has certain distinctive and practical features. When the project was conceived almost a century ago, it was intended to provide the best possible living standard for an affordable price. This subsidized-housing complex is still considered comfortable and inexpensive. Furnished, from the outset, with the most up-to-date electromechanical systems, appliances, and amenities, it also boasts a double orientation and large windows that permit ample natural ventilation and light. Access is via a staircase serving only two apartments per landing. In some instances, there is a link to what was once a workshop. As people have been satisfied with this residence for almost a century, it would serve as a good model for others.

A Cluster of Spaces

However, the model I propose here is more complex than the rue de Prague artefact. It is a residential unit made to fulfil the needs of the twenty-first century. It comprises a network of five discrete spaces: one main living space, called the flat; one underground parking space; one underground storage space; a shared lobby and service room; and one extra room under the roof.

I propose to locate this multiunit residence in a vertical slice of multiunit complex, a large, seven-storey building sitting on the periphery of a city block. The residence forms a crown around a garden used mainly by its residents and other occupants. For demonstration's sake, let us say that the archetypal city block is a 134-by-66-metre rectangle with its longitudinal axis oriented north-south; these measurements define the property lines as well as the outside façade of the complex. Sidewalks two metres wide bordering an eighteen-metre-wide street surround the building. Retail establishments and lobbies occupy the ground floor. The upper floors of the east and west wings contain residential units; the north and south wings house institutional or community facilities and offices. The building is sixteen metres deep; when it houses apartments, the depth includes a two-metre-wide balcony facing the garden.[124] The overall height of the building is twenty-five metres. In cross section, the archetypal building comprises two basement floors, each 2.8 metres high, a six-metre-high retail space directly accessible from the sidewalk, a space that could accommodate a mezzanine (such a mezzanine is what the French call an *entresol*), five three-metre-high residential floors surmounted by a one-metre-high parapet, an attic floor recessed two metres from the parapet, with a two-metre-high exterior wall recessed at forty-five degrees for another vertical meter and recessed further at twenty degrees to form the roof structure. Because of this profile, the building's perceptible height from either the street or the garden is twenty-two metres.

The ground floor and both basement floors cover the entire area of the block; this means that the garden is actually located on the roof of the ground-floor shops. At the midpoint of the block's west and east sides, a covered pedestrian passageway cuts through, linking the two side streets and lengthening the frontage of the shops. All the front doors and windows of these shops face either the sidewalk or the passageway. Also, all front doors open onto the sidewalk; this is not the case at the Fondation Rothschild Residence. By concentrating all front doors and shop windows on the block's public side, we enhance street activity and reinforces security.

The flat component of the residence is a six-by-fourteen-metre rectangle accommodating a household of up to four people. It has windows on both sides, so it gets the morning and the afternoon sun and benefits from cross ventilation. On each floor of each wing, there are seventeen such units; the total number of units is 170; the block's residential population is 680 people;

the block population density is therefore 480 people per hectare. Residential wings have no corridors. Flats are grouped in vertical banks of ten, two per floor, around a staircase and an elevator.

The same staircase provides access to the garden, a well-defined green enclosure with harmonious proportions. The proportions of the city block we are using here are one-half along the east-west axis and one-sixth along the north-south axis; these proportions result from the fact that the garden floor is five metres higher than the surrounding streets, hence 17/34 and 17/102. Although the garden could be designed in a variety of ways, I will suggest certain basic principles. It is not a paved courtyard, but a lawn generously adorned with flowers and bushes. The technology is available today to build such rooftop gardens. This one is a place for small children to play – that is, children who live in the flats as well as those who attend a day-care centre or kindergarten that might be located in the block. The garden is also a place for adult residents to sit and enjoy the sun or read a book – especially if it is adjacent to a public library, which might also be located in the block. Balconies face the garden. The privacy of the lower balconies is preserved by raising their floor level one metre higher than the garden floor. Vines grow on the garden's side walls. Those who come to this semiprivate landscaped enclosure enjoy a safe, quiet, luxurious respite from the feverish activity of the surrounding city.

The activity components of this city block are connected to the rest of the world through a series of high-tech devices: telephone lines, terminal and switching boxes, cable-television hookups, fibre-optic-cable computer-terminal boxes, satellite dishes, shortwave transmitters and receivers, and so on. This communications equipment is located in a section of the attic and relays information to each unit in the complex. Moreover, the entire roof surface is covered with solar-energy panels, and these fulfil a substantial portion of the complex's energy requirements.

The complex's two basement floors are designed to house a set of communal amenities.[125] These include some 350 parking spaces. In addition, two large and high spaces, situated in the centre of the edifice under the garden, are used as secondary retail areas. They have 7.5-metre ceilings beneath the roof structure. As they are located at the same level as the surrounding parking and service areas, their service entrances are easily accessible. At the other end, patrons enter these spaces at an intermediate level, from a mezzanine. Another segment of the basement is a service centre for the complex: garbage is collected, deliveries are made, shipping and receiving is handled here, below ground, away from the street. This facility benefits commercial and residential occupants. The service ramps and lanes in the basement have the width, turning radius, and headroom required by service vehicles. Still another basement area is reserved for storage. The last basement area is used to accommodate electromechanical machinery, which includes an electrical substation, a connection to the city water-supply system with proper pumping and metering equipment, and a mini liquid-waste treatment plant, like the one developed by the Canadian Mortgage and Housing Corporation some years ago and called Canwel. Such a localized water-treatment system has many advantages. It reduces water intake by up to 80 percent, and thereby shrinks the size of the city's aqueduct system. It limits the volume of wastewater returned to the sewer, and thus helps reduce the size of the central treatment plant. And because of its relative autonomy, such a decentralized system is much more secure than the system currently used in our cities. While it is relatively easy to sabotage a network, it is virtually impossible to break scattered, largely independent systems. Finally, the basement contains a solid-waste dispatcher that sorts out recyclable materials from disposable ones, a shredder, a garbage compactor, and fire-fighting equipment.

The buildings in this city-block complex are made with durable materials. Frames are of fireproof reinforced concrete. Exterior walls are of brick, stone, or stucco; there is no exposed concrete or steel because experience is beginning to show that these materials do not age well when they are not protected from the elements. All windows open; all are large and constructed of rustproof materials. Their specific design varies according to specific interior use, climate, orientation, and aesthetic considerations. Interior finishes vary with each dwelling, reflecting the taste and lifestyle of the residents. All building materials are ecologically sound and recyclable.

The residential unit described here is one of a group of ten such units forming a building slice. They are laid out on both sides of a fire-resistant vertical circulation shaft comprised of a staircase, an elevator, and dry vertical ducts for the electrical and communication cables; the wet pipes are grouped in other vertical right-of-ways. On each residential floor, a small hall, separated from the staircase by fire-resistant walls, provides access to two flats.

Entering from the street, we reach the elevator and staircase through a lobby opening directly onto the sidewalk. The lobby is modest, yet spacious enough to serve its purpose. Here we find mailboxes, an information panel, and an interior-communication terminal. On average, the lobby is a three-and-one-half-metre wide, five-metre-deep space. In colder countries, a vestibule may be added to serve as an airlock. The front door is equipped with the proper security devices. The staircase and elevator lead to all levels of the building, including the basement floor and the private garden. A small service room opens into the lobby: it is used for storing bicycles, bulky toys, and the like. The residents of units accessible through this particular lobby share this amenity. All common spaces are built with sturdy and easy-to-maintain materials. Their decor is respectful of residents' aesthetic values.

The front door is, in itself, an archetype. It meets two particular requirements: it harmonizes with the character of the preexisting public dimension that it faces – the street; and it is distinctive enough to invest the building with its own personality. When it comes to the architectural features that make up the interface between a private space and a public one – like a front door or a building façade – the design challenge is always to respond simultaneously to two seemingly conflicting, but in reality complementary, requirements: a respect for the community and a reverence for individuality. The archetype is the device that deals simultaneously with both levels of intention. Its general characteristics cater to the community's common requirements and its particular applications respond to personal desires.

The design of the building façades, the ones facing the street as well as those surrounding the garden, is accomplished by following simple but proven rules of harmonic ratio. A gentle rhythm is created by alternating generous openings with warm-hued, textured masonry and by introducing a wide variety of details.

In its basement, each residential unit has, as a standard feature, one thirty-square-metre parking space.[126] Residents may use this space as they see fit. Also, in each residential-unit basement there is one ten-square-metre storage area per dwelling.

A Double-Orientation Flat

As the typical flat in this complex is of the transverse kind, with eastern and western openings, it welcomes the morning and evening sun. The flat takes the form of a six-by-sixteen-metre-by-three-metre prism. The east and west exterior façades are six metres long. The interior ceiling height is 2.7 metres, allowing thirty centimetres[127] for the reinforced concrete slab, acoustic insulation, electromechanical systems, and resilient floor finish, with or without carpeting. The flat's interior space is fourteen metres deep; on the garden side, a two-metre-deep balcony or *loggia* provides an exterior prolongation. As two adjacent flats are served by a vertical circulation shaft that has a footprint area of twenty-two square metres, the flat's interior area is seventy-three square metres, or eighty-five square metres if the balcony's area is included.[128]

The flat is subdivided into four areas: a twelve-square-metre balcony; a twenty-four-square-metre living/dining room; a twenty-five-square-metre service area comprising an entrance hall, kitchen, toilet, bathroom, washer/dryer closet, and wardrobes; and a twenty-four-square-metre sleeping area, which could be made into two bedrooms. If the street is noisy, the living/dining room is on the street side and the sleeping quarters on the garden side. However, if the street side is quiet at night, a more satisfactory layout can be used: the living/dining room and balcony facing the garden.

The living/dining room is meant to be used in a variety of ways, depending on the household's needs and lifestyle. The space is a well-lit, comfortable rectangle that permits several patterns of furniture distribution.[129] In this common room, residents interact with one another and experience moments of intimacy. It is a place to welcome friends, share food, listen to music, read a book, watch television, and debate personal issues.

At the other end of the flat are two twelve-square-metre bedrooms, each large enough to accommodate a double bed or two single beds, bed tables, a dresser, and a desk and chair. They are quiet, comfortable rooms. Wardrobe closets may be located in the central service area next to the bedrooms. Bedroom windows are large and can be opened in different ways to admit fresh air in all seasons; their sills are sixty to seventy centimetres from the floor so that a piece of furniture may be inserted below.

The unit's attic room is between ten and twelve square metres. It can also be used in a variety of ways: as an extra bedroom, a private office, a workshop, a den, or a study. With the attic room, the residential unit has four different living spaces to accommodate a household of four residents. Three of these rooms can be used for sleeping. Multiple combinations are thus possible. For example, in the case of a young family, the parents may use one of the two bedrooms, the two small children may share the other bedroom, and the attic room may be used as a work space. In the case of an older family, the parents may sleep in one bedroom, the grandmother may take the other bedroom, and the teenage daughter may (to her delight) make the attic room her private quarters. Alternatively, four adults may share the unit: two may sleep together in one of the bedrooms, another may take the second bedroom, and the fourth may occupy the attic room. It is always possible for someone to sleep in the living/dining room, but, as this is designed as common space, it may engender conflicts of use.

The flat comes with a set of standard features and appliances. It has a kitchen, which may open into the entrance hall, or the living/dining room,

A residential archetype of elegance: at the Fondation Rothschild Workers' Residence, large windows let in plenty of sunlight

or both. If they so desire, residents may choose to prepare food while participating in a discussion taking place in the living room. The kitchen is equipped with what are now viewed as standard kitchen appliances: stove with oven, microwave, refrigerator/freezer, double sink with garbage disposal, food-preparation surfaces, safe electrical outlets, cupboards, and closets. It has a mechanical ventilation system.

The bathroom comes with an integrated bath/shower unit, two sinks, appropriate cupboards, mirror, and safe electrical outlets. The toilet is located in its own small room. This standard European-style arrangement, still somewhat unusual in North America, is proposed here because it offers more flexibility. In a flat where up to four people must share one bathroom, it makes a great deal of sense. The room that houses the toilet is also equipped with a small sink. The flat has a washer/dryer unit located in a closet as well as a place to store an ironing board. And it has a series of closets. Well-designed partitions and solid doors create sound barriers within the flat. As is the rule in Parisian residences today, three doors isolate the bedroom from the living/dining room.

Two Innovations

The kitchen, bathroom, and lavatory, amenities that began to be introduced at the end of the nineteenth century, became standard equipment in the twentieth century. In France, the Hygienists' crusade, culminating in the Fondation Rothschild architectural competition, had a major impact on this development. In the archetype I am proposing for the twenty-first century, two more amenities are put forward with a view to making them standard features: a multimedia communications workstation and a private minigarden.

The computer assisted multimedia workstation occupies a six-square-metre area that contains a desk, a computer with one or two monitors, a printer, a fax receiver/transmitter, a telephone with a modem and answering machine, bookshelves, and filing cabinets. This workstation is connected to a worldwide information network. Today, telephone, radio, and television are standard equipment in almost all residential units. In addition, the microcomputer is rapidly infiltrating private homes. Generally speaking, however, what exists today is a chaotic assemblage of discrete pieces of equipment, more or less plugged into one another, more or less connected with various communications networks, and not at all integrated into the architectural configuration of the flat. Except in the homes of rare dedicated computer adepts, these devices do not make up a comprehensive residential workstation. Their installation is still improvised. What I am suggesting with this archetype is to move beyond the current state of improvisation and do for the multimedia station what has been done for the kitchen during the past century: transform it into a well-functioning work area.

The proposed multimedia workstation is a mininetwork of peripherals. For example, more than one telephone, each linked to the main computer, could be located in different rooms. An intercom system could be integrated with the telephone system and serve, also, as the front-door control. A switching device could regulate the electronic-communication traffic and distribute messages through the regular telephone, the modem, and the fax. Regular television sets could be linked with the computer and sometimes transformed into extra workstations. The audio-stereo system could also work as an independent unit, or as the television sound system. Compact laser discs, used for the video or sound systems, could also be part of the computer CD-rom system and its memory bank.

The multimedia main workstation, with the computer and bulky peripherals such as the printer and the fax receiver/transmitter, is ergonomically designed and located either in the attic room or in one corner of the living/dining room. If it is in the attic room, it means that the nineteenth-century concept of a workshop attached to an apartment, as implemented at the Fondation Rothschild Workers' Residence, has now been adapted to meet twenty-first-century needs. The same rationale that was used by the Fondation Rothschild planners to justify a workshop close to workers' homes prevails today with respect to the electronic workstation. It permits a person to earn a living at home while rearing children. Moreover, in an economy that is struggling to find new resources and do more with less, it provides office space without overhead.

The flat's second new standard feature is the minigarden. As I have mentioned, the archetypal flat has an exterior space in the form of a twelve-square-metre balcony or *loggia* facing the living/dining room. This outdoor space is designed to serve many complementary purposes. It is a place to sit, have a drink or a meal with family or friends, or simply take the sun and enjoy the fresh air when the weather is nice. As such, it extends the living/dining function of the flat. But it is also a place for gardening. Living in a high-density artificial environment tends to isolate people from their traditional, natural roots. A minigarden reintroduces nature into the living space in a more meaningful way than tropical plants in pots. Growing herbs and flowers is a highly civilized activity. Herbs add flavour and interest to food and have medicinal properties. Flowers bring happiness. To offer someone fresh flowers, especially from one's own garden, is to make a

A residential archetype of elegance: these balconies could be enlarged to form an indoor/outdoor attachment to a living room

gesture of friendship; in some circumstances, it is to make a declaration of love. Flowers enliven a home. Voltaire was fond of saying that tending one's own garden is the beginning of wisdom.

Either the entire balcony of the archetypal flat or half of it can be transformed into a greenhouse; it is a way of maintaining a garden during the colder season. This means that the apartment's exterior living/dining-room wall – either entirely or just half – is made of two glass partitions at least two metres apart. These partitions can be opened or closed depending on the season and on how the residents intend to use both the living/dining room and the balcony.

Although derived from the Fondation Rothschild Workers' Residence, this residential archetype differs from its inspiration. Its entrance lobbies, unlike those at the rue de Prague complex, open onto the sidewalk rather than the courtyard. There are four reasons behind this modification: it is meant to facilitate accessibility and front-door visibility from the street, to contribute to the street's intense public activity, to increase security on the street, and to have at the back of the building a green space more private than the rue de Prague courtyard. In terms of area, the archetype is much larger than the Fondation Rothschild complex; in this respect, it has more in common with Augustin Rey's original proposal, which was to construct larger flats than the ones that were actually built.

As did the Fondation Rothschild project in its time, the archetype presented here brings to the popular flat the sort of amenities found in many more upscale apartments. However, this archetype also initiates some major improvements. In addition to an increased amount of usable space, which reflects one hundred years of progress, it includes as a standard feature one parking space, one storage area, one attic room, an exterior space or greenhouse with a minigarden, a multimedia computer package and workstation, and a large, semiprivate communal garden.

What I am proposing is an elegant archetype that is compact, practical, and adapted to current needs. It offers all the necessary components of an extremely pleasant, aesthetically appealing home in a high-density inner-city environment. It is an archetype that respects people in a very concrete way.

This archetype is innovative, but not in the sense that it breaks with reality; instead, it improves upon a reality that has already succeeded. My aim in proposing this archetype is not to make something radically different for difference's sake, but, rather, to make something noticeably better as judged by society in the light of the value-based design criteria outlined earlier.

WHERE PEOPLE SOCIALIZE

The other two archetypes of elegance that I am putting forward are models of public places. Without exception, in a city, private activity components connect with the public network of places where all people have the right to be. Simply by walking out of their homes and entering the public domain, people engage in a process of face-to-face socialization. On crowded streets they rub elbows with their fellow citizens. At the marketplace they make deals. In Paris, on New Year's Eve, about a million people stroll up and down the Champs-Élysées just to soak up the festive atmosphere. Every summer on the outdoor plaza at Montreal's Place des Arts and in the surrounding streets, a jazz festival attracts hundreds of thousands music lovers. When Martin Luther King made history by telling America about his dream of hope, he stood in a Washington public place.[130]

Discussing today's urban public places, Kostof made the point that

> within the dense press of the built fabric, the greatest luxury of all is empty space. Whether it is used for the spectacle of pomp or for play, the open frame is politically

charged; the activities encompassed, frightened with consequence. Only here can a representative portion of the populace mass to make its mood known at a glance. Public space as it is successfully reshaped is an artefact of the collective passion that binds society: from civic protest to regimented ceremonies of consensus, to leisure pursued in an Arcadian idyll, or through the ritualized consumption of products and aestheticized environments. Even at its most trivial, the mere presence of a public realm is testimony to the insistence of our need periodically to rediscover the physical fact of community. (Kostof 1992, 172)

Although it is true, as Bernard Rudolfsky asserted, that a "town is not the result of a design program, [but] the reflection of a way of life," the fact remains that architects and urban designers are responsible for designing the sort of place where public activities may flourish in a meaningful way. Unfortunately, not all public areas are conducive to the enhancement of urban endeavours. Some open spaces are not public places in the true sense of the word, but uncared-for leftovers that quickly degenerate into desolate no-man's-lands. People feel uncomfortable or unsafe in these barren areas and repudiate them. The causes of such wasteful treatment of public resources are numerous, but bad design or simply lack of design are two of them. This is especially true in America, where the urban public domain is largely neglected. Rudolfsky convincingly documented this unfortunate situation in his book *Streets for People*. Criticizing a certain negative attitude found in America towards public places in general and streets in particular, he lamented that "the results" of efforts to ameliorate the situation "have proved unmemorable" (Rudolfsky 1969, 20). While we may find high-quality public places in a few cities, such as Boston and San Francisco, the most prevalent public place in American cities is the commercial strip – Las Vegas is its ultimate model. In such a car-oriented environment, the pedestrian is an endangered species.

The two public-place archetypes of elegance presented here are the small urban park and the city square.

The Inspiration of Outremont and the Palais-Royal

The five parks of Outremont provide the inspiration for the first archetype, while the public square in front of the Palais-Royal serves as the departure point for the second.

Observing Joyce, Pratt, Outremont, Saint-Viateur, and Beaubien parks we find common characteristics from which we may compose a community-park archetype. The average size of these parks is 20,400 square metres.

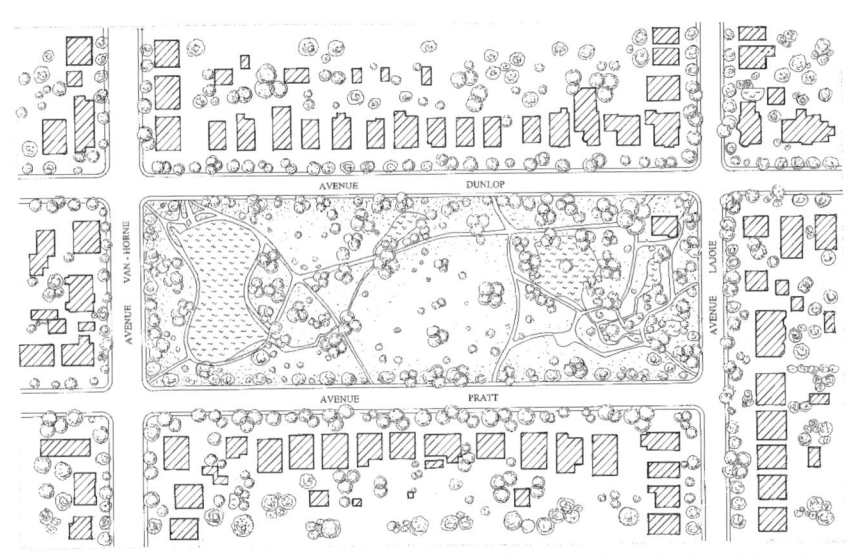

The inspiration for a community park archetype of elegance: schematic plan of Parc Pratt in Outremont

Although they are inserted into a rectilinear street grid, their internal geometry is fluid, *à l'anglaise*. They have meticulously mown lawns adorned with bushes, flowerbeds, and several species of tree. People are allowed to walk, sit, and lie on the grass. In four of the five there are pools that become skating rinks in winter. Although the main function of the Outremont parks is to provide a place to walk away from traffic and noise, other kinds of leisure-activity facilities are provided, such as tennis courts, children's playgrounds, a community centre for teenagers, and a community vegetable garden, also for children. In almost all cases, a sidewalk surrounds the parks. As no fence stands between the sidewalk and the typical Outremont park, one can enter anywhere. And the park is surrounded by the same kind of residence found elsewhere in the neighbourhood.

On its south, formal side, the Palais-Royal faces an ensemble of public places that may inspire the design of future city squares. The premier square in this network is place du Palais-Royal. It is a formal square used in a convivial way, a seemingly rectangular area that, in reality, is a trapezium. Unmistakably public, it forms a well-defined enclosure that flows effortlessly into the adjacent places. It is truly a square for the people; it serves as an urban hub. Most of the time it is crowded. No statues, fountains, trees, or parked cars are found on place du Palais-Royal. Its bare floor provides a smooth surface for the street artist and roller skaters who mingle with the many pedestrians.

Place du Palais-Royal is surrounded by major institutional buildings such as the Louvre, the Conseil d'État palace and the Comédie-Française theatre; it is also encircled by utilitarian buildings such as a hotel, a major store, offices, shops, restaurants, and cafés. All these edifices house facilities that generate intense activity, which, in turn, nourishes the community life of the public place. The square's underground contains an important metro station as well as public amenities such as toilets and small shops. Place du Palais-Royal is easily recognizable and accessible. It displays pleasant proportions on the human scale. With its hard-surfaced floor, its porticoes, and its service aediculae such as metro entrances, newsstands, and flowershops, it is an open-air urban room.

Still unfinished, place du Palais-Royal is presently struggling with a traffic problem: too many pedestrians are trying to share the space with too many cars.

The Small Urban Park

In October of 1989, an international symposium on urban parks and gardens was held in Paris. Its main theme was the parks and gardens of tomorrow. Among the many presentations made by city officials, landscape architects, and municipal engineers was an interesting lecture by J. Gadet, a senior park manager from Amsterdam. He presented the results of a study carried out the year before on users' motivations in Amsterdam's main park, Amsterdamse Bos. Four million visitors go to the Bos every year. Comparing his results with those of an earlier study, Gadet noted two important developments: an increase in visit frequency and a shift from recreational to everyday usage. The Bos users were asked why they went to the park: 51 percent gave walking as the main reason, 17 percent said bicycling, 15 percent said jogging or simply keeping fit, 15 percent said they came to enjoy the scenery, 10 percent said to sit and take the sun, 9 percent said to bring children to play, 9 percent said to walk the dog, and 3 percent said to practise other sports. Calculating the length of their stay at the park, 34.5 percent estimated they stayed one hour or less, 38 percent said between one and two hours, 17 percent said between two and three hours, and 10.5 percent said more than three hours. Gadet's conclusion was that, in view of this evolution, more amenities should be provided in parks.

Perhaps other conclusions can be inferred. If the results of this one Amsterdam study can be generalized for other cities, then we may say that several small, well-distributed parks could advantageously replace one large park and better meet most users' needs. And even though serene streets, such as those found in Outremont, do not replace a large park, it is still true that cycling on well-landscaped city thoroughfares is an agreeable experience that may complement cycling in a park. This is, indeed, what the Dutch do in their beautiful cities and towns. Only a tiny proportion of park users practise "other sports" – mainly tennis, football, and track-and-field activities. No doubt sport facilities are needed in a city, but they can be located on grounds of their own, not necessarily in parks. There is not much of a relationship between these sports and other park activities: those who go to the park to stroll rarely belong to the same group as those who go to play tennis; before or after playing tennis, people do not usually take a walk. In America, the same rationale could be used for softball, baseball, and football facilities. In Paris, it seems clear that the primary reasons people go to the many gardens, squares, and parks are identical to those that emerged as most important in the Amsterdam study: walking, enjoying the scenery, sitting and taking the sun, eating lunch, and bringing the children to play. These needs are successfully met by relatively small green spaces because the way they are distributed in the urban fabric increases their accessibility.

The small, Outremont-style, urban-park archetype of elegance is intended to meet these needs. The archetype is a real small park, not a garden or a square. It is the size of a regular Outremont city block: 256 metres by 96 metres, an area of 2.46 hectares, larger than both the square, which rarely exceeds half a hectare, and the enclosed garden like the one at the Palais-Royal, which has an area of 2.05 hectares. Like the parks of Outremont, its outside shape is rectangular because it is inserted into the street grid.

Even though the small urban park welcomes people from all parts of the city, it is designed primarily to serve neighbourhood residents. The key to the success of this park archetype is pedestrian accessibility. I suggest locating one such park at the centre of a 120-to-150-hectare residential district; it should be inserted well into the urban fabric and kept highly visible and accessible at all times. Neighbourhood residents should be able to walk to the park in ten minutes or less. Why dictate such an access time? The reason is this: it seems that a ten-minute walk is the longest most people will take when embarking on an unplanned visit. A man might say to his wife: "We have half an hour before dinner. Shall we take a walk in the park?" They

A park archetype of elegance: a soft lawn with trees, bushes, and flowers entices people to enter and relax

will take ten minutes to get to the park, ten minutes to meander in it, and ten minutes to return home. This detailed time calculation has been introduced here in order to make a point. In reality, of course, people will not make such a rational plan. They will just know that the park is near and decide, on a whim, to go. If the park is farther away, they will hesitate.

The small urban park is a green space devoted mainly to strolling. It has none of the formality of the Palais-Royal's enclosed garden and none of the perceptible space organization of the Parisian-style square. It is basically a large lawn with a gently rolling terrain. It has an informal, English-style layout that encourages relaxed, informal use. It is designed in such a way that activities can occur there spontaneously without a management organization. It also has a pond and a fountain, but not at its centre. Here and there, a few unobtrusive monuments or sculptures are installed. Trees are plentiful, not aligned, and of multiple species. Tall trees, smaller trees, and bushes provide shade variation and define a range of informal, natural enclosures. Flowers are abundant.

In a way, the small park serves as the community's backyard. Hence, it has to be very informal and very clean. Clean benches are required; a clean lawn is also indispensable because adults lie, and children roll and tumble on it. In this park archetype, a few individuals nap while others study or simply chat with one another. Teenagers may throw a Frisbee. In colder climates, children go to the park to play in the snow. They may skate on the frozen pond, or, if the land slopes, slide on their toboggans.

The park archetype offers a series of services. If there are several such parks in a neighbourhood, as there are Outremont, they provide complementary facilities: one park may have a community vegetable garden while another may have a children's playground with swings.

The residential buildings surrounding the archetypal park are no different than other houses in the neighbourhood and elsewhere in the city. They can be cottages, duplexes, triplexes, or multiapartment houses; it makes no difference. Real-estate-market forces may push their selling price above that of similar properties on the next street. That is unavoidable in our kind of economy. What is avoidable, however, is exacerbating this speculation by placing larger mansions there, by intentionally reserving the best places in the city for the rich.

As it is inserted in the street grid, the park's outside shape is more or less rectangular; but this rectilinearity does not prevail inside the park. This contrast between outside and inside is a vital compositional feature of the park archetype. While a visually perceptible sense of order in the urban street fabric is necessary for the purposes of orientation, the opposite is required in the park. There, people need to experience freedom of movement; they must, for example, have enough unstructured space to fly a kite. In the middle of this open space, people can exist, for a short interval, in a natural setting, somewhat isolated from the built environment. They can temporarily forget the hardness of the streets. In spite of the fact that it is a totally domesticated milieu, it must still give, for a moment, the impression of being an untamed refuge. Of course, the feeling of isolation is an illusion. The wild is really a world away. Between the bushes and the trees, we can always glimpse civilization. As Colette once wrote: "It is so nice to be afraid when we know that there is no danger!"

The small urban park is not a complicated creation. It is a place for simple daily pleasures and safe daydreaming, a gentle haven that brings an element of peace to the city. This fundamental purpose dictates the park's design concept. To be successful, its design must be straightforward. It must not try to convey strange, esoteric meanings, postmodern or otherwise. It should incorporate only a gently rolling lawn, trees and bushes, a few flowerbeds, a pond with a fountain, benches, lampposts, maybe a corner for small children with a few swings, and a few tennis courts – but

A park archetype of elegance: in winter, the pond may be converted into a skating rink

no more. These things, however, must be designed, built, and maintained meticulously, as they have been in Outremont. Elegant landscaping means that a lawn is a lawn, not a hard, dirt surface; a lawn is a soft, natural carpet that invites you to take off your shoes and walk.

A park with "Keep off the grass!" signs should not be considered a park. No such sign appears in the archetype. This is the real humanist, democratic challenge this archetype answers: create a magnificent lawn and ensure that people play on it. If, in order to maintain the lawn, people must be excluded, then there is a deep problem with the park's maintenance policy. A small urban park is not a monument. People do not play in a monument; they pay their respects. Elsewhere in any city there are places for such formal symbolism: a cathedral, a city hall, a university tower. A park is for relaxing.

The small urban-park archetype is bordered by a sidewalk that is a segment of the city's sidewalk network. The interface between the surrounding sidewalk and the park's lawn is continuous. This intimacy between the formal pedestrian system of the sidewalk and the informal pedestrian ground of the park is absolutely necessary if the park is to succeed. Fences and gates between two components of the public realm are the equivalent of "Keep off the grass!" signs, and are a frustrating obstacle. The message delivered by such barriers is this: "You may be good enough to walk on the sidewalk, but 'we' will allow you into the park only when 'we' feel like it. This fence creates two classes of public place, and 'we' are the ones who hold the key to the gate, which means that, 'we' are more important than 'you.'" Such an attitude defeats the purpose of a small park, which is to accommodate everyone.

The City Square

"At best, squares are microcosms of urban life, offering excitement and repose, markets and public ceremonies, a place to meet friends and watch the world go by." It was with these words that British critic Michael Webb opened his book *The City Square*. He went on to define this square by remarking that it comes in an infinite variety of shapes and sizes. He added:

Reduced to basics, a public square can be as simple as a child's drawing: an outdoor room, with walls to enclose space, doors to admit traffic, the sky as ceiling ... Stand in a public space, walk about, sit at its edges. Does the space itself have a presence, a definition, a quality that adds significantly to the architecture and the features that it embraces? And if you decide that, yes, it is a square, does it work well? Does it take your breath away as you enter, and lift your spirits as you stroll around? Is it a place in which you want to meet your friends and observe strangers? Is it the first choice for community celebrations? Does it offer a sense of place, a feeling of historical continuity, a vision of what urban life should be? (Webb 1990, 9–12)

Yes, what *does* it take to make a public square work well? If I am given the responsibility of designing a square, how do I go about it? Are squares even necessary to a city? The authors who have studied the subject unanimously answered "Yes." Kostof, for one, showed that "the essentialness of public space [is] a universal urban trait ... cities of every age have seen fit to make provision for open places that would promote social encounters and serve the conduct of public affairs" (Kostof 1992, 123).

The city-square archetype of elegance warrants a clear definition.

As understood here, the city square is not a place removed from the street, but an integral component of the urban grid. An empty lot, even admirably landscaped, is not the sort of square we are considering here. The London square, – such as Bedford Square, for example – is certainly a charming urban place, but it is not a city square. Neither is the Paris *square*, such as square Armand-Trousseau, which faces the Fondation Rothschild complex; this is a landscaped playground surrounded by streets. Similarly, the Circus in Bath, England, forms a marvellous urban enclosure, but it is not a square because no public activity is allowed in its central green space. A courtyard, such as cour de l'Horloge at the Palais-Royal, is also an enclosure, but it does not constitute a square because it is removed from the street system. An enclosed urban garden, such as that of the Palais-Royal, is not a square, although it may have some similar features. The New England green, such as the one found in Woodstock, Vermont, accommodates the same sort of community functions as a square, but it is not a square because it does not have the same enclosing features. The American shopping mall and the inner-city room, such as Montreal's Complexe Desjardins, are also places where people gather, but they are not squares because they are private places that open their doors to the public for profit. The commercial strip, although lined with commercial establishments, is not a square because it is a car-oriented environment that does not form an enclosure.

To be a true square, and to function successfully as one, the open-space archetype I am putting forward here must possess a combination of complementary characteristics. The city square is a strictly urban construct. It is a component of the urban fabric, and its reality as an open space derives from the dense environment that surrounds it. The square appears in urban settlements of all sizes, in all cultures, and at all times. The reason for this universality is simple. People live together in closely packed environments because they share certain values and require certain services and facilities. They need to come together from time to time to affirm their existence as a community. The square is merely a place, open to all, that serves these needs. Other sorts of open space have fulfilled the same function, but, over the years, the square has done it consistently well. The square is a public place, and understood as such by all citizens. It belongs to all and to no one in particular. It is easy to access and it costs nothing to enter. Its management, policing, and maintenance are the responsibility of the public authority.

Although the square is an integral part of the city's street network, it is a readily recognizable place. It is a concave, positive enclosure. While the street is designed to channel movement – people may pass through or stop to conduct certain activities – the square is, essentially, a place of rest that one may choose to traverse. As Webb wrote, the square is an urban room; it has a floor, and walls, and the sky is its ceiling. As long as it forms an obvious enclosure, the square's actual geometric shape is not very important. A successful square can be rectangular, square, circular, or look like

Archetypes of Elegance

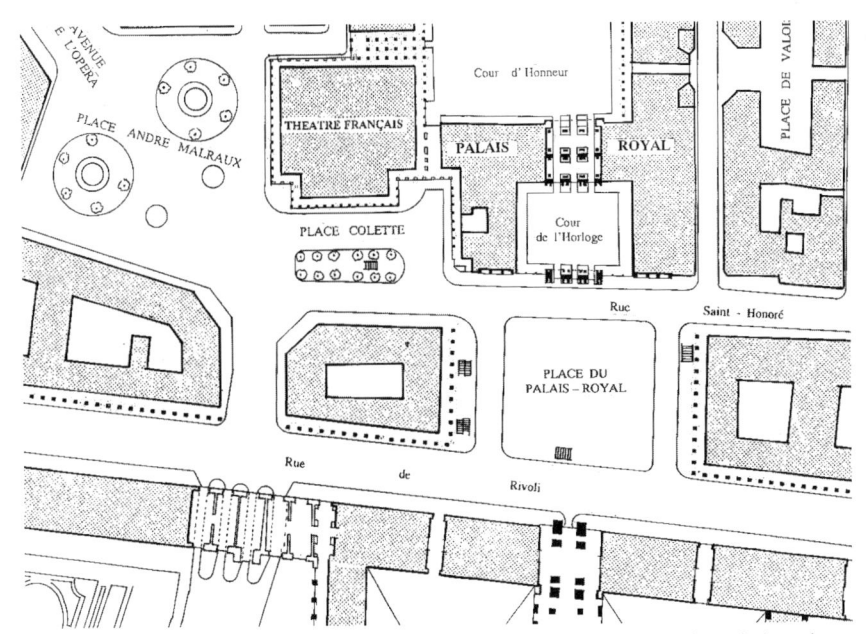

The inspiration for a public square archetype of elegance: schematic plan of place du Palais-Royal

a seashell, as does Sienna's central *piazza*. What is important is that the energy emanating from the users of the square reverberates back to its centre. This is, perhaps, the essential difference between a street and a square. In a street, the reverberations of human energy are channelled in a linear fashion; in a square, the reverberations accumulate in energy waves that complement one another and become collective. It is the positivity of the space that creates this resonance of human energy. What takes people's breath away when entering Venice's Piazza San Marco, Florence's Piazza della Signoria, Sienna's Piazza del Campo, or Brussels's Grande Place is the confluence of human energy returning endlessly upon itself. In this respect, the grand square generates the same sort of feeling a Gothic cathedral does; the only difference is that the former occupies itself with human affairs while the latter inspires heavenly gestures.

Squares come in all sizes, but there is a limit. As Camillo Sitte pointed out, in order for a square to be perceived as an enclosure, a relationship must be established between its size and the height of the surrounding buildings. And these various sets of ratios must respond to the size and sensorial perceptions of humans. A one-kilometre-square open space surrounded by buildings five hundred metres high, although theoretically an enclosure, is not a square because it is too large in relation to human size. At the beginning of his book, Webb compared the size of twelve well-known squares; the largest of this group was Moscow's Red Square (385 by 240 metres) and the smallest was Pienza's Piazza Pio II (20 by 20 metres). Among the other squares mentioned by Webb were Paris's Place Vendôme (130 by 115 metres), Madrid's Plaza Mayor (121 by 96 metres), and Sienna's Piazza del Campo (110 by 88 metres) (Webb 1990, 1). For the sake of comparison, the size of place du Palais-Royal is 80 by 78 metres.

Discussing the proper proportioning of a square, Alberti wrote: "For my part, I would have a Square twice as long as broad, and that the Porticoes and other Buildings about it should answer in some proportion to the open Area in the middle, that it may not seem too large, by means of the lowness of the buildings, nor too small, from their being too high. A proper Height for the Buildings about a Square is one third of the Breadth of the open Area, or one sixth at the least" (Alberti 1986, 173). This means that if we were to take Alberti's suggestion and apply it to place du Palais-Royal, we would be proposing to surround the square with buildings between 20 and 26.6 metres high. For all practical purposes, this is the actual situation: the height of the Palais-Royal varies from 20 to 22 metres, the two side buildings are slightly higher, and the Louvre Richelieu wing is slightly higher again at 26.4 metres.

Another way of looking at the proportioning of a square is to take a theoretical example, say a one-to-two rectangle in plan, with dimensions of between 66 and 75 metres in width and 132 and 150 metres in length. This means that, if we wish to maintain a one-to-three proportion for building height to square breadth, the square is lined with 22-to-25-metre-high buildings along its long sides; and with regard to the square's length, the ratios of 1 on 3, 1 on 4, 1 on 5, and 1 on 6 would call for building heights ranging from 22 to 50 metres. Such buildings would fit the place du Palais-Royal scale. This theoretical rectangle would make a large, formal square. Its 11,250-square-metre area would be comparable to that of Madrid's Plaza Major (11,626 square metres), larger than that of Venice's Piazza San Marco (10,080 square metres, including the *piazzetta*), and smaller than that of place Vendôme (14,950 metres). Most squares, especially those less central or less formal, are smaller than the 75-by-150-metre rectangle I am describing.

The consequence of the size limitation is that successful squares are rarely lined with skyscrapers; that is, they rarely abandon the range of proportions advocated by Alberti. The case of the square at New York's Rockefeller Center is interesting in this context: it is a relatively small square encircled by office towers. A popular place with a strong sense of enclosure, the square was praised by Webb in his essay. There, wrote Webb, "on a warm autumn day, a lunch may be enjoyed out of doors." In winter, it is transformed into a skating rink. In Webb's opinion, the architects have cleverly solved the problem of proportion: "The square should seem oppressive, so extreme is the plot-height ratio. But the architects knew what they were doing. Setbacks and the smaller buildings to the east admit a flood of sunlight at noon, and breezes to set the flags snapping" (Webb 1990, 174). Perhaps the Rockefeller Center square is an exception to the general rule, which calls for a triple relationship: in plan, the width-to-length ratio (or any other relevant measurement depending upon the square's particular shape, diameters, axes, and so on); in cross section, the surrounding buildings' height with respect to the horizontal measurements; and these measurements in relation to human beings.

When the proper balance between the three ratios has been established and a general space configuration obtained, the square vessel is ready to accept its load of human activities. As Kostof, Webb, and Rudolfsky have explained, there are two types of activity on a square: programmed and fortuitous. Only if the square's design permits them to will these activities occur.

A wedding and Sienna's *palio* are two programmed activities that take place on squares. A wedding involving a local celebrity is a much-anticipated event. People love to watch free spectacles, especially if they recognize the people involved. In order for there to be happy people watching happy people, a symbiosis must exist between the spirit of a community and the place where that community gathers. Such a symbiosis emerges only if the gathering place is designed to hold a celebration, such as a wedding, and is able to welcome many people, actors as well as spectators. Over the centuries, it has become apparent that a city square that can prompt a complicity between the stage and the stand, the church and the café, is a public place well equipped to accommodate such an event. A place surrounded by, say, a prison, two office buildings, and a convent may be a pleasant open space if it is well designed, but will probably remain empty most of the time. Notwithstanding the fact that such tranquil public spaces are needed in a city, they do not make good gathering places. Therefore, it is a sine-qua-non characteristic of the city-square archetype I am proposing with this theory that it be lined with activity-generating functions catering to people's immediate needs and generating community festivities.

The *palio* is a horse race held twice a year on Sienna's Piazza del Campo. Horses and "knights" representing the city's various neighbourhoods compete in this colourful and ferocious cavalcade. It is a tradition that dates back to the Middle Ages. Due to its design, the *campo* is a highly appropriate public place in which to hold this event. Surely historians can tell us which came first, the *palio* or the *campo*; but this is not the point here. The point is that both the event and the place are inextricably linked. If it is to organize traditional events that express its spirit, a city must have a public space in which to stage them. The architect is not in a position to conceive and create such community celebrations, but he can propose public places that are suitable sites for them. Not all cities are as old or as culturally rich as Sienna, but all have a history. And all deserve a place in which to express their spirit. This archetype does not advocate the building of a copy of the *campo* elsewhere; instead it promotes the building of a public place that displays the same sort of archetypal characteristics as those found at Sienna's *piazza*.

The second type of activity is the fortuitous event. It occurs on the square if, and only if, many people come and spend time there, and they spend time on the square only if they have things to do. In the course of their daily lives, people rarely go to a place just to have an aesthetic experience. Most of the time, they go for practical reasons. It is while they are conducting their regular business that the fortuitous event happens. For example, a young man will go to a square not for the square's sake, but to have lunch on the terrace of a nice restaurant. Since the weather is fine, he thinks it would be more pleasant to have lunch outdoors than in his company's cafeteria. He chooses to go a restaurant on the square not only because the food is good and the prices reasonable, but also because the establishment is located in an agreeable setting where he will see and be seen by people. By coincidence, a young woman has the same idea. By an added coincidence, so do many other people and the restaurant is full. Only one little corner table is free at the terrace's far end. Being in a gregarious mood, the young man suggests to the young woman that they share the table. Being in a similar mood, she accepts. This, as Humphrey Bogart would say, could be the beginning of a beautiful friendship. A fortuitous encounter requires converging forces: people, spirit, events, and a square to uphold the tension among them.

In the proposed archetype, a portico like the one described earlier surrounds the square. It provides the gallery from which we may watch the square's spectacle. The level of the portico's floor is never lower than the main floor of the square; it can be at the same level, but is preferably one or two steps higher. This slight elevation permits a better view of the centre of the square and enhances the feeling of protection. However, more than three steps would create a physical barrier and this alternative is to be rejected from the model.

A public square archetype of elegance: the square is an integral part of a city's public domain

If a square is to thrive, activity-generating functions must be present, but these alone are not enough. An intimate spatial and functional relationship must also be established and maintained between the walls of the square and its floor: people must be able to walk between the centre of the square and the surrounding buildings without having to deal with physical obstacles. A busy street is the most common of these obstacles. Are cars to be excluded from the square? The answer is partly negative and partly affirmative. Negative because the square is an integral component of the street network, and cars move on streets, hence on squares. Affirmative because, although cars may have access to edge of the square, they should be excluded from its central area. And parking should not be allowed on the square. What remains to be resolved is how the interface between cars and pedestrians should function – that is, the interface between the flow of cars parallel to the edge of the square in front of the surrounding buildings and the perpendicular movement of pedestrians.

The current situation at place du Palais-Royal is a good example of the problem. In this square, streets run between the facing buildings and the central area. Two of these streets are important arteries in the Paris network and support heavy traffic: rue de Rivoli in front of the Louvre and rue

A public square archetype of elegance: one of the challenges for a square designer is to manage the interface between pedestrians and drivers harmoniously

Saint-Honoré in front of the Palais-Royal. The two other streets, in front of Hôtel du Louvre and the Louvre des Antiquaires store, go only from rue de Rivoli to rue Saint-Honoré and bear little traffic. Rue de Rivoli hinders the immense flow of pedestrians generated by the Louvre; the other important pedestrian flow moving towards the Palais-Royal is slowed by rue Saint-Honoré. At present, the street pavement indicates that the four linear areas in front of the buildings belong to cars; and pedestrians are relegated to the central area and the outside sidewalks. When, for example, people wish to go from the centre of the square to the Louvre, they have to invade the territory of the car. This is an uncomfortable situation.

What the archetype proposes is to reverse this situation and have cars invade the pedestrian domain. The interface between cars and pedestrians is easily managed when pedestrians have the right of way and car movement is slow. Three complementary interventions are required to accomplish this: paving the areas of the square where cars are allowed with a material that is clearly distinct from the ordinary texture of the street; slightly raising the level of the square's floor – that is, by no more than two centimetres; and stationing stop signs or traffic lights at the square's entrances.

The square's basement is another important generator of activity. At place du Palais-Royal we find a major metro station together with what are probably the cleanest public toilets in Paris. In the twenty-first-century city, a highly efficient public-transportation system is indispensable, and so it make sense to link the square with the transportation network. In fact, a major square could certainly sit on a multimodal station and become a truly urban hub. In addition to a metro station, there could be a commuter-train station, a bus station, taxi stands, and parking. Exits from the underground are constructed inside the square's enclosure, preferably at its edge. In this way, when people emerge they discover the square in its entirety; the theatrical effect is spectacular, generating the sort of feeling that, as Webb remarked, takes your breath away. Another reason for entering or exiting within the confines of the square is orientation.

A square designed according to the principles outlined in this archetype is a public enclosure suitable for a market. In any city, there are many different sorts of market. One is the regular, daily food market. Another is the bazaar, or fleamarket. A third is a weekly or biweekly event; this type of market is suggested here. It is housed in temporary, portable stalls, which are dismantled after each use. In a dense urban environment with an efficient public-transportation system, most patrons of such a market would come on foot. Public parking could be reduced to a few off-street places; people with a heavy parcel to load could use these lots.

There are no monuments on place du Palais-Royal, despite the fact that squares have traditionally been the places where communities erect their monuments. The present archetype favours the erection of a monument or a fountain. The question of where to locate a monument can be a touchy one. On this point, Sitte is adamant: "The centre of the square [should] be kept free!" (Sitte 1965, 20). He may have a point. Insofar as the square is a public room, it makes sense to leave its main area open to be occupied by people. If large monument commands the centre of the square then people are pushed to the periphery and attention is shifted to the monument and away from the human element. The square then loses its character as a gathering place and becomes more of a theatre-in-the-round in which the play is not community life but a memory of it.

In this archetypal square, statues, sculptures, or fountains are to be situated away from the centre. But where, exactly, should they go? Again, Sitte may have the answer: "Imagine the open square of a small market town in the country, covered in deep snow and criss-crossed by several roads and paths that, shaped by the traffic, form the natural lines of communication. Between them are left irregularly distributed patches untouched by traffic; on these stand our snowmen, because the necessary clean snow was to be found only there. On exactly such spots, undisturbed by the flow of vehicles, rose the fountains and monuments of old communities" (Sitte 1965, 22). To complement the monument, the square may have to possess other features that help define its character and strengthen the feeling of enclosure: archways, gates, portals, masts, columns, lampposts, flagpoles, and bollards. The archetype suggests that generous use is made of these features.

A square is not a garden. It is a paved enclosure where people walk, congregate, and do things. It has no lawns or flowerbeds. If trees or flowers are deemed necessary, they may be placed in boxes that can be moved in response to other needs. However, holding a flower market is an activity well suited to a square because flowers are symbols of friendship. And the sort of city square this archetype will produce is a place for fraternity.

An Unfortunate Modern Architecture Trend

Successful squares designed in the twentieth century are very rare. The square at Rockefeller Center is one Modern Architecture exception. In both Kenneth Frampton's *Modern Architecture: A Critical History* (third edition) and William J. R. Curtis's *Modern Architecture since 1900* (second edition), the Rockefeller Center is named as the only contemporary project that contains a bona fide square (Frampton 1992; Curtis 1987). According to Frampton, the only two other projects containing a public place that resembles a square are in Paris: the Centre Pompidou's *parvis*, and the Grande Arche podium. Curtis's study contains a photograph of Arne Jacobsen's SAS hotel in Copenhagen, built in 1955; in the picture we see some foliage surrounding what appears to be a pleasant open space adorned with a fountain. However, Curtis does not say whether the open space belongs to Jacobsen's project or not.

Twentieth-century architecture is defined by the isolated building and the skyscraper. Certain interesting open spaces have been designed in this century, but they do not meet the definition of a city square. Like Baltimore's Old Port, waterfront esplanades are public areas created more for tourist activity than for civic functions. Faneuil Hall Marketplace in Boston, because of its historical setting, perhaps comes closest to fulfilling the square definition; but it is a historical rehabilitation, not a new design. Each of the various Disney theme parks contains several open spaces that swarm with people; but this is dreamland, not real life, and these spaces are merely gigantic private shopping centres with make-believe decors. Charles Moore's much-publicized Plaza d'Italia in New Orleans is also an anecdotal open space, designed, with its theatre-like decor, as an adjunct to a commercial development.

In addition to rehabilitated or upgraded squares in older cities, the three most common types of public open space designed in the twentieth century are: either gigantic esplanades or platforms on which the sense of enclosure has disappeared; setback areas in front of office towers; and leftover lots surrounded by streets. In the first group, we find, for example, Beijing's Tienanmen Square, originally built in 1651 but quadrupled in size in 1958, and Brasilia's platform, planned by Lucio Costa and designed by Oscar Niemeyer, also in the mid-fifties. While Beijing's great square is thronged with people in spite of a lack of space definition and amenities, Brasilia's platform is relatively deserted. The setback space in front of Mies van der Rohe's Seagram House in New York is a good example of the second group; this space is not a square because it offers no sense of enclosure and no amenities for activity. In fact, such an area is the antithesis of a square because it is designed and used exclusively as a transition space serving no civic purpose. Examples of the third group are countless. Many of these leftover open spaces are well designed and have become cherished gardens. The need for such breathing spaces is well recognized, but a landscaped lot should not be confused with a city square.

Perhaps two factors explain why successful squares have rarely been designed in the twentieth century. First, these squares are unrelated to modern technological development. In an epoch defined by the car, plane, telephone, television, and computer, a public open-air enclosure where people come together either to perform a civic function or simply to enjoy themselves seems out of step with the times. Twentieth-century technology has given people the power to design stupendous structures such as the World Trade Center in New York or the Golden Gate Bridge in San Francisco. A simple square surrounded by five- or six-storey buildings does not make use of this technological might, and is therefore viewed as an outdated artefact, like a horse-drawn carriage. In the twentieth-century-architectural hall of fame, space has been reserved for megastructures or postmodern extravaganzas, not for serene city squares.

The second factor is that influential American architects have viewed squares with contempt and, at least in the second half of the century, America has exerted the strongest global influence in matters of urban design and architecture. In their book *The Intellectual versus the City*, Morton and Lucia White showed that an antagonistic view of the city has long been deeply rooted in American society. The lineage of intellectuals who echo Thomas Jefferson's opinion, "I view great cities as pestilential to the morals, the health and the liberties of man," is long, and includes Frank Lloyd Wright (White and White 1964, 28). The Whites explained that Wright saw the city as "a poisoned [place], a wen, a cancer, a fibrous tumor." They wrote: "As Lewis Mumford has remarked, it never appears to have entered Wright's mind that one might need to profit by the presence of other men within an area compact enough for spontaneous encounters, durable enough for the realisation of long range plans, and attractive enough to stimulate social intercourse. Save for the family, he scarcely recognises the need for social groups or associations; for him, co-operation is a kind of self-betrayal" (White and White 1964, 194, 196).

American postmodern architect Robert Venturi expressed the same sort of contempt for the urban square. He described the scheme he entered in Boston's Copley Square Competition – incidentally, Copley Square is more a *parvis* in front of Trinity Church than a bona fide square – with these words: "So we made a non-piazza; we filled up the space [with trees] to define the space." Venturi added: "But the open piazza is seldom appropriate for an American city today except as a convenience for pedestrians for diagonal short-cuts. The piazza, in fact, is 'un-American.' Americans feel uncomfortable sitting in a square; they should be working at the office or home with the family looking at television" (Venturi 1966, 128, 133).

We must counteract this unfortunate and unfounded negative attitude. Then, may be, the next century will see a renewal of the age-old tradition of designing meaningful, elegant city squares. We need these spaces because technology's revered might has its limits in terms of being a civilizing force, as the current American inner city and the European suburban slum so disturbingly prove.

Meaningful Archetypes Are Needed

Let me repeat that the purpose of this constitution is to give the architect the means of designing a more satisfactory environment. The task is immense. The sad fact remains that, in most cities of the world, we find many more dilapidated and totally inadequate apartments than we do dwellings like the Fondation Rothschild Workers' Residence. We see many more patches of dirt than small and inviting urban parks like those of Outremont. And we see many more empty, dangerous, ill-defined lots than vital squares that cater to the community spirit like place du Palais-Royal. A radical change in attitude towards the designed environment is urgently required. Architectural archetypes such as those I have described may provide a guiding light for this much-needed evolution. I propose these archetypes because they are inspired by places that are respectful of human dignity and that contain the seeds of an architecture of elegance.

10

CONCLUSION
ELEGANCE FOR AN ARCHITECTURE OF SATISFACTION

At the beginning of this book, I maintained that the world is plagued by rampant environmental mediocrity. More than ever, the architect's efforts are required. We urge him to design better places to live and to ensure that they are well built. To help him produce a more satisfactory architecture, I have offered a theory. With it, I suggest answers to the three fundamental questions that were posited at the outset of our journey.

What Is Architecture?

Harnessing the phenomenological method of inquiry, the theory undertakes to answer the first question by defining the architectural artefact: it is a physical object, time and place specific, but always in the present, and it is always conceived as a promise of a better world. Freed from all the current ideologies that blur the way it is perceived, the artefact is found to be an inherent component of the architectural phenomenon, which always comprises people conducting an activity in a cultural shelter inserted in nature and projected through time. What is designed and built is not the phenomenon as a whole, but only the shelter and the part of nature that immediately surrounds it. What is designed is the architectural artefact. However, what always emerges from the architect's creative undertaking is not the artefact by itself, but the fully constituted architectural phenomenon.

That is why it is necessary to probe and penetrate the architectural phenomenon. Twelve veils drape it: people, activity components, surroundings, presence in evolution, materiality, structuring systems, ecology, form and space, economy, energy, character, and projection. An unveiling procedure uncovers an enhanced consciousness of the idea of architecture. Redraped

Should our design objective be to provide a courteous environment at the service of a gentle society?

with its twelve veils, the eidos of architecture is dwelling in a protective place made for the enhancement of human exchange.

What the architect can learn from this phenomenological description of the architectural phenomenon is that, no matter what he professes ideologically or executes in practice, the material result of his creative work always encompasses these twelve veils. This is an apodictic and universal condition of the architectural phenomenon. However, the architect retains his freedom of choice with respect to this reality: he may consciously incorporate all the dimensions into his design process in order to control them or choose to ignore some of them. If he includes them all, he increases his chances of producing a more satisfactory architecture because his design endeavour is more thorough. This statement is not as obvious as it sounds, because current architectural training, attitudes, practises, and ideologies ignore or even reject many of these dimensions of architecture.[131]

Defining the eidos of architecture in useful terms is the first task that the theory accomplishes.

How Do We Assess Architecture?

In answering the second question, the theory tells the architect that the essence of architecture has not one but two dimensions, its eidos and its telos, what architecture is and what it wants to be. Finding a route to architecture's ultimate destiny is the second task of the theory. An epochè of societal values as they are expressed in the various charters of rights that guide human institutions is conducted, and it yields the idea of satisfaction in architecture. The telos of architecture, it is revealed, is a happy one that makes a positive contribution to the most fundamental human motivation: the perpetual pursuit of happiness. A successful architecture is one that respects and satisfies people; it is a general prescription that can be applied to individual cases. A twofold procedure for judging whether or not an architectural artefact satisfies people is proposed. First, the architect is encouraged to solicit users' opinions, a common-sense gesture rarely made today. Second, he is asked to assess an architectural artefact employing the design criteria that have been reconstituted from the telos of the architectural phenomenon, a self-critical approach that is also taken infrequently today. These criteria are not arbitrary, because they are based on societal values. They are universal because they rest on values that constitute the underlying principles of the ethics codes that have guided society since the dawn of civilization.

The architect is told that he is designing an artefact that is meant to be used and experienced by people other than himself. Hence, the assessment of the artefact's validity is shown to be a non-self-referential procedure: this is one of the main demonstrations of the theory, a demonstration that undermines a certain dimension of current architectural discourse. Some architects like to maintain the illusion that the artefact's user can have no say in what they call the architect's "artistic expression." In fact, all people pass judgement on architecture because that is where they live. Insofar as architecture is still considered an art, the artistic challenge faced by the architect is to create a work that responds to people's values, as they themselves understand them. That challenge is not to realize some self-proclaimed vision. The telos of the architectural phenomenon, I am suggesting here, is dwelling in a place of satisfaction by responding positively to the values of society.

If the desire to produce an architecture of satisfaction is to be fulfilled, then an inquiry into the existing architectural reality must be made. An epochè is therefore conducted on three complementary architectural artefacts that have retained, over the years, their original purpose and vitality. Are the Palais-Royal, the Fondation Rothschild Workers' Residence, and Outremont true models of an architecture of satisfaction? The results of the epochè demonstrate that these places are immensely successful and worthy of emulation.

The three places did not spring up overnight; they are, rather, the products of a long gestation period presided over by successive architects. Each of these entities has matured into a socially relevant environment; each has become a cherished component of a specific cultural heritage. In different ways, but with the same level of intensity, all three are subtle, convivial, refined, and extremely dignified places that have continuously respected and satisfied their users as well as their communities at large.

In short, the three places are found to be artefacts of excellence and magnificence, that is, artefacts of elegance. If the rest of the world were designed with the same degree of elegance as they exhibit, it would be a better place to live.

How Do We Design Architecture?

As these places emerge as models, the theory tackles the third issue: design strategy. We need to formulate the procedure for making an architecture that displays the sort of characteristics from which the three entities have fashioned their success. Three successive constitutions are necessary for charting the road to a more satisfactory architecture. The first starts with a general design strategy, a seven-step proactive phenomenological procedure – proactive in the sense that it affirms that it is more efficient to construct the kind of future that we want today rather than trying to predict the kind of mediocre future that will inevitably impose itself upon us if we fail to intervene. Within this strategy, a specific architectural-design approach is suggested: the hierarchical decomposition-recomposition approach. This approach suggests the epochè/constitution dialectic. It obliges the architect to redrape the architectural artefact consciously; that is, to project his intentionality towards each of the constitutive veils of the architectural phenomenon, in themselves and in relation to the others and to the whole, and to redrape the project with them. When the architectural scheme is conceived, a critical assessment of it is made using the value-based design criteria.

The second constitution of the third task provides the theoretical means of charting a course through the design process. When that is accomplished, the architect will be ready to undertake the task of making an architecture of excellence and magnificence.

The idea of quality is constituted, and this leads to the idea of quality assessment, which, in turn, implies the concept of measurement nourished by some of the value-based criteria outlined earlier. The quality of an architectural artefact is determined by its clarity of purpose, its perdurability, the consistency of its upkeep and improvement, its specificity, and its timeless appearance. Since quality can be measured, we can establish degrees of quality, from mediocrity to excellence. Excellence denotes the highest quality; therefore, the architect's goal is to produce an artefact that reaches the level of excellence. The principle of excellence is the user's ultimate satisfaction.

The idea of beauty is also constituted, and this leads to the idea of beauty appreciation, which, in turn, implies the concept of taste, also nourished by some of the value-based criteria outlined earlier. Beauty is defined as a worthy value that is intrinsic to a thing, a positive, emotional attribute that triggers feelings of pleasure in humans experiencing it. It encompasses elements such as perceived truth, symmetry, measure, equilibrium, appropriateness, harmony, rhythm, contrast, colour, texture, light and shadow, and order. It could imply purity and simplicity and incorporate ornament or decoration. Beauty is both free, like a rose, and dependent, like a Japanese sabre. Joyful and respectful, beauty cannot be created solely through a design process based on deductive or inductive reasoning; sensitivity comes into play, because the attainment of beauty requires a penetration of the realm of the unexplainable and necessitates the tasteful manipulation of proportions. Since beauty can be appreciated, we can establish levels of beauty, from ugliness to magnificence. Magnificence is the level of the greatest beauty. Hence, the architect's goal is to produce a magnificent artefact. The principle of magnificence is aesthetic pleasure of the highest order.

In architecture, things are necessarily connected in a synthetic whole as the veils are intertwined to form the architectural phenomenon. The notion of beauty appears in the definition of quality, and vice versa. The symbiosis of the idea of excellence and the idea of magnificence forms the idea of elegance, which is the ultimate attribute of all architectural works and the highest motivation of any design process or creative endeavour. Elegance, as we have seen, is deeper than physical appearance and finds its true meaning in the artefact's soul. It denotes youthful maturity, subtle appropriateness, powerful refinement, and the sort of graceful boldness that comes from long practice and patient searching. Elegance requires honesty, politeness, and a generosity of feeling.

Furthermore, we have seen that the idea of measurement, in matters of quality, generates the concept of degrees of excellence. Also, the parallel idea of appreciation, in matters of beauty, generates the concept of examples of magnificence. The symbiosis of degree and example, in matters of architecture, engenders the idea of archetype. The archetype acts both as a point of departure for design and an original model. An architectural device, the portico, is used to illustrate the idea of architectural archetype because it responds to the universal human need for a proper distinction and a proper interface between places for private activities and places for public manifestations.

In the third and last constitution of the theory, three archetypes of elegant architecture are proposed. They are presented as design beacons, emerging from the examples of successful architecture described by the epochès of the Palais-Royal, the Fondation Rothschild Workers' Residence, and Outremont. The first archetype deals with private places of residence and the other two with public places for social exchange. What the theory suggests to the architect is that his design is inspired by the architectural reality that surrounds him and that it is to his advantage to be inspired by models that have demonstrated their success. He is not compelled to adopt the archetypes that are presented here, but if he chooses these models, or any other model based on an artefact that demonstrates its elegance, he increases his chances of producing a successful, respectful, and fully satisfactory architecture – an architecture of elegance.

Original Contributions

I hope that this theory makes several original contributions to architectural knowledge. The first may stem from what this work is: a bona fide theory that is neither an apology nor a manifesto but a descriptive and prescriptive mental construct. In an epoch when the gulf between architectural theoreticians and practising architects is widening, this approach counteracts and establishes a conceptual link between theory and practice. I am advocating a theory that is useful, and arguing for social accountability rather than mere intellectual speculation. Contrary to the current postmodernist ideology, which focuses on marginality, this theory concentrates on the mainstream of architecture. Without rejecting distinctiveness and contextualism, it shows that universality is also a dimension of architecture.

Although the theory borrows from phenomenology, a well-entrenched philosophy, it takes an original approach. At the same time, its thesis neither contradicts nor opposes earlier works on the combined topic of phenomenology and architecture. Having positioned itself on a different plane, it goes beyond earlier essays in this field. Key differences distinguish this theory from those of Gaston Bachelard, Christian Norberg-Schulz, and contemporary American existential phenomenologists such as Edward Relph and David Seamon. The theory presented here is a theory of architecture based on phenomenology, while the others are phenomenologies of the man-made environment. Being practice-oriented, it comprises both descriptive and prescriptive elements, while the other works are exclusively descriptive. It is a theory based largely on the central tradition of phenomenology inspired by Edmund Husserl; the other works ignore Husserl and take their inspiration mainly from Heidegger. This theory introduces a new understanding of some of the methodological aspects of phenomenology and its application to architecture. Recapturing the Husserlian tradition and the spirit of its method, notably the epochè, it introduces a new practical interpretation, which is the systematic unveiling. Adopting the position that intuition is as important as rational discourse for the proper description of phenomena and comprehension of the life-world, the theory links with architectural conception, a relationship that has never been discussed before.

In the sense that it retains the rigour of Husserl's intellectual approach while embracing the softer, more open approach of the American existential phenomenologists, this work is very cautious. It insists that extremes are sterile, because purely intellectual reflection tends to draw the discourse away from the reality of architecture and the necessities of practice.

Conversely, it says that the existential approach, even though it is often concrete and perceptive, is too contextual to provide a credible foundation for architectural design.

In this work, epochès of the architectural phenomenon are conducted. This has not been attempted by the other works I mentioned, at least not in such a systematic fashion. To a certain extent, only the studies of Bachelard and Norberg-Schulz display any of the methodological characteristics of the epochè, but these authors never make a methodological reference to Husserl. Moreover, none of the other writers have tried to establish a method for reconstructing the reduced architectural phenomenon; that is, none have tackled the constitution of architecture. The notion of place developed by Relph and discussed by Norberg-Schulz, the archetypal poetic images of the phenomenon of habitation presented by Bachelard, Heidegger's notion of dwelling, and Merleau-Ponty's concept of *espace spatialisant* are all incorporated into this work, but transformed into design beacons. And the issue of design is ignored in the other writings while it is a major concern of this work.

The Essence of Architecture?

At this late juncture, I would like to risk formulating a definition of the essence of architecture. I therefore propose, for future debate, that: *The essence of architecture is the creation of elegant dwelling places that make people happy.* Which brings us back to our departure point. A theory that reaches beyond existing ideologies, that establishes as its legitimate object the entire designed environment, that concentrates on the essential dimensions of the architectural phenomenon, that puts at the helm of its design strategy the quest for elegance, that grounds its design criteria in consensual human values, that sets human happiness as the prime goal of its mission is bound to address people's real architectural needs and aspirations. It is also bound to be relevant. The architect who rises to the challenge of this immense task becomes, once more, a builder of civilizations.

> Instead of a village
> A city and its suburb
> Ten religions twenty languages
> The old folks are silent
> And look at me straight in the eyes
> All these people to make happy.[132]
> — Gilles Vigneault

NOTES

CHAPTER ONE

1 Throughout this work, in sentences such as this one, masculine includes feminine.
2 In his book *A Brief History of Time*, Hawking defines a theory as follows: "A theory is a good theory if it satisfies two requirements: It must accurately describe a large class of observations that contains only a few arbitrary elements, and must make definite predictions about the results of future observations" (Hawking 1988, 9). In architecture, however, one makes rather than predicts.
3 Another, complementary definition of theory was given by Peter Rowe in *Design Thinking*: "Theory is assumed to be about general principles with applicability beyond specific cases, and, whether it comes by way of systematic speculation and codification or by way of more indirect experience, to be well substantiated. To the extent that it has a community of subscribers, theory represents a corpus of principles that are agreed upon and therefore worthy of emulation" (Rowe 1987, 115).
4 In the present work, the idea of architecture is understood as being larger than the idea of urban design, even though urban design usually concerns larger-scale projects. Hence, architecture includes urban design. Unless specified otherwise, each time the words *architecture* and *architect* are used, they mean also *urban design* and *urban designer*.

CHAPTER TWO

5 *The Failure of Modern Architecture* is not only the title of a telling book by Brent Brolin, it is also a well-documented issue. Authors as diverse as Jane

Jacobs, the Prince of Wales (Prince Charles), and Charles Jencks have studied and discussed the devastating effects of the Modern Architecture doctrine on contemporary cities (Jacobs 1961; Wales 1989; Jencks 1984).

6 In addition to Peter Rowe himself, these architects were George Baird, Thomas Fisher, Elizabeth Padjen, Andrew Saint, Carl Sapers, Alexander Caragonne, Margaret Henderson Floyd, and Robert Geddes.

7 For example, it was a repeat of calls made by Otto Wagner in 1895, Le Corbusier in 1923 (Le Corbusier 1958), and Christian Norberg-Schulz in 1965 (Norberg-Schulz 1965).

8 The debate in the U.K. was somewhat more complex because the architectural profession was under two sorts of attack. First, there was an ideological one: proponents of liberalism wanted to deregulate practically all sectors of the economy, including the protected profession of architecture. Second, there was a commercial one: other sectors of the construction industry wanted to do what architects do in an exclusive way. However, the fact remains that it was the weakness of the architectural profession that opened the door to these attacks.

9 In the present context, the main design disciplines are regional and urban planning, urban design, landscape architecture, architecture, interior design, industrial design, and furniture design. There are, of course, many more design disciplines, such as graphic design, fashion design, airplane design, or car design, but these are outside the scope of this work.

10 In this select company, critics such as Sigfried Giedion, Lewis Mumford, Michel Ragon, and Bruno Zevi were brilliant but secondary commentators.

11 Some of these authors are Michel Foucault, Jean-François Lyotard, Jacques Derrida, Gilles Deleuze, Hans Gadamer, Fredric Jameson, David Harvey, Jürgen Habermas.

12 Over the years, several other philosophers have contributed to the development of phenomenology, notably Gaston Berger (1941), Suzanne Bachelard (1968), Marvin Farber (1967), André de Muralt (1974), Martin Heidegger (1971, 1988), Jan Patocka (1988), Leszek Kolakowski (1975), and the team of Rudolf Bernet, Iso Kern, and Edouard Marbach (1993).

13 The *Cartesian Meditations* are a series of lectures that were delivered in Paris in 1929. These lectures were given in German, but translated into French. They are considered by many phenomenologists to be phenomenology's prime text.

14 "I think, therefore I am"; or, "I think, therefore I exist" (author's translation).

15 The author's translation appears in the text. The original quote is: "Mais qu'est-ce donc ce que je suis? Une chose qui pense. Qu'est-ce qu'une chose qui pense? C'est-à-dire une chose qui doute, qui conçoit, qui affirme, qui nie, qui ne veut pas, qui imagine aussi, et qui sent."

16 "Lived experience" is a rather inadequate translation of the more concise French expression, "le vécu."
17 The author's translation appears in the text. The original quote is: "L'épochè est la mise entre parenthèses du monde objectif. Elle ne nous place pas devant un pur néant. Ce qui, en revanche et par là même, devient nôtre, ou mieux, devient mien, à moi sujet méditant, c'est ma vie pure avec l'ensemble de ses états vécus purs et de ses objets intentionnels, c'est-à-dire l'universalité des phénomènes au sens spécial et élargi de la phénoménologie. On peut dire aussi que l'épochè est la méthode universelle et radicale par laquelle je me saisis comme moi pur, avec la vie de conscience pure qui m'est propre, vie dans et par laquelle le monde objectif tout entier existe pour moi, tel justement qu'il existe pour moi. Tout ce qui est monde, tout être spatial et temporel existe pour moi, c'est-à-dire vaut pour moi, du fait même que j'en fais l'expérience, le perçois, le remémore, y pense de quelque manière, porte sur lui des jugements d'existence ou de valeur, le désire, et ainsi de suite. Tout cela, Descartes le désigne, on le sait, par le terme cogito. À vrai dire, le monde n'est pas pour moi autre chose que ce qui existe et vaut pour ma conscience dans un pareil cogito."
18 The author's translation appears in the text. The original quote is: "La réflexion ne se retire pas du monde vers l'unité de la conscience comme fondement du monde, elle prend recul pour voir jaillir les transcendances, elle distend les fils intentionnels qui nous relient au monde pour les faire paraître, elle seule est conscience du monde parce qu'elle le révèle comme étrange et paradoxal."
19 The author's translation appears in the text. The original quote is: "Ces deux idées fondamentales se trouvent dans une sorte d'enchaînement antagonique, l'une récusant, l'autre construisant, l'une ayant pour fonction de mettre à découvert, l'autre s'efforçant de prendre pied dans le terrain nouvellement découvert et d'en effectuer l'exploration exhaustive."
20 The author's translation appears in the text. The original quote is: "Un universel. L'humanité est le genre, l'universel; l'homme Socrate est la réalité singulière."
21 What is architecture made of?

CHAPTER THREE

22 What is called theory of architecture constitutes only one chapter of the knowledge base of architecture. Some of the other chapters are artefact descriptions, high- and low-tech construction techniques, specification manuals, catalogues of building materials and systems, building-science research reports, architectural programs and project briefs, management and maintenance manuals,

bylaws and other construction regulations, noninterpretative historical treatises, and books on empirical traditions.

23 Laugier was obviously following the teachings of Plato and Aristotle in this respect: art finds its foundation in the imitation of nature. But since architecture is not the illustration of something else, is it still art? Aristotle argued that it is not. (Borissavliévitch, 1951, 2).

24 For example, to describe the evolution of Western architecture, historians normally start their discourse with either the Mesopotamian or Ancient Egyptian style. After, they describe the Classical Greek style, then its Roman version. They follow with the Early Christian and Byzantine styles, perhaps the Moorish style; afterward, they describe in succession the Romanesque, Gothic, Renaissance, baroque, neoclassical, and Georgian styles. Reaching the end of the nineteenth century, they discuss the Industrial (Iron and Glass), Arts and Crafts, and Beaux Arts styles.

25 Vitruvius's work also profoundly influenced Alberti's treatise; it was translated into French by Jean Martin (1547) and Claude Perrault (1674), into Italian under Raphael's direction in 1520, and into English in 1692.

26 After Vitruvius, the lineage includes the works of prominent authors such as mastermason Villard de Honnecourt (ca. 1230), Renaissance Italian architects Alberti (1452), Vignola (1562), and Palladio (1570), French architects Phillibert de l'Orme (1567), François Blondel (1688), Amédée Frézier (1739), Germain Boffrand (1745), Jacques-François Blondel (1756, 1777), Pierre Patte (1769), J. N. L. Durand (1805), Viollet-le-Duc (1850), and, in the twentieth century, parts of the written works of Sullivan, Le Corbusier, Frank Lloyd Wright, and the Bauhaus instructors. (Years in parentheses refer to the publication dates of the authors' main works.)

27 In addition to Abbot Suger and Jencks, the list of criticism-oriented architectural theoreticians includes writers such as Androuet du Cerceau (1559), Fréart de Chambray (1650), André Félibien (1666), René Ouvrard (1679), Claude Perrault (1683) and his brother Charles (1688), Michel de Frémin (1702), Jean-Louis de Cordemoy (1714), Père Yves André (1741), Charles-Étienne Briseux (1752), Marc-Antoine Laugier (1753), Étienne-Louis Boullée (around 1790), C. N. Ledoux (1804), Schopenhauer (1818), G.W.F. Hegel (around 1830), Vischer (1851), Rudolf Adamy (1881), Adolf Göller (1887), August Thiersch (1889), Heinrich Wölffin (1886), John Belcher (1810), John Ruskin (1880), Otto Wagner (1895), Adolf Loos (1908), Le Corbusier (1923), the Bauhaus manifestos (1920–30), and Robert Venturi (1966).

28 It is the cultural dimension of the architectural phenomenon that introduces the distinctiveness of each shelter and of each activity in contrast to all others. However, the cultural dimension itself – that is, a man-made thing made

for a purpose – is a universal characteristic of the architectural phenomenon, and it is embedded in the idea of architectural shelter. An architectural shelter, by definition, is cultural.

29 The author's translation appears in the text. The original quote is: "Tout acte humain, toute pensée humaine, n'est que le résultat de la transformation de cette énergie photonique solaire vers une forme plus organisée."

30 Many cities lack meaningful landmarks. For example, the image one often retains of North American cities is one of a chaotic cluster of office towers competing with one another for the privilege of becoming the dominant landmark. In this jungle of private symbols, communal landmarks are submerged. To be recognized as a cultural beacon, a landmark, such as Paris's Eiffel Tower, must be a highly visible signal within its environment.

31 The author's translation appears in the text. The original quote is: "Le temps qui passe et qui transforme la matière inerte qui l'oublie, laisse sa trace dans la matière vivante qui se souvient."

32 These groupings of urban activity components and systems are purely functional and technical. They are based on criteria emerging from more than twenty years of designing and constructing city components. In individual buildings as well as in municipal infrastructures, the plumbing system, for instance, is put in a different category than the power or communication systems, because each requires a very different design approach: different trades, different utility companies, different spatial requirements, and different performance specifications. Fluids are transported through large pipes while electrical power travels via thin wires that can bend and go everywhere. Water-supply and sewer systems may work by gravity, a characteristic that, unfortunately, does not apply to electricity. Oil and gas may be used for heating and cooking – that is, for the same purposes as electricity – but, unlike electricity, they require a piping system to reach their destination. Broken water pipes and gas lines leak fluids into the environment, while damaged electrical cables cause different problems. Fibre-optic cables may transport messages and light by the most circuitous routes, demonstrating a flexibility the plumbing system does not enjoy.

33 The CIAM is Congrès international d'architecture moderne. Created in 1928, and strongly influenced by Le Corbusier and Gropius, it promoted the modernist conception of architecture and city planning. In 1933, it proclaimed a manifesto called the Athens Charter, which outlined the modern urban-planning principles: separation of housing, work, recreation, and transportation; and promotion of the abundant use of natural light, pure air, and greenery.

34 Form in architecture may also be understood in a functional way. This is the thesis of Bill Hillier's "Space Syntax." In Hillier's view, correlations can be

established between the way connected forms are made and the way they function. Form is central to the reality of architecture and urban design: "a theory of the architecture of the urban object itself ... is a theory of the deep structure of the material form of the city" (Hillier 1983).

35 The author's translation appears in the text. The original quote is: "le jeu savant, correct et magnifique des volumes assemblés sous la lumière."

36 For more than a century now, one of the most recognizable urban objects in the streets of Paris has been the colonne Morris, an erect cylinder advertising theatre productions. Only the exterior of this form-only artefact is used and seen. In the fall of 1994, the Champs-Élysées received an extensive face-lift. New colonnes Morris were located on the famous avenue. They were given a second function: they now serve as telephone booths. What used to be a form-only artefact has become a space-and-form artefact.

37 Or it may not. In certain circumstances, a long, naked façade may be appropriate and have a very distinctive look. The bland façade is used here only as an example.

CHAPTER FOUR

38 By introducing evaluation criteria into the architectural discourse, the theory continues to bridge the gap between criticism and design.

39 UN General Assembly, Forty-Third Session, Official Records, Supplement 8, addendum (A/43/8/add. 1).

40 A ninth text, which does not deal directly with housing rights but still has far-reaching implications for architecture, urban design, environmental science, and ecology, is the UNESCO *Convention Concerning the Protection of the World Cultural and Natural Heritage*. By 1997, 147 state-parties had signed this convention and 506 sites had been inscribed on the World Heritage list; these sites are protected by the international community.

41 The eight fundamental texts expressing the housing right are:

a. *The United Nations Universal Declaration of Human Rights* (1948): "Everyone has the right to a standard of living adequate for the health and well-being of himself and his family, including food, clothing, housing, and medical care and necessary social services, and the right to security in the event of unemployment, sickness, disability, widowhood, old age or other lack of livelihood in circumstances beyond his control" (art. 25.1).

b. *The UN Convention Relating to the Status of Refugees* (1951): "As regards to housing, the Contracting States, in so far as the matter is regulated by laws or regulations or is subject to the control of public authorities, shall accord to refugees lawfully staying in their territory treatment as favourable as possible and, in any event, not less favourable than that accorded to aliens generally in the same circumstances" (art. 21).

c. *The UN Declaration on the Rights of the Child* (1959): "The child shall enjoy the benefits of social security. He shall be entitled to grow and develop in health; to this end special care and protection shall be provided to him and his mother, including adequate pre-natal and post-natal care. The child shall have the right to adequate nutrition, housing, recreation and medical services" (par. 4).

d. *The UN International Convention on the Elimination of Racial Discrimination* (1965): "States Parties undertake to prohibit and eliminate racial discrimination in all its forms and to guarantee the right to everyone, without distinction as to race, colour, or national or ethnic origin, to equality before the law, notably in the enjoyment of the following rights ... (e) Economic, Social, and Cultural Rights in particular ... (iii) the right to housing" (art. 5.e.iii).

e. *The UN Covenant on Economic, Social and Cultural Rights* (1966): "The States Parties to the present Covenant recognise the right of everyone to an adequate standard of living for himself and his family, including adequate food, clothing, and housing and to the continuous improvement of living conditions. The States Parties will take appropriate steps to ensure the realisation of this right, recognising to this effect the essential importance of international co-operation based on free consent" (art. 11.1).

f. *The UN Declaration on Social Progress and Development* (1969): "Social progress and development shall aim at the continuous raising of the material and spiritual standards of living of all members of society, with respect for and in compliance with human rights and fundamental freedoms, through the attainment of the following main goals ... (f) the provision for all, particularly persons in low income groups and large families, of adequate housing and community services" (resolution 2,542.XXIV, part II).

g. *The Vancouver Declaration on Human Settlements* (1976): "Adequate shelter and services are a basic human right which places an obligation on governments to ensure their attainment by all people, beginning with direct assistance to the least advantaged through guided programmes of self-help and community action. Governments should endeavour to remove all impediments hindering attainment of these goals. Of special importance is the elimination of social and racial segregation, *inter alia*, through the creation of better balanced communities, which blend different social groups, occupations, housing and amenities" (sec. III.8).

h. *The UN International Convention on the Elimination of Discrimination against Women* (1979): "States Parties shall take all appropriate measures to eliminate discrimination against women in rural areas in order to ensure, on a basis of equality of men and woman, that they participate in and benefit from rural development and, in particular, shall ensure to such women the right ... (h) to enjoy adequate living conditions, particularly in relation to housing, sanitation, electricity and water supply, transport and communication [this housing right expressed for rural areas applies also to urban settlements]" (art. 14.2.h).

42 The first paragraph of the preamble to *The Universal Declaration of Human Rights* reads: "Whereas recognition of the inherent dignity and of the equal and inalienable rights of all members of the human family is the foundation of freedom, justice and peace in the world."

43 I am a Canadian, and fully realize that I write this text from a Western viewpoint; it would be interesting to see a comparable reflection on values by an Oriental or a Muslim author.

44 We could use the plural and talk of civilization*s*. The civilization of mankind may be both the offspring and the synthesis of several discreet civilizations.

45 According to city historian A. E. J. Morris, the early Mesopotamian cities date from about 3800 B.C., the Egyptian cities from about 3200 B.C., the Harappan cities in India from about 2300 B.C., the early Shang cities in China from about 2100 B.C., and the Olmac/Maya cities from about 800 B.C. (Morris 1989).

46 The Noble Eightfold Path of morality comprises: right views, right intention, right speech, right conduct, right livelihood, right effort, right mindfulness, and right concentration (Carus 1983, 48; Flew 1984, 249).

47 Here, also, one may use the plural, and speak of churche*s*.

48 It is interesting to note that the idea of fraternity, established by the Muslims as a social norm, was deployed in a different way by French revolutionaries and redefined by Communists a short century later.

49 Again, Muslims had argued for good health several centuries before it was adopted as a social norm, first in the Occident and later throughout the world; today, the World Health Organization symbolizes the universal acceptance of this value.

50 The worldwide fear of AIDS and the recent mad-cow-disease crisis in Europe constitute a telling demonstration of how important this value is for people today. Good health is a powerful value, capable of mobilizing entire communities.
51 The recent White March in Brussels against paedophilia and mass demonstrations in Spain protesting the murder of a young Basque politician may be among the first signs of the emergence of this new value.
52 The author's translation appears in the text. The original quote is: "L'activité humaine est dominée par la recherche du bonheur. Le bonheur, à son tour, est essentiellement la réalisation de soi, un état dans lequel tous les besoins materiels ou intellectuels se trouvent satisfaits."
53 No sexual meaning is implied here by the word *promiscuity*.
54 It is interesting to note that even temporary structures tend to last longer than expected. As a case in point, in downtown Ottawa, World War II barracks built to be used only for the duration of the war were used extensively for several years afterwards; they were demolished only in the mid-seventies. Other barracks in military compounds were still in use in 1992.

CHAPTER FIVE

55 Together, they form the equivalent of the U.S. Supreme Court.
56 This may soon change. The Ministry of Culture is presently studying a plan to make this central entrance public, in the axis of the Louvre entrance to the recently renovated Richelieu wing.
57 At that moment only the large theatre remained. The small theatre built by Richelieu had been demolished some years before.
58 The author's translation appears in the text. The original quote is: "Le talent de l'architecte s'affirmait par la franchise du parti pris et la netteté, par la clarté de la conception. Point de sécheresse dans les silhouettes; aucune lourdeur dans les détails. La hauteur de ces constructions était admirablement calculée et leurs proportions d'une justesse parfaite: plus basses, les toits des maisons d'alentour auraient pu apparaître; plus élevées, le jardin du Palais Royal aurait eu l'air d'un cloître ou d'une prison. La division des façades, où apparait l'harmonie élégante du pur style Louis XVI, les 180 arcades d'une courbe heureuse, les pilastres finement cannelés, les deux étages et la balustrade dissimulant les mansardes, tout cela garde encore aujourd'hui un caractère de beauté majestueuse et aimable."
59 The author's translation appears in the text. The original quote is: "Citoyens, il n'y a pas un moment à perdre. J'arrive de Versailles; M. Necker est renvoyé: ce renvoi est le tocsin d'une Saint-Barthélémy de patriotes. Ce soir, tous

les bataillons suisses et allemands sortiront du Champ-de-Mars pour nous égorger. Il ne nous reste qu'une ressource, c'est de courir aux armes, et de prendre une cocarde pour nous reconnaître."

60 The author's translation appears in the text. The original quote is: "Aucun lieu du monde ne peut offrir autant d'agréments, les séductions s'y multiplient à chaque pas et les plaisirs semblent s'y être concentrés. Il s'y tient une foire perpétuelle. Chaque étage a sa destination; on y retrouve des cafés et des restaurants, et partout des salons où les plaisirs sont aussi variés que les décors. À tous les instants du jour, on peut s'adresser à des tailleurs, qui prennent mesure et, pendant qu'on déjeune ou qu'on lit les journaux, façonnent les habits. Des marchands de comestibles peuvent offrir les choses les plus recherchées des pays les plus lointains; et comme dans un catalogue on apprend chez un libraire à connaître les livres; ici, à l'aide d'un Almanach, le gastronome connaît les productions de nos fertiles jardins et de nos fécondes forêts; la terre et la mer offrent les tributs de leurs plus rares productions. Le matin, les honnêtes acheteurs flânent aux boutiques et les désœuvrés commencent décemment leur journée chez le restaurateur de leur choix. L'après-midi, les boursicotiers, les fournisseurs, les fonctionnaires et les rentiers parlent haut et gesticulent fort. Vers le soir, toute une foule élégante qui se presse aux magasins luxueux ou se hâte vers les restaurants. La nuit, enfin, surviennent les joueurs, les 'nopceurs,' attardés de salons, de cercles, de théâtres et de tripots, et, se mêlant aux groupes cosmopolites et disparates, les filles galantes, les camelots et les filous. Quiconque s'en retournerait de Paris sans avoir vu et admiré le Palais-Royal ne pourrait avoir qu'une idée très incomplète de la capitale. Il n'est aucun endroit de ce genre dans toute l'Europe."

61 London's Burlington Arcades and Milan's Galeria Vittorio Emmanuelle II also number among the world's finest iron-and-glass structures.

62 The Élysée Palace, designed by Claude Mollet in 1718 and occupied by such celebrities as the Count of Évreux, Madame de Pompadour, Joséphine and Caroline Bonaparte, and Napoléon himself, has been since 1873 the president of France's official residence; Hôtel Matignon, built in 1721 by Jean de Courtonne, has been the prime minister's residence since 1936; and the Luxembourg Palace, designed between 1615 and 1625 by Clément Métezeau for Maris de Médicis, is the seat of the French Senate and residence of its chairperson.

63 Between 1785 and 1830, many of the Palais-Royal apartments, cafés, and restaurants were used in a variety of ways. For example, some apartments became the headquarters of revolutionary clubs and others were used as brokers' offices. Many more were brothels. Most cafés and restaurants were also gambling halls.

64 To a certain extent, one exception is the unpublished historical study by Jacques Boulet and Philippe Gresset (Boulet and Gresset 1985).
65 The main Palais-Royal architects were Jacques Lemercier (1585–1654), Gilles-Marie Oppenord (1676–1742), Jean-Sylvain Cartaud (1675–1758), Pierre Contant d'Ivry (1698–1777), Pierre-Louis Moreau-Desproux, Victor Louis (1731–1811), Percier (1764–1838) and Pierre Fontaine (1762–1853), and Prosper Chabrol.
66 The author's translation appears in the text. The original quote is: "Les enfants occupant les jardins avec leurs caïds. Leur tumulte est traversé par une reine. C'est Madame Colette, le feutre sur une mousse de cheveux, le foulard autour du cou, les pieds nus dans des sandales, la canne à la main et son œil admirable de lionne asséné sévèrement sur des jeux de crimes, de police et de guerre."
67 The author's translation appears in the text. The original quote is: "Entouré de grilles, d'une muraille de Chine où des escaliers à pic conduisent au dehors, le Palais-Royal est une petite ville dans une grande ville. Cette petite ville, gardée par des chats, possède ses mœurs, ses manières, et ses indigènes, indigènes pareils à certains gondoliers de Venise qui n'ont jamais vu un cheval ni une voiture. Les nôtres semblent ne connaître que les voûtes, les lampadaires, les esplanades et les grilles à pointes d'or dans le labyrinthe desquels les échoppes vendent les livres libertins, les timbres poste et les légions d'honneur."
68 The author's translation appears in the text. The original quote is: "Notre chère Colette parlait ainsi: 'Par choix, je suis venus et revenue au Palais-Royal. Y a-t-il dans ce cloître rectangulaire, hanté de pigeons et de chats, des oisifs. Je ne le crois pas. Peut-être le trouverai-je mélancolique, ce jardin prisonnier, si j'avais de longs loisirs. Le 'carré' du Palais-Royal n'est pas une maison de retraite: son aménagement intérieur un peu bâclé, ses cloisons en guingois, ses parquets en montagnes russes, tout ceci, derrière les belles façades rigides, vieillit, joue, périclite et change, semble attirer des hôtes actifs ... Mes veillées régulières font moins de bruit qu'une ronde de feuilles sèches dans un jardin fermé, moins de bruit que les griffes des matous cardant l'écorce des arbres. Le jour, mon gîte épais n'est guère sonore. Mais j'ai la chance qu'une vibration étouffée, merveilleusement identique à celle des hélices, me berce."

CHAPTER SIX

69 Professor of architecture Jean-Paul Flamand, École d'architecture de Paris la Villette, is the author of a book on the history of social housing in France.

70 The historical evidence that the first free cabinetmaker in the faubourg Saint-Germain was actually named Jean Cottillon can be challenged. What is certain, however, is that free artisans arrived in the faubourg around 1472, during the reign of Louis XI (1423–83). A year before, the king of France had granted certain privileges to the faubourg's abbey of Saint-Antoine-des-Champs, including the privileges of rendering justice and protecting cabinetmaking artisans. The abbess was Jeanne IV; at the time, she was considered one of the most powerful figures in Paris (Diwo 1984).

71 In the case of the shops and workshops, these numbers refer to rental units. A tenant may rent two or more adjacent units; he or she then signs one lease per unit. As a rule, all shops and workshops are linked to a residential flat.

72 The current French subsidized-housing standards are, briefly, as follows. Type 1: 20 square metres (this is not a standard for an autonomous apartment, but for an additional room in a larger unit; the extra room may serve as, for example, a bedroom or a workshop); type 1/A: 33 square metres; type 2: 50 square metres; type 3: 63 square metres; type 4: 77 square metres; type 5: 90 square metres; type 6: 110 square metres; type 7: 125 square metres. All units have a fitted kitchen, a toilet, a bathroom/shower, and closets; the three larger units have a second toilet.

73 The approximate height of the building is twenty-four metres.

74 Taken from façade to façade, the width of both rue de Prague and rue du Faubourg-Saint-Antoine is twenty metres, which means that the street cross-section is not exactly a square: it is slightly higher than it is wide.

75 The three courtyards have an irregular shape. The central courtyard, or *grande cour*, is twenty-two by forty metres; the cour Baudelaire is thirty-five by sixteen metres; and the cour Roussel is twenty by twenty-eight metres.

76 At the turn of the century France had 327 private organizations that were devoted to the construction of low-cost housing (Flamand 1989, 109).

77 To this rental fee we must add approximately four hundred francs per month to cover gas (for heating and cooking), electricity, telephone, and janitorial services.

78 This square was named after a nineteenth-century medical doctor.

79 Professional College of the Furniture Arts.

80 The hospital's strange name, which, translated literally, means "Fifteen Twenty," dates back to 1254, when Louis IX founded a hospital/hostel for the blind near the Louvre. The institution was designed to accommodate fifteen groups of twenty patients each, hence its name. Later, under Louis XIV, Cardinal Rohan, who was the hospital's administrator, moved it to its present location, a former army barracks. Today, true to its tradition, the Hôpital des Quinze-Vingt is France's centre for excellence in the field of ophthalmology.

81 The abbey of Saint-Antoine-des-Champs was dismantled during the French Revolution, some fifteen years after this donation. This abbess was the last in a long line of remarkable women, known as "les dames du faubourg," who presided over the destiny of the district for almost five centuries.
82 The FNAC stores are famous in France. The acronym stands for Fédération nationale d'achat des cadres – literally, National Buying Federation for Executives.
83 The name of this establishment is Restaurant Émeraude.
84 *Annals of Public Hygiene and Legal Medicine.*
85 The acronym HBM stands for Habitations à bon marché, that is, low-cost housing.
86 One example was the Cité Napoléon, promoted by Napoléon III, designed by Veugny, and built in 1851 (Dumont 1991, 9). Another was the well-known *Familistère*, built in 1877 by industrialist Godin to house the workers from his cast-iron stove factory, in Guise (Quilliot 1989, 33–41).
87 More precisely, the complex is comprised of 356 "lots," or areas rented with a distinct lease: 297 apartment lots, 40 workshop lots, and 19 shop lots. One tenant may rent and occupy more than one commercial lot; some of the shop and workshop occupants also live at the residence. The complex has 323 mailboxes and 297 actual residents.
88 Two ancillary questions may be asked here: "Why were only seventy-two questionnaires returned?" and "Are the respondents representative of the rue de Prague residence population?" I discussed these questions with French colleagues and the Fondation Rothschild management. Regarding the first, the unanimous comment was that, in Paris, a 22 to 24 percent return was very good – even excellent. (Parisians are swamped with surveys of all kinds and tend to throw away all the junk mail that clutters their mailboxes. To avoid this, I had already asked the head janitor, who is respected by the complex's residents, to initial each questionnaire before depositing it in a mailbox.) Moreover, a 22 to 24 percent return is well within the statistical norms for a survey of this kind. Regarding the second question, the Fondation Rothschild management, which knows its tenants well, agreed that the respondents represented an accurate cross section of the rue de Prague residence population.

CHAPTER SEVEN

89 Strictly speaking, in spite of its cold winters, Montreal is not a northern city. It is located on the forty-fifth parallel, as are, for instance, Bordeaux and Milan.
90 A word on the odd geographic conventions of Montreal and Outremont would be useful at this juncture. In Montreal, boulevard Saint-Laurent is said to run

north-south, although it is actually oriented northwest-southeast. It divides the Island of Montreal into two parts: the east, which is traditionally francophone and poorer, and the west, which is traditionally anglophone and richer. Today's social reality is somewhat more complicated because one finds franco, anglo, and allophones, both rich and poor, on both sides of the great divide. Outremont illustrates this complexity because it is a predominantly francophone neighbourhood located west of Boulevard Saint-Laurent. Montreal's east-west/north-south street designation is maintained in Outremont. For example, avenue Van Horne runs east-west, while avenue de l'Épée is north-south.

In Outremont, all streets are called avenues except for two *chemins* (de la Côte-Sainte-Catherine and Bates), three *boulevards* (Mont-Royal, Dollard, and Saint-Joseph), one *côte* (du Vésinet), and two *places*, which are not city squares (Cambré and du Vésinet). Also, rue Hutchison, which constitutes Outremont's eastern border, retains its Montreal denomination of *rue* (street).

91 The Montreal region is an archipelago in the Saint Lawrence River. The largest island is the Island of Montreal; on it the City of Montreal (one million people) shares territory with twenty-nine other municipalities (together, one million people). The Montreal Urban Community (MUC) is a regional government that encompasses the Island of Montreal municipalities as well as a few small islands. North of the Island of Montreal is another large island: Laval (half a million people), which is not a member of the MUC. There are also many other tiny islands that are not constituents of the MUC. And, to complete the description of the so-called Greater Montreal Region, we must add the northern crescent (80,000 people), across the river north of Laval, and the South Shore (170,000 people), across the river south of Montreal, for a total population of 2,750,000 people (in 1992).

92 These income figures are given in Canadian dollars.

93 This was the title of a Buñuel movie. The Spanish director used it in a derisory, almost cynical way. Such derision and cynicism are not intended here.

94 The plural is used here because there are, in Outremont, several such assemblages of houses. In a way, Outremont is an assemblage of residential assemblages.

95 In 1994, this industrial plant was moved to another municipality, reducing even further Outremont's industrial base.

96 Technically speaking, Bar-B-Q Laurier is in Montreal territory, just outside Outremont city limits. Nonetheless, all Montrealers would agree that this restaurant is "culturally" part of Outremont.

97 I was personally involved in many of these studies.

98 For clarity's sake, I have used the metric system in presenting these measurements, although the metric system was not invented until one hundred years after this subdivision was implemented. At that time, the basic unit of measurement in France and in the French colonies was the *pied*, the "foot," which was longer than the English foot – 0.324 metres compared to 0.304,8 metres.

99 Outremont is renowned for harbouring a host of religious order and institutions, among them the Clercs de Saint-Viateur, the Sisters of the Holy Names of Jesus and Mary, the Maronite Church, the Dominican Church of Saint Albert the Great, the Armenian Church of Saint Gregory the Illuminator, several Catholic churches, and many synagogues.

100 There are, of course, some illustrious exceptions: San Francisco, Philadelphia, Boston, and Manhattan.

101 These are: the diagonal chemin de la Côte-Sainte-Catherine; avenue Van Horne, which is the main east-west axis; and avenue Davaar, avenue McEachran, and avenue Rockland, which are the main north-south axes.

102 These lower ceilings were perhaps introduced before World War II by Gropius, Frank Lloyd Wright, and other Modern architects. But it was well after the war that the Modern architectural ideology influenced the architecture of Outremont. By that time, however, most of the town was already built.

103 The current recession in Canada started in 1990, and, although things had begun to improve by 1994, unemployment was still high in 1997.

104 Prior to this text, and the extensive work of architectural historian Richard Bisson, Outremont had never been studied, even less examined, in print, as an urban-design, architectural, or landscape architectural paradigm.

105 Although it is very strong in Outremont, I am sure that such a feeling of belonging is not exclusive to this city. Within the Montreal area alone, one hears similar expressions of fidelity from residents of Saint-Lambert, Boucherville, Westmount, Ville Mont-Royal, and Saint-Laurent, for example.

CHAPTER EIGHT

106 In this work, no attempt has been made to produce a comprehensive review of the literature on the composite field of architectural design process. Suffice it to say that a considerable amount of knowledge exists about this rather vaguely defined topic. Today, this knowledge resides in two distinct, and most of the time mutually impermeable, domains: architectural practice and so-called architectural theory. In architectural practice, design knowledge is

often acquired incrementally, through firsthand experience, and transmitted orally. Computer-aided expert systems are beginning to codify this knowledge, but few are operational and used by practitioners. It is an empirical knowledge, supported by numerous technical manuals such as *Graphic Standards*. In universities, a further split exists: studio instructors and the authors of design-process essays (especially since about 1950) rarely communicate. Many of the people now writing on this topic are individuals who have rarely, if ever, designed and built a building. Their writings are numerous, and most are interesting in their own way. None are to be rejected, only put in phenomenological suspension, as all contribute in some way to the mastery of architectural design. These writings may be grouped in four broad categories:

1. The first category includes what some may call old-fashioned architectural procedures. Most of these were textbooks for architectural students written before World War II and inspired by the classical tradition of architecture. Some examples of these essays are: Percy Marks's *The Principles of Architectural Design* (1907), Ernest Pickering's *Architectural Design* (1941), Donald Fletcher's *Introduction to Architectural Design* (1947), and Harlan McClure's *The Study of Architectural Design* (1949). Two of these, the ones by Pickering and Fletcher, are remarkable works, and should be required reading in today's architectural-design studios. All of these books were written by architects who give the impression that they have practical experience in their trade.

2. The second category includes works that characterize what could be called the scientific approach to architectural design. These were written after World War II and came out of the rationalistic Modern Architecture ideology. Examples are: Herbert Simon (1992), Geoffrey Broadbent (1973), (editor) Dean Hawkes (1975), Clovis Heimsath (1977), B. Hillier and J. Hanson (1984), William Mitchell (1990), and Donald Schön (1983). Howard Robertson's *Modern Architectural Design* (1952) stands apart from this group because it is not a scientific-process essay in the true sense of the term. It is, as the author writes in the introduction, a manual written "from the point of view of the practicing architect," which advocates, however, a thoroughly functional, rational approach.

3. The third category includes works by authors who explored various issues related to the architectural-design process, or the process itself. These are essays that do not advocate a particular approach, but, rather, analyse the problem. Two remarkable books may be cited here: Peter Collins's *Architec-*

tural Judgement (1971) and Peter Rowe's *Design Thinking* (1987). These should also be required reading in design studios.

4. Probably alone in its category is the treatise on architectural design training, *Enseigner la conception architecturale*, written by a team of French architects, Philippe Boudon, Philippe Deshayes, Frédérique Poussin, and Françoise Schatz (1994). It is a manual that proposes a pedagogical method for teaching and learning how to design an architectural project.

107 The notion of site becomes subtle in odd situations. For example, a space station's habitable capsule could be considered a bona-fide architectural artefact. What, then, would be the site of a space station? Could it be the specific position of the habitable module on the larger station? Or, if we take the entire space station as the architectural artefact, is it a point in space? And is this point in space a material entity? On the earth's surface, these nuances disappear. Even the site of a mobile home is an evident physical reality, because even though it moves it can never escape the fact that it is always somewhere.

108 In phenomenology, description is broader and more meaningful than either analysis or explanation.

109 I was personally involved in both examples cited here. The ice-cream stand was made by my Georgia Tech students in Paris during the fall of 1994. And I took part in the Tokyo project in two different ways: as a consultant and as a professor with the Japan-U.S.A. Academic Exchange Program International Urban Design Studio. The project grouped students and faculty from the Université de Montréal, MIT, Tokyo University, and the Catholic University of Santiago, Chile. Also, the judgement regarding the simplicity or complexity of projects is relative. An ice-cream stand can be very complicated in its own way.

110 Just as the word *architecture* refers to both a process and a product, the word *project* refers to both the act of making a thing and the resulting thing. Here, to avoid confusion, the word *project* is reserved for the activity, and the word *scheme* is used to designate the product resulting from the project. In everyday conversation, *architectural project* and *architectural scheme* are synonymous.

111 The act of buying grapes at the fruit store may be an illustration of such a judgement. Examining several sorts of grapes, the consumer sees that certain kinds are less expensive than others, and since her financial ressources are limited, selects the cheaper ones – provided, of course, that their flavour is acceptable. However, between two kinds of grapes offered at the same price, selection becomes an emotional judgement. The buyer may judge that

one particular variety of grapes looks fresher than the other, or simply tastes better. Another buyer may choose the more expensive grapes if, in his critical judgement, their good flavour or their freshness warrant the higher price.

112 The notion of value also has two predominant meanings, that of worth, as used in this chapter, and that of social principle, as used in chapter 4.

113 Expensive silver and gold models are also offered, as are special limited editions.

114 The only possible exception may be some of the current postmodern architects who base their designs on linguistic considerations. Attempting to make a building beautiful is not part of their conscious design approach.

115 The author's translation appears in the text. The original quote is: "L'ordonnance, en Latin ordinatio, qui est la combinaison des diverses parties de l'ouvrage pour que l'ensemble et les parties aient, les unes et les autres (et les unes par rapport aux autres), une grandeur qui convienne à la satisfaction des besoins du programme."

116 The author's translation appears in the text. The original quote is: "La pureté abstraite de la matière quant à la forme, à la couleur, au son, etc., constitue ... l'essentiel [de l'œuvre]. Des lignes nettement tracées, s'étendant d'une façon uniforme, sans dévier à droite ni à gauche, des surfaces lisses, etc., nous satisfont par leur ferme précision et leur uniforme unité."

117 In his *Cours d'architecture*, François Blondel wrote: "Le génie ne suffit pas pour faire un architecte, et qu'il faut que par l'étude, l'application, le long usage et l'expérience, il s'acquière une connaissance parfaite des règles de son art et des proportions, et qu'il ait la science d'en faire le discernement et le choix, afin de s'en pouvoir servir à propos et les mettre utilement en pratique en toutes sortes d'occasions" (Blondel in Fichet 1979, 172). Author's translation: "Genius alone is not sufficient to make an architect. It is necessary that, through study, diligence, and long practice, he acquire a thorough knowledge of the rules of his art and of proportions; and that he develop the science of using these rules with discernment in order that he may be able to apply them judiciously in all sorts of circumstances."

118 The same sort of quality measurement is made constantly in industry: a brand of car that breaks down once every 25,000 kilometres is thought to be of a higher quality than one that breaks down three times within the same distance. Such a comparison has a meaning only if all other quality variables remain stable. A car that costs $100,000 is expected to break down less often than one that sells for $10,000.

119 Translation by Jonathan Clements. "She is elegant. I am not speaking of that secondary elegance which is nothing but a woman's instinct for the toilet that becomes her. What woman does not posses to some degree the concern and

talent for adorning her person? What I mean is a more refined elegence, the elegance that so well harmonizes manners with inner finesse and pride, rather than clothing with the body; this is an added gift. Ease is a sign of superiority, just as presumptuous assurance is a mark of mediocrity. But this ease must be made of grace in order to be accepted, that is to say, it must be natural. Elegance flows easily, it is the gesture of a noble soul. It is not learned, it is spontaneous, yet it knows itself, and in that it verges on taste. Thus, it is not far from elegence to seeking. Seeking can still be elegant, but where affectation begins, elegance ends. How well these nuances, subtle in appearance, are captured in a woman! In the woman I am thinking of I believe I have found pure elegance; it is half her beauty. Her toilet is full of invention and devoid of pretention; I am convinced that she would consider she was doing herself a serious wrong were she to draw attention to herself by something in her appearance; she knows that it is not a matter of drawing attention to oneself, but of being distinguished, that one must not look like any other while remaining oneself. Indeed, one is oneself by one's entire person, not by the exaggeration of a detail, for everything is held within us and, therefore, everything must be harmonized in our exteriors. Elegance in little things is simply grace; in large things it is dignity, but this must always be from within. This quality [elegance] exercises an extraordinary power of seduction over me, although it often humbles me somewhat. Oh, how I wish I could write a verse which resembles her!"

120 The author's translation appears in the text. The original quote is: "Mme Swann apparaissait, épanouissant autour d'elle une toilette toujours différente, une large ombrelle de la même nuance que l'effeuillaison des pétales de sa robe … souriante, heureuse du beau temps … certaine que sa toilette était la plus élégante de toutes."

121 The author's translation appears in the text. The original quote is: "Dis-moi (puisque tu es si sensible aux effets de l'architecture), n'as-tu pas observé en te promenant dans cette ville que d'entre les édifices dont elle est peuplée, les uns sont muets, les autres parlent; et d'autres enfin, qui sont les plus rares, chantent?"

122 Here are some examples of Knapp's ten essays: Ibsent's *The Master Builder* is examined in "The Emptiness, an Architectural Archetype"; James's "The Jolly Corner" is addressed in "The Entrapped Shadow in the Architectural House"; and Kafka's *The Castle* is analysed in "The Archetypical Land Surveyor."

123 Even the process of ordering food by phone and having it delivered to one's home involves contact with other members of society. It is therefore an activity that requires a movement into the public realm.

CHAPTER NINE

124 The garden's dimensions are 102 metres by 34 metres.

125 Together, the two basement floors form a gross area of 17,688 square metres. The block's 350 parking spaces may be broken down this way: 1 space per housing unit, making 170 spaces; 1 space per 100 square metres of retail or office space, making 170 spaces; and, say, 10 additional spaces for visitors. In all, given that each parking spot is thirty square metres, 10,500 square metres of basement space is consigned to parking. It is anticipated that most office workers coming to the complex would use the public-transportation system.

126 In Europe, a thirty-square-metre parking space is a generously proportioned one; it corresponds to a norm used in North America where cars are larger; in France, a twenty-five-square-metre parking space is quite acceptable.

127 For residential buildings, it is possible to build a reinforced-concrete floor slab that is twenty centimetres thick, or even slightly thinner.

128 The same 85-square-metre space can be divided into two 39.5-square-metre single-orientation bachelor apartments plus a six-square-metre lobby. It can also remain as a single 85-square-metre unit, occupied, however, by a household of three, or a couple, or even a single person. In the latter case, the flat becomes a more upscale apartment, even a luxury one. Also, the flat's width, which is six metres, could be increased by one, two, or three additional metres, creating a much more generous and expensive residence.

129 Including the balcony, the living/dining room has a depth of six metres. Some may consider this depth excessive, but it is not for at least three reasons. First, the ceiling is high: 2.7 metres. In cross section, and counting the width of the exterior wall and the interior-partition width, it has almost a one-on-two proportion. Second, in plan, it is almost a square and it is wider than its depth if the balcony is excluded. Third, almost the entire façade is glazed. Not all the activities that take place in a apartment living/dining room require intense natural light; and, for the most part, a living/dining room in an high-density inner-city apartment is used mainly at night. A western orientation for the living/dining room is desirable in terms of lighting because the warm light of the setting sun can penetrate deep into the apartment. Of course, it is possible to design shallower buildings, but this would entail a lower overall density.

130 Public places take many forms. In cities today, we find simple hallways, plush lobbies, grand *gallerias* (the Galleria Vittorio Emanuele in Milan), distinguished arcades (the Burlington Arcade in London), and *passages* (in Brussels, Paris, or Kyoto). The urban public network comprises kilometres of

narrow and wide sidewalks and streets, pedestrian-only walkways and motor vehicle-only roadways, bus stops, taxi stands, and parking lots where pedestrians become motorists and motorists pedestrians. It includes cluttered back alleys, busy commercial streets, lavish avenues, romantic mews, neon-lit boulevards, and humble courts where a bench is the dominant feature. The urban public realm is where we discover bustling market-places and railway-station halls, metro and commuter-train stations, monumental grounds, *parvis*, *corso*, malls, esplanades, and squares for celebrating, parading, or simply walking. The word *square* describes at least three different kinds of public space: a city square, plaza, or *piazza*, like Sienna's Piazza del Campo; a semi private garden, such as the London square; or a French garden-playground. There are many kinds of leisure-oriented places in cities: gardens, parks, sports fields, playgrounds, bicycle paths, riverbanks, and oceanfront promenades.

CHAPTER TEN

131 For example, the veils of economy, ecology, and energy are never discussed in the writings of Venturi or Jencks. Also, the skills involved in assessing a project's costs or conducting a financial feasibility study are rarely, if ever, taught in architecture schools.
132 These lines are from a song, called "Fer et titane," by Québécois singer Gilles Vigneault. The author's translation appears in the text. The original quote is:
"À la place d'un village
Une ville et sa banlieue
Dix religions vingt langages
Les petits vieux silencieux
Puis regarde-moi bien dans les yeux
Tout ce monde à rendre heureux."

BIBLIOGRAPHY

This bibliography is presented under five headings:
1. Theory/History of Architecture and Urban Design
2. Phenomenology, Philosophy, and Human Sciences
3. Palais-Royal
4. Fondation Rothschild Workers' Residence
5. Outremont

I THEORY/HISTORY OF ARCHITECTURE AND URBAN DESIGN

Alberti, Leon Battista. *De Re Aedificatoria*. New York: Dover Publications, 1986.
Architecture in the Year 2000. Ottawa: Royal Architectural Institute of Canada, 1991.
Bacon, Edmund. *Design of Cities*. New York: Penguin Books, 1976.
Ballon, Hilary. *The Paris of Henry IV, 1589/1610*. Cambridge: MIT Press, 1991.
Barnard, Peter. *The Barnard Report: Architecture in Difficult Times/L'architecture en période difficile*. Ottawa: Government of Canada, Ministry of Regional Economic Expansion, 1986.
Bayer, Brian. "A Sketch of Architectural Education." *CRIT 29: The Journal of the American Institute of Architectural Students* fall 1992.
Blondel, François. "Cours d'architecte, 1675–1688." In *La théorie architecturale à l'âge classique*. By Françoise Fichet. Paris: Pierre Mardaga Éditeur, 1979.
Blondel, Jacques-François. *L'architecture françoise*. Paris: Librairie centrale des beaux-arts-Émile Lévy Éditeur, 1905.
Borissavliévitch, M. *Les théories de l'architecture*. Paris: Payot, 1951.
Borsi, Franco. *Leon Battista Alberti: The Complete Works*. New York: Electra-Rizzoli, 1973.

———. *Le Piaze: Monumenti d'Italia*. Edited by Geno Pampaloni. Novara: Instituto Geographico de Agostini, 1975.

Boudon, Philippe, Philippe Deshayes, Frédérique Poussin, and Françoise Schatz. *Enseigner la conception architecturale: Cours d'architecturologie*. Paris: Les Éditions de la Villette, 1994.

Broadbent, Geoffrey. *Design in Architecture: Architecture and the Human Sciences*. London: John Wiley and Sons, 1973.

Broadbent, Geoffrey, *Design Methods in Architecture*. Edited by Antony Ward. New York: George Wittenborn, 1980.

Brolin, Brent. *The Failure of Modern Architecture*. Scarborough, ON: Van Nostrand Reinhlold, 1976.

Burns, Amy Stechler, and Ken Burns. *The Shakers: Hands to Work, Hearts to God*. New York: Aperture Books, 1986.

Chaput, Marcel, and Tony LeSauteur. *Dossier pollution*. Montreal: Éditions du Jour, 1971.

Ching, Francis. *Architecture: Form, Space and Order*. New York: Van Nostrand Reinhold, 1979.

Collins, Peter. *Architectural Judgement*. Montreal: McGill-Queen's University Press, 1971.

Coulton, J. J. *Ancient Greek Architects at Work*. Ithaca: Cornell University Press, 1977.

Crosbie, Michael J. "The Schools: How They're Failing the Profession." *Progressive Architecture* September 1995.

Crump, Ralph W., and Martin J. Harms. *The Design Connection: Energy and Technology in Architecture*. New York: Van Nostrand Reinhold, 1981.

Cuff, Dana. *Architecture: The Story of Practice*. Cambridge: MIT Press, 1991.

Curtis, William, J. R. *Modern Architecture since 1900*. Englewood Cliffs, NJ: Prentice-Hall, 1987.

Dansereau, Pierre. "La pondération écologique du patrimoine." In *Environment et développement: Questions éthiques et problèmes socio-politiques.*" Edited by José A. Prades, Jean-Guy Vaillancourt, and Robert Tessier. Montreal: Éditions Fides, 1991.

———. "An Ethical Preparation for Global Change." In *The Proceedings of the Third UNESCO Science and Culture Forum on Toward Eco-Ethics: Alternative Visions of Culture, Science, Technology and Nature*. Edited by Ubiratan D'Ambrosio and Vladislav Kotchetkov. Balem, Brazil: UNESCO Publications, 1992.

———. "Repères pour une éthique de l'environnement, avec une méditation sur la paix." In *Actualiser la morale*. By Rodrigue Bélanger and Simonne Plourde. Paris: Éditions du Cerf, 1992.

———. "Une projection éthique sur la prise de possession de la planète." In *Violence et coexistence humaine: Proceedings of the Second World Congress of the*

ASEVICO, 1992, Montreal. Edited by Venant Gauchy. Montreal: Éditions Montmorency, 1994.

Dehan, Philippe. *Jean Ginsberg, 1905–1983: La modernité naturelle*. Paris: Éditions Connivences, 1987.

Dennis, Michel. *Court and Garden: From the French Hotel to the City of Paris Modern Architecture*. Cambridge: MIT Press, 1986.

Doczi, Gyögy. *The Power of Limits: Proportional Harmonies in Nature, Art and Architecture*. Boston: Shambhala, 1981.

Dupuy, Gabriel. *L'urbanisme des réseaux*. Paris: Armand Collin, 1991.

Eisenman, Peter. "Provocateur et architecte." *Le Devoir* [Montreal] 28 February 1994.

Erlande-Brandenburg, Alain. *Quand les cathédrales étaient peintes*. Paris: Gallimard, 1993.

Fichet, Françoise. *La théorie architecturale à l'âge classique*. Paris: Pierre Mardaga Éditeur, 1979.

Fisher, Thomas. "Symposium on Architectural Practice." *GSD News* [Harvard University Graduate School of Design publication] winter/spring 1994.

Fleming, J., H. Honour, and N. Pevsner. *Dictionary of Architecture*. London: Penguin Books, 1991.

Fletcher, D. A. *Introduction to Architectural Design*. New York: D. A. Fletcher, 1947.

Frampton, Kenneth. *Modern Architecture: A Critical History*. London: Thames and Hudson, 1992.

Gallet, Michel. *Stately Mansions: Eighteenth Century Paris Architecture*. New York: Praeger Publishers, 1972.

Giedion, Sigfried. *Space, Time and Architecture*. Cambridge: Harvard University Press, 1962.

Girouard, Mark. *Cities and People: A Social and Architectural History*. New Haven: Yale University Press, 1985.

Gromort, Georges. *Initiation à l'architecture*. Paris: Librairie d'art R. Ducher, 1938.

Gropius, Walter. *The New Architecture and the Bauhaus*, translated by P. Morton Shand. Cambridge: MIT Press, 1965.

Hawkes, D., ed. *Models and Systems in Architecture and Building*. Lancaster, England: Construction Press, 1975.

Heimsath, Clovis. *Behavioral Architecture: Toward an Accountable Design Process*. New York: McGraw-Hill, 1977.

Hillier, B., and J. Hanson. *The Social Logic of Space*. Cambridge: Cambridge University Press, 1984.

Hillier, Bill. "Space Syntax." *Architectural Journal* (London), November 1983.

Jacobs, Jane. *The Death and Life of Great American Cities*. New York: Vintage-Random House, 1961.

Jacques, Annie, and J. P. Mouilleseaux. *Les architectes de la liberté*. Paris: Gallimard, 1988.

Jaffâe, Hans Ludwig, ed. *De Stijl*. New York: Abram, 1971.

Jencks, Charles, *The Language of Post-Modern Architecture*, 4TH ed. New York: Rizzoli, 1984.

———. *The Prince, The Architect and the New Wave Monarchy*. New York: Rizzoli, 1988.

———. *Post-Modernism on Trial*. Edited by Andreas C. Papadakis. London: Design Publication-Academy Editions, 1990.

Jones, Michael. "Models for Educating Architects in this Century and the Next." Ph.D. diss., Georgia Institute of Technology College of Architecture, 1989.

Kandall-Thompson, Eliza. *Apartments, Townhouses and Condominiums*. New York: Architectural Record, 1975.

Kostof, Spiro. *The City Shaped: Urban Patterns and Meanings through History*. Boston: Bulfinch Press-Little, Brown, 1991.

———. *The City Assembled: The Elements of Urban Form through History*. Boston: Bulfinch Press-Little, Brown, 1992.

Krier, Rob. *Architectural Composition*. New York: Rizzoli, 1989.

Lavedan, Pierre. *Histoire de Paris*. Paris: Presses Universitaires de France, 1960.

Lebovich, William L. *Design for Dignity: Studies in Accessibility*. New York: John Wiley and Sons, 1993.

Le Corbusier. *Le modulor*. Paris: Collection Ascoral-Éditions de *l'Architecture d'aujourd'hui*, 1948.

———. "Œuvres." *Architecture d'aujourd'hui*. April 1948.

———. *Modulor 2*. Paris: Collection Ascoral-Éditions de *l'Architecture d'aujourd'hui*, 1955.

———. *Vers une architecture*. Paris: Éditions Vincent, Fréal, 1958.

Letartre, Pierre A. *La recherche en architecture: Une argumentation économique*. Montreal: Institut de recherche en architecture du Canada et l'Université Laval, 1992.

Lincourt, Michel. *Le mésodesign: Théorie d'organisation du milieu physique et modèle conceptuel de ville*. Montreal: Les Presses de l'Université de Montréal, 1972.

Lincourt, Michel, and Claude Parisel. *Institut de recherche en architecture du Canada et son réseau*. Montreal: Ordre des architectes du Québec-Association des architectes en pratique privée du Québec, 1989.

Lincourt, Michel, and Harry Parnass. *Métro-éducation*. Montreal: Université de Montréal, Faculté de l'aménagement, 1970.

Lobell, Mimi. "Spatial Archetypes." *ReVision* 6, no. 2 (1983).

Marks, Percy L. *The Principles of Architectural Design*. London: Swan, Sonnenschein, 1907.

Martin, John Rupert. "The Baroque from the Point of View of the Art Historian." *Journal of Aesthetics and Art Criticism* 14 (1955).

McClure, Harlan. *The Study of Architectural Design*. Minneapolis: Burgess Publishing, 1949.

Michel, André, ed. *Histoire de l'art*. Paris: Librairie Armand Colin, 1906.

Millon, Henry. *Baroque Architecture*. New York: George Braziller, 1965.

Mitchell, William J. *The Logic of Architecture*. Cambridge: MIT Press, 1990.

Morris, A. E. J. *History of Urban Form*. Essex, England: Longman Scientific and Technical- John Wiley and Sons, 1989.

Moynihan, Daniel P., ed. *Urban America: The Expert Looks at the City*. Washington: Voice of America Forum Lecture-U.S. Information Service, 1970.

Mumford, Lewis, *The City in History: Its Origins, Its Transformations, and Its Prospects*. New York: Harcourt, Brace and World, 1961.

Norberg-Schulz, Christian. *Intentions in Architecture*. Cambridge: MIT Press, 1965.

———. *Genius Loci: Toward a Phenomenology of Architecture*. New York: Rizzoli, 1980.

———. *Meaning in Western Architecture*. New York: Rizzoli, 1980.

———. *The Concept of Dwelling: On the Way to Figurative Architecture*. New York: Electra-Rizzoli, 1985.

Otto, Christian F. *Space into Light: The Church Architecture of Balthasar Newmann*. New York: New York Architectural Foundation, 1979.

Padjen, Elizabeth. "Symposium on Architectural Practice." *GSD News* [Harvard University Graduate School of Design publication] winter/spring 1994.

Palladio, Andrea. *I Quattro Libri dell' Architettura/The Four Books of Architecture*. Translated by Isaac Ware. New York: Dover Publications, 1965.

Papadakis, Andreas C., ed. *Post-Modernism on Trial*. London: Architectural Design-Academy Editions, 1990.

Papageorgiou, Alex. *Continuity and Change: Preservation in City Planning*. New York: Praeger Publishers, 1971.

Pérez-Gómez, Alberto. *Architecture and the Crisis of Modern Science*. Cambridge: MIT Press, 1983.

Perrault, Claude. Preface. In Vitruvius 1965.

Pickering, Ernest. *Architectural Design*. New York: John Wiley and Sons-Chapman and Hall, 1941.

Picon, Antoine. *Architectes et ingénieurs au siècle des lumières*. Marseille: Éditions Parenthèses, 1988.

Piel, Gerard, et al., eds. *Cities*. New York: Scientific American Alfred A. Knopf, 1965.

Procos, Dimitri. *Mixed Land Use: From Revival to Innovation*. Stroudsburg, PA: Dowden, Hutchinson and Ross, 1976.

Rasmussen, Steen Eiler. *Experiencing Architecture*. Cambridge: MIT Press, 1959.

Read, Alice G., and Peter C. Doo. *Via 6: Architecture and Visual Perception*. Philadelphia: University of Pennsylvania Graduate School of Fine Arts MIT Press, 1983.

Relph, Edward. *Place and Placelessness*. London: Pion, 1976.

Robertson, Howard. *Modern Architectural Design*. London: Architectural Press, 1952.

Rowe, Peter. *Design Thinking*. Cambridge: MIT Press, 1987.

———. "The Harvard Graduate School of Design: Directions for the Near Future." *GSD News* [Harvard Graduate School of Design publication] winter/spring 1993.

———. "Introduction to the Symposium on Architectural Practice" *GSD News* [Harvard University Graduate School of Design publication] winter/spring 1994.

Rudolfsky, Bernard. *Streets for People*. New York: Rizzoli, 1969.

Ruskin, John. *The Seven Lamps of Architecture*. New York: Dover Publications, 1989.

Rykwert, Joseph. *The First Moderns: The Architects of the Eighteenth Century*. Cambridge: MIT Press, 1980.

Saint, Andrew. "Symposium on Architectural Practice." *GSD News* [Harvard University Graduate School of Design publication] winter/spring 1994.

Samaran, Charles. *Les très riches heures du Duc de Berry*. Chantilly: Musée Condé-Draeger Éditeur, 1969.

Sapers, Carl. "Symposium on Architectural Practice." *GSD News* [Harvard University Graduate School of Design publication] winter/spring 1994.

Schinz, Marina, and Susan Littlefield. *Visions of Paradise: Themes and Variations on the Garden*. Toronto: Stoddart, 1985.

Schorske, Carl E. *Vienne, fin de siècle: Politique et culture*. Paris: Seuil Éditeur 1983.

Schmitt, Karl W. *Multistorey Housing*. New York: Frederick A. Praeger Publisher, 1966.

Schön, Donald. *The Reflective Practitioner: How Professionals Think in Architecture*. New York: Basics Books, 1983.

———. *Problems, Frames and Perspectives on Design*. New York: *Design Research*, 1984.

Scruton, Roger. *The Aesthetics of Architecture*. Princeton: Princeton University Press, 1990.

Seamon, David, ed. *Dwelling, Seeing, and Designing: Toward a Phenomenological Ecology*. New York: State University of New York Press, 1993.

Seamon, David, and Robert Mugerauer, eds. *Dwelling, Place and Environment: Toward a Phenomenology of Person and World*. New York: Columbia University Press, 1989.

Simon, Herbert A. *The Sciences of the Artificial*. Cambridge: MIT Press, 1992.

Sitte, Camillo. *City Planning According to Artistic Principles*. Translated by George R. Collins and Christiane Chasemann Collins. Toronto: Random House, 1965.

Skira, Albert, ed. *The Greek Painting: The Great Centuries of Painting.* New York: Skira, 1950.

Sprigg, June. *Shaker Design.* New York: Whitney Museum-W. W. Norton and Company, 1986.

St. John, Andrew. *The Source Book for Sustainable Design: A Guide to Environmentally Responsible Building Materials and Processes, Architects for Social Responsibility.* Boston: Boston Society of Architects, 1992.

Stitt, Fred A. *Production Systems for Architects and Designers.* New York: Van Nostrand Reinhold, 1994.

Stratton, Arthur. *The Orders of Architecture.* London: Studio Editions, 1986.

Sullivan, Louis H. *Kindergarten Chats.* New York: Dover, 1979.

Summerson, John. *The Architecture of the Eighteenth Century.* London: Thames and Hudson, 1969.

Szambien, Werner. *De la rue des Colonnes à la rue de Rivoli.* Paris: Délégation à l'Action Artistique de la Ville de Paris, 1992.

Tange, Kenzo. *Katsura: Tradition and Creation in Japanese Architecture.* Tokyo: Jokeisha-Yale University Press, 1960.

Taylor, Mark C. "Deadline Approaching Anarchetecture." In *Restructuring Architectural Theory.* Edited by Marco Diani and Catherine Ingraham. Evanston: Northwestern University Press, 1988.

Thiis-Evensen, Thomas. *Archetypes in Architecture.* London: Oxford University Press-Norwegian University Press, 1987.

Tilly, Charles. *An Urban World.* Boston: Little, Brown, 1974.

Venturi, Robert. *Complexity and Contradiction in Architecture.* New York: Museum of Modern Art, 1966.

Vidler, Anthony. *The Writing on the Walls.* Princeton: Princeton Architectural Press, 1987.

———. *The Architectural Uncanny.* Cambridge: MIT Press, 1992.

Viollet-le-Duc. *Histoire d'une maison.* Paris: J. Hetzel, 1874.

Vitruvius, Marcus V. Pollio. *Les dix livres d'architecture de Vitruve.* Translated by Claude Perrault. Paris: Les Libraires Associés, 1965.

Wales, HRH The Prince of. *A Vision of Britain: A Personal View of Architecture.* London: Doubleday, 1989.

Ward, W. H. *The Architecture of the Renaissance in France.* New York: Hacker Art Books, 1976.

Webb, Michael. *The City Square: A Historical Evolution.* New York: Whitney Library of Design-Watson-Guptill Publications, 1990.

Weber, Max. *The City.* Edited and translated by Don Martindale and Gertrud Neuwirth. New York: Free Press-Collier-Macmillan, 1958.

Wegener, Michael. "Operational Urban Models: State of the Arts." *Journal of the American Planning Association* 60, no. 1 (1994).

Wentworth, Eldredge H., ed. *Taming Megalopolis*. 2 vols. New York: Anchor-Doubleday, 1967.

White, Morton, and Lucia White. *The Intellectual Versus the City: From Thomas Jefferson to Frank Lloyd Wright*. Toronto: Mentor-New American Library of Canada, 1964.

Wittkower, Rudolf. *Architectural Principles in the Age of Humanism*. London: Academy Editions-St. Martin's Press, 1988.

Wolfe, Tom. *From Bauhaus to Our House*. New York: Washington Square Press, 1981.

Wright, Frank Lloyd. *The Living City*. New York: Mentor-New American Library, 1963.

Wundram, M., T. Pape, and P. Marton. *Palladio*. Cologne: Benedikt Taschen, 1989.

Yorke, F. R. S., and Frederick Gibberd. *The Modern Flat*. London: Architectural Press, 1937.

2 PHENOMENOLOGY, PHILOSOPHY, AND HUMAN SCIENCES

Aristotle, *Politics and Poetics*. Translated by Benjamin Jowett and S. H. Butcher. Norwalk, CT: Easton Press, 1979.

Attali, Jacques. *Au propre et au figuré*. Paris: Librairie Arthème Fayard, 1988.

Auroux, Sylvain, et al. *Encyclopédie philosophique universelle: Les notions philosophiques*. Vols. 1 and 2. Paris: Presses Universitaires de France, 1990.

Bachelard, Gaston, *Le nouvel esprit scientifique*. Paris: Quadrige-Presses Universitaires de France, 1934.

———. *La psychanalyse du feu*. Paris: Gallimard, 1949.

———. *La poétique de l'espace*. Paris: Presses Universitaires de France, 1964.

———. *L'eau et les rêves: Essai sur l'imagination de la matière*. Paris: Librairie José Corti, 1973.

Bachelard, Suzanne. *A Study of Husserl's Formal and Transcendental Logic*. Translated by Lester E. Embree. Evanston: Northwestern University Press, 1968.

Berger, Gaston. *Le Cogito dans la philosophie de Husserl*. Paris: Presses Universitaires de France, 1941.

Bernet, R., I. Kern, and E. Marbach. *An Introduction to Husserlian Phenomenology*. Evanston: Northwestern University Press, 1993.

Bernstein, Richard J., ed. *Habermas and Modernity*. Cambridge: MIT Press, 1985.

Berque, Jacques, ed. *Le Coran*. Translated by Jacques Berque. Paris: Éditions Sinbad, 1990.

Blackburn, Pierre. *Logique de l'argumentation*. Montreal: Éditions du Renouveau Pédagogique, 1989.

BIBLIOGRAPHY

Blanché, Robert. *La logique et son histoire: d'Aristote à Russel.* Paris: Armand Colin Éditeur, 1970.

Boileau, Nicolas. L'art poétique. In *Encyclopédie des citations.* Edited by P. Dupré. Paris: Éditions de Trévisse,1 1959.

Bürger, Peter. *Theory of the Avant-Garde.* Translated by Michael Shaw. Minneapolis: University of Minnesota Press, 1984.

Capaldi, Nicholas. *The Art of Deception: An Introduction to Critical Thinking.* New York: Prometheus Books, 1987.

Carbonell, Charles-Olivier. *L'historiographie.* Paris: Presses Universitaires de France, 1991.

Carus, Paul. *L'évangile du Bouddha, raconté d'après les anciens documents.* Translated by L. de Milloué. Geneva: Éditions Aquarius, 1983.

Cayla, Fabien. *Routes et déroutes de l'intentionalité, précédé de Correspondance sur l'intentionalité de Wilfred Sellers-Roderick Chisholm.* Paris: Éditions de l'Éclat, 1991.

"Cities: Back to Basics." *US News and World Report,* 1 November 1993.

Cumming, Robert Denoon. *Phenomenology and Deconstruction.* Chicago: University of Chicago Press, 1991.

Deming, Edwards. "Hors de la crise." In *La conquête de la qualité.* Montreal: Royal Bank of Canada, 1991.

de Muralt, André. *The Idea of Phenomenology: Husserlian Exemplarism.* Translated by G. Breckon. Evanston: Northwestern University Press, 1974.

Derrida, Jacques. *La voix et le phénomène.* Paris: Presses Universitaires de France-Épiméthée, 1967.

——. *Heidegger et la question.* Paris: Flammarion, 1990.

Descartes, René. *Méditations métaphysiques.* Paris: GF-Flammarion, 1979.

——. *Discours de la méthode.* Paris: Gallimard, 1991.

Diderot, Denis. *Œuvres.* Paris: Bibliothèque de la Pléiade-Gallimard, 1946.

Dufrenne, Mikel. *The Phenomenology of Aesthetic Experience.* Translated by Edward S. Casey. Evanston: Northwestern University Press, 1973.

Dumas, Jean-Louis. *Histoire de la pensée: Philosophies et philosophes.* Paris: Éditions Taillandier-Livre de Poche-Références, 1990.

Farber, Marvin. *Phenomenology and Existence: Toward a Philosophy within Nature.* New York: Academy Library-Harper Torchbooks, 1967.

Flew, Antony. *A Dictionary of Philosophy.* Rev. ed. New York: St. Martin's Press, 1984.

Gadamer, Hans Georg. "Un entretien avec Hans Georg Gadamer," Interview by Jacques Poulin. Translated by Elfie Poulin. *Le Monde,* 3 January 1995.

Glassé, Cyril. *Dictionnaire encyclopédique de l'Islam.* Paris: Éditions Bordas, 1991.

Habermas, Jürgen. *The Philosophical Discourse of Modernity.* Translated by Frederick Lawrence. Cambridge: MIT Press, 1990.

Hachette. *Dictionnaire: Langue, encyclopédie, noms propres.* 1990.
Hall, Edward T. *The Hidden Dimension.* Garden City, NY: Doubleday, 1966.
———. *The Silent Language.* Greenwich, CT: Fawcett, 1966.
Harvey, David. *The Condition of Postmodernity: An Inquiry into the Origins of Cultural Change.* Oxford: Blackwell, 1990.
Hawking, Stephen W. *A Brief History of Time.* London: Bantam Books, 1988.
Hegel, G. W. F. *Introduction à l'esthétique/L'idée du beau.* Paris: Champs-Flammarion, 1979.
Hofstadter, Douglas R. *Gödel, Escher, Bach: An Eternal Golden Braid.* New York: Vintage-Random House, 1980.
Heidegger, Martin. *Le principe de raison.* Paris: Gallimard, 1957.
———. *Building Dwelling Thinking.* New York: Harper and Rowe, 1971.
———. *The Basic Problems of Phenomenology.* Translated by Albert Hofstadter. Bloomington: Indiana University Press, 1988.
Huisman, Denis. *L'esthétique.* Paris: Presses Universitaires de France, 1954.
Husserl, Edmund. *Idées directrices pour une phénoménologie.* Translated by Paul Ricoeur. Paris: Tel-Gallimard, 1950.
———. *Recherches logiques/3.* Translated by Hubert Élie, Arion L. Kelkel, and René Schérer. Paris: Presses Universitaires de France-Épiméthée, 1963.
———. *The Crisis of European Sciences and Transcendental Phenomenology.* Translated by David Carr. Evanston: Northwestern University Press, 1970.
———. *L'idée de la phénoménologie.* Translated by Alexandre Lowit. Paris: Presses Universitaires de France-Épiméthée, 1970.
———. *Méditations cartésiennes: Introduction à la phénoménologie.* Paris: Librairie Philosophique J. Vrin, 1986.
Impressions of Montblanc. Germany: Montblanc, 1995.
Jameson, Fredric. *Postmodernism or the Cultural Logic of Late Capitalism.* Durham: Duke University Press, 1991.
Kalinowski, Georges. *La phénoménologie de l'homme chez Husserl, Ingarden et Schiller.* Paris: Éditions Universitaires, 1991.
———. *Expérience et Phénoménologie.* Paris: Éditions Universitaires, 1992.
Kallen, Horace M. Introduction. In Aristotle 1979.
Kant, Immanuel, *Critique de la raison pure.* Translated by A. Delamarre, F. Marty, and J. Barni. Paris: Gallimard, 1980.
———. *Critique de la faculté de juger.* Translated by A. Delamarre, J. R. Ladmiral, Marc B. de Launay, J. M. Vaysse, L. Ferry, and H. Wismann. Paris: Gallimard, 1985.
———. *Critique de la raison pratique.* Translated by Luc Ferry and Heinz Wismann. Paris: Gallimard, 1985.
Knapp, Bettina L., *Archetype, Architecture and the Writer.* Bloomington: Indiana University Press, 1986.

Kolakowski, Leszek. *Husserl and the Search for Certitude*. Chicago: University of Chicago Press, 1975.
Kremer-Marietti, Angèle. *La philosophie cognitive*. Paris: Presses Universitaires de France, 1994.
Laborit, Henri. *Biologie et structure*. Paris: Gallimard, 1968.
———. *L'agressivité détournée*. Paris: Union Générale d'Éditions, 1970.
———. *L'homme imaginant*. Paris: Union Générale d'Éditions, 1970.
———. *La nouvelle grille*. Paris: Gallimard-Éditions Robert Laffont, 1974.
Lachelier, Jules. *Cours de logique: École normale supérieure, 1866–1867*. Paris: Éditions Universitaires, 1990.
Larousse. *Grand Larousse de langue française*. 1972.
Lavine, T. Z. *From Socrates to Sartre: The Philosophic Quest*. New York: Bantam Books, 1989.
Leckie, Scott. "The UN Committee on Economic, Social and Cultural Rights and the Right to Adequate Housing: Toward an Appropriate Approach." *Human Rights Quarterly* 11, no. 4 (1989).
Lowen, Alexandre. *Le plaisir*. Paris: Éditions Sands, 1991.
Lyotard, Jean-François. *La phénoménologie*. Paris: Presses Universitaires de France, 1954.
———. *The Postmodern Condition: A Report on Knowledge*. Minneapolis: University of Minnesota Press, 1984.
———. *Phenomenology*. Translated by Brian Beakley. New York: State University of New York Press, 1991.
Machiavelli, Niccolo. *Le prince*. Paris: Gallimars, 1983.
Madan Sarup. *An Introductory Guide to Post-Structuralism and Post-Modernism*. Athens: University of Georgia Press, 1989.
McLuhan, Marshall. *Understanding Media: The Extensions of Man*. New York: McGraw-Hill, 1965.
McLuhan, Marshall, and Quentin Fiore. *The Medium Is the Massage*. New York, Bantam Books, 1967.
McLuhan, Marshall, and W. Watson. *Du cliché à l'archétype: La foire des sens*. Translated by Derrick de Kerckove. Montreal: Éditions Hurtubise HMH-Maison Mame, 1973.
Merleau-Ponty, Maurice. *Phénoménologie de la perception*. Paris: Tel-Gallimard, 1945.
Michelet, Jules. *Histoire de France*. Lausanne: Éditions Rencontre, 1966.
Michelin France. 1995 ed.
Montesquieu. *Essai sur le goût*. Paris: Rivage Poche-Petite Bibliothèque, 1993.
Mucchielli, Alex. *Les méthodes qualitatives*. Paris: Presses Universitaires de France, 1991.

Oléron, Pierre. *L'argumentation*. Paris: Presses Universitaires de France, 1983.
Patocka, Jan. *Qu'est-ce que la phénoménologie?* Grenoble: Éditions Jérôme Million, 1988.
Périllier, Louis. *La patrie planétaire*. Paris: Robert Laffont, 1976.
Peters, Tom. *Thriving on Chaos: Handbook for Management Revolution*. New York: Perennial Library-Harper and Row, 1987.
Piaget, Jean. *Le structuralisme*. Paris: Presses Universitaires de France, 1968.
Poulin, Jacques, ed. *Critique de la raison phénoménologique*. Paris: Les Éditions du Cerf, 1991.
Proust, Marcel. *À la recherche du temps perdu*. Paris. Gallimard, 1954.
Reich, Charles A. *The Greening of America*. New York: Random House, 1970.
Resweber, Jean-Paul. *La philosophie des valeurs*. Paris: Presses Universitaires de France, 1992.
Ricoeur, Paul. *De l'interprétation: Essai sur Freud*. Paris: Édition du Seuil, 1965.
——. *Le conflit des interprétations: Essai d'herméneutique*. Paris: Édition du Seuil, 1969.
Robertson, Robin. *C. G. Jung and the Archetypes of the Collective Unconscious*. New York: Peter Lang, 1987.
Rosenau, Pauline Marie. *Post-Modernism and the Social Sciences: Insights, Inroads, and Intrusions*. Princeton: Princeton University Press, 1992.
Ruhlen, Merritt. *L'Origine des langues*. Translated by Pierre Baucel. Paris: Éditions Bélin, 1997.
Sachar, Rajindar. *The Realization of Economic, Social and Cultural Rights: The Right to Adequate Housing*. Working paper. United Nations Economic and Social Council, Commission on Human Rights, Subcommission on Prevention of Discrimination and Protection of Minorities. UN General Assembly, Forty-Fifth Session, E/CN.4/sub.2/1993/15, 22 June 1993.
Santayana, George. *The Sense of Beauty, Being the Outline of Aesthetic Theory*. New York: Dover 1955.
Saussure, Ferdinand. *Cours de linguistique générale*. Genève: Bally and Séchehaye Éditeurs, 1916.
Selye, Hans. *Stress sans détresse*. Montreal: Les Éditions *La Presse*, 1974.
Sénèque. *La vie heureuse*. Trans. François Rosso Paris: Arléa, 1989.
Stewart, D., and A. Mickunas. *Exploring Phenomenology*. Chicago: American Library Association, 1974.
Sully Prudhomme. *Journal intime: 1862–1869*. Paris: Les Presses du Compagnonnage-Éditions Rombaldi, 1960.
Suzuki, Daisetz Teitaro. *Essai sur le Bouddhisme Zen*. Translated by Jean Hébert. Paris: Éditions Albin Lichel, 1972.

Torrelli, Maurice, and Renée Baudouin. *Les droits de l'homme et les libertés publiques, par les textes*. Montreal: Les Presses de l'Université du Québec, 1972.

Touchard-Lafosse, G. *Chroniques de l'œil-de-bœuf, 1829–1830*. Paris: Le Livre Club du Libraire, 1964.

Thuillier, Guy, and Jean Tulard. *La méthode en histoire*. Paris: Presses Universitaires de France, 1986.

———. *Les écoles historiques*. Paris: Presses Universitaires de France, 1990.

Trotignon, Pierre. *Les philosophes français d'aujourd'hui*. Paris: Presses Universitaires de France, 1967.

Valéry, Paul. *Eupalinos ou l'architecte*. Paris: NRF-Gallimard, 1944.

Vigneault, Gilles. *Le grand cerf-volant: Poèmes, contes et chansons*. Ottawa: Nouvelles Éditions de l'Arc, 1983.

UNESCO. *Universal Declaration of Human Rights: The Fortieth Anniversary, 1948–1988*. Preface by Federico Mayor. Ed. Glen Johnson and Janusz symonides. Paris: UNESCO, 1990.

———. *The Vancouver Declaration: A Programme for Survival*. Ottawa: Canadian National Commission for UNESCO, 1989.

Webster's. The New Lexicon: Encyclopédic Dictionary of the English Language. Canadian ed. 1988.

Wunenburger, J. F. *L'imagination*. Paris: Presses Universitaires de France, 1991.

3 PALAIS-ROYAL

Archives. In France, historical documentation of the Palais-Royal is found in many sources, notably: National Archives of France, Ministère de l'éducation nationale; National Library of France and Cabinet des estampes, Bibliothèque Nationale; Cabinet des estampes, Musée Carnavalet; Department of Archives, Ministère de la culture; Bibliothèque du Patrimoine, Ministère de la culture; Bibliothèque Historique, Ville de Paris.

The main reference catalogues are: *Les Archives nationales, État général des fonds*, tome I, série H, [...] *Travaux de la Ville de Paris, 1536–1789*; série K, [...] *Ville de Paris*; série R4, *Apanage d'Orléans*; tome IV, *Versement de la direction de l'architecture*. M. Hébert and J. Thirion, *Catalogue général des cartes, plans et dessins d'architecture*, tome premier, série N, Paris et le Département de la Seine, Ministère de l'éducation nationale, Direction des archives de France, Imprimerie nationale, Paris, 1958. Mireille Rambaud, *Les sources de l'histoire de l'art aux Archives nationales*, Imprimerie nationale, Paris, 1955.

Abbot, J. *Le Prince Napoléon et le Palais-Royal*. London: n. p., 1866.

Augé de Lassus, L. *La vie au Palais-Royal*. Paris: H. Daragon Éditeur, 1904.

Beaujoint, J. *Histoire du Palais-Royal et de ses galeries*. Paris: A. Fayard Éditeur, n. d.

Bercé, Françoise. *Marchés pour le Palais-Royal de 1628 à 1642*. Vol. 26 of Archives de l'Art français, Nouvelle Période. Paris: Éditions Jacques Laget, 1984.

———. *Le Palais-Cardinal: Richelieu et le monde de l'esprit*. Paris: Bibliothèque du Patrimoine, 1990.

Boulet, Jacques. "Buren's Stripped Columns at the Palais-Royal." *Daidalos*, 15 December 1987.

Boulet, Jacques, and Philippe Gresset. "Le Palais-Royal: Un fragment de ville." Unpublished research report. Secrétariat de la recherche architecturale, Paris, exercice 1983, UPAI, 1984.

———. "Le Palais-Royal: Un inachèvement classique." Unpublished research report. Contract no. 84 01370 00 223 75 01, École d'architecture Paris-Villemin, 1985.

Bouvet, Vincent. "Le Palais-Royal." *Monuments historique de France*, 1982.

Briffaut, E. "Le Palais-Royal." In *Rues de Paris: Paris ancien et moderne* Vol. 1. Paris: n. p., 1844.

Chabrol, W. *Le Palais-Royal: Inventaire général des richesses d'art de la France*. Vol. 1. Paris: Paris/Monuments Civils, 1879.

Champier, V., and R. Sandoz. *Le Palais-Royal d'après des documents inédits: 1629–1900*. Paris: Éditions Henri Veyrier, 1991.

Cocteau, J. *Le Palais-Royal raconté par ... vu par ... Véronique Filozof*. Heidelberg: Éditions Lambert Schneider, 1960.

Colette. Untitled text on the Palais-Royal. In *Guttenberg Informations: Chronicles of the Publishing and Graphic Arts Industry in France*. Paris: Guttenberg, 1987–88.

Constantin, M. *Histoire des cafés de Paris: Mémoires d'un viveur*. Paris: Desloges Éditeur, 1857.

Cottaz, Maurice. "Palais-Royal." *Le spectacle du monde*, July 1988.

Cuisin, P. *Les nymphes du Palais-Royal: Leurs mœurs, leurs expressions*. Paris: Roux Éditeur, 1815.

Dufresne, Claude. *Les Orléans*. Paris: Critérion Éditeur, 1991.

Dulaure, Jacques-Antoine. *Nouvelles descriptions des curiosités de Paris*. Paris: Lejay Éditeur, 1791.

Dupezard, Émile. *Le Palais-Royal de Paris*. Paris: Eggimain Éditeur, 1911.

———. *Protestation contre un projet de transformation du Palais-Royal*. Paris: Hadar Éditeur, 1912.

Espézel, Pierre d'. *Le Palais-Royal*. Paris: Calman-Lévy Éditeur, 1936.

Exhibition Catalogue, 9 May–4 September 1988. Paris: Musée Carnavalet, 1988.

Fontaine, Pierre-François. *Le Palais-Royal*. Paris: Gaultier-Laguinie Éditeur, 1829.

———. *Journal*. Vol. 1 (1799–1823); vol. 2 (1824–1853). Paris: École nationale supérieure des beaux-arts-Institut français d'architecture-Société de l'histoire de l'art français, 1987.

Fournier, A. "Le Palais-Royal." In Hoffbauer 1982.

Gallet, Michel. "Les dessins de l'architecture Henri Piètre pour la décoration du Palais-Royal." *Bulletin du Musée Carnavalet* 1 (1960).

Gaullieur, Hardy. *Portefeuille iconographie de Victor Louis*. Paris: Bibliothèque du Patrimoine de France, 1828.

Gourret, Jean. *Histoire des salles d'Opéra de Paris*. Paris: G. Trédaniel Éditeur, 1986.

Green, Julien. *Paris*. Paris: Champ Vallon Éditeur, 1983.

Guerin, M., and M. Schwartz. *Vues et descriptions du jardin du Palais-Royal*. Paris: Guerin and Schwartz Éditeurs, 1813.

Guéry, Christian. "Immobilier." *Le Figaro Magazine*, 10 December 1994; 21 January 1995.

Hartmann, G. "La merveilleuse vie au Palais-Royal." *La Revue artistique française*, 1929.

———. "Le Palais-Royal: Ses attractions autrefois." *Bulletin de l'union artistique française*, 1929.

Hénard, E. *Études sur les transformations de Paris, fascicule 5. La percée du Palais-Royal: La nouvelle grande croisée de Paris*. Paris: Motteroz Éditeur, 1904.

Hoffbauer, F. *Paris à travers les âges*, 1885. Paris: Firmin-Didot Éditeur, 1982.

Joudiou, Gabrielle. *Constructions et projets de Contant d'Ivry. Bulletin de la société historique de Paris et de l'Île de France*, 1986.

Kimball, Fiske. *Oppenord au Palais-Royal. Guide des Bâtiments Anciens*, February 1936.

Lavalé, M. *Du Palais-Royal et des moyens de lui rendre son ancienne splendeur*. Paris: Bibliothèque historique de la Ville de Paris, 1843.

Lefeuve, Charles. *Histoire des galeries du Palais-Royal*. 4TH ed. Paris: J. Martinon Éditeur, 1863.

Lemonnier, Henry. *Procès-verbaux de l'Académie Royale d'Architecture, 1671–1793*. Vol. 9. Paris: Archives nationales de France, 1926.

Lévesque, J. Jacques. *Jardins de Paris*. Paris: Hachette Éditeur, 1982.

Louis XVI. *Palais-Royal: Lettres patentes du 13 août 1784, et clauses et conditions insérées aux actes de vente des maisons du pourtour du jardin du Palais-Royal, 5 février 1785*. Paris: Archives of the Ministry of Culture, France, 1785.

Lurine, Louis. *Le Palais-Royal*. Paris: G. Havard Éditeur, 1855.

Marionneau, Charles. *Victor Louis: Sa vie, ses travaux et sa correspondance 1731–1800*. Bordeaux: Société historique, 1881.

Mayeur de Saint-Paul, F. M. *Tabeau du nouveau Palais-Royal*. Paris: Éditeur Maradan, 1788.

Mercier, Louis-Sébastien. *Tableau de Paris*. Paris: Louis Michaud Éditeur, 1789.

Moreau-Desproux, P. C. "Dessins de P.-C. Moreau-Desproux pour les édifices parisiens." *Bulletin du Musée Carnavalet* 1 (1962).

Nadal, V. *Le Palais-Royal*. Paris: Bibliothèque historique de la Ville de Paris, 1855.

Niclot, Colette. *Le Palais-Royal*. Paris: A. Morance Éditeur, n. d.

Notice historique sur le Palais-Royal et description des salles d'exposition et des appartements intérieurs. Paris: Musée Carnavalet, 1851.

Ordonnance concernant les passages et les galeries du Palais-Royal, Paris, 16/VIII/1819. Paris: Archives of the Ministère de la culture, France, 1819.

Palais-Royal: Règlement de police du 17 mai 1782. Paris: Archives of the Ministère de la culture, France, 1782.

Pariset, François-Georges. *Victor Louis 1731–1800: Dessins et gravures. Revue Historique de Bordeaux*, 1980.

Sennet, Richard. *Palais-Royal*. New York: Alfred A. Knopf, 1986.

Solinas, M. *Pour une renaissance du Palais-Royal*. Paris: Paris Projet, 1975.

Vatout, Jean. *Histoire du Palais-Royal*. Paris: Gaultier-Laguionie Éditeur, 1830.

4 FONDATION ROTHSCHILD WORKERS' RESIDENCE

Archives. Archives of the Fondation Rothschild. An extensive search of the Fondation Rothschild's archives was conducted by historian of architecture Marie-Jeanne Dumont. What was found in the eighth manuscript of the Régistre des délibérations (the foundation board meetings book of minutes) were plans for three projects other than the Rue de Prague project (Belleville, Trousseau, and Marcadet), construction documents, and building permits for the Belleville and Popincourt projects. All other files, although properly registered, have disappeared. In other words, practically nothing was found on the Rue de Prague project.

Benevolo, L. *Histoire de l'architecture moderne*. Paris: Dunod Éditeur, 1984.

Dantel, Madeleine. *Le logement social en France dans la presse destinée aux architectes et constructeurs d'habitations à bon marché (1878–1979)*. Entries on the Fondation Rothschild: ar43, ar47–50, ar157, aco7, au4, ai1, cpa2–6, cl19, ch121, ch122, ch125, ch127–129, ch132, ch187, h3, hf6, mba4, md4. Paris: École des hautes études en sciences sociales, 1979.

Diwo, Jean. *Les Dames du Faubourg*. Paris: Éditions Denoël, 1984.

Dumont, Marie-Jeanne. "La Fondation Rothschild et les premières habitations à bon marché de Paris, 1900–1925." Unpublished research report. Ministry of

Urbanism and Housing of France, Secretariat for Research in Architecture, research contract no. 81.01520.00.223.75.01, 1984.

——. *Le logement social à Paris, 1850–1930: Les habitations à bon marché*. Paris: Mardaga Éditeur, 1991.

Flamand, Jean-Paul. *Loger le peuple: Essai sur l'histoire du logement social*. Paris: Éditions La Découverte, 1989.

Fortier, Bruno, et al. *La politique de l'espace parisien (à la fin de l'Ancien Régime)*. Paris: Corda, 1975.

Foucault, Michel, et al. *Les machines à guérir*. Paris: Pierre Mardaga Éditeur, 1979.

Hervé, Jean-Pierre. Interviews, the Fondation Rothschild Workers' Residence. Paris, 1994, 1995.

Hillairet, Jacques. *Dictionnaire historique des rues de Paris*. Paris: Les Éditions de Minuit, 1957.

Quilliot, Roger, and Roger-Henri Guerrand. *Cent ans d'habitat social: Une utopie réaliste*. Paris: Éditions Albin Michel, 1989.

Trélat, M. E. "Paris salubre." Public lecture. Paris, 24 February 1901. Permanent exhibit of the Centre national des arts et métiers.

5 OUTREMONT

Beaugrand-Champagne, Aristide. "Le chemin d'Hochelaga." In Bisson 1993.

Biggar, H. P. *The Voyages of Jacques-Cartier*. In Bisson 1993.

Bisson, Pierre-Richard. *Outremont et son patrimoine: Inventaire et mise en valeur du patrimoine d'Outremont*. Montreal: Ministry of Culture, Quebec-City of Outremont, 1993.

City of Outremont. Several reports and miscellaneous documents regarding the affairs of Outremont. 1993, 1994.

Continuité. 2 (1991). (Special issue on Outremont and its heritage).

Guenet, Michel, Marie Lessard, and Michel Lincourt. *Hydro-Québec/Efficacité énergétique: Identification d'éléments préparatoires aux interventions d'Hydro-Québec en matière de maîtrise de l'énergie auprès des municipalités*. Research report. Institut d'urbanisme, Faculté d'aménagement, Université de Montréal, 1992.

"Les parcs d'Outremont donnent le bon exemple à Montréal." *La Presse* [Montreal], 8 December 1991.

Rumilly, Robert. *Histoire d'Outremont, 1875–1975*. Montreal: Leméac Éditeur, 1975.

Statistics Canada (Stats Can). *Demographic, Economic, Social and Linguistic Data on Outremont*. 1993–94.

Tessier, Père Hector. *Saint-Viateur d'Outremont, 1954*. In Bisson 1993.

"Westmount Richest Area in Canada." *Gazette* [Montreal], 21 July 1993.

APPENDIX

Sample of the questionnaire used for the survey conducted at the Fondation Rothschild Workers' Residence

SONDAGE

auprès des résidents de l'ensemble immobilier du 8 Rue de Prague, à Paris, 12ᵉ.

Effectué par Michel Lincourt, architecte et urbaniste
Professeur invité, École d'architecture de Paris La Villette
Doctoral Fellow, College of Architecture, Georgia Institute of Technology
dans le cadre d'une recherche pour une thèse de doctorat
Avec l'autorisation de la Direction des immeubles de la Fondation Rothschild

Madame, Monsieur, s'il vous plait:

1ère question: **Depuis combien de temps demeurez-vous ici?** *1951 (43 ans)*

2e question: **Compte-tenu du prix de votre loyer, êtes-vous satisfait de vivre ici?**
Veuillez cocher la réponse de votre choix
  Oui, très satisfait: ✗
  Oui, satisfait:
  Non, insatisfait:
  Non, très insatisfait:

3e question: **Si oui, [très satisfait ou satisfait], donnez, par ordre de priorité, les trois principales raisons qui appuient votre satisfaction.**
Première raison: *l'ENVIRONNEMENT*

Deuxième raison: *l'excellent entretien des immeubles*

Troisième raison: *le sens de l'humain vis à vis des occupants*

4e question: **Si non, [insatisfait ou très insatisfait], indiquez, par ordre de priorité, les trois principales améliorations à apporter.**
  Première amélioration:
  Deuxième amélioration:
  Troisième amélioration:

le Surveillant-Chef
Mr MOURIER

4 NOV. 1994

Verso

APPENDIX

5e question: Êtes-vous satisfait du quartier?
Veuillez cocher la réponse de votre choix **Oui, satisfait:**
~~Non~~, insatisfait:

6e question: Selon votre réponse [satisfait ou insatisfait], donnez, par ordre de priorité, les trois principales raisons qui appuient votre satisfaction ou votre insatisfaction.

Première raison: Situation par rapport aux grands axes de PARIS

Deuxième raison: DESSERTE par trois stations du Métropolitain (Ledru Rollin - Bastille - Gare de Lyon) et en même temps autobus par rapport à ces stations

Troisième raison: Proximité des gares SNCF = Paris Lyon et Paris Austerlitz

Autres commentaires:
Par rapport à la 2ème question : "oui très satisfaite" - Je dis plus que satisfaite
Il faut avoir à l'encontre de la Fondation Rothschild beaucoup de RECONNAISSANCE pour son souci constant de l'amélioration de l'HABITAT

Veuillez, s'il vous plait, remettre vos réponses chez le gardien au plus tard, jeudi le 17 novembre 1994. Merci.

INDEX

Aalto, Alvar, 33
absolute (as a value), 99. *See also* values
accountability (social), 10
activity components, 58. *See also* veils
Afro-Americans, *see* East Lake Meadows
Alberti, Leon Battista, 48, 118, 273-74, 342
Amsterdamse Bos, 334. *See also* Gadet, J.
Annales d'hygiène publique et de médecine légale, 191
appreciation (in beauty): 265, 356; example, 282; only comparison possible, 285. *See also* taste
archetype, 5, 38, 41, 123, 265, 301-6, 356; of elegance, 319-50; of elegance idea, 317; meaningful archetypes needed, 350; mental construct, 303
architect, 3, 351-55: as medical doctor, 271; as builder of civilization, 358; credibility of, 3; destiny of, 9; essential activities, 24; foundation of his design decision, 37; how he can design a successful environment, 37; ill equipped, 15; mission, 3, 9; obligation to succeed, 264; sine qua non undertaking, 3; thinking and doubting, 23
architects of Outremont: many architects, 224, 230; Barnes, Thomas (horticulturist), 234; Beaugrand-Champagne, Aristide (two small parks), 234-35; Betts, R.C. (Sévère-Godin mansion), 214; Doucet and Morissette (Ozias-Lamoureux house), 214; Dumas, Roland (Parent residence), 214; Lacroix, Émile (engineer), 234; Olmstead, Frederick Law (landscape architect, Parc Mont-Royal), 232
architects of the Fondation Rothschild Workers' Residence: Nénot, Henri-Paul, 195-96; Provensal, Henri, 196; Rey, Augustin, 195-96
architects of the Palais-Royal: Cartaud, Jacques-Sylvain, 135; Chabrol, Prosper, 139, 143; Contant, Pierre (dit Contant d'Ivry), 135, 142; de Champagne, Philippe, 132; Desgots (landscape architect), 134-35; Desgots, Claude (landscape architect), 132; d'Orbay, 133; Le Mercier, Jacques, 131; Le Nôtre, André (landscape architect), 133; Le Pautre, 133; Louis, Victor, 136, 141, 142, 149, 155; Mansart, Jules-Hardouin, 133; Moreau-Desproux, Pierre-Louis, 135, 136, 142, 155, 190; Oppenord (two architects), 134; Percier and Fontaine, 138, 141
architectural doctrines, 47: idées reçues, 47; theoreticians, 47-48; traditions, 81
architecture, 3-4, 9, 20, 36; of elegance, 356; how to assess it, 353-54; how to

INDEX

design it, 354–56; multifaceted reality, 10; as organization of activities, 59; in Outremont, 242; of respect (at the Palais-Royal), 141; of satisfaction, 354, 356; successful architecture at the Palais-Royal, 163–66; at the Foundation Rothschild, 204–5; what it is, 351–53
Aristotle, 7, 9
artefact (architectural), 37, 41, 62, 73, 198: of elegance, 354; nature transformed, 72; proportions, 281, 351
Attic amphora (as example of elegance), 295
attitude (of author), 6

Bachelard, Gaston, 20, 21, 32, 36, 83, 140, 159, 320, 357
Bachelard, Suzanne, 53
Balthasar Neumann's baroque churches (as examples of elegance), 297
Barnard, Peter (*The Barnard Report*), 16
Bauhaus, 18, 48
beauty, 20, 37, 166, 242, 247, 264–65, 271–82, 355: based on good proportions, 281–82; definitions of (Kant), 275; as emotional element (Santayana), 279; in harmony (Alberti), 274; as joyful and respectful, 280; as more than ornamental, 274; pleasure as its principle, 286, 355
Beethoven, 27, 52–53, 78
Berger, Gaston, 27
Blondel, François, 79, 154: beauty in good proportions, 281; his idea of symmetry, 274
Blondel, Jacques-François, 79, 109, 274, 284
Blumenfeld, Hans, 56
Boileau, Nicolas, 157
Botticelli's *Primavera* (as example of elegance), 297
Boulet, Jacques, 168
Brentano, Franz, 25
brief (architectural), 61
Buddha, 94–97. *See also* values

character, 78. *See also* veils

Cheysson, Émile, 192–95
Ching, Francis, 73
chopsticks (as example of elegance), 297
CIAM, 73
City Beautiful movement, 221, 229
Cocteau, Jean, 159, 162
Colette, 159, 162, 166, 337
common good (as a value), 96. *See also* values
compassion (as a value), 94. *See also* values
complexity, 10
Confucius. *See* Venerable Master K'ung
constitution (phenomenological), 5, 29–30, 36, 355: of design criteria, 107–21; of design strategy, 246–64; of idea of archetype, 301–17; of ideas of quality, beauty, and elegance, 264–301; as part of the theory's procedure, 38–43; of three archetypes of elegance, 319–50
Control (as a value), 105. *See also* values
Corinthian Order (as example of elegance), 295
crise de conscience (of architects), 9
criteria (design), 5, 37, 247, 353–55: non-self-referential, 121; value-based, 85–86, 107–21. *See also* constitution

Dansereau, Pierre, 71–72
Déclaration des droits de l'homme et du citoyen, France, 90
Declaration of Independence and Constitution, United States of America, 90
decomposition-recomposition (design method), 258
Deming, Edwards, 268–69
democracy, 96. *See also* values
de Muralt, André, 22, 25–27, 53
Descartes, René, 6, 23–27: *Discours de la méthode*, 6, 25; four precepts, 26, 35; his advice, 62; his suggestions followed, 53
design objective, 3. *See also* elegance
designed environment, 9, 37, 62: its network character, 63; what is it made of, 37
De Stijl Manifesto, 49–50

INDEX

Diderot, Denis, 157, 179, 271
dignity (as a value), 96. *See also* values
Dufrenne, Mikel, 21, 286
dwelling, 32, 33, 35, 81–83, 107, 353–54, 358: at the Fondation Rothschild Worker' Residence, 205–7; in Outremont, 242–43; at the Palais-Royal, 166. *See also* eidos; essence; telos

East Lake Meadows, 13, 16, 255
ecology, 71. *See also* veils
economy, 75. *See also* veils
efficacy (as a value), 104. *See also* values
eidos of architecture, 31: architectural phenomenon, 81–83, 353; dwelling in a place, 82. *See also* essence
elegance: convivial, in Outremont, 209; definition of, 5; as generosity of feeling, 286; as gesture of the noblest soul, 290; grace in small things, dignity in great things, 292; as grounded in the *esprit* of a person, 290; honest, at the Fondation Rothschild, 169; as honesty and humility, 290; illustrations of, 294–99; as natural grace, 290; notion of, 286–92; perennial, at the Palais-Royal, 123; phenomenological view of, 292–94; as politeness, 286; as predominant design objective, 3, 20, 37–38, 41; of studied artefacts, 299
energy, 77. *See also* veils
Enlightenment philosophers (redefining values), 102
entitlements, 87–89
epochè, 5, 27, 36, 245–46, 355: architectural doctrines, 47–48; of the architectural phenomenon (unveiling architecture), 51–83; of architectural theories, 45–46; of current design criteria, human rights and values, 85–106; definition of, 28; of the Fondation Rothschild Workers' Residence, 169–207; of historical interpretations, 46–47; of Outremont, 209–43; of the Palais-Royal, 123–68; as part of the theory's procedure, 38–43; of the three artefacts, 121–22

equality (as a value), 103. *See also* values
equity (as a value), 95. *See also* values
essence, 31, 140: of architecture, first formulation, 51; for future debate, 358. *See also* eidos; telos
European Community, 90
excellence, 5, 107, 168, 265, 266–69, 271, 286, 355–56. *See also* elegance; quality
existential phenomenologists (American writers), 34

Farber, Marvin, 29
Fell, Joseph, 81
Ferry, Jules, 175
Filibien, André, 157
Fink, Eugen, 28
Fondation Rothschild Workers' Residence, 4, 38, 41, 121, 169–207, 255, 261, 263, 299, 301, 319, 350, 356: architectural competition, 194; demonstration of satisfaction with (questionnaire), 201–3; inconspicuous presence of, 169; as inspiration for archetypes, 321; location of, 177; as a no-frills project, but not a simplistic one, 207; as not constricting powerful sense of enclosure, 185; ordinary charm of, 198; as a public-hygiene result, 187, 191, 204; as a solid structure, 182; as a sophisticated arrangement of multiple shapes, 184
form and space, 73. *See also* veils
Fortier, Bruno, 190
fraternity (as a value), 101. *See also* values
freedom (as a value), 102. *See also* values

Gadamer, Hans, 21
Gadet, J., 334. *See also* Amsterdamse Bos
Garden City movement, 221, 229
Gautama (Siddartha). *See* Buddha
Georgia Institute of Technology, 13
Global Strategy for Shelter to the Year 2000, 87. *See also* United Nations
good health (as a value), 103. *See also* values

goodness and beauty (as a value), 97. *See also* values
Greek (Ancient), 95–98. *See also* values
Green, Julien, 130
Gropius, Walter, 18, 49

Hall, Edward T., 59, 74
Halprin, Lawrence, 55
happiness, 106, 358
Harvard Graduate School of Design, 14, 15, 18
Harvard symposium panellists, 15
Hawking, Stephen, 4
Heidegger, Martin, 6, 21, 32, 81–82, 86, 357
history, 64. *See also* presence in evolution
hope (as a value), 99. *See also* values
hospitality (as a value), 101. *See also* values
Howard, Sir Ebenezer, 221
human rights, 90–91
humans, seven universal characteristics of, 57
Husserl, Edmund, 5, 20–36; *Cartesian Meditations*, 22, 28, 45–46, 357. *See also* phenomenology
Hygienists, 191–95, 205

Industrial Revolution, 104. *See also* values
intention, 3
Islam, 100. *See also* values

Jameson, Fredric, 15
Jencks, Charles, 18, 47, 48, 49, 73, 261
Jesus, 98. *See also* values
Jones, Michael, 16–17
Jung, Carl Gustav, 302–4
justice (as a value), 96. *See also* values

Kahn, Louis, 33
Kallen, Horace, 7
Kant, Immanuel, 275
Knapp, Bettina, 304–5
Kostof, Spiro, 314–15, 331–32, 339, 343
Krier, Rob, 281

Laborit, Henri, 57, 65

Lang, Richard, 320
Laugier, Marc-Antoine (Abbé), 46, 112
Leckie, Scott, 12
Le Corbusier, 13, 48, 49, 65, 74, 82, 199: Esprit Nouveau, 18; his aesthetic discourse, 275–79; his Plan Voisin, 13
Les très riches heures du Duc de Berry (as example of elegance), 296
Lincourt, Michel, 302
Loos, Adolf, 48
love (as a value), 98. *See also* values
Lowen, Alexander, 106
Lynch, Kevin, 57
Lyotard, Jean-François, 21, 22, 28, 29, 31

Magna Carta, 90
magnificence, 5, 107, 168, 265, 271–82, 286, 356: as great beauty, 280. *See also* beauty; elegance
Marché de Bauveau, 180, 203
materiality, 65. *See also* veils
meaning, 80. *See also* projection and place
measurement, 265, 356: as quality assessment, 269. *See also* excellence; quality
medieval Islamic philosophers, 100
medieval world, 99. *See also* values
mediocrity (of the designed environment), 11
Merleau-Ponty, Maurice, 21, 28, 29, 31, 82, 358
Michelangelo's Campidoglio, 55
Mickunas, Algis, 20. *See also* Stewart, David
Mies van der Rohe, Ludwig, 18, 49, 349
mission (of the architect), 3, 9
Modern Architecture ideology, 14
Montblanc pen (as example of quality), 266–69
Montesquieu, 283
Mont-Royal, 209, 232
Mugerauer, Robert, 34
Mumford, Lewis, 56, 350

nature, 72: domesticated, at the Palais Royal, 154; given, enhanced in Outremont, 232–36. *See also* ecology;

Fondation Rothschild Workers' Residence; Outremont; Palais-Royal
neglect, 14
Nénot, Henri-Paul, 195–96
Norberg-Schulz, Christian, 32, 33, 47, 82, 120, 157, 301, 357, 358

Organization of American States, 90
original contribution (of the theory), 357–58
Outremont, 4, 38, 41, 121, 209–43, 261, 299, 301, 319, 335, 356: beautification of, 221; bikini crisis, 239–41; as city within a city, 211; cross-section of a typical street, 227; distinctiveness in continuity, 217; eighteen open spaces, 233; as a frugal town, 236; as hidden under a forest, 236; history of, 218–21; as intense community, 230; its parks as inspiration for archetype of elegance, 332; as locus of values, 239; landmarks facilitate orientation, 229; in Montreal, 209; multipurpose public places, 227; nature given, nature enhanced, 232; parking issue, 223; people, 211–13; rectilinear city blocks, 228; red brick and white woodwork, 224, 237; as residential neighbourhood, 214; three commercial avenues, 216; vaulted street space, 225; walking to places within, 222

Padgen, Elizabeth, 15, 16, 19
Palais-Royal, 4, 38, 41, 121, 123–68, 261, 299, 301, 319, 350, 356: as best second-best place, 148; character, 161; commercial bonanza, 152; convenient conviviality, 145; discreet sensuality, 157; domesticated nature, 154; dwelling at the, 166; easy access to, 145; garden, a strong enclosure, 144; as gentle object in nature, 154; history in the present, 131; human scale, 145; informal formality, 125; as most private public place, 144; as multi-use complex, 123; as offering many delights, 138; and Parisians, 125; pedestrian area, 127, 145; as place for all, 162; as porous domain at the centre, 129; rectilinearity, 156; as regal place, 123; rhythmic portico, 160; sexual metaphors, 159; as simple, unified composition, 141; stones of gold, 140; subtle proportions, 155; tradition of theatre, 151; unity transcends perception, 142
Palladio, Andrea, 48, 309
Pantheon, 74
Paris 63: *esprit de*, 121
parks (of Outremont), 335: as inspiration for archetype of elegance, 332; Parc Beaubien, 235; Parc Joyce, 234; Parc Outremont, 235; Parc Pratt, 234; Parc Saint-Viateur, 235. *See also* Outremont
Parthenon, 54, 74, 78
Patocka, Jan, 29
Payet, Bernard, 190
peace (as a value), 96. *See also* values
Pérez-Gomez, Alberto, 35–36, 156–57
Perrault, Claude, 35, 48, 273
personal creative expression (as a value), 105. *See also* values
personal sense of collective responsibility (as a value), 105. *See also* values
Peters, Tom, 269–70
Petit Trianon (as example of elegance), 296
Petronius (as example of elegance), 294
phenomenology, 3, 5, 36: consciousness, 24; constitution, 29; eidic concepts, 29; essence, 31; facts, 21; imagination, 26; intentionality, 24; intuition, 26; lifeworld, 22; logic, 25; many contributing philosophers, 21; as a method, 20–43; *noema*, 26; *noesis*, 26; phenomena, 22; reflection, 25; subject, 23; universals, 30
phenomenology and architecture, 31–36
phenomenon (architectural), 5, 22, 37, 38, 45, 51–52, 62–63, 66, 74, 77: its foundation, 81–83. *See also* phenomenology
Picot, Georges, 192–94
place (meaning of), 33, 35, 81–83, 358
place d'Aligre, 180–81, 203

place du Palais-Royal, 125, 127, 130: among the better-designed Paris squares, 148; as inspiration for archetype of elegance, 332. *See also* Palais-Royal
Plato, 73, 96, 97, 271
plenty (as a value), 104. *See also* values
portico, 312: at the Palais-Royal, 149, 160; ambiguity of, 309; as arcade, 309; as architectural archetype, 306–17; as buffer space, 308; as colonnade, 309, 312; example of archetype, 265; as *loggia*, 314; private and public, 308; to protect pedestrians, 310
post-World War II architectural theoreticians, 18
presence in evolution, 64. *See also* veils
pre-World War II architectural theoreticians, 18
privacy (as a value), 93. *See also* values
procedure (of the theory), 38–43, 353–54
progress (as a value), 102. *See also* values
property (as a value), 93. *See also* values
Proust, Marcel (as example of elegance), 297
Provensal, Henri, 196
public places (as archetypes of elegance), 331: city squares, 339–50; small urban parks, 334–39

quality, 20, 37, 166, 242, 247, 264, 265, 266–69: appearance of, 268; clear purpose of, 266; expressing satisfaction with, 271; focus of, 267; as measurable, 270; ongoing improvement of, 267; perdurability of, 267; satisfaction as principle of, 270

Rasmussen, Eiler, 74
reduction of eidos of architecture, 27, 81–83: bare architectural phenomenon, 50–51; telos of architecture, 106–7. *See also* eidos; epochè; essence; phenomenology; telos
Relph, Edwards, 32, 33, 34–35, 81, 301, 320, 357
Renaissance thinkers (their redefinition of), 101–2

residential flat, to meet twenty-first century needs, 321: as archetype of elegance, 325; two innovations, 328–29
respect for traditions (as a value), 95. *See also* values
Rey, Augustin, 195, 196
Ricœur, Paul, 21, 27
Robertson, Robin, 302–3
Rockefeller Center square, 348
Romans, 98
Rothschilds, 171, 173, 205
Rowe, Peter, 14–15, 257
Rudolsky, Bernard, 332, 343
Ruskin, John, 48
Rykwert, Joseph, 36

Sachar, Rajindar, 11, 87
Sainte-Chapelle (as example of elegance), 295. *See also* elegance
Santayana, George, 279–80
satisfaction, 5, 20, 106, 108, 163: demonstration of, 201–3, 242, 247; as principle of quality, 270–71, 355
Seamon, David, 34, 357
servomechanism, 70
Shaker design (as example of elegance), 298. *See also* elegance
Siegfried, Jules, 192–94
Sienna's *palio*, 343
Simon, Jules, 192
Sitte, Camillo, 341, 347
social bonding (as a value), 103. *See also* values
Société des HBM, 192
society, 3, 353: driven by values, 106
Socrates, 96–97
square Armand-Trousseau, 177, 178, 340. *See also* Fondation Rothschild Workers' Residence
Stevens, S. S., 269
Stewart, David, 20
strategy (design), 37, 246–64: phenomenological action-oriented prescriptive approach, 246; seven steps, 247, 354–56
style, 47, 224
Suger, Abbot, 48
Sully Prudhomme, 288–92

surroundings, 62. *See also* veils
systems, 66–70. *See also* veils
Szent-Györgyi, Albert, 106

tasks (three fundamental), 37
taste, 143, 207, 224, 282–85, 355
Taylor, Mark, 23
telos (of architecture), 31, 92, 106–7, 353–54: a happy architecture, 106. *See also* essence; reduction of eidos of architecture
theory of architecture, 3, 10, 21 38, 45, 351–58: definition of, 4; as needed, 19; as phenomenological underpinning, 36
theory-practice schism, 18
Thiis-Evensen, Thomas, 65, 302, 306
Tilly, Charles, 63
truth (as a value), 94, 100; see also values

United Nations, 11, 89, 91: agenda 21, 154, 259; Centre for Human Settlements, 11; Commission of Human Rights, 11, 87; Conference on the Environment, 154; Economic and Social Committee, 11; eight basic agreements, 89; Universal Declaration of Human Rights, 85, 90–92
universals, 30
urban design (definition), 5
usefulness (as a value), 104. *See also* values

Valéry, Paul, 140, 297
values, 5, 85, 92–106, 239, 353: of Anciens Greece, 95; of Buddha, 94; of late twentieth century, 104; first, 92; of the Industrial Revolution, 104; of Islam, 100; of Jesus, 98; of Medieval world, 99; of the Renaissance and the Enlightenment, 101; of society, 92; of Venerable Master K'ung, 95
Vancouver Declaration on the Survival of Humanity, UNESCO, 71, 90
veils, 52–81, 351–52
Venerable Master K'ung, 95. *See also* values
Venturi, Robert, 18, 33, 48–49, 73, 114, 350
Vidler, Anthony, 46
Vignola, Giacomo Barozzi da, 48, 274
Vitruvius, 37, 47, 48, 109, 112, 273
Voltaire, 134, 293

Wagner, Otto, 48
Wales, HRH (Prince Charles), 110, 112, 114, 116, 261, 281
Webb, Michael, 339–40, 343
White, Morton and Lucia, 349–50
wisdom (as a value), 94, 97. *See also* values
Wittkower, Rudolf, 274
World Health Organization, 12
Wright, Frank Lloyd, 13: Broadacre City, 13, 349–50